ANCIENT PEOPLES

A REVISION OF MOREY'S
"OUTLINES OF ANCIENT HISTORY"

BY

WILLIAM C. MOREY, Ph.D., D.C.L.

PROFESSOR OF HISTORY AND POLITICAL SCIENCE, UNIVERSITY
OF ROCHESTER
AUTHOR OF "OUTLINES OF ROMAN HISTORY," "OUTLINES OF ROMAN LAW"
"OUTLINES OF GREEK HISTORY," ETC.

AMERICAN BOOK COMPANY

NEW YORK   CINCINNATI   CHICAGO

PREFACE

IN this revision of the author's "Outlines of Ancient History" it has been the purpose to review the various phases of national life among ancient peoples. More attention has therefore been paid to the life and customs of the people; and this has been done without losing sight of the fact that the real history of a people deals with its *progressive development*, and not simply with its *antiquities*. The materials of the previous book have been used so far as available, and adapted to the needs of first year pupils of the high school.

In making a selection from the great variety of subjects connected with the life of ancient peoples, the relative importance of these subjects has been determined by their bearing, either direct or remote, upon human progress. The subject of the early man, for instance, has been treated not as a distinct discussion in anthropology, but simply to illustrate the steps of human progress before the dawn of history. In the study of Oriental peoples, the civilization of each nation is considered in connection with the history of the nation itself, to show what each of these nations has contributed to the general improvement of mankind. In the treatment of the Greek and Roman peoples, emphasis has been laid upon those features of the national life which have had the greatest influence upon the progress of the world, — in the case of Greece, political liberty and intellectual and æsthetic culture, — in the case of Rome, political organization and the development of a world empire. The life and customs, as well as the art culture of these peoples, have been considered in connection with the different periods of their history, thus showing the various stages in the development of their social and intellectual life.

The great value of historical study comes from the capacity of seeing how the things which *are* have come to *be*. Even the most elementary pupil may be taught to see how historical events are related to one another, and to understand that history is not simply a series of disconnected and unrelated facts. To aid the pupil to coördinate the various facts and events under discussion, each chapter is prefaced with a " Synopsis " indicating the relation of the subjects to be considered. Special attention has also been paid to the geographical setting of historical facts. The maps have been prepared for the sole purpose of illustrating the text, and to enable the pupil to locate the places mentioned — frequent references being made to the maps where such places may be found. The " Selections for Reading," which follow each chapter, are intended for the use both of the pupil and of the teacher ; the more elementary books are placed in the early part of the lists, and are followed by the more standard works. As references are made to particular chapters by number and title, they show exactly what subjects are discussed, and can readily be assigned for separate classroom reports. The " Special Study " at the close of each chapter is given as a specimen of what may be done with other topics which may be suggested by the teacher.

A textbook at best can be regarded as scarcely more than a guide-book, which must be supplemented by the voice and presence of the living teacher.

W. C. M.

University of Rochester,
  Rochester, N. Y.

CONTENTS

Contents

APPENDIX

IMPORTANT MAPS

ANCIENT PEOPLES

CHAPTER I

INTRODUCTION: THE EARLY MAN AND THE DAWN OF HISTORY

Synopsis

I. THE EARLY MAN AND EARLY AGES. — Looking Backward. — How do we Know the Past? — Traces of the Early Man. — The Age of Stone. — The Age of Bronze. — The Age of Iron.

II. PROGRESS TOWARD CIVILIZED LIFE. — How the Earliest Men Lived. — The Pastoral Life. — The Agricultural Life. — The Manufacturing and Mercantile Life. — The Art of Writing. — The Dawn of History: Written Records.

III. HISTORIC LANDS AND HISTORIC PEOPLES. — Geography as an Aid to History. — The Historical Zone of the Ancient World. — Classification of Ancient Peoples. — The Hamitic Peoples. — The Semitic Peoples. — The Aryan, or Indo-European, Peoples.

I. THE EARLY MAN AND EARLY AGES

Looking Backward. — When we look about us and see the many things that make up our daily lives, we may at first be inclined to think that the world was always just as we see it to-day. But of course we all know that this cannot be true. We know that old things are passing away, and new things are continually coming to light. If we had the magic power to turn back the years and centuries like the hands of a clock, the many things that we now see would, one by one, fade from our view. We should come to a time when there were no telephones, no telegraphs, no railroads — a time when no use was made of electricity and steam; when there were no great ships to plow the sea, no machines to cut our grain and drive our mills, no newspapers and printed books. We should come to a time when our country did not exist, when the places where now stand great cities, with their beautiful churches, their splendid public buildings, their immense factories, were the homes of rude savages roaming the forest. If we continued to turn back the clock of time, we might come at last to an age that would startle us — when we should see scarcely anything made by human hands, and when men were struggling for existence with the beasts of the field. We should then have come to what we might call the " childhood of the world," — when men were beginning to learn their first rude lessons from the book of nature.

We might, perhaps, draw in our minds such a picture as this. But as a matter of fact, no one has this magic power of discovering the past by simply looking into his own mind. We really have to get this knowledge in a less fanciful and more practical way.

How do we Know the Past? — Some one will ask, How then do we know the past — how can we find out anything about the men who lived ages ago? We may best answer this question by first answering a simpler one. How, for example, do we know anything about our own ancestors whom no person now living has ever seen? In the first place, we may have pictures or ornaments or some other relics that they once possessed which have come down to us. Such old pictures and relics would tell us something of the looks and the character of persons who lived before we were born. In the next place, we may have heard our fathers and mothers tell stories about their fathers and grandfathers, — stories that have been handed down from one generation to another. Such stories may not always be entirely true; but they do show us what people have generally thought and believed. Finally, we may have in our possession letters or other papers which our ancestors themselves have written, or which other people have written about them. In such ways as these we may learn something about the people who have lived in the past, and whom we ourselves have never seen. It is, in fact, in quite similar ways that we get our knowledge of the past ages of mankind. And in quite a similar way we may group the sources of our knowledge of the past, as follows:

(1) *Material remains*, or the relics of ancient peoples. Such remains include the weapons that the people used in war, and the tools they used in peace; the remains of dwellings and other buildings; vases, sculptures, pictures, and other works of art. All these go to show something of the character of the people that produced them.

(2) *Oral traditions*, or legends, myths, and stories of any kind that have been handed down from generation to generation. They are of value to show what people have generally believed; although they cannot be accepted as telling the whole truth and nothing but the truth.

(3) *Written records*, including inscriptions, manuscripts, and books. Such records may have been written by those living at the time of the events described, or they may have been written by persons living at a later period but having knowledge of such events.

Traces of the Early Man. — Our knowledge of the earliest men who lived upon the earth is derived entirely from material remains. These men had no books. They did not even leave behind them stories telling us who they were or what they did. It is scarcely more than fifty or sixty years since we began to have any definite knowledge of these primitive people. Whatever relics they left — their weapons, their tools, and even their bones — had lain for ages buried in the earth. When these re-

PREHISTORIC SKETCH OF
EXTINCT MAMMOTH
(Found in a cave in
France)

mains began to be dug up, it seemed like the discovery of a new world — of an early people who lived before the dawn of history. Such traces of a prehistoric people were found in France, in England, in America, and in many other parts of the world. They were found under gravel beds, under deep layers of clay, and under limestone deposits in the caverns of rocks. They were found alongside of the bones of animals now extinct; and among the relics were rude drawings of such animals. These traces of early man showed that the earth had been inhabited many thousands of years ago by a people that has long since passed away.

The Age of Stone. — If we go into a museum containing what is called an " archæological " collection, we find arranged upon shelves a great variety of objects made of stone. Among such objects are stone hammers, axes, knives, arrowheads,

and spear points. Some of these are coarse and rough, showing that the stone was chipped off to bring it into proper shape. Other ob-

FLINT ARROWHEAD FROM DENMARK

jects are smooth and polished, showing a greater degree of skill and taste. But all these pieces of stone show that they were worked by human hands. The fact that these relics were found in places where there were no objects made of any kind of metal, indicates that stone was the chief material from which the early people made their implements. These people represent the lowest stage of human development; and the long period in which they lived is called the " age of stone." Certain of the descendants of such ancient people have remained savages until the present day, and it may be said that they are still living in the " stone age," — for example, the wild tribes in some parts of Africa and in some islands of the Pacific.

The Age of Bronze. — An important step in human progress was made by the discovery and use of metals. If we look over the many metal articles that we need to-day, we are convinced that without the use of the different metals we could scarcely live. We can then see that the discovery of metals and of the method of preparing them for use, must have been a great step toward a civilized life. It is said that the metal that first attracted the attention of men was gold, on account of its glittering appearance. But this simply pleased the eye, and was chiefly used for ornaments.

The first really useful metal was copper. This was used by the American Indians at the time of their discovery by Columbus. But copper is too soft for the making of many articles. When, however, it is mixed with tin, it makes a harder metal, called bronze. It is impossible to tell when and just how men discovered this fact. The mixing of tin with copper required the use of

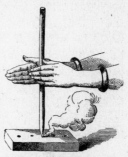

ANCIENT FIRE DRILL

fire and some kind of forge. Men had the use of fire, from the earliest times; primitive people were skillful in producing fire by rubbing two pieces of wood together, or by means of the "fire drill." But the use of fire for the forging of metals was a later discovery. However this process may have been invented, bronze came to be for many centuries the chief metal used by man. Countless articles of this metal have been

BRONZE KNIFE FROM DENMARK

dug up in different parts of the world. It was used for the making of weapons of war, such as swords, daggers, and arrow points; it was used for ordinary tools, such as hammers, saws, and knives; and for ornaments, such as breastpins, earrings, and bracelets. The period when this metal took the place of stone is called the "age of bronze."

The Age of Iron. — A still greater advance was made by the discovery and use of iron. This is a much harder metal than ·bronze and better suited for pointed and cutting implements. Although bronze was still used for purposes of ornament, iron came to be regarded as the " king of metals." Men were now able to make better weapons and to gain a new advantage over the beasts of the field and over their hostile neighbors. They could also make scythes and sickles, spades and iron-tipped plows, and could become better farmers. It would be impossible to name all the ways in which iron has helped to benefit mankind. Before the close of the prehistoric period it had come into general use among all those nations that were becoming civilized. When we consider the immense benefits that men have received from the use of bronze and iron we may readily believe that " without metals man would have remained forever in a state of barbarism."

II. Progress toward Civilized Life

How the Earliest Men Lived. — The first thing needed by every human being that comes into the world is *food*, something to eat. The next thing is *clothing*, something to wear and to protect the body. The next thing is *shelter*, some place in which to live and to be shielded from the weather. These are the three primary wants of man, and are called the " necessaries " of life. To the first men life was indeed a struggle for existence. They were obliged to get the necessaries of life

HARPOON TIP OF REINDEER'S HORN
(From France)

from the natural products of the earth. They had no means of cultivating the soil. They dug in the ground to find roots that might support life. They picked the wild berries where they happened to find them. They climbed the trees for the wild fruit that hung from the branches. Living near the water, they were able to catch fish, either with a hook made of bone or with a harpoon sharpened to a point or tipped with bone or flint. They also lived upon the flesh of wild beasts and became expert hunters. Their principal occupations came to be hunting and fishing. They made their clothing from the leaves of trees, or from grasses matted together, or from the skins of wild animals. To protect themselves from the weather and from the wild beasts and sometimes from hostile neighbors, some of these men lived in caves, and are called " cave dwellers." Some lived in the clefts and hollows of mountain cliffs, such as are now seen in Arizona and New Mexico, and are called " cliff dwellers." Others, as in Switzerland, lived in dwellings built on the surface of lakes and placed upon piles made from the trunks of trees, and are hence called " lake dwellers."

The Pastoral Life. — But after a time men learned that they might make friends of some animals instead of treating them as enemies. This led to what is called the " domestication of animals." The first animals that were brought into the service of man were the dog, the goat, the cow, the sheep, and the horse. Men now became shepherds and herdsmen. They could get their food not simply by following wild animals in the chase, but from the milk and flesh of some

PREHISTORIC SKETCH OF A MAN AND TWO HORSES' HEADS
(From a cave in France)

of their own domestic animals. But the animals needed food as well as their masters. The flocks and herds fed upon the natural pastures of the place where the people were staying. When these were used up, the people, under their chief, would move off and find fresh pastures for their flocks ; and so they came to be a wandering or " nomad " people. They lived in tents, which could easily be taken down and moved from place to place. Their clothing could now be made from the wool sheared from their sheep and colored with natural dyes.

The Agricultural Life. — With the growth of population

and the increase of the flocks and herds the time came when the pasture lands would not supply all their needs. Now came a great discovery — a discovery which has had a wonderful influence upon human progress. Some persons, more observant than the rest, saw that seed dropped into the ground would grow up; that every seed would bring forth after its own kind; and also that seed would be more likely to grow where the soil was soft and broken up. Men thus learned to till the soil and to raise crops. Cereals, such as wheat and barley, had heretofore grown wild. Now they also became "domesticated." But when seed is planted, it is of course necessary

PRIMITIVE HOE AND PLOW USED IN EGYPT

for the people to remain in the same place in order to gather the harvest at the close of the season. Agriculture thus brought about a great change in the life of the people. Men now became farmers, and ceased the wandering life of shepherds and herdsmen; they settled down in villages while they cultivated the outlying lands.

The land was at first cultivated in common by the whole village community. Every one furnished his share of the work at seed time, and received his share of the crops at harvest time. The lands at a distance, or upon hillsides that could not be plowed, would still be used for the grazing of flocks and herds. The ancient occupations of hunting and fishing would not entirely cease, but might still be pursued as a pastime or even as a business. The people now ceased to live in tents, and built more permanent dwellings. They began to live upon ⸱⸱⸱table foods, and to weave their clothes from vegetable fibers. Thus it came about that the introduction of agriculture led to the adoption of settled life, and prepared the way for the growth of towns and cities.

The Manufacturing and Mercantile Life. — If we stand near the center of a small city or village and look at the various buildings, we shall see that not one of them perhaps is used for a dwelling. On one corner is a bank; on the opposite corner is a store; farther down the street perhaps is a carpenter's shop; still farther down a blacksmith shop. By keeping these buildings in mind we may perhaps see clearly how new occupations grew up in prehistoric times, — that is, occupations different from those of the hunter and fisherman, the shepherd and herdsman, and the farmer. When men settled down to agricultural pursuits, the farmer began to need more and better tools, — a better plow, a better harrow; or those that he already had might need repairing. As he had not the time or skill to do this work himself, some man especially expert would undertake to do the work for him and for the other farmers of the village. One man might do the ironwork — make and repair plows, spades, cooking utensils, etc. He would become the blacksmith. Another might do the woodwork — make and repair carts, furniture, and houses. He would become the carpenter. This would be the beginning of an artisan or manufacturing class.

Again, the farmer would produce more grain than he could use, and the herdsman would breed more cattle than he needed. The farmer would then trade a certain amount of his grain for one of the herdsman's cattle. This would be the exchange of one thing for another — that is, barter. Moreover, the farmer might take his broken plow to the blacksmith for repair, giving him some wheat for his work. This would be an exchange of a thing for a service — which is the same thing as barter. There might now be a certain man who would say to the villagers, " I will take and store up your surplus goods, and trade them off to any persons who want them, receiving a little profit for my services." This man would be a store-keeper or merchant.

During all this time goods have been exchanged for goods or services. Such barter is very inconvenient. It would be more convenient if men had some one thing by which they could estimate the value of other things, and which could be used as a " go-between " in making their exchanges. This go-between is money. Different people have used different things for money. Fishermen have used shells; hunters, the skins of animals; shepherds and herdsmen, sheep and cattle. With the discovery of metals some kind of metallic

money came into use, and this was very convenient, both for the storekeepers and for their customers. And now comes a certain man, something like the storekeeper, who says, " I will receive your surplus money

EARLY GOLD COIN FROM GREECE [1]

for safe-keeping, and return it to you whenever you wish it; in the meantime, if you do not wish to use it, I will lend it to those who need it and will pay you a part of the interest I receive." This is the money merchant, or banker. The use of money thus led to the growth of a mercantile class.

These simple illustrations will serve to show the origin of various industrial classes — the beginnings of man's economic life. The four buildings that were pointed out at the beginning of this section stand for the earliest trades and the earliest forms of mercantile life that were developed in prehistoric society.

The Art of Writing. — When a boy cuts notches on a stick so as to "keep tally," he is using the most primitive form of writing. When a girl ties a knot in her handkerchief to aid her memory, she is doing the same thing. Both the boy and the girl are making signs that appeal to the eye and convey

[1] The winged horse on this coin is Pegasus (p. 88).

an idea. It is none the less writing because it is so entirely different from the kind of writing we are accustomed to use. Such notches and knots were used by the most primitive people; and this was the only way in which some early savages knew how to convey their ideas. The origin and growth of writing illustrate in a remarkable way the early progress of mankind. When the savage holds up his outstretched hand to express the number five, that is sign language. But when he draws five marks on a piece of stone, that is writing.

The earliest kind of writing that came into general use was writing by means of pictures. Picture writing was used by people as far removed from each other as the ancient Egyp'-tians and the American Indians. Pictures at first denoted simply the thing itself that was represented, as a lion or an eagle. Then they were used as symbols suggestive of some idea, as a lion of *strength;* an eagle of *flight* or *swiftness;* the sun of *light* or *brightness.* In the process of time these pictures came to be reduced to mere signs that would scarcely remind one of their origin. The change from crude pictures to signs is well illustrated in the earlier and later Chinese characters.

	Sun	Moon	Mountain	Tree	Dog	Horse	Man
ANCIENT							
MODERN							

CHINESE WRITING

But a great change took place when written signs were used to express the sounds of spoken language. In the Chinese language a written sign corresponds to an entire word; in the Babylo'nian to a single syllable; in the Egyptian, sometimes to a word or syllable, but sometimes to a single letter. Finally, the Phœni'cian language was written with an entire alphabet of letters. It was from the Phœnicians that the principal modern nations derive their alphabets. Every early people had already developed some form of written language before the dawn of history.

The Dawn of History: Written Records. — History, in the proper sense of the word, begins with the use of writing for the purpose of recording facts and events. When a people begin to make a record of themselves that can be read by others, they begin to have a history. Before that time they are regarded as a prehistoric people. We have seen that some men made considerable progress in the arts of civilized life before they had any historical records. We know that the Babylonians and Egyptians were not savages or barbarians, but civilized peoples, when they began to make written records.

Written records may take different forms. The earliest form is that of inscriptions, — writings cut on stone or impressed on brick, or sometimes cut on plates of bronze. They may be found on tablets, on monuments, on the outside and inside of buildings. Written records may also be found in the form of manuscripts. These may be written on some kind of paper made from a plant, such as the Egyptian papy'-rus; or they may be made on parchment made from the skins of animals. We think of a book as a piece of literature printed on many pages and bound in

THE PAPYRUS PLANT

cloth or leather. The ancients had no such books. All their books were in writing. The Egyptian books were written on rolls of papyrus; the Babylonian books were written on clay tablets burnt in the kilns. The beginning of such written records marks what we may call the " dawn of history."

III. Historic Lands and Historic Peoples

Geography as an Aid to History. — It has been said that " Chronology and Geography are the two eyes of History." Chronology helps us to see the *time* when events have occurred, Geography helps us to see the *place* where they occurred. We fix the time by means of *dates*. We fix the place by means of *maps*. The study of geography by the help of maps is one of the most important aids to the study of history. We know that men are influenced to a large extent by their surroundings — by the localities in which they live. For example, the climate of a given place has much to do with the character of the people. Too much heat, or too much cold, tends to weaken or benumb their powers. A temperate climate is most favorable to progress. Moreover, men are most likely to advance in those places where they can obtain the best means of living — where the soil is most fertile, and where the earth furnishes the largest amount of natural resources; also where peoples can most easily exchange their products with one another by land or by water routes.

On the other hand, the progress of man may be hindered by unfavorable surroundings. A barren soil tends to keep men in poverty. Mountain barriers often hem them in and narrow their lives. And so in the early periods of history, especially, man is largely the creature of his circumstances. But with the growth of a higher civilization he may rise above nature, and become to a certain extent its master.

The Historical Zone of the Ancient World. — Let us now trace on the map that strip of territory which contained the lands of the Old World best fitted for early human progress, and upon which the old civilizations flourished. This strip we may call " the historical zone of the ancient world " (see

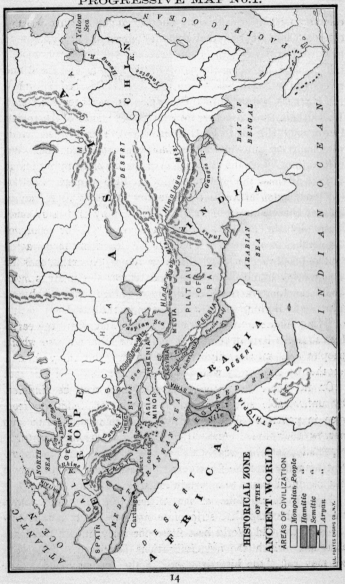

HISTORICAL ZONE
OF THE
ANCIENT WORLD

AREAS OF CIVILIZATION
Mongolian People
Hamitic   "
Semitic   "
Aryan   "

J.L. FOATES ENG'RG CO., N.Y.

colored portions of the map on p. 14). Beginning on the coast of China, let us follow along the line of the Hwang River; then westward along the Hima'laya and the Cau'casus mountains, and finally along the banks of the Danube and the Rhine rivers to the North Sea, — and the line thus traced will mark the northern boundary of the civilized world in ancient times. Its southern boundaries are, in general, the shores of the Indian Ocean and the deserts of Arabia and Africa. The lands thus marked out possess the climate, soil, and other conditions most favorable for human progress; and they became in ancient times the homes of many civilized peoples.

Classification of Ancient Peoples. — The most usual way to classify the various races and peoples of the world is by *color*. Thus we have (1) the black, or Negro, race; (2) the yellow, or Mongolian, race; and (3) the white, or Caucasian, race.

The black race is found chiefly in Africa, Australia, and the neighboring islands. In those lands it includes many peoples that stand low in the scale of human beings; they have done practically nothing for the civilization of the world.

The yellow, or Mongolian, race has occupied the central and eastern parts of Asia, and has made some advance in the arts of civilized life. But it early became stationary, and its contributions to human progress have been few. Of this race the most important people in ancient times were the Chinese. Their country, though great and civilized, was shut off from the rest of the civilized world by its remote situation and the barriers formed by the Himalayas and other mountains.

The most progressive peoples of the world have belonged to the white, or Caucasian, race. There are many Caucasian peoples, and when we attempt to arrange them into distinct groups, we find it difficult, because they were often intermingled with one another. It is, therefore, usual to group them merely according to their *language*. Peoples who speak the same language, or similar languages, even if they are not of the same blood, are closely related to one another in their culture and historical development. By the study of their different languages, we are able to group the white, or Caucasian, peoples into three divisions; namely, (1) the Hamit'ic, (2) the Semit'ic, and (3) the Ar'yan, or Indo-European, peoples.

The Hamitic Peoples. — In early times, the Ham'ites probably occupied all the northern coasts of Africa. But it was only in Egypt, on the rich alluvial soil of the Nile valley, that they found the conditions most favorable to their development. In this gifted land they attained a high place among the nations of the Old World.

The Semitic Peoples. — The original home of the Sem'ites was probably in Arabia. This remarkable race furnished some of the most important historical peoples of the ancient world. The Babylonians and the Assyr'ians settled in the fertile valley of the Ti'gris and Euphra'tes rivers; and the Hebrews and the Phœnicians found a home on the eastern shores of the Mediterranean. From the Phœnicians sprang the Carthagin'-ians, who founded a commercial empire on the northern coasts of Africa. In later times, the Arabians built up a great Mohammedan empire, which covered western Asia and northern Africa and encroached upon southern Europe.

The Aryan, or Indo-European, Peoples. — The peoples that carried ancient civilization to its highest stage were Aryans, or Indo-Europeans. In ancient times they extended from the Gan'ges River to the Atlantic Ocean. They mingled with other peoples whom they conquered and absorbed. But wherever they went they preserved the marks of an ancient common language [1] and of a common primitive culture. To this division of the white race belonged the ancient Hindus of

---

[1] The various groups of Indo-European languages, and the most important peoples speaking them, may be stated as follows: (1) *In'dic*, — peoples of India. (2) *Iran'ic*, — Medes, Persians. (3) *Hellen'ic*, — Greeks, Macedonians. (4) *Ital'ic*, — ancient Romans and their historical descendants, the Italians, French, Spaniards, Portuguese, Roumanians. (5) *Slavon'ic*, — Russians, Bohemians, Poles, Bulgarians, Serbs. (6) *Teuton'ic*, — Germans, Scandinavians, English, Dutch. (7) *Celtic*, — Gaels, Welsh, Irish, Highland Scotch.

India, the Medes and Persians of central Asia, and the Greeks and the Romans of southern Europe. The Indo-European peoples also include the Germans, and other peoples whose history is not so important in the ancient period.

In ancient times India, like China, stood nearly alone. It was separated from the peoples of western Asia by the wide, dry plateau of Iran'. It was the home of civilized peoples, but they did not have much influence upon the rest of the ancient world. Ancient history is, for the most part, a record of the white peoples who occupied the Euphrates and Nile valleys and the coasts of the Mediterranean Sea.

Selections for Reading

Seignobos, Ch. 1, "Origins of Civilization"; Ch. 2, "History and the Records" (1).[1]

Clodd, Part I., "Early History of Mankind" (2).

Hoernes, § 8, "Metals" (2).

Starr, Chs. 3, 4, "Food Getting" (2).

Tylor, Anthropology, Ch. 1, "Man, Ancient and Modern"; Ch. 3, "Races of Mankind" (2).

Ducoudray, Ch. 1, "Beginnings of Civilization" (1).

Keary, Ch. 1, "Earliest Traces of Man"; Ch. 5, "The Nations of the Old World" (2).

Joly, Part II., "Primitive Civilization" (2).

Boughton, Ch. 1, "Primeval Man" (4).

Myres, Ch. 1, "Peoples which have no History"; Ch. 2, "The Dawn of History: the Stage and Actors" (1).

Smith, P., Intro., "The Nations and their Abodes" (4).

Haberlandt, Ch. 9, "Nations of the Mediterranean Race" (2).

Special Study

PICTURE WRITING. — Starr, "First Steps," Ch. 2 (2); Joly, "Man before Metals," pp. 320–326 (2); Keary, "Dawn of History," Ch. 12 (2); Tylor, "Anthropology," Ch. 7, and "Early History," Ch. 5 (2).

---

[1] The figure in parenthesis refers to the number of the topic in the Appendix, where a fuller title of the book will be found.

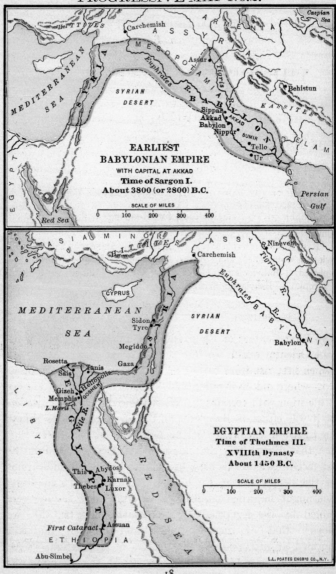

EARLIEST
BABYLONIAN EMPIRE
WITH CAPITAL AT AKKAD
Time of Sargon I.
About 3800 (or 2800) B.C.

SCALE OF MILES
0   100   200   300   400

EGYPTIAN EMPIRE
Time of Thothmes III.
XVIIIth Dynasty
About 1450 B.C.

SCALE OF MILES
0   100   200   300   400

L.L. POATES ENGR'G CO., N.Y.

THE ORIENTAL PEOPLES

CHAPTER II

THE TIGRIS–EUPHRATES VALLEY — THE BABYLONIANS

Synopsis

I. GROWTH OF THE BABYLONIAN EMPIRE. — The First Centers of Civilization. — The Tigris-Euphrates Valley. — Sources of Babylonian History. — The Early City States: Sargon I. — The Old Babylonian Empire: Hammurabi.

II. BABYLONIAN CIVILIZATION. — Babylonian Industry and Art. — Babylonian Government and Laws. — Babylonian Writing and How it was Deciphered. — Babylonian Tablets and Literature. — Babylonian Religion and Temples. — Babylonian Science.

I. GROWTH OF THE BABYLONIAN EMPIRE

The First Centers of Civilization. — In beginning our study of the Oriental world, we may ask, In what part of the East did men first rise from barbarism to a civilized life — in other words, where did civilization first appear? We cannot answer this question with certainty. We may be quite sure, however, that it was either in Babylonia in the lower Euphrates valley, or in Egypt in the valley of the Nile. It has long been supposed that Egypt was the oldest civilized country. But the most recent excavations have brought to light some indications that the people of the Euphrates valley reached a condition which might be called civilized, as early as these results were attained by the Egyptians. However this may be, the two valleys — that of the Euphrates and that of the Nile — formed at first two distinct centers of civilization. Separated as they were by an intervening desert, the Egyptian and

Babylonian peoples took the first steps in the direction of a more civilized life, each unaided by the other. For a long period of time they did not know each other. It was only when they had each broken through their early boundaries and extended their conquests along the eastern coast of the Mediterranean Sea — that is, in Syria — that they began to get acquainted with each other. The first to extend their conquests to this middle land of Syria were the Babylonians. Whether or not they were the first to emerge from barbarism, the Babylonians, or the peoples of the Tigris-Euphrates valley, were the first to extend their culture to lands beyond their own, and to obtain importance as a civilizing people.

The Tigris-Euphrates Valley. — The Tigris and Euphrates rivers rise in the mountains of Armenia and flow southward, pouring their united waters into the Persian Gulf. The valley formed by these rivers — sometimes called Mesopota'mia — we may divide into two parts: the southern or the lowlands, and the northern or the highlands. The southern part, which has received the name of Babylonia, has its chief historical center at Bab'ylon on the Euphrates. Its most marked features are its soft climate and its rich alluvial soil. The northern part of the valley, called Assyria, had its chief center first at Assur on the Tigris, and afterward at Nin'eveh on the same river. Its climate is more rugged than that of the south; and its land, though less fertile, furnishes large supplies of minerals and precious stones.

It was the people who found their way into the southern part, or the lower valley, that first developed a civilized state. It is certain that the lower valley was in very early times settled by a very ancient, non-Semitic race — now called the Sume'rians — who laid the basis of the Babylonian culture. But the territory became at last the home of a Semitic people, who probably came from Arabia. They conquered and absorbed the earlier peoples, taking up their customs and institutions, and becoming the principal race. It is this mixed people that we call the Babylonians.   The date of the earliest occupation of the country by the Semites cannot be accurately fixed; but it can hardly be much later than 5000 B.C.

Sources of Babylonian History. — Not many years ago our knowledge of this ancient people was derived chiefly from the Greek historian Herod'otus and the Chaldæ'an priest Bero'sus. The accounts of these writers, so far as the earliest history was concerned, were based upon traditions, which were of course not very trustworthy. In recent years, however, our knowledge has been greatly increased and made more definite by the large number of excavations made among the ruins of ancient cities.   The remains of palaces and temples have been brought to light, and inscriptions have been deciphered which show the great antiquity of this people, and reveal much regarding their history, their arts, and their institutions.

The Early City States: Sargon I. —The first light that falls upon the Euphrates valley reveals the existence of many cities of more or less importance, each under its own government and ruled by its own king.[1]   At a very early day the rulers of some of these city states sought to establish for themselves something like an empire by bringing other cities under their power.   So far as we know the first successful attempt to create an empire was made by Sargon I., king of Akkad, who is said to have flourished in 3800 B.C. — or as recent scholars say, 2800 B.C.[2]   With Akkad as his capital Sargon extended his authority to the upper part of the Mesopotamian valley and as far west as the Mediterranean Sea.   Other cities, such as Ur and Babylon, afterward vied with one another in taking the lead.   But the early cities of Babylonia finally (about 2300 B.C.) passed under the foreign dominion of the E'lamites — a people who came from east of the Tigris.

---

[1] A few of these ancient cities were Sippar, Akkad, Babylon, Nippur, Tello (ancient Lagash), and Ur (see map, p. 18).

[2] It may be noticed that the older date is not yet abandoned by some Oriental scholars, for example, Jastrow, Driver, Sayce, and Rogers.

The Old Babylonian Empire : Hammurabi. — Although the earliest empire of Babylonia was really established by Sargon I., the most prosperous period of what is usually called the " Old Babylonian Empire " began with Hammura'bi, one of the greatest of ancient kings. He not only drove out the Elamites, but he again brought the whole territory under a single rule. He made the city of Babylon his capital, and labored for the welfare of his people. He constructed dikes to control the waters of the Euphrates, and built a network of canals to irrigate the arid lands. The most remarkable monument of this king is the " Code of Hammurabi," which has been but recently discovered, and is regarded as the oldest code of laws in the world.

During this most prosperous period of its history, the early Babylonian empire was not devoted to the arts of war so much as to the arts of peace. The people were more active in subduing nature than in conquering their neighbors; and hence we find that they made great progress in the development of a civilized life.

II. Babylonian Civilization

Babylonian Industry and Art. — The life of the Babylonian people was greatly influenced by the country in which they lived. Their civilization was based upon the character of their soil, which was made fertile by the waters of the Euphrates. They were primarily a pastoral and agricultural people, grazing their flocks and herds upon the natural pastures of the valley, or raising by artificial means the grains and fruits necessary for food. Their principal grains were wheat and barley. They dug canals to irrigate the outlying fields. They built sewers for drainage, and were the first people to use the arch. In the absence of stone and timber they built their houses of clay, which became hardened in the sun. They soon learned to manufacture bricks burnt in the kiln, from which they constructed their more important buildings. The wool shorn from their flocks they wove into cloths and rugs. As they extended their territory up the valley, they obtained supplies of wood, metals, and precious stones, and from these they wrought new articles for use as well as for ornament. There thus arose a class of traders and merchants, who exchanged the native products of the lower Euphrates with the products of other lands. The Babylonians developed remarkable skill in the working of clay and metals, and also in the carving of precious stones — which acquired the character of a fine art. This is seen in their vases of alabaster, of terra cotta, and of silver, their statuettes of copper and bronze, and especially in their fine intaglio work cut in onyx, jasper, and other precious stones. The intaglio

A CYLINDER SEAL

work was often cut upon cylinder seals, which revolved upon a metallic axis and were used to make an impression upon the clay tablets used for writing.

Babylonian Government and Laws. — The government of Babylonia centered about the king. From the time of the early city kings to the imperial monarchy of Hammurabi we do not find that the people had any share in the government. The king was the source of all authority. He was supposed to derive his authority from the gods. He was the one to determine what was necessary for the welfare of the people. It was under his direction that the wars were carried on, the public works were constructed, the lands were irrigated, the palaces and temples were built, and the laws were administered.

The character of the Babylonian laws is seen in the recently discovered Code of Hammurabi. In this code we meet with three classes of persons, whose names we may translate as patricians, plebeians, and slaves. In reading this law we find it somewhat similar to that of other very early nations, in dealing especially with injuries to persons and property. If a man injured some other person, he was liable to the penalty of " an eye for an eye and a tooth for a tooth." If he injured the property of another, he was required to make good the loss. If an animal caused an injury, the owner was liable. Fines were graded according to the rank of the person injured. The death penalty was inflicted for many offenses besides murder — for theft from a temple or palace, for robbery, bearing false witness, assisting a slave to escape. Some of these laws remind one of the Hebrew laws, which may have been derived in part from the Code of Hammurabi.

The legal customs of the Babylonians may also be seen in the documents which are found inscribed on brick tablets. These show the rules relating to marriage and divorce, property and inheritance, partnership and loans, and also the fact that nearly all contracts required some kind of written evidence.

Babylonian Writing and How it was Deciphered. — The writing employed by the Babylonians was peculiar to this

AN INSCRIPTION IN
CUNEIFORM

part of the Orient. It is what is called " cune'iform," because expressed in wedge-shaped characters (from *cuneus*, a wedge). The writing took this shape because the only writing material of the lower valley was the clay tablet, or cylinder, and because the instrument used in writing was a three-cornered stylus, a sort of gouge, which made a wedge-shaped mark on the surface of the moistened clay. The cuneiform characters were probably first used by the Sumerians; but they were employed by all the peoples of the middle Orient: not only by the Babylonians, but afterward by the Assyrians, and by the Medes and the Persians.

This peculiar method of writing was for a long time a puzzle to modern scholars, but it was at last solved by the eminent English scholar, Sir Henry Rawlinson. As he was traveling through western Persia he found a curious inscription carved upon the face of a high perpendicular rock near the ruins of an old town named Behistun'. The rock rose to a height of 1700 feet, and the inscription was at least 300 feet from the ground. Upon examination he found that it contained a record of the exploits of the great Persian king, Darius I. The record was inscribed in three different languages, — one of these was the ancient Persian, another was the ancient Babylonian. As the Persian was better known, Rawlinson began the work of deciphering with that language. After a vast amount of labor he succeeded in tracing copies of the mysterious characters. But it was only after eleven years of hard work (1835–1846) that he was able to decipher the Persian part of the inscription and to publish it to the world. After five years more (1851) the rest of the cuneiform characters were deciphered; and so from the " Behistun inscription " the curious kind of writing came to be understood. This was a great work. It was now possible to read the written tablets that had come down to us from the ancient Babylonian people.

Babylonian Tablets and Literature. — The clay tablets inscribed with cuneiform characters had been baked in a peculiar way, making them almost indestructible. Thousands of them have now been dug up, revealing the thought and spirit of this ancient people. They really embody an extensive literature — writings on religion and science, history and law, also hymns, penitential psalms,

BABYLONIAN CYLINDER SUPPOSED TO REPRESENT "THE FALL"

and epic poems. They show the beliefs of the people in the form of myths and legends. Some of the stories bear a striking likeness to the stories preserved in the Hebrew Scriptures — such as the accounts of the Garden of Eden, the Deluge, the Tower of Babel, and the confusion of tongues.

Babylonian Religion and Temples. — The Babylonians were a very religious people, although they had many superstitious ideas. Their religion was a form of nature worship. Their

supreme deities were the gods of the heaven, the earth, and the sea (*Anu, Bel,* and *Ea*). Other objects of worship were the sun, the moon, and the several planets. Ishtar, who corresponded to the planet Venus, was the favorite goddess, and was sometimes called "the Queen of Babylon." The people believed that every

BABYLONIAN GODDESS, ISHTAR
(From an Assyrian cylinder)

object has its spirit, good or evil, and that these spirits can be appeased only by the priests and sorcerers through charms.

As the greater gods were supposed to dwell in the heavens, the temples dedicated to them (which were constructed of brick) were built in the form of towers, with a number of receding stories, reaching toward the sky. The temples were presided over by the priests, who were able to exercise a great influence over the people.

FORM OF THE TEMPLE TOWER

Babylonian Science. — The science of the Babylonians was closely connected with their religion. As the gods were supposed to preside over the movement of the heavenly bodies, the position and motion of these bodies were matters of deep concern. From their observations the priests developed a system of astrology, by which it was thought that the will of the gods could be determined and human events could be predicted. As they discovered the regular movement of the heavenly bodies, they acquired some knowledge of astronomical science. They marked out the constellations and gave names to the stars. They divided the year into months, weeks, days, hours, minutes, and seconds. They measured the hours of the day by the sundial, and the hours of the night by the water clock. In their mathematics they adopted the decimal notation; but they also used another system of notation, that is, a system based on the number sixty — which we have inherited from them in our division of the hour and the minute into sixty parts. Besides acquiring considerable knowledge of mathematics, the Babylonians were the first to devise a regular system of weights and measures.

The progress made by the early Babylonians in architecture, science, and the mechanic arts exercised a great influence upon later nations. Indeed, it would be difficult to overestimate the importance of these early steps in the world's civilization.

CUNEIFORM
NUMERALS

Selections for Reading

Knowlton, Topic A 3, "The Tigris-Euphrates Valley" (1).[1]
Goodspeed, Ancient World, pp. 28–32, "Early Babylonian Empire" (1).
Murison, Ch. 1, "Ancient Babylonia"; Ch. 2, "United Babylonia" (5).
Budge, Ch. 3, "Babylonian History from about 3800 B.C." (5).
Myres, Ch. 4, "The Dawn of History in Babylonia" (1).
Ragozin, Chaldea, Ch. 5, "The Babylonian Religion" (5).
Ducoudray, Ch. 3, "The Babylonians and Assyrians" (1).
Boughton, pp. 493–508, "Mesopotamian Institutions" (4).
Smith, P., Ch. 16, "Art and Civilization in Babylonia"; Ch. 17, "Cuneiform Writing and Literature" (4).

Special Study

USES OF CLAY AND BRICK IN THE TIGRIS-EUPHRATES VALLEY. — Smith, P., Ch. 16, § 3 (4); Rawlinson, Vol. I., pp. 67–69, 70–73, 82, 86, 279, 340, 348 (4); Sayce, pp. 90–93, 137–139, 208–213 (5).

[1] The figure in parenthesis refers to the number of the topic in the Appendix, where a fuller title of the book will be found.

CHAPTER III

THE VALLEY OF THE NILE—THE ANCIENT EGYPTIANS

Synopsis

I. EGYPT AND THE EGYPTIAN EMPIRE. — The Valley of the Nile. — The People of the Nile. — Sources of Egyptian History. — Egypt at the Dawn of History. — Growth of the Egyptian Kingdom. — The Egyptian Empire.

II. EGYPTIAN CIVILIZATION. — Egyptian Society and Government. — Egyptian Industry and Industrial Arts. — Egyptian Religion and Science. — Egyptian Architecture and Monuments. — Egyptian Sculpture, Painting, and Music. — Egyptian Writing and Literature. — The Influence of Egypt.

I. EGYPT AND THE EGYPTIAN EMPIRE

The Valley of the Nile. — Nearly every one who thinks of Egypt is likely to quote the oft-repeated words of Herodotus, " Egypt is the gift of the Nile." This is still the best text ever written for a description of the geography of Egypt. Without the Nile, Egypt would have been a desert. Its wonderful monuments would never have been built, and its thousands of inscriptions would not have been written. This river is one of the longest in the world. Rising in the distant lakes of central Africa, it pursues a course of about 4000 miles on its way to the sea. But the part of the valley occupied by the Egyptians extends only about six hundred miles from the mouth of the river — that is, to the rapids called the " First Cataract " near the borders of Ethiopia (map, p. 18). The main part of the valley is only about ten miles wide, being inclosed on either side by a low range of mountains. But at the Delta it spreads out into a wide, open plain, with a coast line of nearly six hundred miles on the Mediterranean.

This valley has not only been cut by the Nile, but its fertility is due to the annual overflow of the river. Outside of the valley, Egypt is a barren waste of sand. The people have obtained their living from the rich soil brought to them from other lands, — from the vast country drained by the sources of the Nile. The ancient Egyptians had an excellent system of irrigation — that is, of distributing the overflow of the Nile by means of canals and large reservoirs. In very recent times the British government has sought still further to control

PART OF THE ASSUAN DAM

these fertilizing waters by building an immense storage dam, over a mile in length, across the river at Assuan', near the First Cataract. From their rich soil the Egyptians were able to raise wheat, oats, barley, and rice in great abundance; so that the country became the granary of the ancient world. From the mountains on either side of the valley they were able to obtain stone suitable for building. This gave them a great advantage over the Babylonians, who were obliged to use the less durable materials, clay and brick.

Egypt may be divided into two principal parts. The lower, or northern, part includes the extended plain about the Delta. Here the soil is most fertile, and it was here that the earliest civilization was developed. It was here that the first empire was established, with its center at Memphis. The upper, or southern, part includes the rest of the valley as far as the First Cataract. In very ancient times both parts of Egypt became dotted with towns and villages, each one of which was a seat of industry and art.

The People of the Nile. — As to the origin of the Egyptians we have very little definite knowledge, except that they belonged for the most part to the Hamitic branch of the white race. It is supposed that in the earliest times — during the Stone Age — the land was inhabited by an uncivilized black people, of whom we know little. The Hamites probably came from the lands along the southern coasts of the Red Sea, either from eastern Africa or from southwestern Arabia. It is also supposed by some writers that the early Hamites, before coming to Egypt, were acquainted with the primitive culture of the people living in the Tigris-Euphrates valley. But whatever may be said regarding the origin of the Egyptian people is very largely a matter of guess.

Sources of Egyptian History. — To travelers visiting Egypt, in ancient as well as in modern times, this land has always been a land of wonders. On every side are seen the monuments left by a great people. Here are gigantic, timeworn columns pointing to the sky; majestic temples laid in ruins; colossal statues mutilated by some barbarian invader; great cities of the dead wrapped in gloom; stupendous monuments of stone which seem impossible to build. And everywhere, upon columns and slabs of stone, are strange writings which for many hundred years no one could read. If these inscriptions could only be deciphered, perhaps the mysteries of Egypt would be solved.

Previous to the nineteenth century little was known about the ancient Egyptians, except what was contained in the fanciful stories of Herodotus, the Greek historian, or might be gathered from the fragmentary writings of Man'etho, an old Egyptian priest. It seemed almost an accident that a key was finally found which furnished to the world a new source of knowledge regarding Egypt. When Napoleon was making his campaign in Egypt, a slab of black stone was found near Roset'ta, at one of the mouths of the Nile. This contained a royal decree written in three kinds of characters. One of these was in "hieroglyphics," the ancient writing of Egypt; and another was in Greek, which all scholars knew. With this inscription as a key the French scholar Champollion deciphered the hieroglyphic characters (in 1821). It was the "Rosetta stone" which opened up new sources of Egyptian history. The many excavations made during the last seventy-five years have also added vastly to our store of knowledge.

Egypt at the Dawn of History. — No one is able to tell the time when Egyptian civilization began. It is generally supposed to have been somewhere between 3000 and 4000 years before Christ. There is no doubt that the civilization of Egypt, like that of every other ancient country, grew up from small beginnings. It is quite clear that Egypt did not always form one country. At first, little villages and towns grew up along the banks of the Nile, in which the people lived a quiet, independent life. They cultivated the rich soil of the valley. They pastured their flocks and herds on the broad fields of the Delta. They built their small rude hovels of straw and mud. They needed very little clothing in that warm climate. They fashioned their tools from polished stones and sometimes from bronze. They sailed up and down the Nile, exchanging their goods with one another. Each village was governed by its own chief and elders. They were contented with their humble lot, as is generally the case with uncultured barbarians who have not much fighting to do.

Growth of the Egyptian Kingdom. — So far as we know the first important step in the development of Egyptian civilization was the union of the different towns under one king. This king is known as Me'nes. The united kingdom was probably established about 3400 B.C., and this date is generally reckoned as the beginning of Egyptian history. The people were so thoroughly imbued with religious ideas that they believed Menes and the later kings were descended from the gods, or at least had received their authority from the gods. The king's power was supreme and was upheld by the priests. The common people were not only his subjects but his servants. The labor of the people belonged to the king. The king, by impressing this labor, was able to build great works in the vicinity of his capital at Memphis, on the lower Nile. Here were built, by a king known as Che'ops (kē'ops), or Khu'fu,

SPHINX AND PYRAMID AT GIZEH

the great pyramids at Gizeh (gē'zĕ), which have withstood the storms of centuries. Here was fashioned that colossus of stone, the Sphinx, which even to-day from his bed of sand seems the " monarch of all he surveys." If we had the miraculous power of vision to trace at a glance a thousand years of progress, we might see the steps in the growth of the ancient kingdom. We should see cities springing up — temples being built — vast stone cemeteries laid out — reservoirs and canals constructed. We should see Egypt growing in population and wealth, and reaching a high degree of prosperity. This prosperity continued until the land was conquered and ruled by a line of foreign kings, called the Hyk'sos — an event that put a stop to the progress of Egypt for nearly two hundred years.

The Egyptian Empire. — After this time of darkness Egypt recovered her independence and entered upon a new period of prosperity. She now extended her authority over other lands and became an empire. She conquered Ethiopia on the south and Syria on the north, under the great warrior-king, Thothmes III. (about 1450 B.C.). She came into contact with the Hit'tites, a mysterious people to the north of Syria. She also came into contact with the culture of the Babylonians, who had previously occupied the Syrian lands. She now acquired a taste for the finer mechanical arts, for a more palatial style of architecture, and for a more luxurious life like that of Babylon.[1] It was during the reign of Ram'eses II. (about 1300 B.C.) that Egypt reaped the glorious results of these conquests. Under this renowned king the civilization of Egypt surpassed that of the other countries of the world. We have

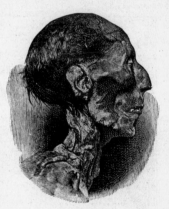

MUMMY HEAD OF RAMESES II.

evidence of the glory of this period in the wonderful monuments erected by Rameses II. at Thebes, the new capital of the Empire.

II. EGYPTIAN CIVILIZATION

Egyptian Society and Government. — The people of ancient Egypt were divided into certain distinct classes. The upper classes included the priests, whose office was hereditary, and

[1] The great influence of Babylonia upon Egypt is shown in the now famous Tel-el-Amarna Tablets discovered near the Nile in 1887 — about three hundred in all, written in Babylonian characters — containing correspondence between the Egyptian king (Amenho'tep IV., the "heretic king") and the kings of Assyria and Babylonia; also letters between Egyptian officials, showing that the Babylonian was the official diplomatic language in Egypt at the time. See Goodspeed, Babylonians and Assyrians, p. 134.

the warriors, who were devoted exclusively to military pursuits. The lower classes comprised the common people, including the artisans, the farmers, and the herdsmen. The land was generally owned by the upper classes, and let out to peasants, who paid their rent in the products of the soil.

Above all these classes was the king, or Pharaoh (fā′rō), who was looked upon as a divine person. He was the fountain of

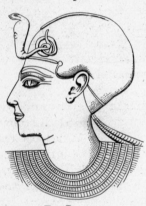

THE PHARAOH

all authority; and the labor, the property, and the lives of the people were at his disposal. The king was assisted in his government by a body of councilors, who carried out his will. The highest offices of the state were held by the priests, who were exempted from all taxes and held the best parts of the land. The government was supported by the army, or warrior class, which was also exempt from taxes and held large landed estates. The great body of government officials preyed upon the common people, who were obliged to furnish their tribute and labor. The government of such a body of taxgatherers and taskmasters necessarily became corrupt and oppressive. We read of workmen, goaded by tyrannical masters, rising in revolt in the manner of a modern "strike" and refusing to continue their work. Sometimes their tasks were lightened, but quite as often they were made more heavy — as in the case of the Israelites in the time of Moses.

Egyptian Industry and Industrial Arts. — The Egyptians, like the Babylonians, were first of all an agricultural people. It was to make their soil more productive that they made the Nile their servant, and developed their remarkable system of irrigation. Their agricultural life is depicted on their ancient tombs. In these pictures one may see men plowing and hoeing

(p. 8), harvesting their crops, threshing and winnowing their grain. One may also see their domestic animals, cattle, sheep, geese, and swine. The Egyptians also acquired great skill in the industrial arts, — working in clay, stone, and glass; in wood, leather, ivory, and in the manufacture of cloths. They were also skillful in the working of the various metals — of the coarser metals, bronze, lead, and iron, and the precious metals, gold and silver. The upper classes wore garments of fine texture, often embroidered

EGYPTIAN SHOEMAKER'S SHOP

with gold. The people exchanged their products with one another by boats plying up and down the Nile, which became an artery of domestic commerce. They also carried on considerable commerce with foreign nations. The articles they did not produce themselves, such as fine woods, ivory, spices, and incense, were generally brought by foreign merchants, who established trading posts on the Mediterranean coast near the mouths of the Nile.

Egyptian Religion and Science. — The religion of Egypt was a strange mixture of various kinds of worship. The lowest form of religion was animal worship, such as was prevalent among the primitive tribes of Africa. The crocodile, the serpent, the hawk, the cow, the cat, and many other animals were held as sacred. For many centuries the bull Apis was worshiped as an important god at Memphis. This low form of worship survived in Egypt even after the development of higher religious ideas. Beside

SERAPIS

this animal worship we find a certain kind of nature worship. The forces of nature were worshiped as gods, and represented in human forms. The mixture of these two

forms of religion — animal worship and nature worship — is seen in the representation of the gods with human bodies and the heads of animals. The animal features came afterward to be regarded as simply symbolical of spiritual qualities. In the higher gods, however, human heads were joined to human bodies.

AMMON

PTAH

The chief object of nature worship was the sun, the source of light and life, whose journey through the heavens was the cause of day and night and an emblem of life and death. The sun god was worshiped under different names at different places — as Ptah at Memphis, as Am'mon at Thebes, as Osi'ris at certain other cities. The gods were often joined in " triads " — the most noted of which was that of Osiris the father, Isis the mother,

JUDGMENT OF THE SOUL BEFORE OSIRIS

and Horus the son. With the recognition of a supreme god, the most learned men of Egypt attained an idea which approached that of monotheism. We sometimes find in the old records such statements as this: " Before all things which actually exist, and before all beginnings, there is one God, unmoved in the singleness of his own Unity."

The Egyptians believed in the continued existence of the soul after death. This belief led to the practice of embalming the body of the deceased, that the mummy might be preserved for the return of the spirit. The Egyptians also believed in a system of future rewards and punishments, and that every soul must be judged before Osiris for the deeds done in the body. The priests of Egypt, who had charge of the religion, were also the learned class. They studied philosophy and the various sciences — astronomy, geometry, arithmetic, and medicine — which here attained a considerable degree of development.

Egyptian Architecture and Monuments. — The religious spirit of the Egyptians is seen especially in their architecture, — the chief examples being their tombs and temples. The most ancient tombs were simply mounds of stone in the shape of pyramids. Such small pyramids are still seen scattered about on the plains in Lower Egypt. Larger and larger pyramids were erected until at last they reached the gigantic proportions that still remain at Gizeh. The Great Pyramid is a vast royal tomb. Tombs were also cut in the rock on the hillsides along the Nile. Such rock sepulchers increased in number until they became a real " city of the dead." The tomb was looked upon as the home of the departed. It contained, first of all,

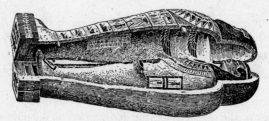

MUMMY CASE

the " mummy," or the embalmed body of the deceased. The body was filled with spices, wound with cloths, and drenched with a peculiar liquid to preserve it from decay. It was then placed in a closely fitting wooden coffin, or " mummy case."

The tomb also contained numerous articles supposed to minister to the wants of the deceased, — jars containing food, chairs, mirrors, and even musical instruments. Sometimes there is found an image of the dead person, together with statuettes of servants who might wait upon him in the future life. The walls of the tomb might be decorated with inscriptions, and pictures illustrating the life of the deceased person. But such elaborate tombs were for the princes and the better classes only; the poorer people were buried in shallow graves marked perhaps by an upright stone.

The most impressive architecture of the Egyptians is seen in their temples — those massive buildings of stone, the ruins

TEMPLE AT LUXOR (Restoration)

of which even to-day excite our wonder. The chief ruins are now found in the vicinity of Thebes — at Karnak and Luxor — and farther up the Nile at Abu-Sim′bel (Ipsambul). The great temples at Karnak and Luxor, dedicated to the god Ammon, with their halls of gigantic columns, were many years in building and were the work of many successive kings. But the greatest of the royal builders was Rameses II. His name and works are the most familiar to the traveler of to-day. One of the mammoth temples built by him was called after his name the "Ramesse′um." But perhaps the most remarkable of his works is the rock temple the remains of which are now seen at Abu-Simbel. Standing before it, one sees the face of the temple cut from solid rock, nearly 120 feet long

ROCK TEMPLE AT ABU-SIMBEL

and 100 feet high. This is decorated with four colossal statues of the great king, 65 feet high. The interior of the temple reaches back into the rock for 180 feet. It contains two immense halls and twelve smaller chambers. Upon the walls are carved drawings and inscriptions celebrating the exploits of the king. All these buildings impress one with their grandeur and immensity; they are seemingly built for all time.

OBELISK NOW IN
NEW YORK

We should also notice the obelisks of Egypt, those graceful monuments of stone covered with inscriptions and pointing to the sky, and in many cases standing near the temples. Two of the most noted of these were erected at Heliop'olis in Lower

Egypt. These were in later times taken to Alexandria; afterward, one was carried to London, and the other to the city of New York.

Egyptian architecture is distinguished by simplicity of general design, but especially by grandeur of proportions and great elaborateness of decoration. It is also distinguished, in some cases, by the use of columns as a means of supporting the roof — a feature which was afterward adopted by the Greeks.

Egyptian Sculpture, Painting, and Music. — The other arts were also cultivated by the Egyptians. This people was probably the first to make sculpture an independent art, — that is,

EGYPTIAN PORTRAIT STATUE

not joined to architecture. Some of the best of their statues belong to a very early period. The colossal Sphinx is perhaps the most striking example of independent sculpture existing in the world. But a less pretentious form of statuary grew up in the form of portrait statues, which were placed in the tombs to preserve the image of the deceased. Many of these portrait statues show a considerable degree of artistic skill. But Egyptian sculpture came to lose its independent character and to be used for the decoration of buildings. It appears in immense figures affixed to tombs and temples, and also in the multitude of bas-reliefs which adorned the walls of buildings. These sculptured designs were almost always colored; and this addition of color to carving was probably the earliest step in the growth of painting. The subjects of these paintings are almost infinite in variety, from

EGYPTIAN GUITAR, HARP, AND PIPES

the representation of the gods to scenes of domestic life. The Egyptians also attained some skill in music; they possessed such instruments as the guitar, the harp, and the pipe, and the drum and the trumpet inspired the Egyptian soldier on his march.

Egyptian Writing and Literature. — The great number of inscriptions cut upon the buildings and monuments of Egypt make them veritable books in stone. But they remained practically sealed books until a key to the peculiar Egyptian writing was found in the "Rosetta stone" (p. 30). The Egyptians first wrote by means of pictures. The characters they used were called "hieroglyphics," that is, sacred writings, which evidently grew out of picture writing. One may see in the hieroglyphic characters some evidence of their origin. For instance, one can find pictures in this line taken from the Rosetta stone: [1]

The Egyptian wrote not only upon stone, but also upon a sort of paper made from the papyrus plant. A roll of written paper would make a "book"; a collection of these rolls would make a library. There thus grew up a vast body of literature — books upon all subjects, — religion, science, art, and upon special subjects, such as geometry, astronomy, music, etc. One of the most remarkable of these books is the so-called "Book of the Dead." It consists of a collection of various writings deposited with the mummy at burial. Some of these contain the words which the soul was expected to say at the judgment-seat of Osiris, for example:

"I have not done evil in place of good . . . I have not defrauded any one of his property . . . I have not caused pain . . . I have made no man to suffer hunger . . . I have done no murder . . . I have not borne false

[1] The line is read *from right to left*, and is translated thus: "**Raising | statue |** of king of Egypt | Ptolemy eternal beloved of **Ptah.**"

witness . . . I have given bread to the hungry, drink to the thirsty, and clothing to the naked, and a boat to the shipwrecked mariner . . . Let no one then make accusation against me in the presence of the great God."

The Influence of Egypt. — Egypt held a place in the valley of the Nile somewhat similar to that held by Babylonia in the Tigris-Euphrates valley. They both represent the earliest stages in the world's civilization, and contributed much to the progress of later nations. But the culture of Egypt was not at first so widely extended as was that of Babylonia. Egypt, however, formed one of the great sources of Oriental culture, from which Europe and modern countries have received valuable materials. Egypt taught the world the principles of a durable architecture. It is true that the Babylonians built massive structures of brick, but these have well-nigh perished; while the stone buildings of Egypt have withstood in a wonderful manner the destructive influences of time. Indeed, we might say that one great difference between the material civilization of Babylonia and that of Egypt was the fact that one was wrought in *clay* and the other in *stone*. The Greeks, no doubt, derived much of their early knowledge of architecture from the Egyptians. The Egyptians have also exercised a strong intellectual influence upon the world. The progress made by them in some of the sciences — especially in geometry and astronomy — was appreciated by later nations, and formed a basis for further scientific achievements. Their higher religious ideas — for example, their idea of a Supreme Being and of a future life — may have had some influence upon the religion of the Hebrews, and even upon that of Christian nations. We may, therefore, look upon Egypt as one of the sources of modern thought and culture.

Selections for Reading

Knowlton, Topic A 2, " The Nile Valley and its Gifts to Civilization " (1).[1]
Seignobos, Ch. 3, "The Egyptians"; Ch. 4, "Assyrians and Babylonians" (1).

[1] The figure in parenthesis refers to the number of the topic in the Appendix, where a fuller title of the book will be found.

Murison, Egypt, Ch. 1, "Introductory"; Ch. 2, "The Ancient Kingdom"; Ch. 3, "The Middle Kingdom"; Ch. 4, "Eighteenth Dynasty"; Ch. 12, "The Book of the Dead" (6).

Myres, Ch. 3, "The Dawn of History in Egypt" (1).

Ducoudray, Ch. 5, "The Monuments and Arts of Egypt" (1).

Lenormant, Vol. I., Bk. III., Ch. 5, "Civilization, Manners, and Monuments of Egypt" (4).

Boughton, pp. 211–250, "The New Empire — XVIIIth and XIXth Dynasties"; pp. 428–450, "The Mesopotamians" (4).

Sayce, Ancient Empires, Part I., "Egypt" (4).

Maspero, Egyptian Archæology, Ch. 5, "The Industrial Arts" (6).

Smith, P., Ch. 1, §§ 3, 8 (sources and inundations of the Nile); Ch. 2 (authorities for the history of Egypt); Ch. 3, § 9 (the Sphinx); Ch. 9, "Industry, Religion, and Arts of Egypt" (4).

Breasted, Ch. 3, "Earliest Egypt"; see also Index, "Obelisk" (6).

Herodotus, Bk. II., Chs. 35–99 (manners and customs of the Egyptians); Bk. III., Chs. 147–152 (accession of Psammetichus) (17).

Special Study

THE PYRAMIDS. — Smith, P., pp. 62–67 (4); Rawlinson, Story of Egypt, Ch. 4 (6); Rawlinson, History of Ancient Egypt, Vol. I., Ch. 7; Breasted, Egypt, from the Earliest Times, Ch. 6 (6); Encyclopedias, Article "Pyramid."

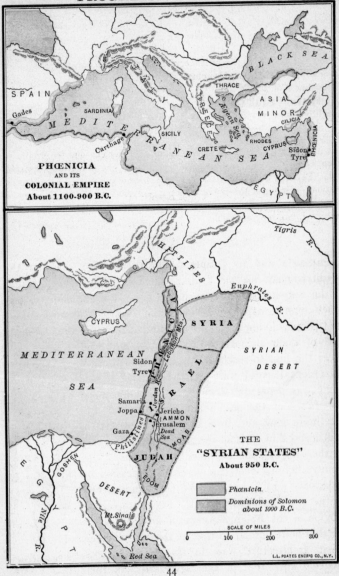

PHŒNICIA
AND ITS
COLONIAL EMPIRE
About 1100-900 B.C.

SPAIN

Gades

MEDITERRANEAN SEA

SARDINIA

Carthage

SICILY

THRACE

CRETE

RHODES

CYPRUS

BLACK SEA

ASIA MINOR

CILICIA

PHŒNICIA

Sidon
Tyre

EGYPT

THE
"SYRIAN STATES"
About 950 B.C.

Phœnicia

Dominions of Solomon
about 1000 B.C.

SCALE OF MILES

0   100   200   300

HITTITES

Tigris R.

Euphrates R.

CYPRUS

SYRIA

MEDITERRANEAN

SEA

Sidon
Tyre

PHŒNICIA

ISRAEL

SYRIAN

DESERT

Samaria
Joppa

Jericho
AMMON
Jerusalem

Gaza

Dead
Sea

MOAB

Philistines

JUDAH

EDOM

EGYPT

GOSHEN

DESERT

Nile R.

Mt. Sinai

Red Sea

L.L. POATES ENG'G CO., N.Y.

44

CHAPTER IV

SYRIAN STATES — THE PHŒNICIANS AND HEBREWS

Synopsis

I. Phœnicia and Ancient Commerce. — Phœnicia and its People. — Phœnician Commerce. — Phœnician Colonies. — The Phœnician Alphabet.

II. Palestine and the Hebrews. — Historical Importance of the Hebrew Nation. — Origin of the Hebrew People. — Periods of Hebrew History. — The Hebrew Prophets. — The Hebrew Religion; Monotheism. — The Hebrew Literature; the Bible.

I. Phœnicia and Ancient Commerce

Phœnicia and its People. — On the eastern coast of the Mediterranean Sea was a land which was the meeting ground of the Babylonians and the Egyptians. For the want of any other common name we call this land Syria. The most important peoples living here were the Phœnicians and the Hebrews, both of whom belonged to the Semitic race. Of these the first to reach an important position in the Oriental world were the Phœnicians. Their home was a narrow strip of land bordering on the shores of the sea, about one hundred and fifty miles long and from ten to fifteen miles in width, and shut off from the interior of the country by the range of the Leb'anon Mountains. This country, having been conquered in succession by Babylonia and Egypt, became the common heir of the two older civilizations. For example, the religion of the Phœnicians was a form of nature worship quite similar to that of the Babylonians. Their architecture was, in its main features, modeled upon that of the Egyptians. In their

PHŒNICIAN
GOLD EARRING

45

mechanic arts they also showed the same refined skill as their older neighbors. The Phœnicians were noted for their fine glass and metal work, their pottery, their textile fabrics, and especially for their purple dyes, which they obtained from a sea snail that was found along the Mediterranean coasts. Besides obtaining many scientific ideas from Babylonia and Egypt, they are said to have discovered the relation between the tides

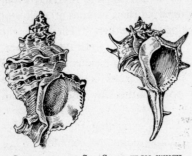

SHELLS OF THE SEA SNAIL FROM WHICH THE PURPLE DYE WAS MADE

of the sea and the motions of the moon. In their limited territory they had no passion for military glory or political dominion; they preferred to pay tribute to others, and pursue their industry. Their government was mainly a government of separate cities, but sometimes these were grouped into loose confederacies. Their greatest cities were Sidon and Tyre, which were in succession the chief seats of Phœnician civilization.

Phœnician Commerce. — The great distinction of this people was their genius for trade and commerce. Upon the sea the Phœnicians established an empire perhaps equal in importance to that which any other Oriental people had established upon the land. The cedars of Lebanon furnished timber for their ships; and with these they became the first masters of the Mediterranean, and the leading commercial nation of ancient times. Their fleets established an early commercial inter-

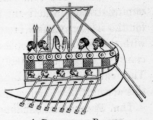

A PHŒNICIAN BIREME

course between Europe, Asia, and Africa. They not only exported their own products to other countries, but they became the common carriers for the known world. From India they brought ivory, jewels, spices, and scented wood. From Arabia they brought gold, precious stones, incense, and myrrh. From the coasts of Ethiopia they added to their cargoes of gold and ivory, supplies of ebony and ostrich feathers. They brought from the shores of the Baltic yellow amber; from Spain, silver, iron, lead, and copper; from Africa the precious metals; and from Britain tin. Thus the different parts of the world were brought into relation with one another by the Phœnician mariners and merchants.

Phœnician Colonies. — To aid in extending their commerce the Phœnicians established trading posts, or colonies, in all the countries visited by their ships and merchants. Not only were these established in the civilized countries of the East for the purchase and exchange of wares; they were also established among the uncivilized peoples of the West for the development of the resources of new lands. The coasts of the Mediterranean became dotted with Phœnician colonies. The most famous of these

PHŒNICIAN COIN

colonies was Carthage (founded about 850 B.C.), which itself established a commercial empire on the northern coast of Africa, and which in later times came into a bitter conflict with Rome. The colonies on the Mediterranean were largely mining stations, where the metals were extracted from the earth for the use of eastern factories. By thus coming into contact with the barbarous people on the European coasts, the Phœnicians spread among them a taste for the arts of civilized life. They carried not only commodities but culture. They have on this account been called the first "missionaries of civilization."

The Phœnician Alphabet. — Perhaps the greatest gift of the Phœnicians to the world was a true phonetic alphabet. It is said that the Phœnicians used their alphabetical writing as a common language of commerce. Wherever they sailed and carried their cargoes, they also carried their alphabet, which Renan aptly calls one of their " exports." The alphabet was, however, the result of a long process of growth. The earliest writing was in the form of pictures to represent material objects, and then in the form of symbols to represent abstract ideas (p. 11). The Egyptians made great progress by using signs to represent syllables, and afterward to represent elementary sounds. This was the beginning of alphabetic writing; but the signs used by the Egyptians were very indefinite and largely pictorial; for example, the sound of *A* was represented by the picture of a feather or by that of an eagle. It was reserved for the

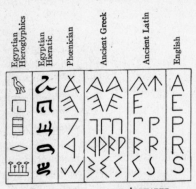

DEVELOPMENT OF THE ALPHABET

Phœnicians to develop a better alphabet, in which the chief elementary sounds were represented by separated and well-defined characters. This alphabet was adopted by many peoples, especially by the Greeks, who gave it to the Romans, by whom it was given to modern nations.

Thus the Phœnicians promoted commerce; they developed a well-defined alphabet; they took up the culture of the Orient and carried it to the West; they must, hence, be regarded as one of the most important of ancient nations.

II. PALESTINE AND THE HEBREWS

Historical Importance of the Hebrew Nation. — South of Phœnicia in Palestine there grew up another Semitic nation, which was in many respects different from every other Oriental people (see map, p. 44). This was the Hebrew nation. Having no great river like that of the Egyptians and that of the Babylonians, and not taking to the sea like the Phœnicians, they did not attain distinction in the industrial or commercial arts. Their greatness did not depend upon art or science, or upon their capacity for political organization. Yet they have perhaps done for civilization as much as any other people of the East, for they became the moral and religious teachers of the world.

Origin of the Hebrew People. — For many years our only knowledge of the ancient Hebrews was derived from the Old Testament. But inscriptions discovered in Egypt and Assyria have thrown much light upon their early history. Such discoveries have also confirmed in many ways the Old Testament records. The Hebrews were at first a pastoral people. They wandered about, like other peoples in Arabia, seeking new pastures for their flocks and herds. They traced their descent from Abraham, who, it was said, came from Ur, a city in Babylonia (map, p. 18). Like the majority of the people in that country, he belonged to the Semitic race. He became dissatisfied with the prevailing religion of his countrymen (p. 26). He was inspired with higher ideas regarding God. He was led to seek a new home in some land that would be pointed out to him. In his wanderings to the west he visited Egypt, and finally settled with his family and followers in Ca'naan. This he looked upon as the " promised land." Here his descendants grew in numbers until they formed the " twelve tribes of Israel." After many years a famine drove them to seek food in Egypt. In time they received a fertile portion of land in Go'shen, near the Delta of the Nile (map, p. 44).

At first their life in Egypt was happy and peaceful. But later there arose a new dynasty of kings, who sorely oppressed them. They were forced to do the work of slaves. Their complaints served only to increase their burdens. At last a great leader appeared, who, like our own Lincoln, inspired the oppressed people with the hope of deliverance. This leader was Moses, who was recognized as divinely appointed for this work. At a time when the Egyptians were suffering from a series of plagues, Moses gathered together his people and led them out from the land of bondage. They crossed the headwaters of the Red Sea, and became once more homeless wanderers in the desert. But they now came to feel that they were at least an independent people, with a destiny of their own.

Periods of Hebrew History. — From the time of their escape, or " exodus," from the tyranny of the Egyptian Pharaoh, the history of the Hebrews falls into three quite distinct periods:

(1) *From the Exodus to the Establishment of the Monarchy.* (about 1300–1095 B.C.) — For forty years the "children of Israel " — for so they called themselves — wandered hither and thither amid all sorts of trials and discouragements. They were held together only by the strong hand of their leader. They were trained to believe that their hope of final deliverance was in Jehovah, whom they must worship as their only God. They were kept to their faith by a series of rites and ceremonies which they were compelled to observe. They carried with them a movable temple, the Tabernacle, which they looked upon as the " dwelling place of the God of Israel."

THE TABERNACLE (Restoration)

Near Mt. Sinai they received the Ten Commandments. These set forth their moral duties — their duties to Jehovah and their duties to one another. They were also taught many rules as to how they should take care of their health, so that they might become a vigorous nation. At last they found themselves on the eastern banks of the river Jordan opposite the city of Jer'icho (map, p. 44). Here Moses, their great leader and lawgiver, died.

Moses was succeeded by Joshua, the Israelitish warrior. Under him they crossed the Jordan, captured Jericho, and began

the conquest of Palestine (or Canaan, as they then called it).
The land was parceled out among the twelve tribes. The people
now began to settle down in villages and cities, like their heathen
neighbors. They became an agricultural, and no longer a
merely pastoral, people. They tilled the ground and raised
crops for their living. But their chief occupation was war
with their enemies and strife among themselves. They at
length became dissatisfied with their present leaders, or " judges "
as they were called, and demanded a king to rule over them.

(2) *From the Establishment of the Monarchy to the Division
of the Kingdom* (1095-975 B.C.). — During this period the
nation was ruled by three distinguished kings. The first of
these was Saul, who carried on war with the neighboring tribes,
the Am'monites, the Philis'tines, and others. The second king
was David, who captured Jerusalem and made it the capital of
the kingdom, building a royal palace, with the aid of Phœnician architects. By his conquests he established an empire
extending from the Euphrates on the north to the Red Sea on
the south. The third and last king of the united monarchy
was Solomon, who gave his kingdom an air of Oriental magnificence. He built a splendid temple at Jerusalem, and adorned
the city with sumptuous palaces. He amassed enormous

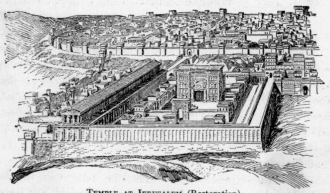

TEMPLE AT JERUSALEM (Restoration)

wealth and surrounded his throne with pomp and splendor.
He married an Egyptian princess, and established a luxurious
court like that of the Eastern kings. But his glory was purchased at the expense of justice and his nation's honor. He
laid heavy burdens upon his subjects and impoverished them.
He disregarded the laws of Moses, and the Hebrew kingdom
became practically an Oriental monarchy like that of Babylon.

(3) *From the Division of the Kingdom to the Babylonish
Captivity* (975–586 B.C.). — During this time the Hebrew nation formed two distinct kingdoms. Ten tribes revolted and
formed the kingdom of Israel, with its capital at Sama′ria; the
remaining two tribes formed the kingdom of Judah, with its
capital at Jerusalem. The kingdom of Israel was finally conquered by the Assyrian king Sargon II. (722 B.C.), and the
people were removed to Nineveh, where they were " lost " as a
separate people. The kingdom of Judah was destroyed by
the Babylonian king Nebuchadnez′zar (586 B.C.), and the inhabitants were carried away as captives to Babylon; but they
were afterward allowed to return to Jerusalem (537 B.C.) as
subjects of Cyrus, the Persian king.

The Hebrew Prophets. — During those troublesome times
there arose a class of men who have held high place in the world's
history. They were not statesmen. They were not warriors.
They were the teachers of morality, and called " prophets,"
or seers — men such as Eli′jah, Eze′kiel, Isa′iah, and Micah.
In the midst of a sinful generation they preached the words
of righteousness. They deplored the fact that their own people
were drawn away after the false gods of other nations; that
they were deceived with false ideas of religion — with mere
burnt offerings — and failed to heed the duties of men to one
another. It is for this, said the prophets, that Jehovah has
" afflicted them and delivered them into the hands of those that
plundered them." Isaiah appealed to the people: " Hear
the word of Jehovah. To what purpose is the multitude of
your sacrifices? I delight not in the blood of bullocks and

lambs. Wash you, make you clean, cease to do evil, learn to do good; relieve the oppressed, be just to the fatherless, plead for the widow." Thus the Hebrew prophets were the preachers of charity and justice not only to their own people, but to all men and to every age.

The Hebrew Religion; Monotheism. — In spite of the fact that the people and the rulers were often led astray by the influence of foreign religious ideas, still the highest and most distinctive feature of the Jewish civilization was the growth of monotheism. We must judge of the real character of the Jewish religion, not by the practices of those who departed from it, but by the teachings of those who were its highest expounders — Moses and the prophets. In these great teachers we find the true idea of monotheism. This is not simply the idea of the Egyptians, that there is one god higher than other gods; it is the idea that there is only one Supreme God. Another feature of the Jewish religion was the fact that it was closely linked to morality. Religious worship and moral duty were regarded as two

HEBREW HIGH PRIEST

sides of a complete life. The history of the nation was a constant struggle against false ideas of religion and false ideas of morality. When the priests were carried away with the idea that religion consisted simply in rites and ceremonies, and the kings were seeking the pomp and luxury of the East, and the people were falling into wickedness and idolatry, it was left to the later prophets to become the true expounders of religion and the moral law.

The Hebrew Literature; the Bible. — The idea of monotheism was the inspiring idea of the Hebrew literature, as it was of the Hebrew religion. This literature is contained in what we call the Old Testament, and comprises (1) the Pentateuch, or the legal books; (2) the historical books; (3) the poetical books; and (4) the books of the prophets. In their literary genius the Hebrews surpassed all other Oriental nations. In the writings of their poets and prophets we find the highest examples of religious fervor and imaginative description. The Psalms of David, the Book of Job, and the Prophecy of Isaiah, considered merely as literary compositions, are unsurpassed in the literature of any people. When we consider the writings of the Hebrews and their religious influence upon the civilized world, we must assign to this nation a high place among the historical peoples of ancient times.

Selections for Reading

Knowlton, Topic A 4, "The Early Peoples of the Mediterranean" (1).[1]

Seignobos, Ch. 7, "The Phœnicians"; Ch. 8, "The Hebrews" (1).

Sayce, Ancient Empires, Part II., "Phœnicia" (4).

Rawlinson, History of Phœnicia, Ch. 18, "Phœnician Manufactures" (7).

Lenormant, Vol. II., Bk. VI., Ch. 4, "Civilization and Influence of the Phœnicians" (4).

Ducoudray, Ch. 4, "Religion and Social State of the Jews" (1).

Goodspeed, Ancient World, pp. 43–50, "The Syrian Empires" (1).

Ottley, Ch. 3, "Israel in Egypt and in the Wilderness"; Ch. 5, "The Age of the Judges"; Ch. 7, "Solomon and the Division of the Kingdom" (7).

Petrie, Ch. 2, "Israel in Egypt"; Ch. 4, "The Period of the Judges" (7).

Kent, Hebrew People, Vol. I., Part I., § 5, "Genesis of the Hebrew People"; Part III., § 13, "The Palace and Temple of Solomon " (7).

The Bible, Numbers, Ch. 4 (the Levites and their duties); Ezekiel, Chs. 26–28 (Exaltation of Tyre).

Special Study

PHŒNICIAN COMMERCE. — Rawlinson, Phœnicia, Chs. 5, 10 (7); Ducoudray, Ch. 5 (1); Lenormant, Vol. II., pp. 199–206 (4); Encyclopedias, Articles "Phœnicia," "Commerce."

[1] The figure in parenthesis refers to the number of the topic in the Appendix, where a fuller title of the book will be found.

CHAPTER V

THE FIRST WORLD EMPIRE — THE ASSYRIANS

Synopsis

I. ASSYRIA AND THE ASSYRIAN CONQUESTS. — The Rise of Assyria. — The First Assyrian Empire. — The Second Assyrian Empire. — The Fall of the Assyrian Empire. — Babylon under Nebuchadnezzar.

II. ASSYRIO-BABYLONIAN CIVILIZATION. — Assyria the Heir of Babylonia. — The Assyrian Government and the Provinces. — Assyrian Architecture; Royal Palaces. — Assyrian Sculpture and Painting. — The People of the Mesopotamian Valley.

I. ASSYRIA AND THE ASSYRIAN CONQUESTS

The Rise of Assyria. — We have seen how the Babylonians and the Egyptians, the Phœnicians and the Hebrews grew up as independent nations. We shall now see how they were all absorbed into one great world empire. The people who established this empire were the Assyrians. They belonged to the Semitic race, like the Babylonians, and dwelt in the upper part of the Tigris-Euphrates, or Mesopotamian, valley. In the rugged climate of the north they developed

ASSYRIAN WAR CHARIOT

a hardy and warlike character. The Assyrians have been compared to the Romans as a military and conquering people. They cultivated the arts of war, having well-organized bodies of infantry, cavalry, and war chariots.

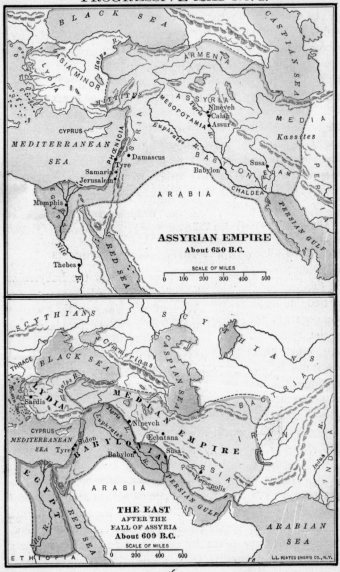

BLACK SEA

LYDIA ASIA MINOR

ARMENIA

CASPIAN SEA

HITTITES

Halle R.

ASSYRIA

MESOPOTAMIA

Tigris R.

Nineveh
Calah
Assur

MEDIA

Kassites

CYPRUS

PHENICIA

SYRIA

Euphrates R.

BABYLONIA

Susa

ELAM

PERSIA

MEDITERRANEAN SEA

Damascus
Tyre
Samaria
Jerusalem

Babylon

CHALDEA

EGYPT

ARABIA

PERSIAN GULF

Memphis

Nile R.

RED SEA

ASSYRIAN EMPIRE

About 650 B.C.

SCALE OF MILES

0   100   200   300   400   500

Thebes

SCYTHIANS

SCYTHIANS

THRACE

BLACK SEA

Cimmerians

CASPIAN SEA

BACTRIA

LYDIA

Halys R.

MEDIAN EMPIRE

Sardis

CYPRUS

Tigris R.

Nineveh

IRAN

MEDITERRANEAN SEA

Sidon
Tyre

BABYLONIA

Euphrates R.

Ecbatana

Babylon

Susa

PERSIA

Indus R.

INDIA

EGYPT

Nile R.

RED SEA

ARABIA

Persepolis

PERSIAN GULF

THE EAST

AFTER THE
FALL OF ASSYRIA

About 609 B.C.

SCALE OF MILES

0   200   400   600

ETHIOPIA

ARABIAN SEA

L.L. POATES ENGR'G CO., N.Y.

The center of Assyrian power was at first the city of Assur; this was a colony of Babylonia situated on the upper Tigris River and the seat of the worship of the god Assur. The city obtained its independence from Babylonia, and gave the name "Assyria" to the whole surrounding country. After a time, the Assyrian capital was transferred from Assur to Nineveh. The new capital became the permanent seat of the empire. The external history of Assyria is a history of almost continual war. A desire for conquest under their ambitious kings seemed the ruling passion of the Assyrian people. The long names of these kings have no special interest for us, except as warriors and conquerors.

The First Assyrian Empire (1120–745 B.C.). — The founder of the first Assyrian empire was the great warrior king of Nineveh, Tiglath-Pile′ser I. He subdued the surrounding cities, and carried his arms to the west. After many wars he finally reached the coasts of the Mediterranean. In an inscription (now preserved in the British Museum), he calls himself "the king of kings, the lord of lords, the ever victorious hero." The merciless char-

ASSUR-NAZIR-PAL

Relief in British Museum

acter of Assyrian warfare is seen in the career of another noted king, Assur-nazir-pal, whom, in spite of his fame, we may regard as one of the most cruel of conquerors. The lands which he conquered, he desolated, ravaging the fields and killing the people. In his own words, which have come down to us, we may read his boasting of the pyramids he has built of human heads, of the captives flayed alive, and of the children burned to death. The conquests of this king were continued by Shalmaneser II., whose deeds are recorded on the famous "black obelisk" which he built. On one side of this obelisk we may

BLACK OBELISK OF
SHALMANESER II.

see a procession of subjects bringing their gifts and tribute to the king. The many wars of the period were intended to bring into subjection the neighboring countries — especially Babylonia to the south, and Syria to the west. But these conquests were not permanent, and the first empire fell into a state of decline.

The Second Assyrian Empire (745–606 B.C.). — The failure of the first empire was due to the lack of an efficient mode of governing the subjects. When a people were once conquered and made tributary, they were left to themselves; and consequently they were tempted to rise in rebellion against the king when he demanded further tribute. This policy was changed by a distinguished king who is regarded as the founder of the second Assyrian empire — Tiglath-Pileser III. He adopted the policy of organizing the conquered cities into districts, or provinces, each subject to a governor of his own appointment. He also adopted the practice of "deportation" — that is, of scattering rebellious peoples into different parts of the empire, thus preventing any united efforts at revolt. In accordance with this practice, Sargon II., when he had conquered Samaria, carried away the "Ten Tribes" of Israel and scattered them among the towns of Media, where they were forever

SEAL OF SENNACHERIB

"lost" as a separate people. The success which attended the campaigns of Sargon in Israel led his successor, the more famous King Sennach'erib, to continue these expeditions. He accord-

ingly attempted to reduce the cities of Phœnicia and Judah.
The story of the destruction of his army by a pestilence at
Jerusalem forms a noted chapter in Old Testament history
(II Kings, Ch. 19). It is also celebrated in the poem by Lord
Byron beginning :

> "The Assyrian came down like a wolf on the fold,
>   And his cohorts were gleaming with purple and gold."

The last years of Sennacherib were devoted to wars with Babylonia, resulting finally in the total destruction of the city of
Babylon (688 B.C.). The conquests of the three kings just
mentioned resulted in bringing nearly the whole of western
Asia under the Assyrian power. The completion of the empire
was effected by the two following kings — Esarhad′don, who
brought Egypt under his control, and
Assur-bani-pal, who reduced the rebellious city of Tyre. Under these
two monarchs the Assyrian empire
reached its greatest extent and its
greatest glory, and became, in fact,
what we may call the first world empire. One of the most remarkable
monuments of this period is the Royal
Library of Assur-bani-pal, which may
be regarded as the first great library
of the world. It was gathered from
various conquered cities, a considerable part of it being plundered from
Babylon. It contained about 30,000
tablets, which have been brought to
light in recent years, and have re-

ASSYRIAN CLAY TABLET

vealed to modern scholars the history and civilization of a people
who flourished more than twenty-five centuries ago.

The Fall of the Assyrian Empire. — But the great empire
of Assyria was not always to last. The subject peoples chafed

under its oppressive rule. Babylonia had frequently tried to throw off the Assyrian yoke, but she failed until she found an ally in a people living east of the Tigris. This people was the Medes, who had themselves been subject to Assyria for more than a century. They had now recovered their independence and established an empire of their own. With the aid of the Medes, the Babylonians succeeded in destroying Nineveh and overthrowing the Assyrian monarchy (606 B.C.). The dominions of Assyria were now divided between the conquerors, — Media ruling the countries to the east of the Tigris, and Babylon the countries to the west.

Babylon under Nebuchadnezzar.— In this way Babylon recovered her ancient power, and ruled with increased splendor. The great king Nebuchadnezzar restored her fallen cities, and

THE NAME NEBUCHADNEZZAR IN CUNEIFORM

made her for a short time the center of Eastern civilization. His dominions extended over the valley of the Euphrates and the countries of Syria to the borders of Egypt (lower map, p. 56). The Jews who refused to respect his authority were treated with severity. Jerusalem was taken and sacked; and the tribes of Judah were carried away into captivity. The great king rebuilt the city of Babylon, surrounded it with massive walls, and adorned it with sumptuous palaces. The walls were said by Herodotus to be 84 feet thick and 320 feet high, containing 100 brazen gates, and making a circuit of 60 miles around the city. To please his queen, a Median princess, Nebuchadnezzar built the famous "hanging gardens," which were artificial hills built in the form of immense terraces and covered with luxuriant shrubs and flowers. During this brief period of her later supremacy Babylon attained, in the highest degree, all the luxury and pomp peculiar to Oriental civilization. But Babylon the Great finally fell before the rising power of Persia (538 B.C.), which absorbed all the countries of western Asia.

II. Assyrio-Babylonian Civilization

Assyria the Heir of Babylonia. — A great part of the civilization of the Assyrians was inherited from the early Babylonians. It is true that these two peoples belonged to the same race; yet they were quite different in spirit. The Babylonians were peaceful in disposition, given to agriculture, fond of literature, well educated, and comparatively humane in the conduct of their wars. The Assyrians cared little for agriculture; their wars were undertaken for plunder and were conducted with ferocity. Still, many of the arts of peace developed by the Babylonians were taken up by the Assyrians. The Assyrians, for example, adopted the cuneiform method of writing used by their older neighbors, and showed something of the same taste for literature. They acquired the same, if not superior, skill in the mechanic arts, and adopted the same scientific ideas. Their religion was in all essential respects the same as that of the Babylonians. They generally adopted the same strict methods in their legal transactions. The advancement which they made upon the Babylonians was principally in the direction of a more highly developed imperial government; a more palatial style of architecture; and a greater appreciation of sculpture as a decorative art.

ASSYRIAN KING IN ROYAL ROBES

The Assyrian Government and the Provinces. — The government of the Assyrians, like that of the Babylonians, centered about the king, who was looked upon as a sort of divine person. He was the supreme source of authority. To exalt his person he was surrounded by a court composed of officers of the palace, such as the grand vizier, the royal cupbearer, the royal treasurer, and the captain of the guards. These officers were ennobled by their service to the king.

The provinces of the empire now received a definite organization. They were divided into two classes — those under governors, or "satraps," appointed by the king; and those under native rulers approved by the king and subject to him. The provinces were all alike obliged to furnish tribute for the

Assyrian Palace at Nineveh (Restoration)

royal treasury and troops for the royal army. Except the priestly class, and the court nobility, on the one hand, and the class of slaves, on the other hand, the subjects of the king possessed a certain degree of equality. But they were all equally the subjects of absolute power. They had no protection against unjust laws; and what we call "political liberty" was unknown.

Assyrian Architecture; Royal Palaces. — The influence of the imperial idea, and the great dignity attached to the king, are seen in the character of the Assyrian architecture. The most important buildings were not the temples, as in Babylonia, but the royal palaces, upon which the wealth of the empire was expended. The temple was merely accessory to the palace, and was still built in the form of a terraced tower. But the palace assumed another form. It was built over an extended area upon the flat surface of an artificial hill or elevation over-looking a plain or river. Although this country furnished stone suitable for building, the Assyrians continued, like the Babylonians, to use brick for architectural purposes. The royal palace consisted of a vast system of courts, corridors, and galleries. In spite of the fact that the Assyrians used the arch in sewers, the roof of the palace was generally supported by wooden beams placed upon massive brick walls. Slender columns, made of stone or of wood covered with metal, were often used for ornamental purposes.

Assyrian Sculpture and Painting. — The Assyrians acquired considerable skill and proficiency in the art of sculpture. This was chiefly employed in the way of ornamentation for the royal palaces. The most conspicuous, but not the most pleasing, examples of Assyrian sculpture are seen in the enormous and grotesque figures that were usually placed at the entrance of the palace. They consisted of winged bulls or lions with human heads, — symbolizing perhaps strength, swiftness, and intelligence. They were supposed to guard the palace from the intrusion of evil spirits. The highest examples of Assyrian art are seen in the bas-reliefs, cut on alabaster slabs and adorning the interior of the royal palaces. Here are represented scenes of war and

WINGED BULL WITH HUMAN HEAD

events in the life of the king. In these sculptured reliefs we may see the best specimens of ancient drawing before the time of the Greeks. From the large number of these reliefs we have obtained much of our knowledge of Assyrian life and customs. The flat and strong colors — often a brilliant vermilion — which were placed upon the Assyrian bas-reliefs show the early steps in painting, which had not yet reached the dignity of an independent art.

ASSYRIAN BAS-RELIEF

The People of the Mesopotamian Valley. — Herodotus, who visited Babylon, tells us that the costume of the people consisted generally of a long linen gown reaching to the feet, over this a woolen mantle, and then a short cape thrown over the shoulders. These garments were more or less richly embroidered. Many of the people were engaged in the manufacture of textile fabrics, such as carpets, rugs, and muslins, which were produced not only for the home market but for the foreign trade. Many persons were employed in the cutting of seals and the engraving of gems, in which the Babylonians and Assyrians greatly excelled. But the great mass of the people were farmers or merchants. Upon the rich soil of the valley were raised abundant harvests of cereals, especially wheat and barley, and large groves of date-bearing palm trees. The Mesopotamian valley was known above all things else as a grain-producing country, and furnished an easy means of subsistence for the people. The agricultural people formed the poorer class, and were generally gathered together in villages. They lived in cone-shaped hovels, built of clay, with no windows and lighted only by an opening in the peak. A village would present much

© *Underwood & Underwood.*

AN ARAB "BEEHIVE" VILLAGE IN MESOPOTAMIA, LIKE THE VILLAGES OF THE
ANCIENT BABYLONIANS

the appearance of a collection of beehives. Next to the agricultural class, the merchant class was the most numerous. The Bible speaks of Babylonia as "a land of traffic," and of Babylon as "a city of merchants." The people, especially on the borders of the Persian Gulf, were devoted to navigation and commerce. The Tigris and Euphrates rivers were highways of communication with the neighboring countries of western Asia.

From this brief review we can see that the Tigris-Euphrates valley was one of the great centers of ancient civilization. By its commercial and political relations its culture was extended to the shores of the Mediterranean Sea. The religious ideas of the Babylonians and Assyrians became the common property of the East. Their notions regarding the origin of the world and the early condition of mankind became entwined with the Hebrew account of creation.   Their progress in certain branches of science, especially in astronomy, formed a contribution to the intellectual development of the ancient world.   Their skill in some of the industrial arts, such as weaving and the cutting of gems, has scarcely been equaled by modern artists. Their political organization formed the basis of the later imperial systems of the East, which were afterward, as we shall see, transferred to Europe under the later Roman Empire.

Selections for Reading

Goodspeed, Ancient World, pp. 51–57, "The World Empire of Assyria" (1).[1]

Murison, Babylonia and Assyria, Ch. 5, "Consolidation of the Assyrian Empire"; Ch. 15, Civilization (of Assyria); pp. 18–20, "The Tel-el-Amarna Tablets" (5).

Sayce, Ancient Empires, Ch. 2, "Babylonia and Assyria" (4).

Lenormant, Vol. II., pp. 417–467, "Civilization, Manners and Monuments of Assyria" (4).

Maspero, Life, Ch. 16, "Assurbanipal's Library" (4).

Rawlinson, Vol. II., pp. 516–520, 553 (the hanging gardens and walls of Babylon) (4).

Josephus, Antiquities, Bk. X., Ch. 8 (capture of Jerusalem by Nebuchadnezzar); Bk. XI., Ch. 1 (return of the Hebrews from captivity) (9).

Herodotus, Bk. I., Chs. 178–183 (description of Babylon) (17).

The Bible, II Kings, Chs. 18, 19 (Sennacherib and Hezekiah); Daniel, Chs. 1–4 (Nebuchadnezzar and Daniel); Ch. 5 (Feast of Belshazzar).

Special Study

ASSYRIAN ARCHITECTURE. — Smith, P., pp. 377–383 (4); Lenormant, Vol. I., pp. 456–465 (4); Maspero, Life, Ch. II, (4); Rawlinson, Vol. I., pp. 277–339 (4).

[1] The figure in parenthesis refers to the number of the topic in the Appendix, where a fuller title of the book will be found.

CHAPTER VI

THE SECOND WORLD EMPIRE — THE PERSIANS

Synopsis

I. THE CONQUESTS OF PERSIA. — The East before the Persian Conquests. — Rise of Persia under Cyrus the Great. — Conquest of Lydia. — Conquest of Babylonia and Egypt. — Conquests in Europe under Darius.

II. THE CIVILIZATION OF PERSIA. — The Government and Provinces. — The Persian Army and Navy. — Persian Art and Literature. — Persian Religion and Morality. — Persian Wealth and Luxury. — Historical Significance of Persia.

III. REVIEW OF ORIENTAL NATIONS. — The Beginnings of Civilization. — The Course of Oriental History. — The Blending of Culture by Conquest and Commerce. — Transmission of Oriental Culture to the West.

I. THE CONQUESTS OF PERSIA

The East before the Persian Conquests. — Herodotus tells us that Persian boys were taught three things — to ride the horse, to shoot the bow, and to speak the truth. The Persians became a nation of soldiers, especially noted for their cavalry, and of men with a high sense of honor and justice. To this may be due the fact that they conquered a great part of the world, and ruled it better than it had ever been ruled before.

If we wish to understand the growth of this great empire, we should first consult the map showing the countries of the East after the fall of Assyria (p. 56). We notice four countries:

(1) The Median empire, which had risen out of the previous empire of Assyria. This extended on the north to the Caspian Sea, on the west to the Ha'lys River, on the south to the Persian Gulf, and on the east to the plains of Iran. It existed only for a brief period; and though extensive in territory it was the shortest-lived of all the great Oriental monarchies.

(2) The new Babylonian empire, in which Babylon, after her long subjection to Assyria, recovered for a brief time her independence. The new empire extended from the Tigris River on the east to the Mediterranean on the west.

(3) The Lydian empire, which covered the western part of Asia Minor from the Halys River almost to the Ægean Sea, on the coasts of which had grown up a number of Greek cities.

(4) Egypt, which had recovered her independence from Assyria through the efforts of a late Egyptian king, Psammet′-ichus, — and now occupied its original territory in the valley of the Nile.

Rise of Persia under Cyrus the Great (558–529 B.C.). — We are now to see how these different countries became absorbed

BAS-RELIEF OF CYRUS

in the new world empire of Persia. Persia had been a small province of the Median empire situated on the Persian Gulf. About the middle of the sixth century B.C. a prince, whom we know as Cyrus the Great, revolted from Media and succeeded in reducing that state to his own authority. Many stories are told about the birth and early life of this great man; but they are largely mythical. His chief significance for us is in the fact that he created the most powerful empire that the world had yet seen, and established a policy which was destined to bring Asia into conflict with Europe. The growth of this empire resulted from the conquests made by three kings — Cyrus, its founder, and his successors, Camby′ses and Dari′us.

Conquest of Lydia. — With the overthrow of the Median empire, Cyrus proceeded to extend his kingdom to the west. This required the conquest of Babylonia, west of the Tigris, and of Lydia, west of the Halys River. Lydia was especially alive to the dangers of Persian aggression. Her energetic king, Crœsus, who had now under his control all of Asia Minor west of the Halys, assumed the part of defender of western Asia. He is said to have consulted the oracle of Apollo at Delphi (p. 137), and to have received the response that "if he crossed the Halys, he would destroy a great empire." Not thinking that this might apply to his own empire, as well as to that

PERSIAN FOOT SOLDIERS

of Cyrus, he crossed the river, and after an indecisive battle retreated into his own territory. Without delay Cyrus invaded Lydia and captured Sardis, the capital. Asia Minor now became a part of the Persian empire.

Conquest of Babylonia and Egypt. — After the conquest of Lydia Cyrus turned his attention to his next great rival, Babylonia. With the fall of Babylon (538 B.C.), this empire also became a part of his dominions. It is to the credit of Cyrus that he permitted the Jews, who had been held in captivity since the days of Nebuchadnezzar (see p. 60), to return to their home in Jerusalem. After the death of Cyrus, his son Cambyses (529–522 B.C.) extended the Persian authority over Phœnicia, Cyprus, and Egypt. But an army sent into Ethiopia perished in the sands of the desert; and an expedition planned against Carthage failed, because the Phœnician sailors, who were in the service of Cambyses, refused to serve against their kinsfolk. The rule of Cambyses was oppressive and often cruel, and was marked by frequent revolts in different parts of the empire.

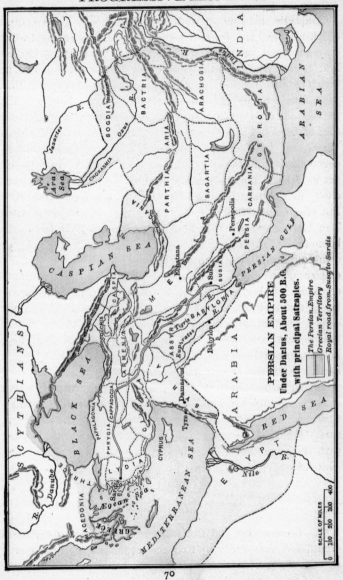

PERSIAN EMPIRE
Under Darius, About 500 B.C.
with principal Satrapies.

The Persian Empire
Grecian Territory
Royal road from Susa to Sardis

SCALE OF MILES
0 100 200 300 400

Conquests in Europe under Darius. — The insurrections which attended the death of Cambyses were quelled by Darius (521–484 B.C.), who was, next to Cyrus, the greatest king of Persia. He has a special interest for us, because he was the first to extend the Persian authority into Europe — and thus paved the way for the subsequent invasion of Greece. The purpose of Darius in entering Europe was, according to Herodotus, to send an expedition against the barbarous Scythians (sĭth´ĭ-anz). So far as the Scythians were concerned, this expedition proved a failure. But on his return to Asia, Darius left in Europe an army which subdued Thrace and the Greek cities to the north of the Ægean Sea, and even compelled Macedonia to acknowledge the supremacy of the great king. The Persian empire was thus extended into Europe to the boundary of Greece.

In its geographical extent Persia surpassed all the previous empires of the East. It not only covered all the lands hitherto occupied by Assyria, Babylonia, Media, Lydia, and Egypt, but added to them other territory not included in these older empires. It extended from the Indus River to the Ægean Sea, a distance of about three thousand miles. It comprised, in fact, the whole civilized world except India and China in the Far East, and Greece and Carthage in the West.

The subsequent history of Persia was closely related to that of Greece, which had by this time developed a distinct civilization of its own and had become the center of a new world culture. We shall hereafter see how Persia came into conflict with the Greek states, and how it was finally overthrown by Alexander the Great (331 B.C.).

II. The Civilization of Persia

The Government and Provinces. — The form of government established over the vast Persian empire was patterned after that of the Assyrians, but strengthened and perfected by the genius of Darius. The person of the king was exalted above that of other men. He sat upon a throne made of gold, silver, and ivory. His garments were of richest silk. To serve him

was the highest mark of nobility. To minister to his comfort, one dignitary was chosen to carry the royal parasol, another the royal fan, while other officers were appointed to perform other equally honorable duties. For the purposes of administration the territory was divided into a number of provinces or "satrapies," each under a provincial governor, or satrap, appointed by the king. The provinces were divided into districts, each under a deputy of the satrap. The provinces were subject to the satraps, and the satraps were subject to the king. The duties of the provincial subjects were to furnish men for the royal army, ships for the royal navy, and money for the royal treasury. The provinces were joined to the capital, Susa, by military roads, the most important of which

THE PERSIAN KING
(with attendants)

was the great royal road from Susa to Sardis, fifteen hundred miles long.

The Persian Army and Navy. — The chief support of the royal authority was the army drawn from the different provinces. When called together, it was marshaled by nations, each with its own costume and subject to royal officers. The footmen were armed with the sword, the spear, and their favorite weapon, the bow, in the use of which they were expert. The cavalry was an important branch of the army, and was very effective when fighting upon an open plain. The king and his officers rode in chariots armed with scythes. The choicest part of the Persian army was the " Ten Thousand Immortals," so called because their numbers were perpetually maintained. On the sea the Persians were able to gather from their subjects a large number of ships, mostly triremes (ships with three banks of oars; p. 184) armed with iron prows. With such an army and navy the Persians had already conquered Asia, and hoped to conquer Greece and Europe.

Persian Art and Literature. — As the Persians were chiefly a conquering and ruling people, they were not distinguished for their intellectual achievements. Whatever art they possessed was mostly a mere reproduction of that of Assyria and Babylon. Their architecture and sculpture, as seen in the ruins at Persep'olis and other places, show no evidences of

RUINS OF PERSEPOLIS

marked originality. While using an Aryan speech the Persians adopted for writing the wedge-shaped characters of the Babylonians. They made no contributions to science; and for many generations they possessed no literature worthy of notice except the "Aves'ta," which was the Persian Bible. This sacred book was a vast collection of prayers, hymns of praise, rites and ceremonies, devotional exercises, and other religious writings. It is said to have been inscribed in gold letters on 12,000 cowhides, and to have contained 2,000,000 lines. It has come down to us in fragments only.

Persian Religion and Morality. — The most distinctive feature of the Persian civilization was its religion. This was doubtless an outgrowth of a lower polytheistic nature worship; but it seems to have reached its highest development under the influence of Zoroas'ter. This religious reformer is supposed to have lived in Bactria about the middle of the seventh century B.C. Some scholars are inclined to believe that his name stands merely for a mythical person; while others strongly assert that " we must accept the historical reality of Zoroaster " (Sayce). He considered the powers of nature as separated into the powers of light and the powers of darkness — the one under the control of the great god of light (Ormuzd), who is the creator of all that is good; and the other under the control of the god of darkness (Ah'riman), who is the father of all that is evil. This is a system of religion which we call Dualism. The whole universe is looked upon as a struggle between light and darkness, between the good and the evil, in other words, between Ormuzd [1] and Ahriman. Human life in the same way is regarded as a perpetual struggle between good and evil; and the duty of man is to cleave to that which is good and to shun that which is evil. Morality was closely related to religion. The Persians believed in truthfulness as a high moral virtue and despised lying and deceit. The higher elements of the Persian religion were corrupted under the influence of a priestly class, the Magi, who were inclined to worship the symbol of fire in place of the god of light, and to regard the performance of religious rites and ceremonies as the chief duty of life.

Persian Wealth and Luxury. — The chief occupation of the Persians was war. By their conquests they gathered to themselves the wealth of the world. They boasted that they need

[1] The upper part of the picture on page 72 shows the symbol of Ormuzd, copied from the Assyrian god Assur.

not toil, for by their skill in arms they could command the products of every foreign land.   Even commerce to them was a
menial and unnecessary occupation.   They could get what
they wished without giving anything in exchange.   All nations
were laid under tribute.   While the Persians were humane in

PERSIAN SUBJECTS BRINGING TRIBUTE TO THE KING

war and made a virtue of telling the truth, their great vice was
in robbing other people.   In this way they accumulated vast
wealth.   They gathered carpets from Babylon, shawls from
India, fine linen from Egypt, coverlets from Damascus, and
gold and silver wherever found.   The people had no need for
home industry, and became fond of indolence and luxury.   Their
swords were decked with gold and studded with gems.   They
wore gold chains about their necks, and gold bracelets upon
their arms.   They wore embroidered robes.   Their floors were
covered with luxurious carpets, their couches were spread with
gorgeous coverlets.   They used cosmetics for their complexions
and spent much time in arranging their hair.   All this luxury was
the fruit of war; but in time it produced a weak and effeminate
people which lost the courage and vigor of their earlier days.

Historical Significance of Persia. — The Persian empire represents the highest unity attained by the ancient Oriental world
before the time of Alexander the Great.   Of all the great monarchies hitherto established — the early Babylonian, the Egyptian, the Assyrian, the Median, and the later Babylonian — no
one except Assyria can be regarded as properly a " world em-

pire." Persia carried to a still higher stage of development the military and political system of Assyria. Although she made no contributions to the finer arts of life, she surpassed all her predecessors as a conquering and ruling power. She withstood the rude barbarians of the North — the Scythians — in their inroads into the civilized South. She developed a more permanent system of provincial government than had before existed. Her religion was perhaps the nearest approach to Jewish monotheism of all the religions of western Asia. But with all her achievements she represented an old and decaying civilization, which appears in its true light when we see it brought into contact, and placed in contrast, with the new and growing civilization of Greece.

III. Review of Oriental Nations

The Beginnings of Civilization. — In reviewing the history of the Oriental nations there are certain general facts which should be impressed upon our minds. In the first place, we see that it is from the Orient that the world received the rudiments of its civilization. It is here that man first passed out of the tribal state and developed a higher form of government, by the erection of cities, kingdoms, and great empires. It is here, also, that we see the early development of religion, which passed from crude forms of animal or ancestral worship to a polytheistic nature worship and finally to a monotheistic religion, as that of the Hebrews. We also find here a great advancement in man's economic life, which began with hunting and fishing or the tending of flocks and herds, and passed to the cultivation of the soil, the growth of manufactures, and the development of commerce. Moreover, the people of the Orient gave to the world the rudiments of some of the important sciences, especially astronomy and mathematics. Still further, we see a remarkable progress made in the art of writing, which began with the expression of ideas in the form of pictures, then advancing to the use of symbolic signs, and at last to the use of a phonetic alphabet such as we use to-day. Finally, these ancient peoples acquired great ability, if not taste, in the art of building, beginning with huts made of sticks or clay, and passing to the use of brick among the Babylonians, and stone among the Egyptians. So thoroughly were they acquainted with the principles of architecture that many of their buildings have remained to the present time as monuments of their skill, and as permanent evidences of that early civilization which we have inherited from the East.

The Course of Oriental History. — A review of the Oriental world will also enable us to distinguish certain periods, or successive stages, which mark the course of its historical progress. We may briefly characterize these periods as follows :

(1) During the first period the rudiments of civilization appeared in two separate and independent centers, — Babylonia and Egypt, — each having a peculiar culture of its own, and each being unaffected, so far as we know, by any influences derived from the other (about 5000–3800 B.C.).[1]

(2) The second period is the time of the Babylonian ascendancy, when Babylonia extended its authority to the Mediterranean coast, and its culture to the lands of Syria (about 3800–1600 B.C.).

(3) Then followed the period of the Egyptian ascendancy, when the authority of Egypt superseded that of Babylonia in the Syrian lands and the Egyptian culture became extended to this territory (about 1600–1100 B.C.).

(4) With the decline of the Egyptian power, we come to the period of Syrian independence, which continued for two centuries (about 1100–900 B.C.). During this time the influence of Phœnicia became predominant over the Mediterranean coasts, and the Hebrew kingdom reached its height under David and Solomon.

[1] These dates are only approximate, and are substantially those adopted by Professor Goodspeed.

(5) This was followed by the ascendancy of Assyria as the first world empire, bringing under its control all the previously mentioned countries of the East, — Babylonia, Egypt, Phœnicia, and Palestine (about 900–600 B.C.). The period of the Assyrian ascendancy closed with the independence of Egypt and the division of the remaining territory between the short-lived empires of later Babylonia and Media (about 600–550 B.C.).

(6) Lastly appeared the second great world empire of Persia, which consolidated under one supreme authority all the countries of the Orient west of the Indus. It comprised not only the nations already noticed, but also the country of the Hittites and Lydia in Asia Minor (about 550–331 B.C.).

The Blending of Culture by Conquest and Commerce. — In connection with the rise and fall of the different Oriental nations, and the general progress in civilization, it is important to notice the fact that the culture of different countries became blended by means of conquests. For example, the successive conquests of Syria by Babylonia and Egypt led to that composite form of culture which marked the Phœnicians. It preserved both Babylonian and Egyptian features, as seen in the Syrian religion and art. Moreover, the conquest of Egypt

PERSIAN COIN

by Assyria did not destroy the existing civilization of Egypt, but rather brought the civilization of the Tigris-Euphrates valley into relation with that of the valley of the Nile. Also, by the extensive conquests of Persia the various centers of culture throughout the Orient were brought into communication with one another.

Again, the civilizations of different peoples became mingled by means of commercial intercourse. Commerce tended to bring about the exchange not only of the products, but of the ideas of various peoples. This we have seen in the case of the

Phœnicians, who became the common carriers not only of commodities but also of culture. Hence, by means of conquests and commerce, the different peoples of the Orient were brought together; and their civilizations became blended into a composite culture, which we may characterize in general as Oriental.

Transmission of Oriental Culture to the West. — The culture of the Eastern world was destined to overflow the boundaries of the Orient, and to find its way at last into the Occident. There were two principal means of communication between the East and the West: the one was by the sea traffic of the Phœnicians, the other was by the land traffic of the peoples of Asia Minor. We can readily see how the Phœnicians, through their commerce and colonies, brought the culture of Asia to the ports of Europe. The peoples of Asia Minor who furnished some means of communication between the East and the West, were the Hittites and the Lydians (map, p. 56). Concerning the Hittites little is definitely known; but that they at one time formed a powerful and influential nation, seems quite certain. They are said to have done much for civilization by taking up the arts and culture of Assyria, Egypt, and Phœnicia, and passing them on to their western neighbors. The Lydians lived on the western frontiers of the Orient and joined hands with the Greeks on the Ægean Sea. It is believed that they received much of the culture of the East, not only through the Phœnicians, but also through their neighbors the Hittites. If this is so, we may see that the peoples of Asia Minor, as well as the Phœnicians, aided in transmitting the ancient culture of the East to the West.

HITTITE RELIEF
(Photographed in situ)

Selections for Reading

Knowlton, Topic A 6, "The Foes of the Greeks" (1).[1]

Goodspeed, Ancient History, pp. 60–65, "The World Empire of Persia" (1).

Myres, Ch. 6, "Upland Neighbors of Babylonia"; Ch. 7, "The Dawn along the Land Bridges" (1).

Lenormant, Vol. II., Bk. V., "The Medes and the Persians" (4).

Benjamin, Ch. 7, "Cyrus"; Ch. 8, "From Cyrus to Darius" (8).

Vaux, Ch. 1, "Cyrus, Cambyses and Darius"; Ch. 4, "Monuments of Persia" (8).

Souttar, pp. 145–190, "Medes and Persians" (1).

Bury, Ch. 6, "Advance of the Persians to the Ægean" (10).

Cox, History, Bk. II., Chs. 1, 2, "The Persian Empire" (10).

Smith, P., Ch. 28, "Decline and Fall of the Persian Empire" (4).

Encyclopædia Britannica, Article "Hittites" (the "Forgotten Empire"); Article "Lydia" (for coinage of Lydia).

Herodotus, Bk. I., Chs. 131–140 (Persian manners and customs); Bk. IV., Chs. 1–8, 28–100 (the Scythians) (17).

Special Study

THE PERSIAN RELIGION. — Clarke, Ten Great Religions, Ch. 5 (3); Rawlinson, Religions, Ch. 3 (3); Rawlinson, Monarchies, Vol. III., The Fifth Monarchy, Persia, Ch. 4 (4); Smith, P., pp. 421–436 (4); Encyclopedias, Articles "Zoroaster," "Avesta."

[1] The figure in parenthesis refers to the number of the topic in the Appendix. where a fuller title of the book will be found.

THE GREEK PEOPLE

CHAPTER VII

GREECE, ITS PEOPLE AND EARLY LEGENDS

Synopsis

I. HELLAS, THE LAND OF THE GREEKS. — Greece and the Orient. — Geographical Features of Greece. — Divisions of Greece. — Greater Hellas.

II. THE HELLENES, THE PEOPLE OF GREECE. — The Earliest Inhabitants of Greece. — Divisions of the Hellenic People. — General Character of the Greek People.

III. THE EARLY LEGENDS OF GREECE. — Importance of the Legends. — Legends of the Founders of Cities. — Legends of Grecian Heroes. — Legends of National Exploits.

I. HELLAS, THE LAND OF THE GREEKS

Greece and the Orient. —As we approach the study of Greece we must first of all notice the close relation of this land to the Oriental countries which we have already studied. Of the three peninsulas of Europe which project into the Mediterranean Sea, Greece lies nearest to the East. Hence it would naturally be the first of European countries to feel the influence of Oriental culture and the first to develop a civilization of its own. The Ægean Sea, which lies between its coasts and those of Asia Minor, can be regarded not as a barrier, but rather as a highway uniting the East and the West, the Orient and the Occident. The numerous islands scattered over this sea aided the early mariners to find their way across its waters; so that these islands have been aptly called the " stepping stones " of the Ægean. Greece was also open to the early commerce of the Phœnicians, who had obtained a foothold upon some of the

Ægean islands. Since the culture of Babylonia and Egypt had
been taken up by Phœnicia and the countries of Asia Minor,
the drift of Oriental civilization was in the direction of the

HELLAS; THE ÆGEAN LANDS. ROUTES ACROSS THE ÆGEAN SEA

Grecian peninsula. For these reasons we may see that Greece
was in a certain sense the heir of the Orient, receiving in some
degree the stimulating influence of Eastern culture.

Geographical Features of Greece. — The Grecian peninsula
presents a striking contrast to the great countries of the East,
with their broad plains and fertile valleys. Greece is a very
small country (about half the size of New York state). Its surface is broken by mountain ranges and small valleys, and drained
by innumerable small streams. The outlines of the country are

as irregular and diversified as its surface. There is no other country of the world of the same area with such an extensive and irregular coast line. It has been called " the most European of European countries." It is said that there is no point in Greece more than forty miles from the coast. The many bays, gulfs, and inlets which indent its shores form the navigable waters of Greece. The climate is generally mild and temperate, but changeable with the seasons and also quite different in different localities. The soil is not very fertile; but under ordinary cultivation, it produced in ancient times wheat, barley, flax, wine, and oil. The trees of Greece range from the pine and oak in the north to the olive, orange, and date palm in the south.

The geographical features of Greece exercised an important influence upon the character of the people and upon their history. The face of nature, with its brilliant skies and beautiful land-scapes, tended to give the people a cheerful temper and a fine æsthetic taste. The broken relief of the country separated the people into distinct communities, and led to the growth of many small states and to the development of a spirit of freedom and local independence. Moreover, the irregular coast line furnished an opportunity for ports and harbors, and thus promoted the commercial spirit of the people. As the bays and gulfs lay mostly upon the eastern coast, Greece may be said to have " faced " toward the Orient, and thus to have been fitted by nature to receive the gifts of her more civilized neighbors.

Divisions of Greece. — To obtain a more definite idea of the peninsula of Greece and of its most noted places, let us glance at its principal divisions.

(1) *Northern Greece* comprised two provinces, Epi′rus and Thes′saly, which were separated by the Pindus Mountains (map, p. 82). Thessaly was a fertile plain, extending northward to Mt. Olym′pus, the highest peak in Greece (nearly 10,000 feet), upon whose summit the gods were supposed to dwell.

(2) *Central Greece* comprised a number of states of varied his-

torical interest, lying north and east of the Gulf of Corinth. In the middle of central Greece were several small provinces separated from one another by mountain barriers. Of these Phocis claimed the highest renown, for it contained the celebrated oracle of the god Apollo at Delphi. Next to Phocis, on the east,

CENTRAL GREECE AND THE PELOPONNESUS

was Bœo'tia; and beyond that province lay At'tica, the most noted country of all Greece. Its most famous point was the Acrop'olis, about which grew up the city of Athens.

(3) *Southern Greece* received the name of the Peloponne'sus or the "Isle of Pelops." This peninsula is connected with central Greece by the narrow Isthmus of Corinth. The central country of the Peloponnesus was Arca'dia; this was surrounded by a wall of mountains, separating it from six other provinces, all of which were important in Greek history (map, above). The

most famous locality in Elis was Olym′pia, the seat of the "Olympian games." Laco′nia was the home of the Spartans, who became the ruling power of the Peloponnesus, and whose chief city, Sparta, became the greatest rival of Athens.

(4) *The Islands* of Greece are also worthy of notice. The large island of Euboe′a stretches along the eastern coast from Thessaly to Attica. Southwest of Attica was the island of Sal′amis, which gave the name to a decisive naval battle between the Greeks and the Persians. Off the eastern coast of the Peloponnesus was a group of islands called the Cyc′lades (map, p. 82). The most noted of this group was the tiny island of Delos, the seat of a celebrated shrine of Apollo. The largest and most important island was Crete, which was a center of the oldest civilization of the Ægean.

Greater Hellas. — The home of the Greeks, which they called Hellas, was not confined to the European peninsula and the neighboring islands. It included also the western coasts of Asia Minor, which were from very early times occupied by a Greek people. This part of the Greek world may be called "Asiatic Greece." Besides these lands about the Ægean Sea, Hellas, in the larger sense, came to include other lands, which we may call "Western Greece." These comprised the eastern and southern part of the island of Sicily, as well as certain territory in the southern part of Italy known as "Magna Græcia." In fact, by the word Hellas the Greeks meant all the lands inhabited by the Greek people — the Hellenes as they called themselves — and these lands were continually widening with the growth of Greek commerce and colonization.

II. The Hellenes, the People of Greece

The Earliest Inhabitants of Greece. — It would be interesting to know precisely when, and how, and by whom all the lands about the Ægean Sea were first settled. But this is a subject concerning which we have no very extensive or definite knowl-

edge. What we do know is that the principal people who inhabited Greece in historical times, were people who spoke an
Aryan, or Indo-European, language. At the time of their settlement in Greece — probably before 2000 B.C. — these early
Greeks were scarcely advanced beyond the stage of barbarism.
They worshiped their ancestors and the gods of nature; chief
among their gods was Zeus, the god of the heavens. They lived
upon their flocks and herds and were beginning to acquire a
knowledge of agriculture, cultivating the cereals and perhaps the
vine. They fought with spears and with the bow and arrow.
They made their implements of stone, beginning perhaps to use
some of the metals. They were acquainted with the art of
navigation, certainly with the use of boats and oars; but the
use of sailing vessels was probably acquired after they settled
upon the Ægean. With the aid of these vessels, the people of
the different shores were able to communicate with one another,
to occupy the intervening islands, and thus to preserve the sense
of their original kinship.

Divisions of the Hellenic People. — The Greeks called themselves "Hellenes" because they professed to believe that they
were descended from a common ancestor, Hellen. From this
common ancestor they traced four lines of descendants, or
tribes — the Achæ'ans, the Io'nians, the Do'rians, and the
Æo'lians. The Achæans were in very early times the leading race
of the Peloponnesus, being regarded by some as the founders of
the ancient kingdoms of Ti'ryns, Myce'næ, and Argos. The early
home of the Ionians is placed on the northern coast of the Peloponnesus, also in Attica and the island of Eubœa. The Dorians
are supposed to have occupied in very early times the plains
of Thessaly. The name Æolian was used to cover the rest of
the Hellenic people. The most important of the tribes during
the historical period were the Dorians and the Ionians. The
Dorians were a simple, practical, and warlike race, represented
by the Spartans. The Ionians were a bright, enterprising, and
artistic people, represented by the Athenians.

General Character of the Greek People. — The Greek people were very different from the people in the Orient. In the first place, they possessed a strong love of freedom, which would endure no restraint except that which they imposed upon themselves, and which made them independent, wide-awake, and original. Their love of freedom resulted in the development of self-governing communities, and made the Greek city something far different from the cities of the East. Moreover, the Greeks were characterized by simplicity and moderation, which were revealed not only in their art, but in their life. This led them to shun all forms of Oriental ostentation and extravagance. Finally, they were gifted with great intellectual activity and a fine æsthetic sense, a taste for beauty for its own sake, which made them the creators of a new form of art.

III. The Early Legends of Greece

Importance of the Legends. — We may see some most interesting qualities of the Greek people in their early legends — the myths and stories which they were accustomed to tell in order to explain the mysteries of nature and the origin of their own institutions. The importance which we attach to these stories will depend very much upon our point of view. If we look at them as giving an account of actual and well-defined events, they have of course little historical value. But if we look at them as indicating the ideas and beliefs of the people, they have a great deal of value. The nature of the early Greek mind is revealed in these traditional stories. Moreover, the stories became a subject for the works of poets, sculptors, and painters. Without a knowledge of them, much of the literature and art of a later period would be meaningless to us.

Legends of the Founders of Cities. — The Greeks surrounded every locality, every mountain, stream, and vale with a halo of song and story. An important group of legends referred to the founders of cities. The foundation of Athens, for example, was ascribed to Cecrops, regarded by some as a native of Egypt; he was said to have introduced into Attica the arts of civilized life. Argos was believed to have been founded by another Egyptian, named Dan'aus, who fled to Greece with his fifty daughters, and who was elected by the people as their king. Thebes, in Bœotia, looked to Cadmus, a Phœnician, as its founder; he was believed to have brought into Greece the art of writing. The Peloponnesus was said to have been settled by, and to have received its name from, Pelops, a man from Phrygia in Asia; he became the king of Mycenæ, and was the father of A'treus, and the grandfather of Agamem'non and Menela'us, chieftains in the Trojan war. Such traditions as these show that the early Greeks had some notion of their dependence upon the Eastern nations.

Legends of Grecian Heroes. — That the early Greeks had a great admiration for physical courage is evident from the legends

BELLEROPHON AND PEGASUS

which they wove about the names of their great heroes. Many fanciful stories were told of their wonderful exploits. We can mention here the names of only a few of these heroes. We read of Per'seus, the slayer of the horrid Medu'sa, whose locks were coiling serpents, and whose looks turned every object to stone (picture, p. 144). We read of Beller'ophon, who slew a terrible fire-breathing monster called the " Chimæra " (kĭ-mē'ra) ; and who also captured the winged steed Peg'asus, on whose back he tried to ascend to heaven. We read of Minos, the king of Crete, who rid the sea of pirates, and gave to his subjects a code of laws received from the god Zeus. We read of The'seus, the king of Athens, who rid the land of robbers, and delivered Athens from the terrible tribute imposed by the king of Crete — a tribute which required the periodical sacrifice of seven youths and seven maidens to a man-eating bull called the "Min'otaur." But the greatest of the Grecian heroes was Her'acles (Her'cules). Strange stories were told of the "twelve labors" of this famous giant, the prodigious tasks imposed upon him by the king of Mycenæ with the approval of Zeus.

HERACLES AND THE NEMEAN LION

Legends of National Exploits. — The legends are not only grouped about particular places and individual heroes but have for their subjects national deeds, marked by courage and fortitude. One of these stories describes the so-called "Argonautic expedition." This is a sea story. It tells of fifty heroes who were said to have set sail from Bœotia under the leadership of Jason, in the ship "Argo," to recover a "golden fleece" which had been carried away to Colchis (kol'kis), a far-distant land on the shores of the Euxine (ūk'sĭn; map, p. 115). But the most famous of the legendary stories related to the Trojan war.

The story of the Trojan war tells us of the expedition of the Greeks against the city of Troy in Asia Minor to rescue their countrywoman Helen, the beautiful wife of Menelaus, king of Sparta. Helen had been stolen away from Greece by Paris, who was the son of the Trojan king Priam. The story tells of the sailing of the Greek fleet under Agamemnon, the king of Mycenæ and brother of Menelaus. It tells of the siege of Troy, which lasted for ten years; the fierce battles between the Greeks and the Trojans; the device of the "wooden horse," which concealed a body of Greek warriors and was dragged into the city by the unsuspecting Trojans; the stealthy opening of the city gates by these warriors and the admission of the Greek army; the capture of the citadel and the burning of the city; the terrible massacre, and the flight of the Trojan hero Æne'as with his aged father, Anchi'ses. The story of the fall of Troy, as told by Homer, is closely connected with the story of the founding of Rome, as told in Vergil's " Æneid."

Selections for Reading

Seignobos, Ch. 9, "Greece and the Greeks" (1).[1]

Smith, Wm., Ch. 1, "Earliest Inhabitants of Greece"; Ch. 2, "Grecian Heroes" (10).

Shuckburgh, Ch. 1, " The Hellenes in Greece " (10).

Cox, History, Bk. I., Ch. 3, "Mythology and Tribal Legends of the Greeks" (10).

Abbott, Vol. I., Ch. 2, "The Earliest Inhabitants"; Ch. 3, "Migrations and Legendary History" (10).

Curtius, Vol. I., Bk. I., Ch. 1, "Land and People" (10).

Grote, Part II., Ch. 16, "Grecian Myths as Understood, Felt and Interpreted by the Greeks Themselves" (10).

Holm, Vol. I., Ch. 4, "The Earliest Traditional History"; Ch. 10, "Most Important Legends of Greece" (10).

Herodotus, Bk. I., Chs. 52–58 (the early inhabitants of Greece) (17).

Thucydides, Bk. I., Chs. 2–12 (early peoples of Greece) (17).

Special Study

THE GEOGRAPHY OF GREECE. — Seignobos, pp. 98–100 (1); Goodspeed, Anc. World, pp. 70–73 (1); Smith, Wm., "Introduction" (10); Oman, Ch. 1 (10); Bury, "Introductory" (10); Abbott, Vol. I, Ch. 1 (10).

[1] The figure in parenthesis refers to the number of the topic in the Appendix, where a fuller title of the book will be found.

CHAPTER VIII

THE PREHISTORIC CULTURE OF GREECE

Synopsis

I. THE ÆGEAN CIVILIZATION. — Recent Excavations in Hellas. — Hissarlik and the City of Troy. — The Citadel of Tiryns. — The Ruins and Relics of Mycenæ. — Excavations in Crete. — Character of the Ægean Civilization.

II. THE GREEKS IN ASIA MINOR. — The So-called Dorian Migration. — The Migrations to Asia Minor. — The New Culture of Asia Minor.

III. THE HOMERIC POEMS AND THE HOMERIC AGE. — The Iliad and the Odyssey. — Historical Value of the Homeric Poems. — The Homeric Society and Government. — Homeric Industry and Art. — The Gods and Goddesses of Olympus. — Ideas of the Future Life. — Religious Rites and Ceremonies. — The Morals of the Homeric Age.

I. THE ÆGEAN CIVILIZATION

Recent Excavations in Hellas. — Not many years ago our knowledge of the early ages of Greece was derived almost entirely from the old legends. These were at one time accepted as giving real facts, but were afterward rejected as purely imaginary. But recent excavations have thrown a new light upon the early ages, and opened a new world to the student of Greek history. The story of these diggings among the ruins of the old cities of the Ægean has an almost romantic interest. The name most closely connected with them is that of Dr. Schliemann, the German archæologist. It was his childlike faith in Homer and the tale of Troy that led him to seek for the Trojan city and the palace of Agamemnon, king of Mycenæ. The excavations made by him (beginning in 1871), together with the work of his successors, have not only given us new ideas regarding the poems of Homer, but have also presented many new problems regarding the early ages of Greece.

Hissarlik and the City of Troy. — The hill of Hissar'lik, situated in Tro'as, in northern Asia Minor, was believed by Dr. Schliemann to be the site of Troy. Here he found the remains of nine different settlements, or so-called " cities," lying one above another and representing different stages of human

THE HILL OF HISSARLIK

progress. The lowest city contained relics of the stone age — stone axes, flint knives, earthen vessels covered with rude decorations. The second city — evidently destroyed by a conflagration and hence called the " burnt city " — was surrounded by walls built of brick and placed upon rough stone foundations. It contained a palace surrounding a court. Among the ruins were found battle-axes, spearheads, and daggers made of copper, showing that its inhabitants belonged to what we call the " age of bronze." There were found also articles of fine workmanship, showing an Eastern influence — cups of silver, diadems, bracelets, earrings made of gold. This " burnt city " was believed by Dr. Schliemann to have been the Troy of Homer. But the later work of Dr. Dörpfeld, the distinguished colleague of Schliemann, has shown that the sixth city — with its great circuit walls, its stately houses of well-dressed stone, and its finely wrought vases — is more likely to be the city described in the Homeric poems.

The Citadel of Tiryns. — Important remains of this prehistoric age have been found not only in Asia Minor, but also in European Greece, especially in two cities of the Peloponnesus — Tiryns and Mycenæ. Tiryns is the older of these, and its walls, too, are better preserved. The citadel of Tiryns was surrounded by massive walls. The palace consisted of an elaborate system of courts, halls, and corridors, suggesting an Oriental palace rather than any building in historic Greece. The most artistic features of the palace were alabaster friezes, carved in rich patterns of rosettes and spirals, such as are described in the Homeric poems (Odyssey, Bk. VII.).

"Lion Gate" at Mycenæ

The Ruins and Relics of Mycenæ. — The prehistoric culture of Greece reached a high stage of development at Mycenæ. One of the most conspicuous objects here was the well-known "lion gate" through which the citadel was entered, and which had been an object of interest to the later Greeks. The form of these rampant lions has often been compared to similar designs in the East, from which they may have been brought into Greece. Within the walls near the gate were found a number of graves. These contained human bodies and a wealth of art treasures — articles of gold, silver, copper, bronze, terra cotta,

Gold Diadem from Mycenæ

glass, ivory, and precious stones; articles of ornament, such as diadems, pendants, and rings of artistic design; articles of use, such as bowls, pitchers, cups, ladles, and spoons. These articles show a high degree of mechanical skill and artistic taste. Some of them may have been brought from the East, and some of them may have been the products of native industry. Below the citadel was found another type of sepulchers, called from their peculiar form "beehive tombs," one of which the archæologists have called the "Treasury of Atreus."[1]

THE SO-CALLED "TREASURY OF ATREUS"

Recent excavations have shown that the kind of culture which existed in the prehistoric cities of Tiryns and Mycenæ prevailed in many other parts of Greece, and in many islands of the Ægean. At Orchom'enus, in Bœotia, was discovered an elaborate and beautiful ceiling said to be of a pure Egyptian pattern. At Va-phi'o (near Sparta) were found two remarkable gold cups covered with finely wrought relief work, and regarded by some, as the most artistic work of the prehistoric age.[2]

[1] Such structures were at first supposed to be places where the kings kept their treasures. The ancient writer Pausanias mentions at Mycenæ "underground structures of Atreus and his sons where they kept their treasuries." But ar-chæologists are now agreed that these structures were not treasure-houses but tombs. See Tsountas and Manatt, "Mycenæan Age," p. 117.

[2] Copies of these beautiful cups may now be seen in the Metropolitan Museum of Art in the city of New York.

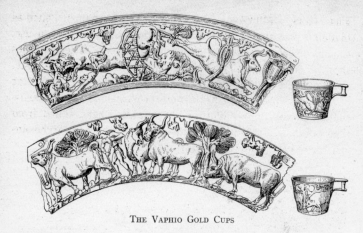

THE VAPHIO GOLD CUPS

Excavations in Crete. — The most interesting of recent excavations have been made in the island of Crete. This work has been carried on in different places, but most extensively at Cnossus (nŏs'us), a town on the northern coast of the island (map, p. 98). Here have been found the remains of a great palace, with massive walls, with many chambers and courts, and marks of kingly splendor, which we might fancy once really belonged to Minos, the royal friend of Zeus, described in the Greek legend (p. 88). So strongly does the name of this king linger about the ruins that the culture of Crete has come to be called "Mino'an." The oldest Minoan period dates back to

MARBLE "THRONE OF MINOS" IN THE PALACE OF CNOSSUS

the time of the early Egyptian kings. Here we see evidences of the stone age — stone vases, stone jars, and carved rocks.

The art of a somewhat later period shows a higher degree of taste. The Cretans seem to have had a special skill in de-

FEMALE FIGURE FROM
CNOSSUS

picting scenes from life. This is shown in their lifelike figures cut in ivory; their vases covered with relief work representing warriors, gladiators, wrestlers, and pugilists. Dr. Evans, the English archæologist, describes " the remains of miniature wall-painting found in the palace at Cnossus, showing a group of court ladies in curiously modern costumes seated on the terraces and balustrades " evidently watching some sort of exhibition.

One of the most important discoveries of Dr. Evans was the fact that the ancient Cretans had made considerable progress in the art of writing. There have been found in the ruins of the great palace of Cnossus many clay tablets covered with inscriptions. When these were examined they were found to consist of some kind of picture writing, and also of what seemed to be alphabetical signs. It is supposed therefore that the Phœnicians may have derived some of their alphabet from the Cretans as well as from

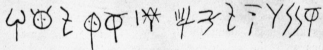

CRETAN WRITING

the Egyptians. To what extent this is true we do not know, because no one has been able as yet to read the Cretan writing.

It seems quite certain that Crete was the center of a prehistoric culture that extended far beyond the limits of that island.

Its influence is seen in Egypt, in Cyprus, and in other parts of the eastern Mediterranean. Objects of Cretan art are found in these places, and the products of other countries are also found in Crete. From this it is inferred that the Cretans had developed an extensive commerce even before the time of the Phœnicians.

JARS FOR OIL AND GRAIN UNDER THE PALACE OF CNOSSUS

Character of the Ægean Civilization. — The type of culture brought to light by these discoveries has been called by some "Mycenæ'an"—a term now restricted to the culture found in Greece proper; more generally it is now called "Ægean," from the fact that it seems to have extended over a large part of the Ægean basin. It is supposed to have reached its culmination perhaps between the years 2000 B.C. and 1500 B.C. But there is reason to believe that in its earlier stages it may have extended back as far as 3000 B.C., or even to an earlier date. Its last and declining stage was evidently closed by the great migrations about 1000 B.C., when it was swept from Greece, its memory still lingering in the minds of those tribes that migrated to the coasts of Asia Minor. Regarding the origin of the ancient culture of Greece, scholars are by no means agreed. It seems likely that this culture — with its strange mingling of crude art, of massive walls, of palatial buildings, of Oriental designs, and

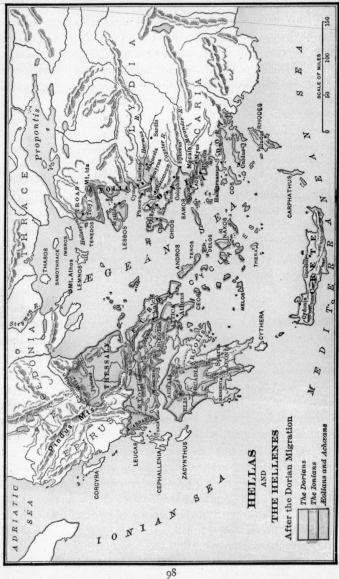

HELLAS
AND
THE HELLENES

After the Dorian Migration

The Dorians
The Ionians
Æolians and Achæans

SCALE OF MILES
0   50   100   150

of objects showing a high mechanical skill and eastern taste — may have been developed by the early people of the Ægean who were brought into close commercial and intellectual relation with the people of the Orient. Whatever we may think of its character and origin, we know that it exercised but slight influence upon the classic art of Greece, but passed away, leaving scarcely more than monuments and memories. These memories, however, furnished an inspiration to the poets and minstrels of the Homeric age.

II. THE GREEKS IN ASIA MINOR

The So-called Dorian Migration. — We have now come to a time when a great change took place in the old Greek world. It seems quite certain that about the year 1000 B.C. there was a general disturbance of the population throughout Greece. This was due to the migration of the northern tribes into the south, resulting in the driving out of the old inhabitants and the destruction of the old civilization. The movement is called the "Dorian migration." Notwithstanding the myths connected with it, it must be regarded as a real movement, which may have extended over many generations. As a result of these changes in the population, we find the Dorians, who formerly occupied Thessaly, now the leading race of the Peloponnesus.

The Migrations to Asia Minor. — The invasion of the Peloponnesus by the Dorians resulted not only in rearranging the tribes in Greece proper, but also in bringing about a closer union between Greece and Asia Minor. The people who had been driven out of their old homes in Greece, or who were not satisfied with their new ones, sought other settlements across the sea. The coasts of Asia Minor now received a new population from the European peninsula. There were, in fact, three streams of migration from Greece to Asia Minor — which we may follow on the map (p. 98).

(1) One stream of migration was made up of the *Æolians*, — which name came to be a general term applied to all who

were not Ionians or Dorians, including even the Achæans. This mixed people took possession of the northern part of the coast of Asia Minor. They also occupied the island of Lesbos, where they founded the important city of Mytile'ne and became noted for their culture, especially in music and poetry.

(2) A second stream of migration comprised many *Ionians*, who settled upon the central part of the coast. They took a course across the sea by way of the Cyclades, leaving on these islands colonies of their own people. They took possession of the islands of Chios (kī'os) and Samos. They established the cities of Mile'tus, noted for its commerce and colonies, and Eph'esus, celebrated for its magnificent temple to the goddess Ar'temis (Dian'a).

(3) A third stream was that of the *Dorians*, who took a southern course by way of Crete, where they left their colonies. They also occupied Rhodes and Cos, and on the mainland they established the noted city of Halicarnas'sus and other less important towns.

The New Culture of Asia Minor. — The invasion of the Dorians and the migrations to Asia Minor mark the decline of the old Mycenæan culture in Greece. But these movements also mark the growth of a new phase of culture in Asia Minor. We shall find that during this transitional period the cities of Asia Minor became the chief centers of Greek intellectual life and activity. But the new culture of Asia Minor did not consist in reproducing the works of Mycenæan art; it consisted rather in rehearsing the traditional glories of that golden age. The bards of Ionia recounted the mythical stories of the gods, the legends of ancient heroes, and the traditions of Troy and Mycenæ. They accompanied their words with regular strokes upon the lyre; and their fanciful stories fell into rhythm and took the form of the hexameter verse. These lays were descriptive in character and inspired with an heroic spirit; they were full of imagination, reciting the deeds of gods and men and throwing a halo about the past.

III. The Homeric Poems and the Homeric Age

The Iliad and the Odyssey. — From the group of poems that sprang up in Asia Minor there arose two great epics, known as the " Il'iad " and the " Od'yssey." Being the fittest expressions of the popular thought and feeling, they survived. They are, in fact, regarded by many critics as the greatest epic poems in the world's literature. The one is a poem of war, and the other is a poem of peace.

The Iliad describes the closing scenes of the Trojan war, and revolves about the wrath of Achil'les, the most valiant of the Grecian heroes. The commander of the Grecian armies was

DEPARTURE OF ACHILLES (From an ancient vase)

Agamemnon, the king of Mycenæ. The poem opens with a quarrel between Achilles and Agamemnon about a captive girl, whom Achilles claims, and Agamemnon takes away from him. Achilles in his wrath sulks in his tent, and refuses to help the Greeks in their battles with the Trojans. In the midst of many conflicts, in which the gods and goddesses take part, Achilles remains aloof. But when his dearest friend Patro'clus is slain by the Trojan warrior Hector, he is aroused to vengeance. Then follows the exciting battle between Achilles and Hector. Hector is slain and his body dragged three times around the walls of Troy behind the chariot of Achilles.

The Odyssey tells of the wanderings of Odys'seus (Ulys'ses), in search of his native island of Ithaca, after the fall of Troy; the anxious waiting of his faithful wife Penel'ope, who was in the meantime beset by many suitors for her hand; the adventures of his son Telem'achus in trying to find him; and his final return to his wife, who was able to recognize the strange guest as her husband because he had the strength to bend the bow that he had left behind him, a feat that none of her many suitors was able to perform.

Historical Value of the Homeric Poems. — It is a question whether the so-called "Homeric poems" were really composed

HOMER

by a single poet called Homer, or were gathered together from various scattered poems and grouped under the name of Homer. But this question does not affect their historical value. It is true that they are made up largely of legends and traditions, and are so far no more valuable than any other legends and traditions. But traditions are not necessarily false. The recently discovered relics of the prehistoric age show how faithfully the memories of "golden Mycenæ" were preserved by the emigrants to Asia Minor and were expressed in the Homeric poems. But the great historical value of these poems does not consist in the narrative of traditional events and the pictures of past glories. It consists rather in the great number of allusions made to the life and customs of the early Greek people.

The Homeric Society and Government. — In the Homeric poems we see the picture of a simple and primitive society, such as we find among other early Aryan peoples. We see the early Greek family, comprising the household father, the mother, the children, and the slaves. The families were grouped into clans and these into tribes. The tribe was governed by a king (*bas'ileus*), who performed the religious rites of the tribe, settled disputes, and commanded the people in time of war. He was assisted by a council (*bou'lê*), made up of the chiefs of the clans. Matters of great importance, such as the declaration of war or the distribution of plunder, might be left to the assembly (*ag'ora*), which comprised all the people capable of bearing arms. In times of war several tribes might unite under a common chieftain; for example, in the expedition against Troy, the Greek tribes were united under the leadership of Agamemnon, king of Mycenæ.

Homeric Industry and Art. — We may also obtain from the Homeric poems an idea of the degree of progress made by the early Greeks in the art of living. They obtained their food not only by hunting and fishing, but also by the domestication of animals and by the cultivation of the soil. They had the use of at least six metals, — gold, silver, iron, lead, copper, and tin, — which they obtained mostly from other lands. They worked the metals in a crude way, and did not possess the fine mechanical skill seen in the more ancient works of the Mycenæan and Oriental art. Their architecture was simple. They had some skill in shipbuilding, and carried on considerable commerce with the neighboring coasts — with Phœnicia and the islands of the sea.

The Gods and Goddesses of Olympus. — The religion of the Homeric age was evidently derived from the nature worship of the early Aryans. The Greeks united with their nature worship an elaborate and beautiful mythology. They saw in their gods beings like themselves, with human feelings and foibles, with human likes and dislikes. The gods were supposed to dwell about the top of Mt. Olympus, where they feasted and held their councils. They took part in the battles of the Trojan war, and assisted the Greeks or the Trojans according to their preferences

ZEUS

for either party. At the head of the divine circle was Zeus, the god of the heavens and the father of gods and men. Around him were gathered the other Olympian deities. The Olympian circle consisted of the greater deities, comprising six gods and six goddesses.

The six gods were: (1) *Zeus* (Jupiter), the supreme god of the heavens, the king and father of mankind; (2) *Apollo*, god of light and of prophecy; (3) *A'res* (Mars), god of war; (4) *Her'mes* (Mercury), the messenger of the gods, the patron of commerce, and the master of cunning; (5) *Posei'don* (Neptune), god of the sea; and (6) *Hephæs'tus* (Vulcan), god of fire.

The six goddesses were: (1) *Hera* (Juno), the wife of Zeus and the queen of heaven; (2) *Athe'na* (Minerva), goddess of wisdom, who was said to have been born from the forehead of Zeus; (3) *Ar'temis* (Diana), goddess of the chase; (4) *Aphrodi'te* (Venus), goddess of love and beauty; (5) *Deme'ter* (Ce'res), goddess of the harvest; and (6) *Hestia* (Vesta), goddess of the hearth.

Besides these superior

HERA

deities there were a large number of inferior gods, as well as mythical beings, with which the Greek imagination peopled the sky, the earth, and the sea.

Ideas of the Future Life. — The religious imagination of the Greeks included pictures of the future life. At death, the soul is conducted to the realm of Ha'des, which is the world of the departed spirits. At its entrance lay the dog Cer'berus, the three-headed monster that prevented the spirits from returning to the upper world. Upon the sentence of Minos, the soul is given a place in Elys'ium (e-lĭzh'i-um), the field of the blest, or is condemned to Tar'tarus, the gulf of torment. The ingenious tortures inflicted upon those who have incurred the anger of the gods are described by Homer (Odyssey, Bk. XI.).

Religious Rites and Ceremonies. — If the anger of the gods may result in eternal misery, the most important thing in life is to retain their favor. This idea lies at the root of the religious rites of the early Greeks. Prayers and sacrifices had to be offered to retain the divine favor. The sacrifices might consist either in offerings of fruit or grain, or in the slaughter of living victims. The will of the gods might be ascertained by divination, that is, by the interpretation of signs presented by natural phenomena, as the flight of birds, the rolling of thunder, etc.; or one might have recourse to an oracle, established at some fixed place, presided over by priests or priestesses. The priestly class, however, never attained in Greece such an exclusive position and authority as it had in the East.

The Morals of the Homeric Age. — The people of the Homeric period were no better and probably no worse than any other early people. Their home life was bright and cheerful; and women were held in high esteem. The men were as courageous in war as any men could well be, without any better organization and discipline than those which then prevailed. We find examples of great individual courage; but we also find instances of vindictive cruelty to a fallen foe. The Greeks were hospitable to the stranger, and listened to the prayer of the suppliant. But they were often tricky and deceitful in their dealings, and even looked upon piracy as an honorable occupation. The question of right and wrong was determined not so much by any proper moral code as by the fear and favor of the gods, which formed the highest motives of human life.

Selections for Reading

Smith, Wm., Ch. 5, "The Poems of Homer" (10).[1]

Myres, Ch. 8, "The Dawn in the Eastern Mediterranean" (1).

Oman, Ch. 2, "Ægean Civilization"; Ch. 5, "The Great Migrations" (10).

Hawes, Ch. 1, " Survey of the Prehistoric Periods of Crete " (13).

Hall, Ch. 7, "Mycenæ's Place in History" (13).

Schuchhardt, Ch. 1, "Life of Dr. Schliemann"; Ch. 2, "Troy"; Ch. 3, "Tiryns"; Ch. 4, "Mycenæ" (13).

Abbott, Vol. I., Ch. 5, "The Homeric Poems" (10).

Grote, Part I., Ch. 21, "Grecian Epic — Homeric Poems" (10).

Weissenborn, pp. 71–103, "Homeric Antiquities" (14).

Mahaffy, Survey, Ch. 2, "The Homeric Age" (10).

Fowler, Ch. 3, "The Homeric Question" (15).

Freeman, Essay, "Homer and the Homeric Age" (3).

Holm, Vol. I., Ch. 13, "Civilization of the Asiatic Greeks — Homeric Poetry" (10).

Jebb, Introduction to Homer, Ch. 2, "The Homeric World."

Keller, Ch. 3, "Religious Ideas and Usages"; Ch. 5, "Marriage and the Family"; Ch. 6, "Government," etc. (14).

Homer, Iliad, Bk. I. (contention of Achilles and Agamemnon); Odyssey, Bk. VI. (the palace of Alcinoüs) (17).

Special Study

HOMERIC SOCIETY. — Smith, Wm., Ch. 3 (10); Oman, Ch. 3 (10); Weissenborn, pp. 58–69 (14); Holm, Vol. I., Ch. 14 (10); Keller, "Homeric Society" (14). See also Appendix (14).

---

[1] The figure in parenthesis refers to the number of the topic in the Appendix, where a fuller title of the book will be found.

CHAPTER IX

EARLY POLITICAL LIFE—THE CITY STATE AND COLONIZATION

Synopsis

I. THE EARLY CITY STATE. — Character of the Greek Cities. — The Beginnings of the City State. — The Government of the City State. — Independence of the City State. — City Leagues, or Amphictyonies.

II. POLITICAL DEVELOPMENT IN GREECE. — Changes in the Government. — The Rise of Aristocracies. — The Rule of Tyrants. — The Growth of Democracy.

III. EXPANSION OF GREECE BY COLONIZATION. — Causes of Colonial Expansion. — Character of the Greek Colony. — The Colonizing Cities. — Areas of Colonization.

I. THE EARLY CITY STATE

Character of the Greek Cities. — When Herodotus visited the Orient he saw cities far different from those he was accustomed to see in Greece. He saw great towns with massive walls stretching over a plain, such as Babylon, miles in extent. He saw sumptuous palaces, several stories in height, filled with a royal court of hundreds of persons, decked in gorgeous robes and ready to prostrate themselves before the king. But he never saw in an Oriental city the people gathered together in a public assembly to discuss the affairs of government, or to vote on matters left to their approval.

The Oriental cities were governed solely by the king, or by viceroys subject to the king; and this resulted in the growth of autocratic and despotic governments, in which the people had no part. In the Greek cities, on the other hand, the people obtained a certain share in the government; and this resulted in the growth of institutions more or less democratic in character. The Greek city was in fact the center of a new political life. We might call it the " cradle of liberty," where was born the idea of popular government. Even at the beginning of the historical period, — about 750 B.C. — we find many centers of city life in different parts of Greece. These cities were in a more or less flourishing condition and could already boast of great age. Most of the early cities, it is true, had kings. But the kings were of the simple Homeric type who consulted the people, and not kings of the Oriental type who ruled with an absolute and despotic authority.

The Beginnings of the City State. — The early Greek state was no doubt the result of a slow process of growth. We may trace its gradual development from the family, the primitive element of Greek society. The family was governed by the father, who presided over its worship, and controlled all its members.

A SACRIFICE

The family expanded naturally into the clan, or gens, which was essentially the larger body of family relatives, held together by a common worship and by a common feeling of kinship. The clan was governed by a council of the household fathers, and by a chief man selected to preside over the common worship, to settle disputes, and to lead the people in time of war. In times of great danger the different clans would be induced to unite in a larger body, called a brotherhood or " phratry." This, too, had its own chief and council, and its armed men might be called together in an assembly to decide on questions of war. To repel a common peril the phratries would league themselves into a still larger body called the " tribe," which would also have its own leader, council, and assembly. By these successive unions was gradually devel-

oped the tribal state such as we find in Homeric times (p. 103);
and this grew into the city state of the historical period.

The Government of the City State. — The city was generally
formed by a union of tribes. The people sought a common
center of defense on some elevated spot — like the Acropolis of
Athens — which could be fortified, and to which they might
retreat in times of danger. They were held together by the
worship of some common deity, whom they regarded as their
protector. The city population comprised not simply the people who lived within the city walls but also those who lived
in the surrounding country — in fact, all those who shared in
the common city worship and were subject to the common city
government. The city government in early times was patterned after that of the tribe, and consisted of the king, the
council, and the assembly.

(1) The city king (*basileus*) was, like the older tribal chief,
the leader of the people in time of war, the priest of the common city religion, and the judge to settle disputes between the
citizens. He governed by no written laws, but tried to uphold
the existing customs of the people and what he supposed to be
the will of the gods.

(2) The city council (*boulê*) was, like the council of the
tribe, made up of the leading men of the community. They
formed a sort of advisory body, which was called together
whenever the king desired. On account of their influence they
might guide or restrain the power of the king; and on account
of their superior birth or position, they came to be an aristocratic class, or what we might call a body of nobles.

(3) The city assembly (*agora*), like the tribal assembly, was
composed of all citizens capable of bearing arms. As the state
was formed originally for the purpose of protection, and as it
thus had primarily a military character, the people were generally consulted only on questions relating to war. But as the
state acquired more of a civil character, the assembly came to
be a more important element in the government.

Independence of the City States. — The Greek world was made up of a large number of these little city states, which for the most part preserved their local independence. This was due largely to the broken nature of the country, which kept the different communities separated from one another. It was due also to the independent spirit of the people themselves. The political life of Greece was thus confined to the cities. The spirit of patriotism consisted in the love of one's own city; and the great achievements of the Greeks were made to glorify the city. The Greek spirit of independence had both a good and a bad effect. On the one hand, it tended to foster free institutions and the forms of local self-government. On the other hand, it prevented the permanent union of Greece and the development of a national state.

City Leagues, or Amphictyonies. — Although the Greek cities were politically independent of one another, they sometimes united themselves into leagues or confederacies, called " amphic'tyonies." These leagues were often formed to maintain the worship of some common deity, or to promote common commercial interests, or to protect the cities against a common foe. The members of the associations often professed to believe that they were descended from some common ancestor, and were under the protection of the same god. Sometimes one city obtained the leadership, or " hegem'ony," over the rest; but if such a leadership became oppressive, it generally provoked a revolt on the part of the subject cities. In the course of our study we shall have our attention called to a number of such Greek confederacies.

II. Political Development in Greece

Changes in the Government. — When we consider the political organization of the Greek city states, we must not suppose that they always remained in the simple and primitive condition which has just been described. Their political life, on the contrary, was one of continual activity and change. One form of government succeeded another as the king, or the nobles, or the people gained the upper hand. Although the different cities presented a great diversity in their political life, we can trace a general tendency in the direction of more democratic ideas and freer institutions.

The Rise of Aristocracies. — When land was the chief source of wealth, those who acquired the more land would come to be richer and more powerful than their neighbors. The poor would come to be dependent upon the rich. In the early Greek states the large landowners and their descendants not only regarded themselves as more " noble " than their neighbors, but they began to get control of the government and to rule the common people for their own benefit. They took away the power hitherto held by the king, and governed in their own name. If the king remained at all he was a mere figurehead. And so in nearly all the cities of Greece the kings lost their ancient power; and this passed into the hands of the aristocracy, or the large landowners. In such cities we see a wide distinction between the governing class and the governed class, — between the nobles and the common people.

The Rule of Tyrants. — There soon grew up a spirit of bitterness between the aristocracy and the common people. Bitterness led to conflicts. The common people strove to get a greater degree of liberty and equality. The nobles strove to maintain their superiority and political power. In the midst of these disturbances there was a chance for some strong man to take up the cause of the people against the nobles, and ride into power himself. Such a man the Greeks called a " tyrant." This word did not necessarily mean, as with us, a despotic ruler. It simply meant a usurper — a man who had obtained the sole power in an illegal way. He might be, and generally was, a friend of the people, but he was always an enemy of the aristocracy. Many of the so-called tyrants were men of liberal spirit and fine culture. They were patrons of literature and art; they adorned their cities with fine buildings and encouraged commerce with foreign states. The time when these rulers were most numerous in Greece is sometimes called the "age of tyrants" (about 650–500 B.C.).

The Growth of Democracy. — But after a time these "tyrants," as is often the case with ambitious men, began to rule for their own sake, and lost sight of the cause of the people. They became tyrants in nature as well as in name. They ruled without regard to law and justice; they came to be distrusted by the people, and were driven from their high places. The killing of a tyrant ("tyrannicide") came to be looked upon as a patriotic duty. The most important work which the tyrants did was to break down the power of the nobles. They thus paved the way for a more democratic form of government.

The many different states of Greece, however, were not equally successful in obtaining a democratic government. In some states we see the power remaining in the hands of a small part of the people, resulting in the permanent establishment of an aristocracy, or oligarchy. In other cities, we see the political power transferred to the great body of citizens, resulting in the growth of a well-organized democratic state. Of the various Greek cities we may look upon Sparta and Athens as typical, for they represented the two extreme tendencies in the political development of Greece — Sparta showing the tendency toward aristocracy, and Athens the tendency toward democracy.

III. EXPANSION OF GREECE BY COLONIZATION

Causes of Colonial Expansion. — At the same time that the cities of Hellas were working out the problem of free government, we see the boundaries of the Hellenic world widening by the establishment of colonies. The causes leading to the colonial expansion of Greece were various. In the first place, the growth of population required the formation of new settlements; and these could be formed only in the unoccupied lands which bordered upon the adjoining seas. In the next place, the political discontent resulting from aristocratic oppression led many people to seek greater freedom in new settlements; hence we find a large number of colonies established by cities subject to aristocratic rule.   Finally, the growing spirit of commerce furnished a strong impulse to colonization.   The coasts of the Ægean were indented with natural harbors; and the Greeks early derived from the Phœnicians the spirit of commerce and shared with them the trade routes of the sea.   With the decline of the Phœnician power, the Greeks became the leading commercial people of the East.   Like the Phœnicians, they dotted the shores of the Mediterranean with their trading posts.   Greece thus became the mother of colonies, and from the eighth to the sixth century B.C. (750–550 B.C.) the territory of Hellas was continually growing wider and wider.

Character of the Greek Colony. — The Greek colony was a community of Greek citizens transported to a new land.   It was generally, though not always, the offshoot of a single city. Wherever it might be planted, it bore the blossoms and fruits of Greek culture.   The founding of a colony was a matter of so much importance that it was customary to consult the oracle at Delphi to find out whether the undertaking would meet with the divine sanction.   If the response was favorable, a " founder " was appointed to lead the colonists to their new home.   The sacred fire taken from the altar of the parent city was carried with the colonists as a symbol of their filial devotion.   The infant colony worshiped the same gods as the parent city, and in every way showed the sacred reverence due from a daughter to a mother.   But in its political life the colony was entirely independent of the parent state.   Though bound by filial affection, it was not subject to parental authority.   It formed its own government, made its own laws, and was expected to work out its own destiny.[1]

---

[1] This statement does not apply to the citizen colonies, or "cle'ruchies," sent out by Athens to maintain her influence in a foreign land.   In a cleruchy the settlers retained their political relations and rights as members of the parent state.

**COLONIES ON THE
NORTHERN ÆGEAN
AND PROPONTIS**

SCALE OF MILES

0 10 20 30 40 50   100

GREATER HELLAS

Sixth Century B.C.

Chief Seats of Colonization.

Ionians   Æolians and Achæans
Dorians   Phoenicians

SCALE OF MILES

50 100   200   300   400

East   25   from   Greenwich   30   35

L.L. POATES, ENGR., N.Y.

The Colonizing Cities. — The cities of Greece were not equally zealous in the planting of colonies. Of the chief cities, Athens was one of the least important in this movement. This may have been due to the fact that she was at first more devoted to politics than to commerce, or to the fact that her citizens were less discontented than those of other cities. Sparta, on account of her distance from the sea, was also not important as a colonizing state. Of the cities of Greece proper the foremost in the colonizing movement was Chalcis (kăl′sis), on the island of Euboea (map, p. 114). This city had a favorable seaboard. It had an extensive trade with the East, and its aristocratic government, too, was a cause of popular discontent. These facts are sufficient to explain its colonizing spirit. Next after Chalcis should be mentioned the neighboring city of Ere′tria; and then Meg′ara and Corinth (map, p. 114),

COIN OF ERETRIA

both of which were favorably situated for commerce, and were often misruled by an oppressive oligarchy. But the city which surpassed all others as a colonizing center was situated not in Europe, but in Asia. This was Miletus, the most celebrated city of Ionia (map, p. 115). It possessed four large harbors, and seems to have fallen heir to the commercial enterprise of the Phœnicians. Miletus is said to have been the mother of eighty colonies.

Areas of Colonization. — The lands open to Greek colonization were the unoccupied coasts of the Mediterranean and Black seas. Some of these lands had already been held by Phœnician colonists; but the decline of Phœnicia gave an opportunity to the Greeks, either to take possession of the old Phœnician sites, or to establish new settlements. The new lands were generally inhabited by a barbarous people; but the native products of these lands afforded a strong inducement to

Grecian traders. There were two general areas open to coloni-zation, which we may distinguish as the eastern and the west-ern. The eastern area comprised the northern coasts of the Ægean Sea; the shores of the Propon'tis with its tributary straits, the Hellespont and the Bosporus; the extensive coast of the Euxine or Black Sea; and also the northeastern coast of Africa. The western area comprised the western coasts of Illyr'icum and Epirus; the coasts of southern Italy (Magna Græcia) and Sicily; and the seaboards of the western Mediter-ranean, including southern Gaul, and extending along the shores of Spain. (For the most important colonies see map, pp. 114, 115.)

Selections for Reading

Seignobos, pp. 108–111, "The Hellenes beyond Sea" (1).[1]

Smith, Wm., Ch. 12, "History of the Greek Colonies" (10).

Oman, Ch. 9, "The Age of Colonization" (10).

Curtius, Vol. I., Bk. II., Ch. 3, "The Hellenes beyond the Archipelago" (10).

Bury, Ch. 2, "The Expansion of Greece"; pp. 95–102 (Sicily) (10).

Allcroft, Vol. I., Ch. 9, "Evolution of Governments"; Ch. 10, "Age of Tyrants" (10).

Abbott, Vol. II., Introduction, "Sketch of Constitutional History"; Ch. 11, "The Greek Colonies" (10).

Holm, Vol. I., Ch. 20, "Political Development of the Greek States"; Ch. 21, "Greek Colonization" (10).

Greenidge, Ch. 2, "Early Development of the Greek Constitutions; Mon-archy, Aristocracy, Tyranny to Constitutional Government"; Ch. 3, "Colonization" (11).

Special Study

THE CITIZEN COLONIES, OR CLERUCHIES. — Smith, Wm., pp. 112, 268 (10); Shuckburgh, p. 215 (10); Oman, pp. 152, 277 (10); Bury, pp. 265–266 (10); Abbott, Vol. II., pp. 376–379 (10); Smith, Dict. Antiqq., "Cleru-chi" (11).

[1] The figure in parenthesis refers to the number of the topic in the Appendix where a fuller title of the book will be found.

CHAPTER X

THE TYPICAL CITY STATES — SPARTA AND ATHENS

Synopsis

I. THE DORIAN CITY STATE, SPARTA. — The Dorians and Sparta. — Classes of the People in Sparta. — The Government of Sparta. — Spartan Education: Training of the Boys. — Education of the Girls. — The Spartan Army. — The Conquests of Sparta: the Peloponnesian League. — Position of Sparta in Greece.

II. THE IONIAN CITY STATE, ATHENS. — The Ionians in Attica. — The Beginning of Athens: the Monarchy. — The Athenian Aristocracy: the Archons. — Condition of the People: Laws of Draco. — The Reforms of Solon. — Solon and the Athenian Discipline. — The Tyranny of Pisistratus. — The End of the Tyranny. — The New Constitution of Clisthenes. — The Triumph of Democracy.

I. THE DORIAN CITY STATE, SPARTA

The Dorians and Sparta. — In their conquest of the Peloponnesus (p. 99), the Dorians took possession of the cities in three important countries — Ar'golis, Laconia, and Messenia (map, p. 84). But all the Dorian cities were at last overshadowed by Sparta, a town of Laconia, which we may study as the chief city state of the Dorian race. It was situated on the Euro'tas River. It was at first a mere military garrison, struggling to maintain itself against a hostile people. By degrees it gained in strength until it became the center of the Dorian civilization. This remarkable city owed its success to its peculiar organization and discipline, said to have been established by Lycur'gus. The stories which are told of Lycurgus are largely mythical. It is said that he reorganized, with the approval of the Delphic oracle, the whole social and political system of Sparta; and that, having obtained from the people a solemn oath to make no changes in his laws during his absence, he left the city and never returned. Without attempting to criticize the " myth of Lycurgus," which is told by Plutarch, let us review the Spartan institutions as they existed in historical times.

LYCURGUS (So-called)

Classes of the People in Sparta. — The first thing we notice in Sparta is the division of the whole population into three classes — which had evidently grown up from the Dorian conquest of the Peloponnesus.

(1) The upper class consisted of the Spartans themselves, the descendants of the Dorian conquerors. They were the free inhabitants of the Spartan city, and were the sole possessors of political rights. They formed, in fact, a comparatively small part of the entire population — not more than ten thousand men capable of bearing arms. They received the best portions of the land; but they were forbidden themselves to till the soil, or to do the work of artisans or traders. Their sole occupation was war and service to the state.

(2) The next class comprised the more favored inhabitants of the surrounding towns that had been conquered by the Spartans. They were hence called Periœ'ci (dwellers around). They were allowed to retain their old lands on condition of paying a fixed tribute to the state, and of furnishing heavy-armed troops for the Spartan army. As long as they fulfilled these duties they were free to do as they pleased; but they had no share in the Spartan government.

(3) The lowest class comprised those people who had stubbornly resisted the Spartans in their conquests, and were hence

reduced almost to the condition of slaves. As the last town to hold out against the Spartans was Helos (map, p. 124), this whole class were known as " Helots." They were deprived of their lands, and were made absolutely subject to the state. They were not exactly slaves, but serfs bound to the soil, from which they could not be sold. They were the tillers of the land. They formed the largest part of the population. They had no rights and their condition was wretched. They even held their lives at the mercy of their masters. It is said that the state appointed a secret police force, made up of Spartan young men, armed with daggers, to go about the country and kill every helot who was looked upon with suspicion. It is no wonder that they were inclined to revolt and to be regarded as a dangerous class. To keep the helots in subjection was one of the great problems of the Spartan government. The story is told that at one time when the Spartans feared an insurrection of the helots they promised liberty to the men who most desired it. Two thousand of the most spirited young men responded. The Spartans pretended to honor them by crowning them with garlands and leading them in a procession around the temples. But it was not long afterward, as the historian Thucydides says, that " the Spartans put them all out of the way and no man knew how any one of them came to his end."

\ **The Government of Sparta.** — The form of the Spartan government was in some respects different from any other in Greece. It consisted of four branches — the kings, the senate, the assembly, and the ephors.

(1) At the head of the state were two kings. They were members of two distinct royal families, and held their office for life. The royal power, however, became very weak, because each king acted as a restraint upon the other. After a time they came to be mere figureheads. Their chief duty was to command the army in the field.

(2) The senate was a sort of council of state. It consisted of twenty-eight members, besides the two kings. Its members

were elected by the assembly. They were at least sixty years
of age, and held their position for life. They were not like our
United States senators, representing different states or localities;
but were all chosen from the city of Sparta. They were elected,
not by ballot, as with us, but by the voice of the people. When
a vacancy occurred the candidates passed one by one through
the assembly; and the one who received the loudest applause
was declared elected. This was decided by persons sitting in a
building near by, who could hear the applause, but could not
see the candidates. The chief duty of the senate was to prepare
measures for the approval of the assembly.

(3) The assembly was the general meeting of all the citizens
above thirty years of age. It was called together every month.
It voted upon the laws submitted to it by the senate. It decided questions of peace and war. It elected not only the
senators but the ephors and other officers.

(4) The ephors, or body of " overseers," were the most peculiar
feature of the Spartan government. They were five in number,
and were chosen each year from the whole body of Spartan
citizens. They were looked upon as the guardians of the state.
They kept watch over the kings, and two of them even accompanied the king when he took command of the army. They
called to account all the magistrates. They even controlled
the manners of the people. It is said that when they entered
upon their office they issued a proclamation to the citizens " to
shave their upper lips and obey the laws " (Bury).

Spartan Education: Training of the Boys. — The Spartans evidently believed that the character of a nation depends upon the
training of its children. If the state is to be prepared for war, the
children must be physically strong and inured to hardships akin
to those of war. The Spartan elders decided whether each child,
at birth, was sufficiently strong to be reared, or whether he should
be exposed to the wild beasts. At the age of seven the boy was
taken from his mother's care and placed in the hands of the
public trainers. From this time he was subject to a training

which was severe, and which to us seems brutal; but to the Spartans it seemed the necessary education for a soldier's life. The boys were compelled to form small companies and to eat, like soldiers, at a common " mess," and each one was obliged to prepare his own meals; to wear the same clothing summer and winter; to sleep on a bed of rushes; to be hardened by the

FOOT RACE (Vase painting)

lash that he might better endure the hardships of the camp. To develop his physical strength and agility, he was trained in gymnastic exercises, in running, wrestling, and throwing the javelin.

The Spartans had little sympathy with higher intellectual culture, with art and science. They approved of music and poetry, if they were inspired with a warlike spirit. Oratory had no charm for them. They insisted upon short, pithy sayings instead of long speeches. We to-day refer to such sayings as " laconic " — a word derived from Laconia, the country of the Spartans.

Education of the Girls. — If the boys were trained to become men in the Spartan sense, the girls were trained to be the mothers of such men, to be strong and healthy. It is said that the Spartan women were the most vigorous and beautiful of all the women of Greece. The girls were trained in much the same manner as the boys. They had their gymnastic exercises in running, jumping, throwing the discus and even the javelin. They were taught to admire the young men who were brave, and to despise those who were cowardly. With such a training the women inspired their sons to be courageous soldiers, to be brave in battle, to choose death rather than dishonor. The story is told of the Spartan mother who sent her boy to the war, telling him to bring back his shield or to be brought back upon it.

The Spartan Army. — We in our day are taught to believe that the state exists for the citizen. The Spartans, on the other hand, were taught that the citizens existed for the state; and they believed that the great end of the state was to be always ready for war. In carrying on war they learned that battles are not to be won by men fighting in a mob, every man for himself. They learned that an army to be effective must be properly organized. They therefore introduced a new arrangement something like our organization of companies, regiments, and brigades. The smallest division was a company of twenty-four men, under a captain. Each division, from the smallest to the largest, was under its own officer. An order of the commander-in-chief was sent down through these officers until it reached every soldier in the ranks. When arranged for battle the main divisions were united in a "phalanx," — which was a solid body of men eight rows deep, presenting an almost irresistible force in the face of the enemy. Every soldier was heavily armed, that is, a "hoplite." He was, in the first place, protected by a defensive armor, consisting of a helmet for the head, a breastplate (or cuirass) for the upper part of the body, greaves

GREEK HOPLITE

for the legs, and a shield carried upon the left arm. Besides this he carried two offensive weapons, — a long spear in his right hand and a short sword in his belt.

The Conquests of Sparta: the Peloponnesian League. — With such military training and discipline Sparta was able to extend and maintain her authority over the Peloponnesus. She first gained possession of the valley of the Eurotas, and brought the whole of Laconia under her authority. After two long and severe wars — each one lasting about twenty years — Sparta subdued the neighboring district of Messe'nia. These conflicts are known as the " Messenian Wars," and belong to the most heroic period of Spartan history (about 750–650 B.C.). Later the territory of Arcadia was subdued. Finally, Sparta gained a controlling influence in Elis, especially in the management of the national games at Olympia.

All the cities of the Peloponnesus, except Argos and the towns of Acha'ia, were joined in a confederacy known as the

THE PELOPONNESUS

" Peloponnesian League." Each city was allowed to retain its local independence, but was joined to Sparta by a treaty, in which the city agreed to furnish to Sparta a certain number of troops in time of war. Every city of the league had an equal voice in a federal council, which met at Sparta and which was supposed to regulate matters of general interest. In this confederacy Sparta was the leader; and she exercised her influence in striving to extend her aristocratic institutions throughout Greece.

Position of Sparta in Greece. — While there are many things that we might criticize in the narrow government, the austere training, and the domineering policy of Sparta, we must confess that she contributed much to the future greatness of Greece. She set an example of simplicity in life, of self-control, of patriotic devotion, of respect for existing institutions. She showed the importance of physical education, of healthy, strong, and symmetrical bodies; and she gave Greece an ideal of physical manhood which furnished an inspiration to Greek sculpture. She also set a pattern of military organization by which in the subsequent period of foreign invasions Greece was saved from destruction. Although Sparta did not represent the highest culture of Greece, she did much to make that highest culture possible.

II. The Ionian City State, Athens

The Ionians in Attica. — As Sparta was the chief city of the Dorian people, Athens came to be the most noted city of the Ionians. The chief settlements of the Ionian people were made in Attica. This was a district on the eastern coast of Greece, jutting out into the Ægean Sea; it was about the size of the state of Delaware. It was a rugged country, broken up by mountains and valleys, with a few plains watered by small streams. It had not a fertile soil. It afforded no special attractions for the stranger. Nobody seemed to know when the Ionians came into Attica, where they came from, or what they came for, -- and so they called themselves the " children of the soil." The territory came to be dotted with villages and towns. Some of the people settled upon the plains — the farmers. Some settled on the hills — the shepherds and the herdsmen. Some drifted down to the seashore, — the fishermen and the mariners. Some collected together into towns — the artisans and merchants. The rugged land did not provoke the envy of warlike neighbors; and these early people had no desire for conquest. And so the people of Attica did not develop a military spirit, as did the Spartans. They preferred to till the soil, to graze their flocks upon the hillsides, to build ships and plow the sea, to gaze into the azure sky and tell wonderful stories about the gods.

The Beginning of Athens : the Monarchy. — One of the Ionian towns grew up near a high rock about four miles from the

ATHENA
(Statue in Parthenon)

southwestern coast. This rock was called the Acropolis. The land here was thought to be under the special guardianship of Athena, the goddess of wisdom; and so the settlement was called Athens. All the people of Attica came to look upon Athena as their guardian deity, and upon Athens as their capital city. While living in their own towns they came to Athens to worship the goddess, and all alike regarded themselves as Athenians. They obeyed the ruler of Athens as their own king, and thus came to be united under a common monarchy.[1] In this way the early city state which grew up about Athens comprised all the towns of Attica united under a common government. Our knowledge of this early period is based almost entirely upon traditions. But we may be quite certain that the earliest government was a monarchy of the Homeric type — with a king, a council, and an assembly.

[1] The union of the different towns of Attica under a single king is the subject of the traditional stories about Theseus, who was said to be the first king of Athens.

The Athenian Aristocracy : the Archons. — The descendants of the old Ionian families were divided into four large groups, or "tribes," which were known as the "four Ionian tribes." They held the largest amount of the land. They had the greatest wealth. They regarded themselves as better born, more "noble," than the rest of the people, who could not trace their pedigree so far back. The nobles called themselves "Eupat'-rids" — meaning the *well-born*. They not only regarded themselves as superior to their neighbors : they also desired to rule and to have the entire control of public affairs. When, therefore, the royal line ran out they chose one of their own number to be ruler in place of the old king.[1] This man was called an "archon," which means a *ruler*. At first the archon was chosen for life, then for ten years, then for one year; and finally there were elected each year nine archons, who were the chief rulers in the state. After their term of office expired they became members of a council, to give their advice on public affairs. The council of ex-archons met on the Hill of A'res (Mars) and hence were known as the "Council of the Areop'agus." In this way Athens came to be an aristocratic government, ruled by the Eupatrids, or the highborn nobles who belonged to the old Ionian families.

Condition of the People : Laws of Draco. — While the old Ionian families were becoming more rich and prosperous, the common people were becoming poorer and more wretched. In the first place, they were taxed nearly to death by the enormous rent they were obliged to pay to their rich landlords. In the next place, if a person owed his landlord for back rent or was in debt for borrowed money, he was liable to be arrested, his land taken away, and he himself with his family reduced to slavery. Again, the laws were unwritten, and nobody but the nobles knew what they were. As the judges were all nobles, the

---

[1] This change in the government is told in the traditional story about Cod'rus, who was said to have sacrificed himself in battle, and to have been the last king of Athens.

common people were at their mercy. In some cases, people even fled from the country to escape the cruelty of their masters.

With much of the land uncultivated and the people reduced to poverty, it seemed necessary that some reforms should be made. The first step was to reduce the laws to a written form. This task was placed in the hands of one of the archons named Dra'co. When the new code was published, the people were shocked at the cruelty of the laws to which they had been subject; and it was afterward said of them that they were "written not in ink, but in blood." It is said that Draco formed a new council of four hundred and one members, based on wealth. But this was of no benefit to the poorer classes.

The Reforms of Solon (about 594 B.C.). — Athens was in need of a real statesman; and one now appeared in the person

SOLON (So-called)

of So'lon. He was called one of the "Seven Wise Men." He was a poet and philosopher, and above all a patriot. Once upon a time the island of Salamis was stolen from the Athenians, by the more warlike people of Meg'aris, and the Athenians showed no disposition to fight for its recovery. To arouse them to action Solon pretended to be mad, and rushed into the market place, railing at them for th ir lack of spirit. "I am ashamed of my country," he exclaimed, "to abandon Salamis. Let us away to Salamis; let us fight for the lovely island and thrust from our shoulders this load of shame." The Athenians responded, and the island was recovered. This was the man who was now called upon to reform the state.

(1) In the first place he freed all those who had been sold into slavery for debt, and called back all those who had fled into exile to escape the cruelty of their masters. He canceled the old debts, and abolished the practice of reducing men to slavery on account of debt.

(2) His next reform was to extend the franchise to the poorer classes. There had already been established (at some time not exactly known) four " census classes," in which the members of the Ionian tribes were arranged according to the amount of income which persons received. These classes had previously been used as a basis for the apportionment of the taxes. Solon now used the classes as a basis for the distribution of political rights. For example, the archons were to be elected from the first class only; and all the inferior officers were to be chosen from the first, second, or third class. But all the classes — including the fourth, called the *The'tes* — received the right to vote in the assembly for all officers. The new plan gave to the assembly a more democratic character. By this reform the right to vote was open to all; but all did not yet have the same right to hold office. Solon also established a popular court (*Heliæ'a*), in which all citizens, including the *Thetes*, could sit as jurors.

(3) The third important reform of Solon was the reorganization of the council. He retained the old council of the Areopagus, which continued to hold its dignified position as " guardian of the constitution." But in place of the council of four hundred and one established by Draco, he created a new council of four hundred members — one hundred members being chosen by lot from each of the four Ionian tribes. This council prepared the laws, which might or might not be submitted to the assembly of the people.

The reforms of Solon were guided by wisdom and moderation. Although he did not entirely overthrow the aristocratic element of the state, he did give a greater importance to the popular element, and paved the way for a more democratic government.

Solon and the Athenian Discipline. — Like the Spartans, Solon believed that the character of the state depended upon some form of discipline. But, unlike the Spartans, he believed that the sources of public virtue were in the home. He held the father responsible for training the son in habits of industry. He believed that education — physical, intellectual, and moral — was a means of preserving the state. " In the shady wrestling-grounds, which spread themselves out in the neighborhood of the city, the young Athenians were to unfold the vigor of their bodies and minds, and grow to be a part of the state, which demanded men not drilled in the Spartan fashion, but fully and freely developed " (Curtius). Solon believed it to be the duty of every citizen to have an interest in public affairs; and he disfranchised the man who refused to take part in political life. He also believed that individual liberty should be restrained in the interests of public morality; and he punished those who led infamous lives, or attempted to corrupt others. The Athenians were thus trained by a discipline, no less than the Spartans. But it was a discipline more rational, and based upon broader ideas of human nature; and it finally led to a higher form of culture.

The Tyranny of Pisistratus (560–527 B.C.). — It is said that Solon bound the people by an oath to observe his laws for ten years, and then departed from the city.[1] But during his absence bitter strifes arose among the various classes of citizens who had different interests. These were: (1) the wealthy landowners, who held their estates on the lowlands, and were called the Men of the Plain; (2) the shepherds and peasants, who

---

[1] He traveled abroad, and is said to have visited Crœsus, the king of Lydia. In response to a question of the king, as to who was the happiest of men, Solon, knowing the fickleness of fortune, is said to have replied that "no one can be counted truly happy until he is dead." Whether this story is true or not, the fate of Crœsus afforded an example of the truth of these words; for he was afterwards driven from his throne. Indeed, Solon also experienced their truth; for when he returned to Athens, he found his native city, for whose happiness he had so faithfully labored, still disturbed by civil strife, and he was led to believe that his work was a failure.

lived in the highlands, and were called the Men of the Hill; and (3) the merchants and traders who lived along the coast, and were called the Men of the Shore.   In the struggles between these parties, the cause of the common people was taken up by an able leader, Pisis'tratus, who seized the government in a manner not sanctioned by law, and governed it as a " tyrant " (p. 111).   Although driven from the city by his enemies, he recovered his power.   The story is told that to insure his safe return, he employed a stratagem.   He approached the city in a splendid chariot, accompanied by a beautiful, stately woman, decked in the armor and costume of Athena ; he was preceded by heralds announcing that the goddess had come to reinstate the banished ruler.   Overawed by this exhibition, it is said, the people quietly submitted.

"His administration," says Aristotle, "was more like a constitutional government than the rule of a tyrant."   He retained the political forms established by Solon, only taking care that his own supporters should be elected to the archonship.   He advanced money to the poorer people to aid them in obtaining a livelihood.   He appointed local judges in the country, so that the rights of the lower classes might be protected without their being obliged to come to the city for justice.   He adorned Athens with public buildings, not only to satisfy his own love of art, but to give work to the unemployed.   He was a patron of literature and collected a library which he threw open to the public.   He is said to have made the first collection of Homer's poems.   He gathered about him the poets and artists of Greece.   He also encouraged commerce and formed alliances with foreign states.   He favored in every way the worship of the gods, and instituted splendid festivals in their honor.   Although a tyrant in name, he was one of the greatest of Athenian rulers, and began the policy that later made Athens the literary and art center of Greece.

The End of the Tyranny. — At the death of Pisistratus the power passed into the hands of his two sons, Hip'pias and Hippar'chus.

ARISTOGITON

They began their rule by following their father's worthy example. But Hipparchus was killed as the result of a private quarrel, and his brother Hippias was embittered. By his despotic rule Hippias made the name of tyrant forever odious to the Athenian people. With the aid of the Spartans, who were directed by the Delphic oracle to help the Athenians, Hippias was overthrown and banished from the city. The tyrannicides, Harmo'dius and Aristogi'ton, who had previously killed Hipparchus. were hailed as the deliverers of their country, and statues of bronze were erected in their honor.[1]

The New Constitution of Clisthenes (508 B.C.) — The man who now appeared as the friend of the people was Clis'thenes, who had taken part in overthrowing the recent tyranny. He was an able and farseeing statesman, and one of the greatest reformers that Greece ever produced. Let us see how he made the government more democratic.

(1) In the first place, Clisthenes extended the right of citizenship to all the people of Attica, regardless of birth. He did this by allowing every one to vote who lived in a certain locality, whether he belonged to the old Ionian tribes or not. The smallest local district in Attica was the township, or *deme*. All

---

[1] The original statues were carried away from Athens by Xerxes, and another group was set up in their place. When Alexander the Great afterward conquered Persia, he restored to Athens the original bronzes, and the two groups were placed side by side on a terrace overlooking the market place.

persons properly enrolled in a *deme* were now to be regarded as citizens. He then arranged these townships — a hundred or more — into ten large groups, known as "local tribes." — something like our own counties. The ten new Attic tribes thus took the place of the four old Ionian tribes. In thus making citizenship depend upon residence instead of blood, Clisthenes gave the vote to many persons who had hitherto been deprived of it — such as enfranchised slaves and resident foreigners.

(2) In the next place, the government was changed so as to rest upon this new arrangement of the people. For example, the assembly (*eccle'sia*) was now made up of all the people of Attica who were enrolled in the various demes. So too, the council, or senate (*boulê*) — instead of consisting of four hundred members, one hundred from each of the four Ionian tribes — was now made to consist of five hundred members, fifty of whom were selected by lot from each of the ten new tribes. The chief magistrates of the state continued to be the nine archons, but soon after the time of Clisthenes they were chosen by lot from candidates presented by all the demes. The military organization also was based upon the new tribal division, ten generals (*strate'gi*) being elected to command the ten tribal regiments, and forming a war council under one of the archons who acted as commander in chief.

(3) Clisthenes also introduced a method to protect the state from dangerous party leaders. If six thousand votes were cast at a special assembly called for that purpose, the man receiving the highest number was obliged to withdraw from the city for ten years. As these votes were written upon pieces of earthenware (*ostraca*) the process was called "ostracism." Although intended as a safeguard to the state, it was yet capable of being abused by being used for partisan purposes. There is a story that Clisthenes himself was the first man to be ostracized; but concerning the later life of this great reformer little is known.

The Triumph of Democracy. — We all no doubt appreciate the privilege of living under our democratic institutions. We ourselves have a " government of the people, by the people, and for the people." But we do not always appreciate the long and painful struggles through which other people have gone in order to obtain such a government. From this review we may see the steps by which the ancient monarchy of Athens was gradually changed into a well-organized democracy. The old king, who held his office by hereditary right, was displaced by the archons, chosen at first from the nobles, and finally from the whole body of the people. The ancient council of elders, or war chiefs, passed into the council of the Areopagus, which consisted of the ex-archons. This was supplemented by new councils, — at first, the council of four hundred and one, established by Draco, and chosen from the wealthy classes; afterward, the council of four hundred, established by Solon, and chosen from the four Ionian tribes; and, finally, the council of five hundred, established by Clisthenes, and chosen from the members of the ten new Attic tribes. The assembly had passed through somewhat similar changes, until it had come to be composed of the whole body of citizens, and to hold the sovereign power of the state.

As Athens came to represent the principle of democracy, she incurred the enmity of the Spartans, as the chief defenders of the aristocratic principle. Under their king, Cleom'enes, they even invaded Attica and attempted to overthrow the new Athenian constitution; but this effort proved a failure. With her democratic institutions firmly established, Athens continued to grow in strength until she became the chief city of Hellas and the champion of Greek liberty and of Greek culture.

Selections for Reading

Seignobos, Ch. 11, "Sparta"; Ch. 12, "Athens" (1).[1]
Shuckburgh, Ch. 4, "Athens and Attica" (10).
Smith, Wm., Ch. 10, "Early History of Athens" (10).
Bury, Ch. 3, "Growth of Sparta"; Ch. 5, "Growth of Athens" (10).

[1] The figure in parenthesis refers to the number of the topic in the Appendix, where a fuller title of the book will be found.

Oman, Ch. 7, "The Dorians in Peloponnesus"; Ch. 12, "Solon and Peisistratus"; Ch. 16, "The Constitution of Cleisthenes" (10).

Cox, History, Ch. 5, "Constitution and Early History of Sparta"; Ch. 9, "Early Constitutional History of Athens"; Ch. 12, "Reforms of Kleisthenes" (10).

Cox, Greek Statesmen, "Solon," "Pisistratus," "Kleisthenes" (26).

Abbott, Vol. I., Ch. 6, "The Spartan State"; Ch. 15, "Pisistratus and Cleisthenes" (10).

Curtius, Vol. I., Bk. II., Ch. 1, "History of the Peloponnesus"; Ch. 2, "History of Attica" (10).

Greenidge, Ch. 5, "Mixed Constitutions" (11).

Gilbert, pp. 81–91, "The Lacedæmonian League" (11).

Abbott, Vol. I., pp. 212, 213, "Spartan Women" (10).

Plutarch, "Lycurgus," "Solon" (26).

Aristotle, Athenian Constitution, Chs. 3–21 (growth of the constitution) (17).

Herodotus, Bk. I., Chs. 29–33 (Solon and Crœsus); Bk. VI., Chs. 126–113 (the wooing of Agariste, the daughter of Clisthenes, tyrant of Sicyon, and mother of Clisthenes, the Athenian statesman) (17).

Special Study

THE CONSTITUTION OF CLISTHENES. — Shuckburgh, pp. 89–94 (10); Smith, pp. 108–111 (10); Oman, Ch. 16 (10); Bury, pp. 211–215 (10); Abbott, Ch. 15 (10); Allcroft, Vol. I., Ch. 15 (10); Curtius, Vol. I., pp. 401–411 (10); Grote, Part I., Ch. 31 (10); Greenidge, pp. 157–162 (11); Gilbert, pp. 145–152 (11).

CHAPTER XI

THE EARLY CULTURE OF THE GREEK PEOPLE

Synopsis

I. THE GREEK RELIGION AND RELIGIOUS INSTITUTIONS. — Religion as a Phase of Greek Culture. — The Delphic Oracle. — The Amphictyonic League. — The Panhellenic Games. — Special Religious Festivals.

II. THE BEGINNINGS OF GREEK ART. — The Greek Temple. — Orders of Greek Architecture. — Architectural Decoration. — Early Greek Sculpture.

III. THE GREEK LANGUAGE AND EARLY LITERATURE. — The Greek Language. — The Poems of Hesiod. — The Early Lyric Poets. — The Early Greek Philosophers.

I. THE GREEK RELIGION AND RELIGIOUS INSTITUTIONS

Religion as a Phase of Greek Culture. — One of the most important elements of the early Greek culture was religion. The religious ideas of the people, their conceptions of the gods and the future life, were essentially the same as those contained in the Homeric poems (pp. 103–105). The stories of the gods and goddesses were woven into a beautiful mythology which appealed to the Greek taste. The deities were inspired with the same feelings as were the Greeks themselves. The Greek religion was, in fact, a reflection of the Greek character. The religion was also a most powerful inspiration of Greek life and thought. It influenced the acts of the warrior and the statesman, and furnished the theme of the poet and the sculptor. Another important feature to be noticed is the fact that it was the strongest bond of union between the different branches of the Greek race. However much they might be embittered by jealousy and war, the Greeks found in their religion a common bond of sympathy.

The Delphic Oracle. — The Greeks believed in oracles — that is, they believed that the gods revealed their will to men. They looked upon Apollo as preëminently the god of revelation, the god of light, of inspiration, and of prophecy. He had many oracles, but no other so renowned as that at Delphi, which was situated at the foot of Mt. Parnas'sus, in Phocis. Here was his most illustrious temple, rich with costly gifts bestowed by his worshipers. Here his breath was supposed to issue from a cleft

RUINS OF THE SHRINE OF APOLLO AT DELPHI

in the rock, over which stood a tripod — the seat of the Pyth'ia, or priestess, who uttered his will. The inspired words of the Pythia were taken down by the attendant priests, and delivered to the people. The oracle was consulted by private persons, as well as by the envoys of cities from every part of Hellas. Answers were given to questions relating to religion and politics, to national disputes, to wars, and to colonization. It is true that these answers often had a double meaning and were difficult to interpret (see p. 69). Still the Delphic priests were able by means of this sacred oracle to exercise a great and generally a beneficial influence upon the Greek people.

The Amphictyonic League. — The influence of the Greek religion, as a bond of union, is also seen in the amphictyonies, or leagues of cities bound together by some common interest, religious, commercial, or political (see p. 110). The most important of these associations in early times was the famous Amphictyonic League organized for the protection of the temple of Apollo at Delphi. It was made up of twelve states of central and northern Greece, which sent to Delphi a number of delegates forming the Amphictyonic council. Although religious in its origin, the league also had a political influence in binding the cities together under a kind of legal code. The cities were bound, not only to protect the temple of the god, but to respect one another's rights in time of war — not to cut off the running water which supplied a city, and not to destroy any Amphictyonic town. The council was a sort of international court, with judicial powers greater than those of our modern tribunal at The Hague. If any city disregarded its duty to the league, the other cities made war upon it and brought it to submission.

The Panhellenic Games. — Other institutions which tended to promote a national unity and a national type of culture were the great public games. These were celebrated in honor of the gods, and they show how closely religion was connected with all the phases of human life, — with art and literature, and even with athletic sports. Chief among these games were those held every four years at Olympia in Elis. The physical contests consisted in running, jumping, throwing the discus or quoit, casting the javelin, wrestling, boxing, and sometimes in chariot racing. The games were not barbarous sports, but were subject to strict rules, intended to promote the restraints of discipline and the sense of honor. The competition was restricted to Greeks of good character, well-trained and unblemished by any physical or moral taint. The reward of the victor was a wreath of olive leaves; high honors were paid him, and a statue might be erected to celebrate his triumph. The games also furnished a field for intellectual culture. Here poets recited their verses, painters displayed their pictures, and men of science explained their discoveries. Olympia became adorned with noble buildings —

especially the temple of Zeus. The multitude which gathered here from every part of Hellas carried back to their homes the feeling of a common kinship, and the love of Greek ideals. We have a living proof in our day of the continued interest in the old Olympic games. Their revival in modern times (beginning with the Olympic games at Athens in 1896) shows that we still admire the Greek ideals as something worthy to be imitated.

Other less noted games were the Pythian, given in honor of Apollo near his shrine at Delphi; the Neme'an, in honor of Zeus at Nemea, in Argolis; and the Isthmian, in honor of Poseidon, on the Isthmus of Corinth.

Special Religious Festivals. — Besides these general celebrations which belonged to the whole of Greece, there were special festivals which were more local in their character. These were holiday entertainments given in honor of certain deities, and for the sake of social recreation. They consisted of processions, singing, dancing, games, and other diversions in which the people took part. There were a number of these festivals in Attica. The most important of them were: the Panathenæ'a, given in honor of Athena; the Diony'sia, in honor of the god of wine, Diony'sus; and the Eleusin'ia, in honor of the goddess Demeter. The last-named festival was of peculiar interest, especially to those who had been initiated into the secret rites of this worship. It consisted of a solemn procession, in which every one might take part, from Athens by the " sacred way " to the city of Eleu'sis, the seat of the mysterious worship of the goddess. The secret ceremonies and doctrines attending this worship were called the " Eleusinian mysteries," of which no one was supposed to have any knowledge except the initiated. All the festivals formed a very important part of Greek life, and were preserved until a very late period.

II. The Beginnings of Greek Art

The Greek Temple. — The art of Greece, like that of the Orient, was closely related to religion. But the religion of the

Greeks appealed more strongly to human sympathy, and their art showed a finer sense of beauty. For the highest expression of Greek art we must look to the temple. In every city the temple was the most beautiful and conspicuous object. In its design the Greek temple was a simple roof supported by columns and covering a space inclosed by four walls. It is supposed that this design grew out of the form of a dwelling house, made of wood, with a front porch.

From this simple beginning the temple came in time to be a most beautiful building constructed of marble. A fine early example of such a building was the temple dedicated to Athena at Ægi′na on the island of the same name, not far south of Athens (map, p. 124). By looking at the

WEST FRONT OF TEMPLE AT ÆGINA

restored front, or " façade," of this temple we may get a good idea of some of its general features. The building rests upon a stone foundation built in the form of steps and supporting the columns. Resting upon the columns is a smooth, horizontal block of marble called the " arch′itrave." Above this is the " frieze," made of a succession of fluted blocks (" tri′glyphs ") with intervening spaces (" met′o-pes "). Between the frieze and the roof is a triangular space, or gable, called the " ped′iment," which, in most temples, was filled with a group of statuary, representing some mythological scene. The inside of the temple was divided into two chambers. The larger chamber contained a statue of the god or goddess in whose honor the temple was dedicated. In the smaller one were placed the treasures offered to the deity by devout worshipers. The purpose of the Greek temple was not, like a Christian church, to afford a place where the people might assemble to listen to sermons or to perform their acts of worship. It was the dwelling place of the god, who was there represented by his carved image.

Orders of Greek Architecture. — As the Greeks broke away from the massive architecture of the Eastern peoples, they developed styles of architecture of their own. These styles, or orders, are distinguished chiefly by the forms of the columns

Doric   *Ionic*   *Corinthian*

ORDERS OF GREEK ARCHITECTURE

and of the capitals. The earliest style was the Doric, so called because it was supposed to have its origin among the Dorian people of the Peloponnesus. This was the simplest and most dignified style. The column had no distinct base, and the capital consisted simply of a circular band surmounted by a square slab. The Doric style was used mostly during the early period, but it was always greatly admired by the Greeks. A later style was the Ionic, in which the column was more slender and rested upon a distinct base, and the capital was adorned with a spiral roll, or volute. A third style, developed still later, was called the Corinthian, which was a mere modification of the Ionic — the capital being somewhat more ornate and embellished with designs taken from the leaves of the acanthus plant. While the architecture of the Greeks did not reach its highest development during this period, it yet acquired a distinctly Hellenic character and showed the Greek taste for simplicity and symmetry.

Architectural Decoration. — If we wish to know what the Greeks meant by simplicity and symmetry, we may see it most clearly in their use of decoration. Indeed, the difference between true art and false art can be most easily seen in the use of ornamental designs. The Greeks did not believe in tawdry show or gaudy colors. They did not use decoration for the mere sake of display or to attract attention to itself, but to beautify the objects upon which it was placed. They used upon their buildings a great variety of ornamental designs, such as the fret, the egg and dart, the bead and fillet, and the honeysuckle. The way in which they arranged these designs is seen in the accompanying illustration. They also adorned their buildings with sculptured figures, which were not made unduly prominent, but were subordinate to the whole structure. Compare the sculpture used on an Egyptian temple (p. 39) with that used on a Greek temple (p. 141).

GREEK DECORATION

1, fret; 2, egg and dart; 3, bead and fillet; 4, honeysuckle

Early Greek Sculpture. — The art of sculpture did not make as rapid progress in this period as did architecture. In fact, most of the examples which are left to us are crude and archaic. But we can see the first efforts to break away from the stiff and conventional forms of the East, and to give to stone some features of life. The influence of religion is seen in the early attempts to represent the gods in the form of men; but these attempts are suggestive of idols rather than statues. The credit of giving to statues a more lifelike appearance is ascribed to the mythical Dæd'alus, who is said to have visited Crete. Schools of sculpture grew up in the cities of Samos and Chios, in Asiatic Greece; at Argos, Ægina, and Athens, in European Greece; and especially at Seli'nus, in Sicily. We have preserved

RELIEF FROM TEMPLE OF SELINUS
(Perseus slaying Medusa, see p. 88)

to us some of the sculptured reliefs from the temple at Selinus. These consist of small groups of figures representing mythological scenes, and are carved in a very rude fashion. They are placed in intervening spaces (metopes) on the frieze. They are interesting, as they show the early way in which sculpture was used for temple decoration. Among the strongest influences which led to the improvement of Greek sculpture were the encouragement given to physical training and the custom of erecting at Olympia statues to successful athletes. But it is not until the close of this period (about 500 B.C.) that we see the sculpture beginning to acquire some of the artistic qualities of the temples upon which they were placed.

III. The Greek Language and Early Literature

The Greek Language. — Another strong bond which united the various branches of the Greek people was their language. This gave them a common means of communication, and preserved among them the feeling of kinship. It also separated them from the outside " barbarian " world, and contributed to the growth of a distinct Hellenic culture. Although a branch of the great Aryan or Indo-European family of languages, the Greek early surpassed the other languages of the group in its capacity of expressing the finer shades of thought and of sincere feeling. By means of this remarkable language the Greeks produced a literature which has given them a high place among the most civilized peoples of the world. We can here take only a hasty glance at the growth of the literature during the early period.

The Poems of Hesiod. — At the beginning of this period (about 750 B.C.) the Greeks still possessed the poems said to have been written by Homer. These had come down from the heroic age. Later, we find an entirely different kind of poetry in the work of He'siod, the " Bœotian farmer." We do not know exactly when he lived, but it was probably two or three generations after the time assigned to Homer. Hesiod tells us in his poems that he was born near Mt. Hel'icon, in Bœotia; that in his youth he watched over his father's flocks on the mountain side; and that he was cheated out of his inheritance by an unjust brother. It is said that he desired to reform the life of his wayward brother; and, inspired by the muses, he wrote his first poem, called " Works and Days." This teaches that it is the duty of a man to be honest and industrious; that the best kind of life is that of a simple farmer. " You must start," says Hesiod " with a house, a wife, and an ox to plow, and have your farming implements ready in the house." He tells what kind of work should be done and the proper days on which to do it; and gives a great amount of good wholesome advice. As a poem this falls far below the heroic spirit of Homer. But in a later poem, called the "Theog'ony," Hesiod was inspired to write upon a more lofty theme — the origin and nature of the gods. The "Theogony" became an accepted guide to Greek mythology.

The Early Lyric Poets. — There soon arose in Greece still another kind of poetry, which consisted of songs expressing personal feeling, and hymns in praise of the gods. These were accompanied by music, especially by the lyre, and hence were called "lyric." The story goes that the lyre was invented by the god Hermes, who first drew strings across the oval hollow of

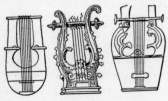

GREEK LYRES

a tortoise shell which he found upon the seashore. From this beginning the Greeks learned to stretch strings across a wooden frame. With the lyre as an accompaniment the poets sang their songs of war, of love, and of the pleasures of life. The first of these poets was Alcæ'us, a native of the island of Lesbos, near the coast of Asia Minor (map, p. 98). Many of his songs were patriotic, directed against the oppressive rule of the tyrants. Where can one find a nobler description of a state than this :

"What constitutes a state?
Not high-raised battlements or labored mound,
    Thick wall or moated gate;
Not cities fair, with spires and turrets crown'd;
    No : — Men, high-minded men —
With powers as far above dull brutes endued
    In forest, brake, or den,
As beasts excel cold rocks and brambles rude —
    Men, who their duties know,
But know their rights, and, knowing, dare maintain."

Another lyrist was Sappho, from the same island of Lesbos. She sang in beautiful strains of love and the tender passions of the heart. To the Greeks she was "the poetess," as Homer was

" the poet." On account of the beauty of her verses she was called " the tenth muse." [1] The English poet, Byron, refers to her in his lines, " The isles of Greece, the isles of Greece, Where burning Sappho loved and sung." Some fragments of her poetry have recently been discovered, but none finer than the little poem beginning with these well-known lines :

> "O Venus, beauty of the skies !
> To whom a thousand altars rise,
> Gaily false in gentle smiles,
> Full of love-perplexing wiles.
> O goddess, from my heart remove
> The wasting cares and pains of Love."

A poet of quite a different character was Anac'reon, who seems to have been inspired by Eros (Cupid), the mischievous little god of love, and Dionysus (Bacchus), the pleasure-loving god of wine. The spirit of his odes might be summed up : " Let us eat, drink, and be merry, for to-morrow we die." This is Anacreon's idea of a happy life :

> "Fill the bowl with rosy wine !
> Around our temples roses twine !
> And let us cheerfully awhile,
> Like the Wine and Roses, smile.
> To-day is ours ; what do we fear ?
> To-day is ours ; we have it here ;
> Let's treat it kindly, that it may
> Wish, at least, with us to stay.
> Let's banish business, banish sorrow ;
> To the gods belongs to-morrow."

There were other lyric poets who wrote hymns in praise of the gods, to be sung by a chorus at public festivals. Many of these choruses were sung in honor of the wine-god Dionysus.

The Early Greek Philosophers. — Another phase of Greek culture is seen in the writings of the early philosophers. We begin to see something like philosophy in the sayings of the

---

[1] The muses were nine goddesses who presided over song, the different kinds of poetry, arts, and sciences.

" Seven Wise Men." These men put into pithy form practical maxims for the guidance of life. Some of these maxims were inscribed upon the temple of Apollo at Delphi and are worthy to be remembered; for example, " Know Thyself," " Do nothing in excess." Other sayings ascribed to them were these: " The greatest blessing is the power to do good." " Pardon is better than punishment." " Unlucky is he who cannot bear ill-luck." " The most difficult things are to keep a secret, to forgive injuries, and to improve one's time." We might almost call Æsop, who lived at this time, one of the wise men; for his " Fables," in the form of stories about animals, contain moral precepts and good sound advice, and have given entertainment and instruction to old and young down to our own day. Besides the words of wise men, the growth of science also prepared the way for philosophy. Mathematics and astronomy were among the earliest of the sciences.

We need notice here the names of only a few men who were called philosophers. The first was Tha′les, one of the " Seven Wise Men." He was first of all a student of mathematics and astronomy. He was a great traveler. He is said to have taught the Egyptians how to measure the height of the pyramids by the shadows. He is also said to have predicted an eclipse of the sun. He believed that the whole universe had been produced from one primitive substance, and that this substance was *water*. Another philosopher, Anaxim′ines, thought it was *air*. Another, Heracli′tus, thought it was *fire*. Still another, Pythagoras, who looked at everything through mathematical eyes, thought that the most important principle of all things was *number*. These philosophers may have failed in their theories; but they excited men to think, and to give up many of their old mythological notions about the gods.

We can thus see in the Greek religion, art, poetry, and philosophy the evidences of a distinctive Hellenic culture, different from that of any other ancient people. The growth of such a common culture shows that the Greeks, although broken up into many small city states, were yet bound together in thought and feeling as one great nation, which extended from the coasts of Asia Minor to the shores of Sicily.

Selections for Reading

Seignobos, Ch. 10, "The Greek Religion" (1).[1]

Fairbanks, Part I., Ch. 2, "The Worship of the Gods" (16).

Smith, Wm., Ch. 13, "History of Literature"; Ch. 14, "History of Art" (10).

Mahaffy, Survey, Ch. 3, "First Two Centuries of Historic Development" (10).

Curtius, Vol. II., Bk. II., Ch. 4, "The Unity of Greece" (10).

Holm, Vol. I., Ch. 24, "Growth of Greek Philosophy, Literature and Art in Asia Minor" (10).

Symonds, Studies of the Greek Poets, Ch. 5, "The Lyric Poets."

Zeller, First Period, Part I., "The Three Earliest Schools" (15).

Tarbell, Ch. 2, "Prehistoric Art in Greece"; Ch. 3, "Greek Architecture" (12).

Collignon, Bk. I., "Origin of Greek Art" (12).

Grote, Part II., Ch. 28, "Pan-Hellenic Festivals" (10).

Gardiner, E. N., "The Olympic Festival" (11).

Harper's Dictionary, "Oracula" (Greek oracles); "Religio" (the religion of Homer and of later times); "Eleusinia" (Eleusis and its mysteries); "Delphi" (and its priesthood) (11).

Special Study

THE GREEK FESTIVALS AND GAMES. — Smith, Ch. 6 (10); Guhl and Koner, pp. 199–231 (11); Gulick, pp. 91–105, 306–308 (11); Blümner, Chs. 8, 11 (11); Holm, Vol. I., Ch. 19 (10); Gardiner, Chs. 9–11 (11), Harper's Dictionary (see names of different festivals and games) (11).

---

[1] The figure in parenthesis refers to the number of the topic in the Appendix, where a fuller title of the book will be found.

CHAPTER XII

THE WARS OF THE GREEKS AND THE PERSIANS

Synopsis

I. THE FIRST PERSIAN INVASION, UNDER DARIUS (492–490 B.C.). — Greece and Persia. — The Asiatic Cities and the Ionian Revolt. — Plans of Darius against Greece. — Persian Invasion under Datis and Artaphernes. — Miltiades and the Battle of Marathon.

II. ATHENS DURING THE TEN YEARS' RESPITE (490–480 B.C.). — Democratic Progress at Athens. — Aristides and Themistocles. — The Naval Program of Themistocles. — Athens Becomes a Maritime Power. — The Congress of Corinth.

III. THE SECOND PERSIAN INVASION, UNDER XERXES (480–479 B.C.). — Preparations and Advance of Xerxes. — Battles at Thermopylæ and Artemisium. — Themistocles and the Battle of Salamis. — The War under Mardonius. — Battles of Platæa and Mycale. — The Carthaginian Attack : Battle of Himera. — The Liberation of Greece.

I. THE FIRST PERSIAN INVASION, UNDER DARIUS (492–490 B.C.)

Greece and Persia. —We have thus far traced the beginnings of the Greek city states, and the first steps in the growth of a common Hellenic culture. We have seen how the Greeks broke away from the old monarchical ideas of the East, and laid the basis of freer and more democratic institutions. We have also seen how they began to develop a higher intellectual life and a finer æsthetic taste than had hitherto existed among the peoples of the Orient. With the extension of their colonies, the influence of this new civilization was beginning to be felt on nearly every shore of the Mediterranean — in Asia Minor, in Thrace, in southern Italy and Sicily. But now came a great crisis in the history of the Greek people, when they were called upon to defend their very existence. Their cities, their colonies, their commerce, their free institutions, and their new culture were all threatened with destruction by the encroachments of Persia. This great world power had already absorbed all the empires of the East, and was now brought into contact with the city states of Greece. Persia had extended her power to the shores of the Ægean. Her armies had crossed the Hellespont into Europe, and held lands upon the very borders of Thessaly.[1]

We are now about to wit-ness a conflict which is per-haps to decide the fate of the world; it will certainly decide the question whether Greek civilization is to sur-vive, or whether Europe is to become a province of the Orient.

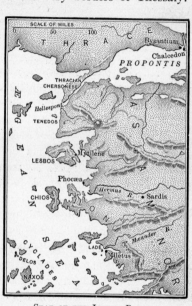

SEAT OF THE IONIAN REVOLT

The Asiatic Cities and the Ionian Revolt. — The great struggle between the East, represented by Persia, and the West, represented by Greece, began with the re-volt of the Greek cities in Asia Minor. We remember that these cities grew up as the result of the early mi-grations of the Greeks across the Ægean Sea (see pp. 99–100). The most important of them were in Ionia; and the most influential of the Ionian cities was Miletus. The Greek cities of Asia Minor maintained their independence for a long time. But when the empire of Lydia arose, they passed under the control of the Lydian kings, the most noted of whom was Crœsus (560–546 B.C.). Under the

[1] For the Persian conquest of Lydia, the Scythian expedition of Darius, and his encroachment upon Europe, see pp. 69–71.

Lydian rule, the Greeks were well treated and their rights respected. A great change, however, occurred when Lydia was conquered by Persia, and the Asiatic Greeks became subject to the Persian empire. They were now ruled by tyrants under the control of the Persian satrap whose capital was at Sardis. The revolt against Persia began at the city of Miletus (500 B.C.); it soon spread to the other cities of Asia Minor, and also to the Greek colonies on the coast of Thrace.

In their extremity the cities appealed to European Greece for assistance. Sparta refused to give any help. But Athens voted to send a fleet of twenty ships to aid their " kin beyond the sea." To the Athenian fleet was added a small squadron of five ships sent by Eretria, on the island of Eubœa. With this aid the Ionians captured and burned the Persian capital, Sardis. But on their retreat from the city the Athenians suffered a severe defeat; and, disheartened, they returned to Greece. The Asiatic cities were now left to fight alone. On account of their relative weakness, and especially their lack of union, they could not cope with the forces of Persia. The Persians gained a decisive naval battle near Miletus. That city was then captured and burned; and the remaining cities of Asia Minor were soon reduced to submission (493 B.C.). The revolt furnished an example of the lack of strength that results from a too great love for local independence and the failure to unite in a common cause.

Plans of Darius against Greece. — Whether or not the Persian king, Darius, had up to this time thought of conquering Greece, he was now determined at least to punish the cities of Athens and Eretria for interfering in the affairs of Asia. For this purpose he organized an expedition (492 B.C.), consisting of land and naval forces, and placed it under the command of his son-in-law Mardo'nius. This expedition was to invade Greece by way of the Hellespont and the coasts of Thrace and Macedonia. But the first attempt to invade Greece was a complete failure; for the fleet of Mardonius was wrecked off the rocky point of Mt. Athos. This failure, however, did not discourage the Persian king. He now determined not simply to punish Athens and Eretria, but to subdue all the cities of Greece. To test them he sent his heralds among them, demanding "earth and water" as a token of their submission. Most of the island states, fearing attacks from the Persian fleet, yielded. But the

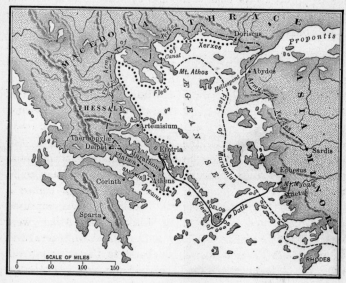

ROUTES OF PERSIAN INVASIONS

heralds sent to Athens were thrown into a deep pit; and those sent to Sparta were cast into a well and told they would find there the earth and water to take to their king. The indignant reply of these leading states showed that Greece might yet be united in the face of its common enemy.

Persian Invasion under Datis and Artaphernes. — The new expedition of Darius was placed in the hands of a Median general, Datis, and the king's nephew Artapher'nes. Instead of following the previous course of Mardonius and risking another disaster at Mt. Athos, the new generals proceeded directly across the sea. Their fleet consisted of six hundred triremes. On their way they captured Naxos and reduced its inhabitants to slavery. They soon landed on the island of Eubœa, and attacked the city of Eretria. After a gallant defense, the city fell by the treachery of two of its citizens. It was burned and its people were enslaved. The Persians now crossed over to Attica to mete out a similar punishment to Athens. By the advice of Hippias, the banished Athenian tyrant (p. 132) now in the enemy's service, the Persians landed on the shore of Attica near the plain of Mar′athon.

MILTIADES (So-called)

Miltiades and the Battle of Marathon (490 B.C.). — Upon Athens now rested the chief duty of defending Greece. She collected an army and sent it to meet the invaders. It was led by the ten generals (*strategi*), who yielded the chief command to Milti′ades. A swift runner [1] was dispatched to Sparta with a request to that city for aid. This aid was promised; but it was delayed on account of a Spartan superstition that an army should not be sent away before the time of the full moon. The only assistance which the Athenians received was from the friendly city of Platæa, which sent its entire army, a thousand fighting men, raising the total force to ten or eleven thousand.

[1] The name of this noted athlete is differently spelled — Phidip′pides, and Philippides. He reached Sparta, 150 miles distant, on the second day — in less than 48 hours. After the battle at Marathon, the story goes, the same (or another) runner hastened to carry the news to Athens, about 25 miles, and so overtaxed himself that he fell dead after delivering the message. This "run" is celebrated in our modern "Marathon races."

The Greeks were drawn up in front of the town of Marathon. Opposite them the Persians were stationed nearer the sea and supported by their fleet. The battle line of the Greeks was equal in length to that of the Persians; but the center was made weak in order to strengthen the wings. At a given signal, the Greeks, heedless of superior numbers and the terrible shower of arrows, rushed upon the enemy. The Persians drove back the weak center of the Athenians and pressed forward in the intervening space. But the strong wings of the Greek army closed upon the enemy and routed them with great slaughter. The Persians were pursued to their ships. Not entirely discouraged, they sailed directly to Athens, hop-

BATTLE OF MARATHON, 490 B.C.

ing to find the city unguarded. But Miltiades made a forced march to Athens; and the Persians, when they arrived, found the city protected by the victorious army. Foiled at every point, Datis and Artaphernes sailed with their defeated forces back to Asia. When the full moon was passed, the Spartan army arrived to find that Marathon had been won.

The Athenians were entitled to look upon Marathon as their own battlefield. The Spartans paid the highest tribute to their valor. The poets of Greece vied with one another in singing the praises of the dead heroes. A monumental mound was thrown up in their honor, which remains to the present day. Two statues were erected to Miltiades, one at Athens and the other at Delphi. Although the battle of Marathon did not end the struggle between the East and the West, it marked an important step toward the ascendancy of Athens in Greece, and of Greece in the civilization of the world.

II. ATHENS DURING THE TEN YEARS' RESPITE (490–480 B.C.)

Democratic Progress at Athens. — After the battle of Marathon there was an interval of ten years before the next Persian invasion. During this time Athens was striving to maintain her democratic institutions, and to strengthen her power for the next attack. As Miltiades was looked upon as a friend of the aristocratic party, he was called upon to answer a charge of deceiving the people. He had induced them to fit out for him a naval expedition, which had failed. On the pretext thus furnished, the popular party condemned him; and the hero of Marathon died in disgrace. The people also drove into exile all the friends of Hippias, the banished tyrant who had aided the Persians in the recent invasion. The popular party overcame all opposition, until they held completely the reins of government. The archons, who had hitherto been chosen from the aristocratic party, were now elected by lot from candidates put up by the people of Attica. All political questions were now reduced to the one problem, how best to maintain and strengthen the Athenian democracy.

Aristides and Themistocles. — But even in the popular party there were different views as to the best way of developing the power of Athens. The conservative view was held by Aristi'-des; the progressive view by Themis'tocles. Aristides was highly esteemed by the people, so that they called him "the Just." He had supported the democratic reforms of Clisthenes, and had commanded the Greek center at Marathon. He believed that the strength of Athens depended upon preserving the institutions and maintaining the policy that had already made her great, and that no change would improve her condition. Themistocles, on the other hand, believed that the state should not rest entirely upon the past, but should prepare itself for the future. The success which Athens had already attained should not blind her eyes to the need of new achievements. These two statesmen, though differing widely in their character and views, were equally conscientious and devoted to the interests of their country.

The Naval Program of Themistocles. — Themistocles no doubt saw more clearly than Aristides the need of preparing for a new struggle with Persia. He also saw that in the coming conflict Athens, the chief object of Persia's hatred, must again bear the brunt of Persia's attack. Persia was both a great military and a great naval power. In any future conflict, if Sparta was to be recognized as the chief military power of Greece, Athens should be recognized as its chief maritime power. There was also another consideration in favor of the policy of Themistocles. Athens was now embroiled in a war with

THEMISTOCLES (So-called)

Ægina, the neighboring island state, which had shown a sympathy with Persia. Ægina had already a strong fleet. The only hope of winning in this war was by meeting ships with ships. With arguments such as these Themistocles enforced upon the people the need of a strong navy. That the new naval project might be carried through without hindrance, Aristides was ostracized, and Themistocles became the leader at Athens without a rival. An old story is told of a poor peasant who cast his vote in the assembly against Aristides, and was asked if Aristides had ever wronged him. "Oh no," he replied, "I am simply tired of hearing him always called ' the Just.' "

Athens Becomes a Maritime Power. — Through the building of a strong fleet and the construction of an adequate harbor, Athens soon became the greatest naval power in Greece. The fleet was built with the aid of the silver mines at Lau'rium, in the south of Attica. It was at first proposed that the product of these mines, which belonged to the state, should be divided among the citizens. But Themistocles appealed to the patriotism of the people and induced them to devote the proceeds of the mines to the building of warships. In a short time Athens possessed a fleet of two hundred triremes, far outnumbering that of Ægina or of any other Greek city. About this time Themistocles also transferred the harbor of Athens from the bay of Phale'rum, which was exposed alike to storms and to enemies, to the Piræ'us, which was far better adapted for a naval station (map, p. 174). The new port was surrounded by natural defenses, but was now further strengthened by fortifications. On account of these works Themistocles may properly be regarded as the founder of the maritime greatness of Athens.

The Congress of Corinth (481 B.C.). — But Themistocles saw that Athens alone, even with her new navy, could not withstand the power of Persia. He saw that the safety of Greece depended upon the union of her states. At his suggestion a congress was called at Corinth to consider the means of a common defense. The principal continental states responded favorably to this call — except Argos and Thebes, who were jealous, the former of Sparta and the latter of Athens. The Greeks in their conference at Corinth agreed to lay aside all internal strife, and act together against the common foe. It was decided to punish any city that should " Medize " — that is, aid the cause of Persia. It was also decided that of the three possible lines of defense—namely, the vale of Tempe in northern Thessaly (p. 153), the pass of Thermop'ylæ, and the isthmus of Corinth—the best place to meet the invader was at the pass of Thermopylæ. The leadership of the new confederation of Greek states was given to Sparta. At no other period did Greece ever come so near to being one nation as it did at this time. It was by the foresight and genius of Themistocles that not only Athens, but all Greece, was made ready for the next great war with Persia.

III. THE SECOND PERSIAN INVASION, UNDER XERXES

Preparations and Advance of Xerxes. — While the Greeks were thus preparing to defend themselves against Persia, the Persians were making the most formidable preparations for their next invasion. These preparations had been begun by Darius, but were interrupted by a revolt in Egypt and were finally cut short by the death of the king himself. Darius was succeeded by his son Xerxes, a man of far greater pretensions and of far less ability than his father. Prompted to take up the task left unfinished by Darius, he called together his nobles and announced his purpose. "As Cyrus, Cambyses, and Darius," he said, " have each enlarged the empire, I wish to do the same. I propose to bridge the Hellespont and march through Europe, and fire Athens for burning Sardis and opposing Datis and Artaphernes. By reducing Attica and Greece, the sky will be the only boundary of Persia " (Herodotus, VII., 8). Four years he spent in preparing for his great expedition. Infantry, cavalry, horse transports, provisions, long ships for bridges, and warships for battles were collected from various Asiatic nations. Three years were spent in cutting a channel through the isthmus of Athos, to avoid the promontory near which the fleet of Mardonius had been wrecked.

After collecting his forces at Sardis, Xerxes marched to the Hellespont. Crossing into Thrace, the army was reënforced by the fleet, which had followed by way of the coast. Here the great king reviewed his immense armament, gathered, it is said, from forty-six different nations. Here were Persians armed with great bows and short javelins. Here were Ethiopians covered with the skins of beasts and having arrows tipped with sharp stones. Here were savages from central Asia, and more civilized warriors from Assyria and Media. According to Herodotus the whole army amounted to more than a million of men — which is probably an exaggeration. The fleet consisted of more than twelve hundred ships collected from Phœnicia,

Egypt, Ionia, Cyprus, and other maritime states. With this prodigious armament Xerxes hoped to appall and overwhelm the little armies and fleets of Greece. He advanced by way of Thrace and Macedonia to the pass at Tempe, and was surprised to find this point abandoned. He then pushed through Thessaly and approached the pass of Thermopylæ.

Battles at Thermopylæ and Artemisium. — It was here that the Greeks had decided to resist the Persian advance. This was no doubt the strongest defensive point in Greece. The pass itself was a very narrow roadway between the mountains and the sea. It could be easily defended by a small force. It was also protected from an attack from the sea by the long island of Eubœa, so that it could be approached from the north only through the strait at Artemis'ium (map, p. 153). The defense of the pass was intrusted to the brave Spartan king Leon'idas; while the strait was guarded by the Grecian fleet under a Spartan admiral — the Athenian division being commanded by Themistocles. Leonidas had with him about four thousand men, including three hundred Spartans. These he stationed behind an old wall which guarded the pass. That the whole Spartan army was not hurried to the defense of this most important position was due to a superstition similar to that

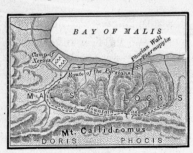

PASS OF THERMOPYLÆ

which had before delayed the arrival of the Spartan troops at Marathon. But with his small force Leonidas determined to hold the pass. For two days Xerxes hurled against him as large detachments of his army as he was able — but in vain. Even the " Ten Thousand Immortals " were repulsed. Then a citizen of Malis, who has been branded as the " Judas of Greece," Ephial'tes by name, revealed to Xerxes a secret path over the mountains, by which a force could be thrown in the rear of the Spartan position. By this act of treachery Thermopylæ was lost. Leonidas and his Spartan band preferred death to dishonor, and perished — examples for all time of courage and patriotic devotion.

At Artemisium the Grecian fleet was held to its duty by the inspiring influence of Themistocles. The fleet comprised nearly three hundred vessels, more than half of which were furnished by Athens. By persuasion, and even by bribery, Themistocles induced the Spartan commander to hold his position. For three successive days the Greeks fought the Persian navy. Although these battles were indecisive, they prevented the Persians from approaching Thermopylæ by the sea.

SEAT OF THE SECOND PERSIAN WAR
Route of Persian Army →→→—
Course of Persian Fleet ——→——

But when Thermopylæ was lost, it was useless to hold this position longer, and the fleet retired to the island of Salamis. All central Greece was now open to the invader.

Themistocles and the Battle of Salamis (480 B.C.). — The army of Xerxes pushed through central Greece into Attica, burned Athens, and destroyed the temples on the Acropolis. The inhabitants fled to the neighboring towns. The Persian fleet meanwhile followed the Greeks to Salamis. It was here that Themistocles, by his influence and adroitness, brought on the decisive battle of the war. The Peloponnesian army had retreated behind a wall thrown across the Isthmus of Corinth, and its leaders insisted that the fleet should retire to the same place. But Themistocles saw the great advantage of fighting in the narrow strait between Salamis and the Attic shore, where only a part of the Persian fleet could be brought into action. A council was called, and in the heat of debate Themistocles was charged with being a "man without a country," now that Athens was lost. But he replied that with a hundred and eighty warships at his command he could found a city anywhere. He threatened to withdraw his vessels and sail to Italy if the allies saw fit to abandon their Athenian comrades. By this threat the allies were persuaded to stand firm and fight in the strait. But to prevent any further indecision, Themistocles sent a messenger to Xerxes, giving the advice, as coming from a friend, that the Greeks must be attacked immediately to prevent their escape. Xerxes accordingly ordered up his fleet, and sent the Egyptian squadron to the strait opposite Megaris, to prevent any escape west of Salamis. At this juncture Aristides arrived from his retirement in Ægina, and pleaded with his old rival that they should now be rivals only in the cause of Greece. He announced that the battle must take place at Salamis, as all means of escape were cut off. This showed Themistocles that his plans had been successful.

BATTLE OF SALAMIS, 480 B.C.

The Greek fleet now held the strait east of Salamis. The Persian squadrons gathered on its front. The Phœnicians moved in heavy columns on the right and the Ionians on the left. The great king sat upon a throne erected on a slope near the shore to watch the conflict. The details of this battle are uncertain, but the victory of the Greeks was decisive. The Phœnician squadron, upon which the king chiefly relied, was shattered. Nearly half of the Persian fleet was destroyed; and a new glory crowned the loyal states of Greece.

The War under Mardonius. — The victory at Salamis had broken the naval power of Persia; but the land forces were still intact. Xerxes, however, seemed to regard the cause of Persia as lost, and ordered a general retreat of the army. He directed the remnants of his fleet to hasten to the Hellespont to guard the bridges by which he might recross into Asia, and which were now threatened by the Greeks. But there was one man who believed that a Persian army might still conquer Greece. This man was Mardonius. He it was who had failed in the first expedition under Darius by the destruction of the fleet off Mt. Athos, and who had encouraged Xerxes to undertake the present invasion. Intrusted with three hundred thousand men, Mardonius was permitted to remain in Greece to retrieve the disaster at Salamis.

Before beginning his campaign the following year, Mardonius sought the alliance of Athens against the rest of Greece. He promised to aid the Athenians to rebuild their city and to give them all the neighboring territory that they desired. But the Athenians sent back the word that " so long as the sun keeps its course, we will never join the cause of Xerxes " (Herodotus, VIII., 143). Attica was once more invaded, and the Athenians were again obliged to flee for safety. Again Greece was called upon to resist the invaders. Athens again called upon Sparta for aid, which was furnished after the usual delay. While the Grecian army was being collected, Mardonius retreated into Bœotia, near Platæa, to await the final contest.

Battles of Platæa and Mycale (479 B.C.). — Against the army of Mardonius the Greeks brought a force of about a hundred thousand men under the command of the Spartan Pausa'-nias. The Athenian division was led by Aristides. The Spartan commander was evidently convinced of the superiority of the Athenian division, for he insisted that it should hold the place of honor and danger against the strongest wing of the Persian army. After fighting and maneuvering in three different positions, the battle was finally decided near the walls of Platæa. The Persian army was nearly annihilated. Mardonius was killed. Another decisive victory was thus added to those of Salamis and Marathon. In commemoration of this victory, the assembled allies made an offering of thanksgiving to Zeus Eleuthe′rios (the Deliverer), and instituted a public festival, called the Eleuthe′ria, to be celebrated once in every four years.

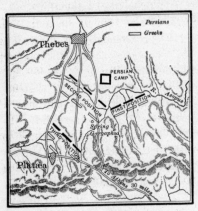

BATTLE OF PLATÆA, 479 B.C.

On the same day, it is said, on which the battle of Platæa was fought, the Grecian fleet, having set out from Delos, gained a signal victory over the Persian navy on the Asiatic coast near the promontory of Myc′ale (map, p. 153). This gave the Ionian Greeks fresh hope that the day of their deliverance was near.

The Carthaginian Attack: Battle of Himera. — While the Persians were trying in vain to conquer Greece, the Carthaginians, who were in alliance with Persia, were trying to conquer Sicily. Carthage, we remember, was a colony of Phœnicia; it had already an extensive empire in northern Africa and held certain cities in the western part of Sicily. Carthage, like Persia, represented the civilization of the Orient; and the struggle in Sicily, as well as that in Greece, was a conflict between Orientalism and the new culture of Europe. The largest part of the coast of Sicily had long before been settled by Greek colonies, and formed a part of what we have called "Western Greece" (which also included the Greek colonies on the southern coasts of Italy). The cities in Sicily had become the centers of Greek civilization, which was now exposed to the attack of Carthage. The leading city in the defense of western Greece was Syracuse, now under the rule of the tyrant Gelon. The decisive battle of this war took place at Him'era (480 B.C.), on the northern coast of Sicily (map, p. 114). Here the Carthaginians suffered a severe defeat at the hands of Gelon. According to tradition the battle of Himera was fought on the same day that the Greeks gained their decisive victory over the Persians at Salamis.

The Liberation of Greece. — We should never lose our interest in the story of these struggles between the Greeks and their foreign enemies; for they belong to the most heroic period of Greek history. The war against Persia and Carthage has been aptly called " the war of liberation." It rescued Greece and Europe from Oriental conquest. It revealed to the Greeks their own character and strength. The battles of Marathon and Thermopylæ and Salamis and Platæa taught them that courage and patriotism are virtues necessary to national independence. They gave to the Greek people the consciousness of unity, and showed them the importance of their own institutions and culture. They also gave a new inspiration to Greek life which was expressed in art and literature. But more than all, the war gave to the Greeks a half century of comparative peace in which they might devote themselves to fulfilling their high mission in the world, unhindered by foreign interference. During this period from the close of the great Persian wars to the beginning of the Peloponnesian War (from 480 to 431 B.C.), we shall see Athens becoming the leading state in Greece.

Selections for Reading

Knowlton, Topic A 7, "The Struggle with Persia and Carthage " (1).[1]
Seignobos, Ch. 11, "The Persian Wars" (1).
Goodspeed, pp. 118–130, "The Persian Wars" (1).
Shuckburgh, Ch. 10, "Salamis and Platæa" (10).

[1] The figure in parenthesis refers to the number of the topic in the Appendix, where a fuller title of the book will be found.

Smith, Wm., Ch. 16, "The Ionic Revolt"; Ch. 17, "The Battle of Marathon"; Ch. 18, "The Battles of Thermopylæ and Artemisium"; Ch. 19, "The Battle of Marathon" (10).

Cox, History, Part II., Ch. 5, "Invasion and Flight of Xerxes" (10).

—— Greeks and Persians. Ch. 5, "The Ionian Revolt" (10).

—— Greek Statesmen, "Miltiades," "Aristides," "Themistocles" (26).

Oman, Chs. 19, 20, "The Invasion of Xerxes" (10).

Allcroft, Vol. II., Ch. 13, "Themistocles and the Naval Programme" (10)

Bury, Ch. 7, "The Perils of Greece" (10).

Abbott, Vol. II., Ch. 3, "The Great Invasions" (10).

Curtius, Vol. II., Bk. III., Ch. 1, "The War of Liberation" (10).

Plutarch, "Aristides," "Themistocles" (26).

Herodotus, Bk. I., Bk. VII., Chs. 1–4 (last days of Darius); Bk. VIII., Chs. 74–95 (battle of Salamis) (17).

Æschylus, Drama of "The Persians" (account of the battle of Salamis) (17).

Special Study

CARTHAGINIAN INVASION OF SICILY. — Smith, Wm., p. 215 (10); Oman, Ch. 21 (10); Abbott, Vol. II., Ch. 14 (10); Holm, Vol. II., Ch. 6 (10); Allcroft, Vol. II., Ch. 14 (10).

outline the persian war naming
battles, leaders and results.

CHAPTER XIII

THE ATHENIAN EMPIRE — AGE OF PERICLES

Synopsis

I. ATHENS AND THE DELIAN CONFEDERACY. — The New Athens under Themistocles. — Fortification of the Piræus. — Athenian Supremacy in the Ægean. — The Delian Confederacy under Aristides. — Growth of Imperialism under Cimon. — Jealousy between Sparta and Athens.

II. PERICLES AND THE ATHENIAN EMPIRE. — Pericles and his Policy. — The Building of the Long Walls. — Attempts at a Land Empire. — Completion of the Maritime Empire. — Restoration and Death of Cimon. — Failure of the Imperial Policy of Athens.

III. THE ATHENIAN CONSTITUTION UNDER PERICLES. — Character of the Athenian Democracy. — Changes made by Pericles. — Classes of the People in Attica. — The Athenian Assembly, or Ecclesia. — The Athenian Council, or Boulé. — The Athenian Magistrates: the Generals. — The Athenian Courts: the Jury System. — The Athenian Army. — The Athenian Fleet. — Public Expenses and Revenues. — The Athenian Money. — The Subject Cities of the Empire.

I. ATHENS AND THE DELIAN CONFEDERACY

The New Athens under Themistocles. — Herodotus tells us that in the great Persian crisis the Athenians were the saviors of Greece — that, next to the gods, they repulsed the invader. It is also true that they were the greatest sufferers in the cause of Greece. Their city had been twice occupied by the enemy and was now a heap of ruins. The inhabitants had been obliged to flee for safety to the neighboring islands of Salamis and Ægina. The first need of the Athenians was now a home. Themistocles was now the leading man in the state. He determined that on the ruins of the old city there should be built a new Athens, surrounded by strong and extensive walls sufficient to protect the people in any future war.

The Athenians brought back their families, and began to rebuild their ruined homes. But Themistocles saw that a defense for the city was quite as important as a shelter for the citizens. Without strong walls their homes would still be defenseless. He therefore urged the people first of all to work on the new fortifications.

The story is told that the neighboring states looked with envy upon the growing power of Athens and appealed to Sparta to put a stop to this work on the city walls. It would make Athens too strong for them. Sparta accordingly sent an embassy to Athens to show her that such fortifications were not necessary for her defense. Sparta had no such walls, and could defend herself without them. Themistocles received the Spartan ambassadors politely and assured them that perhaps they were right; and that he himself would come to Sparta with two colleagues, and talk the matter over. True to his word, Themistocles proceeded to Sparta, but instructed his colleagues to remain behind and push with all speed the building of the walls. The whole population, — men, women and children, — were pressed into the work, toiling day and night, and using in their haste even tombstones and the broken columns from the ruined temples. In the meantime Themistocles put off his talk with the Spartan ephors, on the pretense of waiting for his colleagues. The ephors began to be suspicious and sent a new embassy to Athens to find out the truth. But Themistocles dispatched a secret message to the Athenians to detain the Spartan envoys, and hold them as hostages for his safe return. At last, when the walls had reached sufficient height, Themistocles threw off his mask and declared to the Spartans that Athens was now ready to stand alone and defend her own cause against the rivalry of her neighbors.

Fortification of the Piræus. — When the walls of Athens had been erected, Themistocles turned his attention to strengthening the harbor of Athens. This was located at the Piræus, on the Saron'ic Gulf, about four miles from the city. The fortifications, begun after the first Persian invasion, were now

THE PIRÆUS, THE PORT OF ATHENS (Restoration)

finished, and the Piræus became an important factor in the commercial growth of Athens. There soon grew up here a large commercial population — merchants, sailors, and resident foreigners who carried on trade. Thus Themistocles not only created the naval power of Athens and secured the triumph of Greece during the great Persian war; but he also rescued Athens from the disasters of that war. By rebuilding the city walls and strengthening the harbor at the Piræus he raised her to a position in which she might command the commerce of the sea. To him more than to any other man, Athens was indebted for her maritime and commercial supremacy; upon the foundations which he laid was built the Athenian empire. Although he had many faults, and was at last driven into exile, he was yet one of the greatest statesmen of Greece.

Athenian Supremacy in the Ægean. —We may now see how Athens took another step in the development of her power by getting command of the Grecian fleet in the Ægean Sea. This fleet was engaged in freeing the cities that had fallen under the Persian power during the late war. As Sparta had been, since the congress of Corinth (p. 158), the recognized leader of Greece, the chief command of the Ægean fleet was in the hands of a Spartan admiral — who was no other than Pausanias, the victor of Platæa (p. 163). The Athenian division of the fleet was under the command of Aristides, and with him was associated Cimon, the son of the great Miltiades. Pausanias began his work well, by freeing a part of Cyprus in the eastern Mediterranean, and Byzantium in Thrace. But with the spoils of Byzantium in his hands, Pausanias became arrogant toward the Greeks and friendly toward the Persians. He even offered to marry the daughter of the Persian king, and to betray to him the states of Greece. When the officers of the fleet compared the brutal and treacherous conduct of Pausanias with the upright character of Aristides, they with one accord turned over the command from the Spartan to the Athenian admiral. By thus obtaining the chief command of the Grecian fleet under Aristides, Athens acquired the supreme control of the Ægean Sea. Sparta withdrew from the leadership which she had held since the congress of Corinth, and relapsed into her former position as simply the head of the Peloponnesian League.[1]

The Delian Confederacy under Aristides. — The work of freeing the cities of the Ægean was continued by the new admiral, Aristides. To him it seemed necessary to provide for their common defense against any future encroachments of Persia. He therefore began to organize a confederacy of the Ægean cities under the leadership of Athens. He formed alliances with the cities, not only on the islands, but also on the Asiatic coasts. All members of the confederacy were to be equal; they were to send delegates to a common congress, and they were to furnish ships or money for the common cause.

---

[1] The fate of Pausanias was suited to his crime. He was recalled to Sparta. When the evidence of his crime became clear and he was about to be arrested, he fled for safety into the temple of Athena. But this did not protect him from the vengeance of the people. The door of the temple was closed by a wall, and the traitor was starved to death.

The confederacy was to be a perpetual union, and no member could withdraw without the consent of the others. The island of Delos, the seat of the shrine of Apollo, was selected as the place where the common meetings were to be held, and where the common treasury was to be established. The assessments for the treasury were intrusted to Aristides, in whose justice all had confidence. The Confederacy of Delos thus became an Ionian league under the leadership of Athens; and it was an offset to the Dorian league of the Peloponnesus under the leadership of Sparta. Henceforth the interests of Athens and of Sparta became more and more opposed to each other; and they came to be recognized as the two rival powers of Hellas.

Growth of Imperialism under Cimon. — The work which was begun by Aristides was completed by his colleague and successor, Cimon. Cimon inherited the conservative spirit and military ability of his renowed father Miltiades. His policy comprised peace with Sparta and war with Persia. His chief work was to enlarge and make strong the newly formed confederacy. He proceeded to Thrace and freed many cities on that coast. He reduced the rocky island of Scyros (sī'ros; p. 82), where a nest of pirates threatened the commerce of Athens; and he planted upon it a colony

CIMON (So-called)
From a gem

of Athenian citizens. But his greatest military achievement was the defeat of the land and naval forces of Persia near the mouth of the river Eurym'edon in southern Asia Minor (466 B.C.; map, p. 115). This double victory insured the freedom of the cities on the Asiatic coast, and thus added to the strength of the confederacy.

While the chief purpose of Cimon was to destroy the Persian influence in the Ægean, he was also determined to subdue any dissatisfied members of the league. For example, the island of Naxos wished to withdraw from the league; but Cimon besieged it and reduced it to submission. Again, the island of Thasos, embittered by a quarrel with Athens, revolted; but it was compelled to submit by the allied fleet under Cimon. The result of this policy of coercion was to take away from the dissatisfied cities their previous rights as independent allies, and to reduce them to the condition of tributary subjects. In this way Athens was gradually becoming not simply the leader of a confederacy but the sovereign of an empire.

Jealousy between Sparta and Athens. — The whole course of events at this time was to increase the jealousy between Sparta and Athens. Sparta had complained that the Athenians had shown deceit and an undue spirit of independence in fortifying their city. She was also chagrined at losing the command of the fleet, and was envious of the growing power of Athens. On the other hand, Athens charged the Spartans with a treacherous attempt to assist the people of Thasos in their recent revolt. It was the policy of Cimon to appease, so far as possible, this enmity between the leading states of Greece, and to present a united front to Persia, their common enemy. Sparta was now suffering from the effects of a terrible earthquake, and from a revolt of her subject population, the helots. In their revolt the helots were aided by the Messenians (p. 124). For two years Sparta tried in vain to reduce her rebellious subjects. At last she appealed to Athens for help in putting down the revolt. Cimon was in favor of giving this aid. The new leaders of the democracy, Ephialtes and Per'icles, opposed it. The influence of Cimon prevailed, and the Athenian assembly decided to send an army to assist the Spartans in their distress. When the army arrived and did not succeed immediately in putting down the revolt, the Spartans thought its failure was due to treachery, and dismissed it insolently. This piece of effrontery served to widen the breach between the two states. The party of Cimon, which had favored Sparta, now lost its influence, and Cimon himself was ostracized (461 B.C.).

II. Pericles and the Athenian Empire

Pericles and his Policy. — In the same year in which Cimon was exiled, Ephialtes, the chief leader of the democratic party, was assassinated. By the removal of these two party chiefs Pericles became the leading man in Athens. In his character this great man united many of the best qualities of his predecessors. He was a skillful statesman like Themistocles. He had a high sense of honor and justice like Aristides. He also believed in the military and political supremacy of Athens, like Cimon. But more than this he was the foremost orator of his day, and this gave him almost absolute control of the Athenian as-

PERICLES

sembly. We can best understand the character of Pericles as a statesman if we keep clearly in mind what he attempted to do. His foreign policy was to extend and secure the imperial power of Athens, and to make it the foremost city of the world. This policy included: (1) the extension of the fortifications of Athens; (2) the establishment of a land empire over the continental states of Greece; (3) the completion of the maritime empire over the cities of the Ægean; and (4) the weakening of the power of Persia — not only by protecting the Greek cities in Asia Minor, but also by aiding the Persian subjects in their revolts, especially in Egypt and in Cyprus.

The Building of the Long Walls. — Pericles followed the policy of Themistocles in seeking first of all to make Athens an impregnable city. The fortifications erected by Themistocles about Athens and about the Piræus had created two

separate centers of defense. Pericles desired to unite these
two places by one system of defensive works, and thus to prevent Athens from being
cut off from her harbor
and from the rest of the
world. This defensive
system may have been
begun by Cimon; but
it was completed by
Pericles. One of the
new walls, the southern,
ran from the city to the
Bay of Phalerum; and
another, the northern,

THE WALLS OF ATHENS [1]

ran to the harbor of the Piræus. In a few years a third and
middle wall was erected near and parallel to the northern one,
these two together being known as the " Long Walls." They
formed a wide and secure avenue from the city to the Piræus.
Athens and the Piræus were thus united in a single fortified
area, which formed a military and naval base of operations for
the whole empire.

Attempts at a Land Empire. — Pericles now wished to extend the influence of Athens upon the land as well as upon the
sea. He wished to make Athens the head of a continental as
well as a maritime league. The first step in this direction was
the result of an alliance which had already been formed by
Athens with Argos and Megara. This alliance excited the
jealousy of the neighboring Dorian states, Corinth and Ægina;
a war followed, and Ægina was reduced to the condition of a
tributary state. The next step was the result of an attempt
made by Sparta to interfere in the affairs of central Greece.
This brought on a war between Athens, on the one side, and
Sparta and Bœotia, on the other. After a victorious battle

[1] There is some question as to the exact location of the "Phaleric wall," and
some writers even doubt that there was such a wall.

at Œnoph'yta, on the borders of Bœotia and Attica (456 B.C.; map, p. 178), the cities in Bœotia, except Thebes, were brought under the power of Athens, and compelled to accept democratic governments. By these two movements Pericles succeeded in extending the Athenian power over most of central Greece.

Completion of the Maritime Empire. — While Athens was thus gaining new subjects on the land, she was also obtaining greater power over her allies upon the sea. The members of the Delian Confederacy were at first expected simply to furnish ships and sufficient money to maintain the fleet. Soon they were inclined to make their contributions entirely in money, while retaining their independence. Afterward, the contributions were regarded as tribute due to Athens, which Athens had a right to collect. Again, it was at first expected that the affairs of the confederacy were to be managed by a congress of delegates, meeting at Delos; but the allies soon regarded these meetings as irksome, and the political control of the confederacy gradually passed into the hands of Athens. Finally, the common treasury was transferred from Delos to Athens (about 454 B.C.). By these means Athens was able to get complete control over the cities of the league; and the Delian confederacy became transformed into an Athenian empire. Of all the members of the original confederacy, only three — Chios, Lesbos, and Samos — were allowed to retain their position as equal and independent allies.

Restoration and Death of Cimon. — After the empire was finally established, Cimon, who had been recalled from his banishment, recovered for a brief time his influence over the Athenian assembly. His policy of peace with Sparta and war with Persia again found favor with the people. He accordingly made a Five Years' Truce with Sparta (450 B.C.), by which each party agreed to refrain from war and to respect the rights and possessions of the other. Cimon then set out on a new expedition against Cyprus, in which island Persia was now attempting to reëstablish her authority. This expedition resulted in a decisive victory over the Persians, and also in the death of Cimon (449 B.C.). After Cimon's death, Pericles regained his previous position as the ruling spirit of Athens.

Failure of the Imperial Policy of Athens. — The wonderful energy which Athens displayed at this time is evident from what she accomplished. Within thirty years, she had recovered all the Ægean cities lost during the Persian wars, and had established her authority over a large part of European Greece (study the map on pp. 178, 179). But her ambitious policy to maintain an empire upon the land proved a failure. She was soon beset with difficulties and afflicted with reverses which weakened her influence among her continental allies. News had also come that a fleet of two hundred vessels, sent some time before to free Egypt from Persia, had been annihilated (454 B.C.). Sparta denied the right of Athens to control the affairs of central Greece. Bœotia opposed the effort to establish democratic governments within her borders, and defeated the Athenians in a battle at Corone'a (447 B.C.). The spirit of revolt extended to other cities; and one after another the Athenian land allies renounced their allegiance. Under these depressing circumstances Pericles concluded a Thirty Years' Peace with Sparta (445 B.C.). The freedom of the continental allies was now acknowledged. Athens thus lost her land empire in Argolis, Achaia, and central Greece; but retained her supremacy upon the sea.

III. The Athenian Constitution under Pericles

Character of the Athenian Democracy. — By the term "democracy," the Athenians understood a state in which all the powers of government are exercised directly by the citizens, and in which all citizens are equal before the law. The Athenian idea of democracy differed from our modern idea chiefly in two ways; first, in that the Athenians had very little notion of the modern idea of representation; and second, in that the number of citizens formed a smaller part of the whole population.

It was during the time of Pericles that the democratic constitution of Athens reached its most complete form. We have already seen the gradual steps in the growth of the Athenian democracy. The most important of these steps had been: (1) the establishment of the archonship — which took the place of the ancient monarchy; (2) the reforms of Solon — which broke down the old nobility, by opening the offices to all persons having a certain amount of property, and extending the right to vote to all classes; and (3) the reforms of Clisthenes — by which the rights of all the people were determined not by their membership in the old Ionian families, but by their residence in certain local districts. But Pericles introduced still further changes, which he thought would lead the people to take a greater interest in political affairs.

Changes made by Pericles. — The first change made by Pericles was with reference to the mode of choosing officers. Previous to his time candidates for office had been nominated by the vote of the people in the different townships of Attica, very much as we now nominate officers in our " primary elections." From this select number of candidates the officers were chosen by lot. Pericles did away with the primary elections, so that the officers were now chosen by lot from all eligible citizens who presented themselves. Every one now had an equal chance to hold office.

In the next place, to enable the poorest citizen to serve the state, Pericles adopted a system of state pay. In more ancient times it had been the custom for every one to perform public duties without reward. Now a compensation was given to those in the public service, — the archons, the members of the council, jurymen, soldiers and sailors. Pericles went still further; he used the public money to give assistance to the poor and needy, — grain to the hungry, and even tickets to those who were unable to pay for admission to the theater.

ATHENIAN EMPIRE

ITS GREATEST EXTENT

About 450 B. C.

SCALE OF MILES

0   50   100

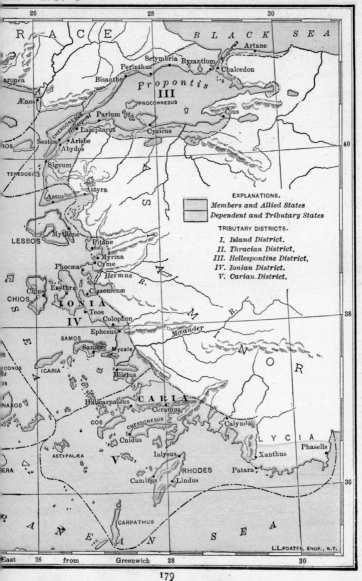

R A C E

B L A C K   S E A

Artane

Selymbria   Byzantium   Chalcedon
Perinthus
Bisanthe

aronea

Propontis

III

Ænos

PROCONNESUS

Cius

ROS

CHERSONESUS   Parium

Lampsacus   Cyzicus

Sestos   Arisbe
Abydos

Sigeum

TENEDOS

Astyra

Assus

LESBOS

Mytilene

Pitane
Myrina
Phocæa   Cyme
Erythræ   Hermus   R.
Chios   Clazomenæ

CHIOS

IONIA   Teos

IV   Colophon

Ephesus

SAMOS

Samos   Mycale

ICARIA

Miletus

CONOS

NAXOS

Halicarnassus

CARIA

Ceramus

COS   CHERSONESUS   Calynda

Cnidus

ASTYPALÆA   Ialysus   L Y C I A

V   Phaselis

ERA   Xanthus

RHODES   Patara

Camirus   Lindus

Mæander

M   R.

O   R

EXPLANATIONS.
Members and Allied States
Dependent and Tributary States

TRIBUTARY DISTRICTS.
I.   Island District.
II. Thracian District.
III. Hellespontine District.
IV. Ionian District.
V.   Carian District.

CARPATHUS

N   E   A   N   S E A

East   26   from   Greenwich   28   30

Another change introduced by Pericles was with regard to citizenship. The right to vote and to hold office was now limited to those born of an Athenian father and an Athenian mother. He evidently believed that too large a foreign population was not good for the state, and he wished to put a higher value upon the privilege of being a citizen of Athens.

Classes of the People in Attica. — We may get an idea of the limited nature of the Athenian democracy by looking at the different classes of persons residing in Attica, the territory of the Athenian city state; namely, the slaves, the resident foreigners, or " metics," and the citizens.

(1) The slaves of Attica have been estimated at about 100,000. They included captives taken in war and persons imported from the slave markets on the Thracian and Scythian coasts. The practice of reducing men to slavery for debt had been abolished by Solon (p. 129). The slaves were employed in domestic and agricultural labor, and were even allowed to work for themselves on consideration of paying their master a yearly sum. The slave, however, had no political or civil rights, although he might be protected from the cruelty of his master, and sometimes, in grave emergencies, might be called upon to serve in the army or the fleet.

(2) The resident foreigners, or " metics," numbered with their families perhaps 50,000. These persons were engaged mostly in trade, and formed a valuable part of the population. But they had no share in the government. They could not hold land in Attica. They were obliged to pay a yearly tax and sometimes to serve in the army and navy; for example, as shield-bearers or rowers. Every resident foreigner was bound to choose a citizen to represent and protect his interests. These foreigners could not now be admitted to the rights of citizenship by any process of " naturalization," like that heretofore adopted by Clisthenes (p. 132).

(3) The class of citizens formed the rest of the population of Attica. The number of Athenian citizens, including men,

women, and children, was at the time of Pericles in the neighborhood of 120,000. Of this population the number of voters is generally estimated as about 30,000. This comparatively small body of persons, scattered through the local districts — that is, the tribes and demes — of Attica, formed the Athenian democracy.

The Athenian Assembly, or Ecclesia. — The most important political body in the state was the Ecclesia, or general assembly of the people. It consisted of the whole body of male citizens above eighteen years of age. It met forty times each year on the Pnyx (nĭks) — a sloping hill backed by a perpendicular

THE BEMA ON THE PNYX

rock. Here was located the *bema*, the stone platform upon which the orators stood to address the people. The assembly was the ultimate source of political authority. Here any citizen could speak and vote upon questions properly submitted by the council. The assembly was often brought under the power of some influential man, whose character and oratorical ability enabled him to sway the multitude and to become the "leader of the people," or, as Aristoph'anes puts it, "the master of the stone on the Pnyx." The Greek historian Thucyd'ides describes Athens at the time of Pericles as "a democracy ruled by its ablest citizen."

The Athenian Council, or Boulé. — Since the decline of the Areopagus, the most important political body, after the assembly, was the Council of Five Hundred. The council was composed of ten sections, being made up of fifty members, at least thirty years of age, chosen annually by lot from each of the ten "local tribes." This body exercised the highest administrative and executive powers in the state. It prepared the measures to be submitted to the assembly. It could itself pass ordinances provided they did not conflict with the existing laws. It had charge of the public buildings, festivals, and religious ceremonies. It had control of the public finances. It saw that the laws of the state were carried into execution, and in certain exceptional cases it exercised judicial functions.

The Athenian Magistrates: the Generals. — The chief officers of the Athenian government were no longer the archons, but the generals (*strategi*). They were ten in number, one from each of the ten "local tribes," elected by the people — not chosen by lot, like other officers. Special qualifications were required for this, the highest office in the state. No one was eligible unless he held landed property in Attica, and was a man of high character. The generals might be chosen for successive terms. It was by virtue of this office that Pericles held his leadership for about thirty years. The first duty of the generals was to command the army and to provide for the public defense. They also had charge of foreign affairs, the negotiation of treaties, and the receiving of ambassadors. They furthermore had the power to call extra sessions of the assembly, if in their judgment the public interests required it.

The Athenian Courts: the Jury System. — If we should go into an Athenian court room as it existed in the time of Pericles we should doubtless be surprised to see that it looked more like a public assembly than like one of our own courts. Instead of a judge and a jury of twelve men we should see a body of two or three hundred men, — in rare cases perhaps a thousand — who were all acting as judges and jurors. We should find that every man who came before this body with a complaint was obliged to plead his own cause, and make his own speech to the jurors. He might have prepared the speech himself, or he might have had some professional speech-maker prepare it for him. The case would be decided by a majority of votes. If we should ask a juror how much he received for his services he would tell us three obols [1] a day. If we expressed any surprise at this he would probably explain that he was a poor man and had nothing else to do; and he could support his family fairly well on that. Such a popular court was strictly in harmony with a pure democracy. It was a direct appeal to the people for law and justice.

The Athenian Army. — The army, like the government, was based upon democratic principles. Every man between the ages of twenty and sixty was liable to be called upon to serve the state as a soldier. The army consisted of three branches: (1) the heavy-armed troops, armed with the defensive equipment, the shield, helmet, breastplate, and greaves, and the offensive weapons, the sword and spear; (2) the light-armed troops, who fought, without the defensive armor, with the sword and spear, and sometimes with the bow and arrow; and (3) the cavalry, which was not much used in Greece, on account of the mountainous character of the country. The army was carefully organized in divisions and subdivisions, each under its own officers; in battle it was usually drawn up in eight ranks, like the Spartan "phalanx." The Greek phalanx was the most effective military organization before the time of the Roman legion.

---

[1] Three obols would contain about as much silver as our dime; but the purchasing power of silver was far greater at that time than at present.

The Athenian Fleet. — Athens was now the mistress of the sea. She used force to maintain her authority over her maritime subjects, who often chafed under the heavy tribute laid upon them. The main strength of Athens lay in her fleet, which now consisted of three hundred vessels always ready for the sea; also about one hundred select ships held in reserve to defend the Piræus. The war vessel of this period was a ship with three banks of oars, called the " trireme."

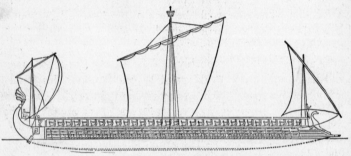

GREEK TRIREME (Restoration)

Each ship was commanded by an officer called a " tri'erarch," and carried about two hundred men. Besides the men who worked the oars, there was a small body of heavy-armed marines. The success of a naval battle depended largely upon the skill of the oarsmen, the effort being made to run down and disable the opposing vessels. The Athenians might well be proud of their navy. It was the creation of Themistocles and had won many noted battles. At the time of Pericles it commanded the eastern Mediterranean and was the chief bulwark of the empire.

Public Expenses and Revenues. — The supervision of the public finances was in the hands of the council. The expenses of the state were due chiefly to (1) the maintenance of religion and the public games and festivals, (2) the payment of civil and military officers, (3) the construction and repair of public buildings, and (4) public bounties paid to poor citizens, and pensions paid to the orphans of deceased soldiers. The revenues of the state were derived principally from (1) the tribute laid upon the subject cities, (2) the rent of state property, like the silver mines at Laurium, (3) duties on goods exported and imported or sold in the market, and (4) the tax on resident foreigners. The state was also accustomed to receive voluntary contributions from patriotic citizens.

The Athenian Money. — To manage the revenues and expenditures of the state, as well as to facilitate the trade among the people, it was necessary to adopt some kind of financial system. And this system in turn required some kind of money by which values could be measured. The Athenian money consisted chiefly of silver — although gold and copper were used to some extent. The chief coin was the silver drachma, which

ATTIC DRACHMA

contained about sixty-seven grains of silver. The other coins and units of money were the obol, the mina, and the talent. The following table gives a rough estimate of their values in silver, in terms of our money:

6 obols = 1 drachma (nearly 20 cents).
100 drachmas = 1 mina (nearly 20 dollars).
60 minas = 1 talent (nearly 1200 dollars).

The Subject Cities of the Empire. — We may well ask, How was the method of raising and spending money regarded by the subject cities of the Athenian empire? These cities were scattered over the islands and coasts of the Ægean Sea. For the purpose of raising the revenue they were grouped in five sections, called "tributary districts" (map, p. 179). When the tax-collector came around to one of these cities, the people began to make complaints. They complained that the tribute was originally a war-tax, to help throw off the yoke of Persia. Now that they were freed from Persia why should they still be obliged to pay the tax? They also complained that most of the money was used solely for the benefit of Athens — to help Athens increase her own power and especially to beautify and adorn her own city. To this Pericles answered that to beautify Athens was to beautify the capital of the empire, in which they should all be interested.

But the subject cities still regarded the tax as very oppressive. They were somewhat in the condition of our American forefathers, who protested against " taxation without representation." But no country in those ancient days understood the modern idea of representation. And so to keep a hold upon the discontented people Pericles planted among them citizen-colonies, or " cleruchies " (p. 113), made up of the poorer class of Athenians. To these he allotted lands and gave arms, making them a sort of military garrison to prevent the danger of revolt. This tax and these citizen or military colonies were the most oppressive features of the policy of Pericles.

Selections for Reading

Knowlton, Topic A 8, "The Age of Pericles" (1).[1]

Seignobos, pp. 142–145, "The Government of Athens" (1).

Shuckburgh, Ch. 12, "Continental and Home Policy of Pericles" (10).

Goodspeed, Ancient History, pp. 131–140, "The Rise of Athens " (1).

Smith, Wm., Ch. 23, "Rise and Growth of the Athenian Empire" (10).

Oman, Ch. 22, "Origin of the Confederacy of Delos"; Ch. 23, "Building of the Athenian Empire"; Ch. 24, "Athens at the Height of Her Power"; Ch. 25, "The Years of Peace" (10).

Bury, pp. 336–342 (Athens's treatment of her subject states) (10).

Allcroft, Vol. II., Ch. 10, "Athens under Pericles"; Ch. 11, "Constitutional Development in Athens"; pp. 145–147 (ethics of Athenian policy) (10).

Curtius, Vol. II., Bk. III., Ch. 2, "Growth and Power of Athens"; Ch. 3, "The Years of Pericles" (10).

[1] The figure in parenthesis refers to the number of the topic in the Appendix, where a fuller title of the book will be found.

Holm, Vol. II., Ch. 14, "Pericles to the Thirty Years Peace"; Ch. 16, "The Government of the City" (10).

Abbott, Pericles, Ch. 6, "The Areopagus and Ephialtes"; Ch. 16, "The Athens of Pericles; the Government" (27).

Greenidge, Ch. 6, "Democracy" (11).

Whibley, Political Parties, Ch. 1, "Athenian Constitution and Empire" (11).

Freeman, Essay, "The Athenian Democracy" (3).

Plutarch, "Cimon," "Pericles" (26).

Aristotle's Constitution, Chs. 23–27 (Ephialtes and Pericles) (17).

Special Study

THE CONFEDERACY OF DELOS. — Smith, Wm., Ch. 22, § 6 (10); Oman, pp. 240, 241 (10); Cox, Ch. 7 (10); Bury, Ch. 8 (10); Abbott, Vol. II., Ch. 8 (10); Allcroft, Vol. II., pp. 91–104, 139–151 (10); Curtius, Vol. II., pp. 376–385, 430–432 (10); Holm, Vol. II., Ch. 17 (10); Greenidge, pp. 189–204 (11); Gilbert, pp. 416–434 (11).

CHAPTER XIV

THE ART AND INTELLECTUAL CULTURE OF ATHENS

Synopsis

I. ATHENS AS THE CENTER OF GREEK ART. — New Spirit of the Greek People. — The City of Athens. — The Athenian Acropolis. — The Parthenon. — The Propylæa. — The Erechtheum. — Athenian Sculpture: Myron. — Phidias and his Works. — Sculptors Outside of Athens. — Later Greek Sculptors. — Gravestone Reliefs. — Athenian Painting.

II. THE THEATER AND DRAMATIC LITERATURE. — Origin of the Greek Theater. — The Theater of Dionysus. — The Two Forms of the Drama. — Æschylus, the Father of Tragedy. — Sophocles, the Dramatic Artist. — Euripides, the Dramatist of the People. — The Attic Comedy: Aristophanes.

III. PROSE LITERATURE: HISTORY AND ORATORY. — Herodotus, the Father of History. — Thucydides, the Scientific Historian. — Xenophon, the Historical Essayist. — The Orators of Athens.

IV. THE PHILOSOPHY OF ATHENS. — Anaxagoras, the First Athenian Philosopher. — The Greek Sophists as Teachers. — The Teachings of Socrates. — Plato and the Academic School. — Aristotle and the Peripatetic School.

I. ATHENS AS THE CENTER OF GREEK ART

New Spirit of the Greek People. — The Persian wars had a wonderful effect upon the intellectual life of the Athenian people. The memory of that great conflict stirred their patriotism and pride. It made them feel that they were living in a new heroic age. The poems of Homer became more popular than ever before. The people began to believe that their own heroes were in the same class as the heroes of the old Trojan war, and should be celebrated with equal honor. We may see the influence of the new spirit in the loftier tone given to lyric poetry. The poet who more than any other expressed this patriotic feeling was Simon'ides. Born in Ceos, an island near Attica (map, p. 178), he spent most of his life in Athens. He wrote many noble epitaphs in honor of those who fell in the Persian wars. In one of these he sings:

> "In dark Thermopylæ they lie,
> Oh, death of glory thus to die!
> Their tomb an altar is, their name
> A mighty heritage of fame."

But the greatest lyric poet of this time was Pindar, a native of Bœotia. He received his education at Athens and was honored by all the free cities of Greece. He sang not so much of the glories of war as of the victories of peace. He celebrated the national institutions — the festivals, the games, the shrines of the gods, and the higher religious beliefs of the people. He exalted the moral duties of men. He thus expressed his belief in future rewards and punishments:

> "The deeds that stubborn mortals do
> In this disordered nook of Jove's domain
> All find their meed; and there's a judge below
> Whose hateful doom inflicts th' inevitable pain."

The spirit of the new age is seen most of all in the higher artistic and literary culture of Athens. This it is that entitles the Age of Pericles to be called one of the " golden ages " of the world.

The City of Athens. — Our chief interest in Greece must always be centered in Athens, because it was in this renowned city that the culture of Greece found its highest expression. Let us first of all look at some of its most important features. With the Acropolis as its center, the limits of the city had been gradually widening from the earliest times. At the time of the Persian wars, the " old line " of the city had been reached. With the building of the new wall of Themistocles, the circumference of the city was enlarged to five or six miles. During the times of Cimon and Pericles the city was still further extended by the erection of the Long Walls so as to take in the Piræus (p. 174). A walk about the city walls at this time would make a tour of perhaps twenty miles. The chief entrance to the city was the Dip'ylon gate, to the northwest.

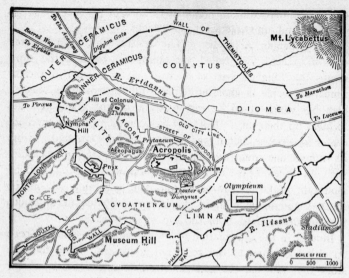

PLAN OF ATHENS, TIME OF PERICLES

The city contained a number of hills, the most important of which were the following: (1) the Acropolis, the central pinnacle of Athens, — formed of limestone rock rising abruptly to the height of two hundred feet, with a length of about a thousand feet, upon or near which were the most important buildings of the city; (2) the Pnyx, to the west, upon which the assembly, or Ecclesia, held its meetings; (3) the Areopagus, a little to the north, where the old council of the Areopagus held its sessions; (4) the Colo′nus, still further to the north, upon which is located the so-called These′um, said to be to-day the best preserved temple of Greece. Between the hill of Colonus and the Areopagus was the Ag′ora, the public square or market place, lined with beautiful trees and porticoes, where the people gathered for business and pleasure. The whole city was divided into certain districts, or wards, corresponding to the "demes" of Attica. Beyond the city walls to the east was the Lyce′um, and to the northwest the Academy; both of these were places of resort and amusement for the people.

The Athenian Acropolis. — The central and most revered spot in Athens was called the Acropolis, because the word means the "highest part of a city." It was usual in ancient times for people in choosing a place for settlement to select a high hill which could be easily defended, and about this hill to build up their city. Not only was the Acropolis an excellent center for defense, but it was most beautifully situated. From its summit one could see the most charming of landscapes, — with its green fields and winding streams — surrounded by mountain peaks on the north and the glistening sea on the south — and above, a liquid sky in which floated fleecy clouds that seemed wafted from the top of Olympus.

Indeed, in the imagination of the Greeks, this spot had been an object of envy to the gods and goddesses. They told the story that Athena, the goddess of wisdom, and Poseidon, the god of the sea, had each claimed to be its rightful possessor. A dispute once arose between them as to which one had first discovered it. As they stood upon the hill, Poseidon pointed to a salt-spring issuing from the rock and claimed that many years ago he had caused that spring to burst forth by the stroke of his trident. Athena, on her part, pointed to an olive tree growing by the side of the spring, and claimed that long before the visit of Poseidon she had caused that tree to grow by a single word of command. This dispute, it was said, was finally settled by an assembly of the gods, who decided in favor of Athena. So firmly did the Athenians believe the story that Pericles caused to be erected there a colossal bronze statue of the goddess, holding in her hand a spear, so high that its shining point was a welcome sight to the mariners far out at sea. But the greatest work of Pericles was the construction of the buildings that covered the summit of this sacred hill.

The Parthenon. — The ancient buildings of the Acropolis — whatever they were — had been destroyed by the Persians.

Erechtheum   Propylæa   Parthenon

THE ACROPOLIS OF ATHENS (Restoration)

Athens had now won from Persia her " years of peace," and
Pericles determined to celebrate these years by giving honor
to Athena, who had helped deliver Athens from the enemy.
The tribute received from the subject cities was used for this
purpose. First of all, there should be built a magnificent
temple dedicated to the Virgin Goddess. Pericles wished it
to be the most beautiful structure that had ever been erected.
This building was the " Par'thenon," a temple which has ever
since excited the wonder and admiration of the world. It was
built of the purest marble, brought from the neighboring Mt.
Pentel'icus. It was in the Doric style, surrounded by forty-six
columns of the finest workmanship. The frieze, pediments,

THREE SISTERS OR THREE FATES (From the eastern pediment)

and other architectural features were decorated with colors
to withstand the glaring rays of the sun. The building was
adorned with the finest statuary that could be produced by the
hand, or under the direction, of Phid'ias, the greatest of Athenian
sculptors.

The small spaces (metopes) in the frieze that surrounded the
temple were filled with sculptured reliefs, representing well-
known mythological scenes. In the pediments on either end
were placed splendid groups of statuary. The eastern pedi-

WEST FRONT OF THE PARTHENON (Restoration)

ment contained a representation of the birth of Athena from
the forehead of her father Zeus. The group in the western
pediment represented the contest of the goddess with Poseidon
for the possession of the Acropolis and the territory of Attica.
The so-called " inner frieze " — which ran just behind the row
of columns, and round the walls of the temple — contained a
remarkable series of reliefs carved in marble. On this frieze
was represented the long procession which on the birthday of
the goddess carried her robe through the streets of Athens to
the Acropolis. This wonderful frieze seemed alive with a vast
variety of figures — prancing horses held in check by the hands of
their riders, beautiful maidens and dignified magistrates, a group
of Olympian deities, and many other subjects (p. 197). The
total length of this frieze was more than five hundred feet, and
it was elevated about forty feet from the pavement of the
temple. Lord Elgin, by permission of the Turkish government, removed about half of these reliefs, with other sculptures
from the Parthenon, to the British Museum, where they are

now deposited under the name of the "Elgin Marbles." The interior of the temple contained only two chambers, of unequal dimensions. The smaller one, to the west, received the treasures of the temple; in the larger one, to the east, Phidias erected a majestic gold and ivory statue of the goddess herself (picture, p. 126).

The supreme beauty of the whole structure was due not to its great size, but to its graceful outlines and exquisite proportions. It was about 225 feet in length, 100 feet in width, and 60 feet in height. It is universally regarded as the most beautiful building of the ancient world.[1] One of the greatest losses that the world of art has ever suffered was the partial destruction of the Parthenon by the havoc of war. In 1687 the Venetians were attacking the city of Athens, then occupied by the Turks. The Parthenon was used as a powder magazine. A shot fired during the attack caused the magazine to explode, shattering the roof and the walls, and leaving the temple a hopeless wreck. But in its ruin it is still the greatest monument of the Age of Pericles.

The Propylæa. — The next important building on the Acropolis erected by Pericles was the Propylæ'a, the entrance to the sacred hill. To one approaching this building it had the appearance of a Doric temple, with its row of columns and its triangular pediment. But the passageway through the Propylæa was lined with Ionic columns, with their curling capitals (p. 142). On the left of the entrance was a gal-

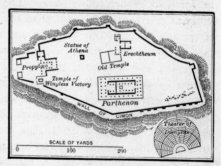

PLAN OF THE ACROPOLIS

[1] A remarkable miniature reproduction of the Parthenon, restored with its many features, may be seen in the Metropolitan Museum of Art in the city of New York.

lery of mythological paintings by the greatest of Athenian painters, Polygno'tus. On the right and front was a beautiful little temple to Athena Ni'ke, generally known as the "Temple of the Wingless Victory." It is said to have been built by Cimon, and Pericles allowed it to remain at the request of its priestly guardians. The whole effect of the Propylæa was beautiful and imposing. At the time of Pericles the Propylæa was approached not by a flight of steps, but by inclined walks leading up from the foot of the hill (p. 192). The steps now seen in the ruins were built long after this by the Romans.

ONE OF THE MAIDENS OF THE ERECHTHEUM

The Erechtheum. — Another notable building of the Acropolis was the Erechthe'um, which Pericles built near the site of an older temple of Athena destroyed by the Persians. Its name was derived from one of the ancient mythical kings of Athens, Erech'theus, who had a shrine near that of Athena. As the new temple was intended to cover both of the sacred spots, its plan was the most irregular of all the temples of Greece. It is supported by beautiful Ionic columns; except that a small porch on the south has for its support six carved female figures (caryat'ides), and is known as the "Porch of the Maidens."

Athenian Sculpture: Myron. — In looking at these buildings we have already noticed some splendid specimens of sculpture. It was not until after the Persian wars that the sculpture of the Greeks began to lose its early crudeness and to acquire more lifelike features. One of the reasons of this improvement was the greater interest that was now shown in gymnastics and athletic sports. To have a healthy and well-developed body was a praiseworthy ambition of the Greeks. No people probably ever had such an admiration of the " human form divine." The influence of gymnastics upon the sculptor's art is clearly shown in the work of the first sculptor of this period, My'ron, a native of Attica. He was especially successful in representing the human figure in action. His best known work is called the " Discob'olus " (the discus thrower). In this we see the young athlete holding the discus, or quoit, just ready to hurl it forward with all his strength. The statue was originally made in bronze; but we can see it to-day only in marble or plaster copies (p. 235).

PART OF THE FRIEZE OF THE PARTHENON, BY PHIDIAS

Phidias and his Works. — The most renowned of all Athenian sculptors was Phidias, who assisted Pericles in the adornment of the Acropolis. His art was inspired by a high religious purpose, like that which led to the building of the Parthenon, —

namely, the worship of the goddess Athena. We have already noticed some of his important works — the statue of Athena in the Parthenon (*Athena Parthenos*) and the sculptured groups in the pediments of that building, and also the figures in the Parthenon frieze. These show a wonderful knowledge of the human form, whether in repose or in action. His work was not confined to Athens. His noble statue of Zeus in the temple at Olympia was regarded by many as his masterpiece, and one of the "wonders of the world." We have no copy of this great work. Our only idea of its grandeur is obtained from its representation upon coins, and the descriptions of it by ancient writers. Many of the works ascribed to Phidias were no doubt the work of his pupils; but they show the spirit and skill of the great master.

Sculptors Outside of Athens. — The influence of Phidias is to be seen not only in the work of his pupils, but in the work

of his rivals outside of Athens. The greatest rival of Phidias was Polycli'tus, of Argos. Like Phidias, he made statues of gold and ivory, which some regarded as quite equal to those of the great Athenian sculptor. His figures were not so grand as those of Phidias, but they were considered by many just as beautiful. He worked mainly in bronze. One of the best known of his statues is the "Wounded Amazon." This is preserved to us only in marble copies; but in these we can judge of the remarkable skill with which the artist has given to the human figure the appearance of natural grace and repose.

WOUNDED AMAZON
(Style of Polyclitus)

Far away from Athens, in the remote city of Mende in the "Thracian district" (map, p. 178), appeared another noted sculptor, Pæo'nius. He lived at the same time as Phidias; and, like Phidias, helped to adorn the sacred city of Olympia. Here was found his most beautiful statue, the "Winged Victory." Though in a mutilated condition, it has been restored with great success. It represents the goddess just alighting upon the earth, her feet scarcely touching the ground, and her drapery blown by the breeze, — a figure bold in design and beautiful in its execution.

Later Greek Sculptors. — Moreover, the influence of Phidias, with that of his pupils and rivals, did not cease with their death. They had, indeed, shown that sculpture was one of the finest of the fine arts. They had furnished examples for those who came after them. Even after Athens became plunged in a civil war, the art of the

VICTORY OF PÆONIUS (Restored)

sculptor still flourished, and in fact has given to us some of the finest statues of the world. If we should seek a name to rival that of Phidias it would be the name of Praxit'eles, a native of Athens. He lived many years after the time of Phidias, and we know little of his life. But we know something of his works. One of the most famous of his statues was the "Aphrodite" of Cnidus (ni'dus; a city in southwestern Asia Minor), which was visited by its admirers from all parts of Greece. But critics have been inclined to give the place of honor to his "Hermes with the Infant Dionysus." This has come down to us only in a mutilated form; but with the aid of early descriptions we may restore the subject in our imagination. The god Hermes is carrying the infant, according to the story, to be reared by the nymphs. He has stopped for a time by the wayside and is now amusing the youngster by holding in his right hand a bunch of grapes. The form of the infant Dionysus is not especially admired; but the figure

HERMES OF PRAXITELES

of Hermes is considered by critics the most nearly perfect human body ever carved in marble.

NIOBE AND CHILD

Another of the later sculptors was Scopas, a native of the island of Paros (one of the Cyclades; p. 179). His name has become famous because to him is attributed the wonderful group of "Ni'obe and her Children." This represents the mother in an attitude of supplication, imploring the gods to stay the vengeance they have pronounced upon her and her children. In the picture before us we see only the figures of Niobe and her youngest child. The child is clinging in terror to the mother's garments and shielded by her protecting arm.

The face of Niobe is unequaled in art as the expression of prayerful grief. The group is so nearly perfect that it is sometimes thought to have been the work of Praxiteles.

The last name on this list of later sculptors is that of Lysip'-pus, of Sicyon (sĭsh'ĭ-on; a city near Corinth). His works are said to have been entirely of bronze. He was especially noted for his selection of human subjects. He was also distinguished for his portrait statues, one of which — that of Soph'ocles (see p. 208) — is regarded as the finest ancient work of its kind.

Gravestone Reliefs. — It was the custom of the Athenians to bury their dead outside of the city walls, along the highways leading from the city gates. The most important of the cemeteries was beyond the Dipylon gate, on a road near the Sacred Way leading to Eleusis (map, p. 190). On either side of the road might be seen the marble monuments intended to preserve the memory of those who had passed away. These gravestones furnish another evidence of the artistic taste of the people. Upon them were carved reliefs calling to mind some personal qualities of the deceased, or indicating some feeling of admiration or affection which lingered about his memory. The warrior might be represented upon a prancing steed, the statesman as addressing an assembly, a friend as holding converse with friends. In these reliefs we see no violent expression of grief. There was "nothing in excess." Here, as elsewhere, are shown the marks of the Greek taste — simplicity and moderation.

GRAVESTONE RELIEF

Athenian Painting. — It is difficult for us to form a very clear idea of the paintings at or near the time of Pericles; for painting is the least durable of the arts. The greatest painter of the time was Polygnotus, a native of the island of Thasos (off the coast of Thrace; p. 178). He lived the most of his life in Athens. His most notable paintings were placed upon the walls of temples, porticoes, or other public buildings. Many of them were to be found in the picture gallery of the Propylæa (p. 196). His subjects were mostly imaginary scenes from Greek mythology. In later times the subjects of the Greek paintings came to be more real. The artists' skill in representing actual things is illustrated in the story often told of the great painters Zeux′is and Parrha′sius. They were rivals, and agreed to make a test of their relative skill. Zeuxis painted a cluster of grapes that deceived the birds, which came and pecked at them. He reported his success to Parrhasius, who told him

GREEK VASE

that his own work could be seen behind a curtain. Zeuxis attempted to draw this aside, and found it was only a painted curtain. And so while Zeuxis had deceived the birds, Parrhasius had deceived the rival painter himself.

A more durable kind of painting one can see in the colored decorations placed upon vases. These represent a vast variety of subjects. While the coloring is very simple the drawing is often very fine. Excellent examples of vase-painting may be found in many of our museums; and from them we learn much of the life and customs of the Greek people (see pictures, pp. 101, 122, 226, 228).

II. THE THEATER AND DRAMATIC LITERATURE

Origin of the Greek Theater. — When we go into our modern theaters we notice that nearly all seem to have one plan of arrangement. In the front is the stage; in the rear and at the sides are rising tiers of seats for the audience. In the center is a semicircular space which we call the "orchestra"; this also, with us, is filled in with seats for the audience. We scarcely ever think, perhaps, that the Greeks gave us this plan. But this is entirely true,— except that the Greeks did not use the orchestra for seats as we do. In a Grecian theater the orchestra was the place where an important part of the performance was given. The Greek word *orchestra* does not mean a place for seats, or even a body of musicians, as we understand it. It meant a *dance*, or a space for dancing.

We may be curious to know how the theater and the drama grew out of a dance. In ancient times at the festivals given in honor of Dionysus, the wine-god, the people were accustomed to gather in the open air to see the dancing and hear the songs which formed a part of his worship. Soon they found it more convenient to sit upon a hillside, while the dancing took place and the choruses were sung in front of them. Afterward, a place on the southeastern side of the Acropolis was rounded out and furnished with wooden benches. While the dancers and singers were resting, the leader of the chorus would relate a story of the god, or explain to the people the meaning of the performance. Later, an actor was introduced who carried on a dialogue with the leader of the chorus; then a second and a third actor came to be introduced, and the dialogue came to be more and more important. A platform or stage was set up that the actors might be better heard by the people. This was the oldest theater. But still, all through these changes, the central part of the theater was reserved for the altar of Dionysus and the "chorus," that is, for the songs and dances. In the time of Pericles the seats were still of wood, rising tier above tier. It was long after his time when these were replaced by stone seats. The Romans copied the Greek theater, but they dispensed with the chorus or dance; and so the semicircular orchestra was reserved for the senators and other distinguished persons. In our day it is reserved for those who can pay a high price for their tickets. We have made a more extensive stage and have added galleries for the audience; but the orchestra still remains as the central part of the theater, just as it was in the days of Pericles.

THE THEATER OF DIONYSUS (Restoration)

The Theater of Dionysus. — There was only one theater in Athens where plays were given. That was the theater of Dionysus, — its name showing that the plays were a part of the festival of the wine-god. The tiers of seats would hold sixteen or seventeen thousand people. The front tier was reserved for the public magistrates, the center seat for the priest of Dionysus. In early times there was an admission fee of one drachma (about twenty cents); Pericles reduced this to two obols (about six cents), and also provided that any citizen too poor to pay should receive a free ticket. The tiers were numbered, and the tickets were numbered to correspond with them.

The performances did not take place every day of the year, but at the festivals of Dionysus. These festivals were great occasions. They lasted several days, and included hilarious processions through the streets of Athens, in which women and children took part. But the most important part of the festival was the performance within the theater. This began at dawn and continued until dusk, so that the people brought their lunches with them.

If we were seated upon one of the tiers we should notice first of all that the whole theater was open to the sky — only a screen perhaps being drawn in some places to shut off the bright rays of the sun. We should see in the center of the orchestra the altar of Dionysus; around it, the chorus composed of from fifteen to twenty-four men, who sang the hymns in honor of the god, and who were trained to dance in set figures as an accompaniment to the songs. On the stage we should see not more than three actors, each one of whom might, however, take more than one part. The scenery on the stage was very simple indeed. But the actors, as well as the singers and dancers, were dressed in elaborate costumes, and all wore masks

MASKS USED IN TRAGEDY

which concealed their faces. The actors wore buskins, or high boots, to give a greater dignity to their figure. All the parts, male and female, were taken by men. All alike, singers, dancers, and actors, were specially trained to take their various parts; the actors especially had to cultivate a rich, powerful voice, with a perfect intonation and accent. The audience was very critical and demonstrative, cheering at what they admired and jeering at what they disliked.

The Two Forms of the Drama. — The theatrical performances took the name of " drama." The Greek word *drama* literally means " a performance." We have seen how the drama grew up with the theater from the festivals given in honor of the wine-god. But we must bear in mind one important fact — there were two of these festivals, quite different in character, one in spring and the other in mid-winter.

The one in the springtime was more serious and religious in character, when the people were grateful to the gods for giving to nature a new life, fresh leaves and buds and blossoms. This festival was celebrated in the theater by more sacred hymns, more measured dances, more somber costumes, and more serious talk by the actors; and so the spring festival gave rise to the more serious drama, — tragedy.

The winter festival, on the other hand, came when the people, especially in the country, were tired of their gloomy life. They wished to wake up the sleeping year. They wanted diversion and amusement; nothing could be too hilarious to suit them. It was a time for general merrymaking. In the theater one would hear lively and rollicking songs, and one would see frolic-some dances and grotesque costumes, while the actors indulged in humorous jokes. And so this festival gave rise to the humor-ous drama, — comedy.

Comedy did not at first succeed so well as tragedy. All dialogues and choruses were carefully written before being pre-sented. The best writers would naturally prefer to dwell upon high and noble subjects; and these were the subjects of tragedy. Prizes were offered for the best dramatic pieces; and in these contests tragedies appealed most strongly to the people as well as to the official judges. Pericles encouraged this form of litera-ture as a means of moral education and culture.

Æschylus, the Father of Tragedy. — It was Æs'chylus who made the dialogue the most important part of the drama, and hence he may properly be called the " Father of the Greek Tragedy." He it was who introduced a second actor. As the

dialogue became more important the chorus became less prominent, and came in at intervals as a sort of accompaniment to
the play. Æschylus was a man inspired with a strong religious
and patriotic spirit. He was a soldier in the Persian wars and
was present at the battles of Marathon and Salamis. One of
his earliest tragedies was called "The Persians." In this he
showed the terrible effect which the battle of Salamis produced
upon the Persian court. The subjects of his later tragedies
were taken from Greek mythology — the stories of the gods —
inspiring his audience with a deep religious sentiment and showing the danger of disobeying the divine will. Over all, he believed, was a supreme Fate, or Providence, to which men and
even the gods were responsible. In one of his greatest plays,
"Prome'theus Bound," he depicts the punishment of Prometheus, who disobeyed the command of Zeus by stealing fire from
heaven and giving it to men. For this Prometheus is represented
as chained to a rock and compelled to suffer by being made the
prey of a devouring eagle. This is the soliloquy of Prometheus
when first left alone on the rock:

> "O, Air divine! and ye swift winged Winds!
> Ye River-fountains! and ye countless smiles
> Of dimpling Ocean! Mother earth! and thou
> Far-piercing Eye of day! On you I call,
> Witness what I, a god, from gods endure."

Æschylus was the most sublime of all the Greek tragedians.
In the portrayal of profound grief and intense suffering no
modern writer — except perhaps Shakespeare in his King Lear
— has equaled him. He produced over seventy tragedies, of
which we have remaining only seven. He introduced the "trilogy"; that is, a series of three plays, closely related by a common
subject and plot. In his early years he received the prize in a
dramatic contest. In one of his later contests the prize was
taken from him by a younger competitor, Soph'ocles.

Sophocles, the Dramatic Artist. — We call Sophocles "the
dramatic artist" because his works were the most beautiful

of all tragedies; they might be called perfect specimens of literary art. As he extracted sweetness from all he touched, he was called the " Attic Bee." The beauty of his tragedies may be due somewhat to his great love of music. In his early youth he was chosen to lead the chorus of boys in a celebration of the victory at Salamis. He devoted himself to training the singers, the dancers, and the actors in the theater, that they might give the finest rendering of the various parts. He added a third actor, that the dialogue might give a better effect. He brought the hymns of the chorus into greater harmony with the sentiment of the play. He composed over a hundred dramas, of which only seven have come down to us. Among these the greatest, perhaps, are " King Œd'ipus," " Œdipus at Colonus," and " Antig'one," — the three being called the " Theban Trilogy," because they were all based upon stories relating to Thebes.

SOPHOCLES

The character of Antigone is one of the most beautiful in literature. This is the story that is told in the play : Antigone is the daughter of Œdipus, the late king of Thebes. The present king is Creon, whose son is betrothed to Antigone. The brother of Antigone has been killed in a war against Thebes, and the king in his wrath has commanded that his body shall never be buried — which the Greeks regarded as the most terrible of calamities. In spite of the king's command Antigone covers with earth the dead body of her brother. As a penalty for her sisterly affection and her disobedience of the king's command, she is condemned to a lingering death in a cavern, watched by the royal guards and without food. She is consoled by the thought that she has been true to her own conscience and the love she owed to her brother. The chorus intercedes and the king relents. But on entering the cave they find Antigone dead, clasped in the arms of her lover, who had evaded the guards to save the life of his expected bride. Hear the words of this beautiful maiden when, standing in the presence of the king, she received her sentence:

"Behold me, princes of my native land!
I tread the last sad path,
And gaze upon the latest beam
Of yon resplendent sun,
To see no more forever. Ah! the hand
Of all-entombing Death
Drives me to Acheron's bleak shore,
Ungraced by nuptial rites; no song
Hath hymned my hour of bliss,
And joyless Death will be my bridegroom now."

Euripides, the Dramatist of the People. — The latest of the great tragedians was Eurip'ides. He was born, it was said, on the island of Salamis on the very day of the great naval battle with the Persians (p. 162). He grew up among the common people and learned to sympathize with them. He had no love for active politics; he preferred the retired life of a student. At the age of twenty-five he began to write tragedies; but in his first dramatic contest he received only the third prize, and it was fourteen years

EURIPIDES

before he obtained a first prize. During this time the ideas of the Athenian people were changing. They began to take more interest in plays that dealt with the affairs of everyday life. Euripides appealed to their hearts; even the gods were represented by him more like human beings with human sympathies. He therefore became the favorite of the common people. Of his ninety-two plays we have remaining eighteen.

One of his beautiful characters is the maiden Iphigeni'a, who was doomed to be sacrificed to appease the spite of the goddess Artemis — this goddess having detained the Grecian fleet when on its way to Troy. When expecting to die she thus addressed her weeping mother:

> "My mother, weep not thus. I gladly bow
> To meet my fate; for all the powers of Greece
> Have now their eyes on me; on me depends
> The sailing of the fleet, the fall of Troy.
> By dying, all these things shall I achieve;
> And on me blessings will forever rest,
> For giving life my land to serve."

The Attic Comedy: Aristophanes. — The greatest of all the comic writers of the Greeks was Aristoph'anes, who was about thirty years younger than Euripides. He mingled in the political life of Athens, and belonged to the party which was " against the government." His comedies might give us the best picture we have of Athenian life, if they contained less of caricature and satire. From other sources we may learn that some of his pictures are fairly just, while others are marked by the grossest injustice. Among his most noted works are the " Clouds," the " Knights," the " Wasps," and the " Birds." The " Clouds " is chiefly noted for the unjust attack which it makes upon the philosopher Soc'rates, whom Aristophanes mistook for a sophist. The " Knights " describes with brilliant satire the coarse demagogue Cle'on, who came into power after the death of Pericles; though not an admirable character, perhaps he does not merit all the abuse he received. The " Wasps " is an amusing picture of the Athenian jury system, in which every man is represented as trying to get a day's pay without a day's work. The "Birds" is "a fantastic satire upon the Athenian habit of building castles in the air, and of indulging in extravagant dreams of conquest."

MASKS USED IN COMEDY

With all his ribaldry, Aristophanes was a poet of real genius, of sparkling wit, and sometimes of exquisite beauty. Here is a brief "chorus" in which he refers to tragedy and the great tragedians:

> "Pipe and lute and dance are there,
> Tragic pomp and stately air;
> With the Sophocle'an strain,
> When he's in his noblest vein,
> And the daintier lays that please
> Falling from Euripides."

III. Prose Literature: History and Oratory

Herodotus, the Father of History. — In Greece, as elsewhere, poetry preceded prose in the order of development. The epic, lyric, and dramatic poetry had been cultivated before any noteworthy works in prose were written. The first really great work of prose literature in the Greek language was the history written by Herodotus, a native of Halicarnassus in Asia Minor. Herodotus was born during the period of the Persian wars. The great conflict between the Greeks and the Persians was to him the greatest of all events. It became the subject of his history, and furnishes to us our chief knowledge of that struggle. He traveled extensively, and became acquainted with the manners, institutions, and legends of many countries. He came to

HERODOTUS

Athens when the culture of that city was at its height; and he became a close friend of Sophocles and an ardent admirer of Pericles. Under these influences his history became inspired with an Athenian spirit, and acquired the character of an artistic literary composition. Into his work are skillfully woven the narrative of historical events and the description of foreign countries, — facts which he himself observed as well as stories and myths told him by others. The critical accuracy of Herodotus has often been questioned; but the charming qualities of his simple graphic style have always been admired.

Thucydides, the Scientific Historian. — The greatest historian of Greece was Thucyd'ides, a native of Attica. He wrote the history of the Peloponnesian war, — the great struggle between Athens and Sparta (p. 241). He himself took part in this war. He was placed in command of a naval expedition; on account of its failure he was condemned to death for treason; but he escaped from Athens and lived in exile for the next twenty years. During this time he collected the material for his great historical work. He desired especially to be impartial, siding with neither party, and telling only the truth. He was careful to ascertain the facts, and to explain them. He gave vivid descriptions of battles and of military movements, and reports of speeches. On account of his accuracy and love of truth, he may be called the scientific historian.

THUCYDIDES

Xenophon, the Historical Essayist. — Following in the path of Thucydides was the genial historical writer Xen'ophon. Although he can hardly be compared with Thucydides as an historian, he wrote in an easy and interesting manner upon a great variety of subjects. His " Anab'asis " tells the story of a famous Greek expedition in Persia, in which he himself took part (p. 250). His " Hellen'ica " continues that part of the Peloponnesian war left unfinished by Thucydides. His " Memorabil'ia " draws a lifelike portrait of his great master, Socrates. His " Cyropædi'a " professes to describe the education of Cyrus the Great, but is quite as much a description of what the author regards as a just prince. His " Œconom'icus " gives us an insight into the home life of the Greeks. He wrote interesting works upon other subjects, the variety of which might justify us in calling him an essayist as well as an historian.

The Orators of Athens. — That branch of prose literature which is distinctively Greek in its origin is oratory. Indeed, it may be said that oratory was the product of the democratic institutions of Athens. The greatest orator of the age of Pericles was no doubt Pericles himself; for by his eloquence he controlled for thirty years the Athenian assembly. But his speeches have been preserved to us only in the reports contained in the history of Thucydides. Not only the Athenian assembly, but the Athenian courts afforded a field for the cultivation of eloquence, for here every man was compelled to plead his own cause. Of the many Athenian orators who attained distinction, we may select three as the most representative — Lys'ias, Isoc'rates, and Demos'thenes.

Lysias was employed, like many others, to write speeches for those who were obliged to plead their own

LYSIAS

cause in the courts. The purpose of his orations was to convince the jurors. As he wrote for plain men, he used a plain, direct, and simple style. By writing clearly and distinctly, he became a master of vivid and effective speech.

Isocrates wrote in a style somewhat different from that of Lysias. He was primarily a teacher of rhetoric, and hence the orations which he wrote — but did not deliver — have more of a rhetorical finish, and are perhaps more attractive in language than effective in thought.

ISOCRATES

But the last and greatest of the famous orators of Greece was Demosthenes, a native of Attica. In his early years he devoted himself to the study of the laws and politics of Athens and to the history of Greece. But he aspired to be an orator, that he might move the assembly as Pericles had done, and to inspire the people to do their duty as Athenian citizens. His first speech was a failure; the people laughed at his awkward figure and his harsh, tremulous voice. But this only spurred him to greater efforts. We are told that he practiced before the mirror that he might overcome his awkward manners; that he declaimed to the waves on the seashore that he might be heard above the clamor of the assembly; that he studied for days and nights the history of Thucydides that he might acquire a vigorous style. He received the reward of his perseverance. He became not only the greatest orator of Greece, but one of the greatest in the world's history. We shall hear more of him hereafter — how he used his great oratorical powers in defense of Greece against Philip of Macedon (pp. 261–262).

IV. The Philosophy of Athens

Anaxagoras, the First Athenian Philosopher. — It was not until after the Persian wars that Athens became the philosophical center of Greece. The first thinker who belonged to what we might call the Athenian school was Anaxag′oras. Although born in Asia Minor, he early came to Athens, where he spent the most of his life, and numbered among his pupils Pericles and Euripides. His name marks a turning point in the history of philosophy, because he seems to have been the first to recognize the controlling influence of mind and reason in the universe. He believed in a supreme overruling Intelligence. This doctrine was opposed to the old mythology; and as the people were jealous of their ancient beliefs, Anaxagoras was charged with atheism and banished from the city. On his departure he proudly said. "It is not I who have lost Athens; it is Athens which has lost me." He died at Lamp′sacus, a town in the north of Asia Minor. On his deathbed the citizens of this place asked him how they could best honor his memory. He begged that the day of his death might be annually kept as a holiday in all the schools of the city.

The Greek Sophists as Teachers. — There grew up in Athens a certain class of men known as "sophists." They were not so much philosophers in the old sense as thinkers. That is, they did not seek to discover the laws of the universe so much as the laws of the human mind. They sought to find out the methods in which men reason. They gained their living by teaching the subjects of grammar, rhetoric, and logic, and preparing young men for the practical affairs of life. It was often charged against them that their learning was more of a pretense than a reality; and it was asserted that their art of reasoning degenerated into mere quibbling, or the attempt "to make the worse appear the better reason." But with all the faults charged against them, they no doubt exercised some beneficial influence, both upon Greek education and upon Greek philosophy.

The Teachings of Socrates. — In the streets of Athens might be seen a man walking to and fro, with no pretense of learning, but talking with any one who wished to hear him — a man who is regarded to-day as one of the greatest moral teachers of the

SOCRATES

world. Everybody knew him, because of his eccentric appearance. He was barefooted, in humble garb, wearing the same clothes summer and winter. He was the son of a poor sculptor. One might see gathered about him a circle of men, young and old — some making fun of his homely face, and some listening intently to his words of wisdom. Some thought him insane because he professed to have with him a spirit, or "Dæmon," as he called it, to whose voice he always listened. Some thought him a sophist, because he was always asking questions and was trying to entangle people in their answers — but he took no fees as the sophists did. And some saw in him a strange teacher, and as they listened to him they were astonished at the method of his teaching. He did not instruct them by telling them what he believed. He rather led them to think for themselves. He drew out from them their own ideas, and by continual questions led them to see the difference between what was false and what was true. He showed them how foolish it was to follow the method of the old philosophers and to speculate about things which cannot be known. His first maxim was, "Know thyself." He taught men that true wisdom consists in knowing that which is good and doing that which is right. He taught them the difference between justice and injustice, between virtue and vice, between courage and cowardice. He taught them their duties to themselves, to their fellow-men, and to God.

But there were men who did not understand these new teachings. They charged the teacher with introducing new gods into the state, and claimed that such doctrines would corrupt the youth. On such a charge he was brought before a jury-court of five hundred of his fellow-citizens. They were surprised that he made no serious defense of himself; and some thought that this was an evidence of his guilt. And so, by a small majority, they condemned him to death — to drink the fatal hemlock. As he was about to be led to prison to await his doom, he addressed those who had condemned him, saying:

"O judges, be of good cheer about death and know this of a truth — that no evil can happen to a good man, either in life or after death. The hour of departure has come, and we go our ways — I to die, you to live, which is better God knows."

He remained in prison for thirty days, spending his time in meditation and in conversing with his friends on the life to come. At the end of this time he cheerfully drank the poisoned cup, and died — a martyr to the cause of truth. This wonderful man was Socrates.

Plato and the Academic School. — Socrates left behind him many disciples who founded new schools. But the most distinguished of these was Plato, the founder of the "Academic school," so called because he generally taught in the Academy (see p. 191). He followed somewhat the method of Socrates. He studied the human mind. He believed that the highest ideas which we have must have

PLATO

been born with us — for example, our ideas of the true, the beautiful, and the good. They could not have had a human origin, he maintained; they must have come from a divine source. By such reasoning, Plato constructed a system of *ideal* philosophy.

The writings of Plato are in the form of dialogues, in which Socrates is often represented as the chief speaker. Some of the dialogues are named after particular persons; for example, the "Protag'oras," which discusses the nature of virtue; the "Phædo," which sets forth the arguments in favor of immortality. One of the most celebrated of Plato's dialogues is "The Republic," which discusses the principles that should govern the ideal state.

ARISTOTLE

From the political conflicts of the time Plato stood aloof; and hence he shows to us the Greek mind in its purest and most tranquil frame.

Aristotle and the Peripatetic School. — Ar'istotle was born in far-off Chalcid'ice.[1] His father was a physician, and he inherited a love for the natural sciences. When he was seventeen years old he went to Athens, and became a pupil of Plato. On account of his zeal in his studies, Plato likened him to a colt that needed the bit more than the spur. He established a school of his own at the Lyceum (p. 190), where he walked back and forth while giving his instructions. And so his school was called the "Peripatet'ic" school — a word meaning "walking about." He professed to be a follower of Plato, but his method was quite different from that of his master. Instead of beginning with *ideas* as Plato had done, he began with *facts;* and he tried to discover the general laws that govern the facts of nature. He was therefore a man of wide observation and general learning.

[1] In the town of Stagi'ra (or Stagirus; map, p. 178). For this reason he is sometimes called "the Stagirite" (stăj'ĭ-rīt).

He gathered and classified a vast number of facts, and became the founder of many sciences — of Logic, which treats of the laws of thought; of Psychology, or the science of the human mind; of Biology, or the science of living things; of Politics, or the science of the state. He is said to have studied the constitutions of many of the states of Greece. A work on the Athenian constitution, which is attributed to him, has added much to our knowledge of that government.

Selections for Reading

Knowlton, Topic A 9, "Age of Pericles: Art and Literature" (1).[1]

Seignobos, Ch. 14, "The Arts in Greece" (1).

Shuckburgh, Ch. 13, "The New Athens" (10).

Smith, Wm., Ch. 34, "Athens and Athenian and Grecian Art during the Period of her Empire"; Ch. 35, "History of Athenian Literature to the End of the Peloponnesian War" (10).

Lawton, Bk. III., "The Attic Drama"; Bk. IV., "Classic Prose" (15).

Abbott, Pericles, Ch. 17, "The Athens of Pericles" (27).

Allcroft, Vol. II., Ch. 13, "The Imperial City"; Ch. 15, "Literature" (10).

Ducoudray, Ch. 9, "Greek Literature and Art" (1).

Guhl and Koner, § 30, "The Theater" (11).

Bury, Ch. 11, § 6, "The Restoration of the Temples"; § 11, "Higher Education; the Sophists" (10).

Curtius, Vol. II., pp. 592–641, "Athens the Center of Intellectual Life" (10).

Holm, Vol. II., Ch. 20, "Athens under Pericles"; Ch. 26, "The New Culture, Rhetoric and Sophistry"; Ch. 29, "Art and Literature" (10).

Fowler and Wheeler, Ch. 2, "Architecture"; Ch. 3, "Sculpture" (12).

Richardson, Ch. 3, "The Fifth Century: Age of the Great Masters" (12).

Tarbell, Chs. 8, 9, "Great Age of Greek Sculpture" (12).

Special Study

THE GREEK THEATER. — Seignobos, pp. 165–167 (1); Tucker, Ch. 12 (11); Blümner, Ch. 12 (11); Guhl and Koner, pp. 121–133, 275–281 (11); Becker, pp. 403–412 (11); Harper's Dictionary, "Theatrum" (11); Smith, Dict. Antiqq., "Theatrum" (11).

[1] The figure in parenthesis refers to the number of the topic in the Appendix, where a fuller title of the book will be found.

CHAPTER XV

LIFE AND CUSTOMS OF THE ATHENIAN PEOPLE

Synopsis

I. DOMESTIC LIFE OF THE ATHENIANS. — The Athenian Home. — The House and its Furniture. — Dress and Ornaments. — The Meals and Articles of Food. — Marriage and the Position of Women. — Home Training and Education. — Funeral Ceremonies.

II. INDUSTRIAL LIFE AT ATHENS. — Occupations of the People. — Agriculture and Agricultural Products. — Manufactures and Industrial Arts. — Commerce and Trade. — Professional Pursuits. — Greek Slavery.

III. SOCIAL LIFE IN ATHENS. — Athenian Sociability. — Society of the Street. — Social and Political Clubs. — The Banquet and Symposium.

IV. AMUSEMENTS AND ATHLETIC GAMES. — The Greek Fondness for Amusements. — The Gymnasium and Athletic Sports. — The Stadium and Public Exhibitions. — The Five Athletic Events. The Hippodrome: Horse and Chariot Racing. — The Pan-Athenian Festival.

I. DOMESTIC LIFE OF THE ATHENIANS

The Athenian Home. — We have now had a view of the political and intellectual life of Athens, and of the distinguished men who took part in that life. Let us look at the more ordinary life of the people. The beginnings of all highly civilized life must be found in the home, and it is true that the center of Athenian life was the home. Here the family gathered to take their daily meals and to offer their daily prayers. While the Athenians worshiped the great gods of the state in their public festivals, they still had a family worship — that of their own ancestors — which they sacredly observed in the privacy of their own homes. As the Athenian gentleman spent a large part of his time at the Agora and other resorts, we might suppose that his home life would be a matter of small concern. But he naturally returned to his home when he had nowhere else to go; and there he entertained his friends and stored his goods. In his own house he was the supreme master, and the law did not interfere with his authority. In his absence the management of the household was left entirely to the housewife and her retinue of servants. To her the home was not merely the center but the entire sphere of her existence. In spite of her social restrictions she was yet the mistress of her own little world. To her was left the care and training of the young children who were to become the future citizens of the state.

The House and its Furniture. — The ordinary dwelling house was an unpretentious structure, as compared with the magnificent public buildings on which the Athenians lavished their wealth. As we approach the house we see nothing but a plain

INTERIOR OF A GREEK HOUSE (Restoration)

stone or brick wall facing the street, and entered by a single door, upon which is hung a metal knocker. In its plan the house was simply a series of rooms surrounding a court, which was open to the sky. The court was usually surrounded by a series of columns, which in the finer houses produced a dignified and artistic effect. Sometimes there might be a second court in the rear, surrounded by the women's apartments; and often the house might be constructed with a second story. The roof was flat and covered with clay tiles. The rooms were warmed by fireplaces or by portable

GREEK LAMP

braziers filled with glowing charcoal; they were lighted by day from the open court and at night by small oil lamps. The decoration and furniture of the house corresponded, of course, to the wealth of the occupant. The Greeks generally preferred comfort to luxury. But the furnishings, however simple they might be, showed a refined taste. The chairs, stools, and couches were made of ornamental woodwork. The lamps, made of metal or terra-cotta, were especially artistic. In different places around the court we might see bronze or marble statuettes and vases of precious metal and of elegant workmanship.

Dress and Ornaments. — The Greeks also showed their simple taste in their dress, which was in strong contrast to the elaborate and gaudy apparel of the Oriental people. The dress of the men and women was quite similar, although that of the women was more full and flowing. It consisted of two garments; first, a tunic called *chiton* (kī'ton) held in place by clasps upon the shoulder, and a belt or girdle about the waist; and second, a broad cloak called *himat'ion*, thrown in loose folds about the body. The mode of adjusting the himation often showed the skill and taste of the wearer (see p. 208). The feet might or might not be protected by sandals. The elaborate ornaments worn

URANIA

DEMETER

by the Greeks at the time of Homer were discarded by men at the time of Pericles. The Athenian gentleman, dressed in his tunic and cloak, with sandals, a ring upon his finger, and a walking stick in his hand, was fully equipped for the street. The Athenian women still retained a taste for ornaments. They wore a fillet for confining the hair, earrings of various designs, necklaces, and bracelets and anklets. They also carried fans and parasols, either for use or for ornament. The general effect of the simple female costume of the Greeks may be seen in the pictures here given of statues representing different mythological characters.

ATHENA

The Meals and Articles of Food. — The Greeks at their meals were noted for their moderation — as in everything else. They evidently knew that gluttony was not conducive to good health or to that physical perfection which they highly prized. The first meal of the day, or breakfast, was taken soon after rising, and consisted of a barley cake or roll dipped in a little wine. The midday meal, or luncheon, was of the same simple character, with perhaps some salt fish or sausages, or ham. The chief meal, or dinner, was taken about sunset, after the day's work or recreation was finished. At this formal repast, the master

POLYMNIA

of the house reclined on a couch, with his wife and children sitting near him on chairs or stools.

The bread was made of wheat or barley, the principal grain raised in Attica. The vegetables at the disposal of the Greeks included spinach, lettuce, and cabbages, also peas and beans, together with radishes and onions, — but no potatoes, corn, tomatoes, squashes, or melons. Fish, both fresh water and salt, were highly esteemed. Meats were not so often eaten. But when oxen, sheep, pigs, and goats were offered in sacrifice at public festivals the flesh of these animals was obtained by the people at nominal prices. The chief fruits of Attica were figs, olives, and grapes. The only drinks used by the Athenians were water and wine. It was not expected that wine should ever be drunk without being mixed with water, and hence the Athenians were noted as a temperate people. Only at special banquets, when the wife and children were absent, did they venture to overstep this rule.

Marriage and the Position of Women. — As the father was the master of the household, he provided for the marriage of his children, and the betrothal was really an engagement made between the parents of the bride and groom. Although marriage was a legal contract, the wedding was a sacred, as well as a festive, ceremony. The parties purified themselves with the water brought from a sacred spring, and the bride's father offered a sacrifice to the gods of marriage. Then followed a banquet, in which the guests partook of the wedding cake. The banquet closed with kind wishes for the newly married couple, who were attended to their future home by a procession of friends and attendants, garlanded with flowers and singing the nuptial song to the music of flutes.

The Athenians believed that the proper sphere of woman was the home; and she was hence deprived of the liberty which she enjoyed in Homeric times, and even at this time in Sparta. Her world was the little world of household duties. For this sphere she had been trained by her mother, and she was taught that politics and the turmoil of the street should be left to men. Her employments, — spinning, weaving, embroidery, and the cultivation of her personal charms, — were not of course conducive to a high intellectual culture. The women of Athens are therefore sometimes satirized by certain comic poets and other writers. But we must remember that while the women of Athens may not have had the social freedom of the women of to-day, they were by no means held in low esteem. The Athenians worshiped Athena as the guardian of their city, and venerated their goddesses quite as highly as their gods; feminine beauty was one of the most exalted subjects of the best Athenian art; and female characters, such as the Antigone of Sophocles and the Iphigenia of Euripides, are among the most noble in the whole range of Athenian literature. These facts show that the Athenians were not entirely insensible to the attractions of feminine charms and of feminine virtues.

Home Training and Education. — Education formed a very important part of Greek life. Its aim was to develop as far as possible a perfect physical, intellectual, and moral manhood, and to prepare young men for the duties which belong to free citizens. It began with home training and continued until the boy reached the age of manhood. Until seven years of age the boy was under the supervision of his mother, who taught him good manners and the care of his health. He might then be sent to a private school. The Athenians were thoroughly impressed with the importance of training the body, the mind, and the character. Gymnastics, mental discipline, and moral inspiration were the chief features of their educational methods. The boy was not only taught by his teacher at school, but was constantly under the supervision of his " pedagogue," a trusty servant who accompanied him to school and watched over him elsewhere. The elementary training consisted of reading, writing, and arithmetic. The boy committed to memory the wise sayings of the old poets, and copied these proverbs upon a waxen tablet by means of the stylus. He became familiar with the heroic lines of Homer, the sayings of wise men, and the animal stories of Æsop's Fables. His arithmetical computations were

A LESSON IN THE POETS

made with the aid of the abacus, or counting board. He studied music, for the cultivation of the feelings; and his systematic exercise in the gymnasium was intended to give him a sound, symmetrical, and vigorous body. Besides the elementary discipline there was added the more advanced education obtained from the conversation and lectures of professional teachers, like the sophists. Such instruction was given in the porches of the Agora, the Academy, the Lyceum, and other public places. It included all branches of practical and theoretical knowledge; and its aim was to give a liberal education — to make broad-minded men and enlightened citizens.

Funeral Ceremonies. — The Athenians had a great respect for the dead. To give a proper burial to one's relatives was one of the most sacred of duties. Even a stranger who found a dead body was required to cover it with earth. The funeral ceremonies were strictly defined. The body was washed, anointed,

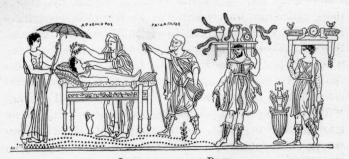

LAYING OUT OF THE DEAD

clothed, crowned with a chaplet, and laid out in the vestibule. An obol was placed in the mouth as a fee to Charon (kā'ron), who was supposed to row the departed spirit across the river Styx. Then were brought together and deposited near the body vases and other personal effects, to be placed in the grave. Over the bier were uttered loud lamentations. On the third day the funeral procession, made up of the mourning relatives and their friends, attended the body to the spot where it was to be burned or buried. If the corpse was burned, the ashes were collected in an urn. If it was buried, it was placed in a coffin, and above the grave was erected some kind of monument (p. 201).

II. Industrial Life at Athens

Occupations of the People. — We may now ask, How did the Athenians get their living? Many of them received some compensation by serving the state. The higher officials, it is true, received no reward except the honor which attended the position. But pay was given to the members of the council, to the jurors when serving at court, to all citizens attending the assembly, and to those who served in the army and the fleet. The mass of citizens, however, obtained their living at Athens, as in other communities, by engaging in some agricultural, manufacturing, commercial, or professional pursuit.

Agriculture and Agricultural Products. — From the earliest times agriculture was regarded as an honorable occupation. No one but a free citizen could own land in Attica. Although the land was not very fertile, and was generally worked by slaves, it yielded a fair income to its owner. The soil was adapted to the cultivation of olives, figs, and grapes; wheat and barley; and the different kinds of vegetables which the Athenians used (p. 224). With the cutting down of the forests, much land was also used for grazing. Bees were kept, and the honey of Mt. Hymet'tus was famous. The farmers produced most of the food required for the people.

Manufactures and Industrial Arts. — Although a certain amount of industry was carried on in the household, — such as spinning, weaving, and embroidery, — there grew up in Athens a great variety of trades in which separate classes of artisans were employed. There were millers and bakers; makers of cloth, fullers and dyers; workers in wood, such as furniture, cabinet and wagon makers; workers in iron, such as blacksmiths and makers of arms and armor; artisans in clay, glass, silver, and gold. In consequence of the flourishing condition of the Attic trades, the articles were sought everywhere, as, for example, the Attic metal and leather wares, lamps, utensils of all kinds, especially of earthenware.

IRON WORKERS (Vase painting)

Commerce and Trade. — Like many other cities of Greece, Athens became an important commercial center, especially after the building of her famous seaport, the Piræus. But as a large part of the commercial business was carried on by resident foreigners, this occupation was not in so high repute as those of the farmer or the manufacturer. The exports were mostly manufactured articles, including olive oil and wine. The imports included grain from Syria and Egypt, and wood, iron, and copper from Macedonia and Thrace. An important mercantile occupation was that of the banker, whose business was to change, borrow, and lend money, and also to assist people in making investments.

Professional Pursuits. — Certain people gained their living by pursuits which we should call "professional." For example, the physician, who was supposed to derive his knowledge from the god Ascle′pius (Æscula′pius), was held in great esteem; he received fees for his services, and sometimes had a fixed salary paid by the state. Although the ordinary schoolmaster was regarded as hardly better than a servant, the higher teachers, such as the sophists, were honored and received considerable pay for their instruction. The common sculptor was looked upon merely as a stonecutter; but there were noted artists and painters, like the great Phidias, and Polygnotus, whose position ranked as a profession, accompanied with honor and large remuneration. A similar difference existed between the lower and the better class of actors and musicians. In the matter of law, every man was expected to plead his own cause; but in the course of time men assumed the part of counselors, to give advice to litigants and to prepare speeches to be delivered by them in the courts of justice, and this became a lucrative profession.

ASCLEPIUS

Greek Slavery. — In Athens, as well as in the other parts of Greece, and in fact in all the nations of antiquity, a large part of the industry, especially that of a menial character, was performed by slaves (see p. 180). There were slaves in almost every household; on the farms and in every mine; even policemen and clerks in public offices were slaves. Many of the slaves at Athens belonged to the same race as their masters, having been taken in war with other Greek states. Their lot was not extremely wretched. They were generally well, if not kindly, treated by their masters. They held positions of trust both in the household and in public places. But still they were deprived of all political and civil rights, and, worst of all, might be subjected to torture when giving testimony before a court. Generally the slave received no compensation for his work except his support; but occasionally he might be intrusted with a certain amount of money and allowed a percentage on what he made from it, and with his profits he might even purchase his freedom. The worst effect of slavery was to throw a kind of reproach upon almost all forms of manual labor, and thus to degrade the poor class of freemen who were obliged to work for a living.

III. Social Life in Athens

Athenian Sociability. — The Athenians were a very sociable people. This is seen in their hospitality, which they possessed in common with all other Greeks, but especially in their love of companionship and of social entertainments, and also in their love of conversation. Of all the Greek peoples the Athenians excelled in the power to talk in an interesting manner. With their high intellectual tastes, they liked to compare their ideas upon literature and art and philosophy; and with their strong democratic spirit, they cared little for the aristocracy of blood or wealth. The marks of a gentleman were refined manners, a bright intellect, a good education, and, not the least, the capacity to converse well upon many topics.

Society of the Street. — The open air was, in many respects, the home of the Greek gentleman. In the streets he could always find his friends, with whom he was accustomed to pass many hours of the day. The chief center of the social life of Athens — as it was of the political and commercial life — was the Agora. Outside the city walls were the exercising grounds called the Lyceum and the Academy. At any of these centers, under the shade of plane trees, or within the neighboring porches and porticoes, one could find comfort and the companionship of friends. Here one could discuss the policy of Pericles, the art of Phidias, the plays of Sophocles, the ideas of Anaxagoras and the sophists, or engage in talk of a lighter strain. A great deal of the intellectual culture of Athens was developed by this kind of social intercourse, which we might call the " society of the street."

Social and Political Clubs. — Another feature of the social life of Athens is seen in the organization of clubs. These grew out of the early custom of forming parties, like picnics, at which each person contributed his portion of the viands. But in time they came to be permanent organizations of persons, made up generally of young men, who shared in the expense of maintaining the club. The club was organized primarily for social purposes, to cultivate companionship; and one of its features was a stated dinner or banquet given perhaps once a month. But from the social clubs there grew up political clubs, made up usually of aristocratic young men, devoted to the interest of the oligarchical party; and they came to exercise some influence upon the political life of Athens.

The Banquet and Symposium. — The banquet was not simply a special feature of the social clubs; it was a general feature of Athenian society. As there were no places of public amusement open after sunset, the banquet was the chief form of entertainment for the evening. It was generally a dinner

SYMPOSIUM

party given by a gentleman at his own house to his friends. It differed from the ordinary dinner in being more elaborate and in being restricted to men, and also in being followed by a "symposium." The character of the symposium varied, of course, with the character and culture of the guests. With the most highly cultivated, it was indeed a "feast of reason and flow of soul," accompanied as it was by refined conversation, dashes of oratory, sparks of wit, relieved by rehearsals from the poets and the music of the flute or lyre. A less cultivated class would be entertained by enigmas and riddles, jests and jokes at the expense of friends, and games of skill or chance. With the most convivial and least cultivated, the symposium might descend to ribaldry, the singing of boisterous songs; and with the exhaustion of their own resources of entertainment, the guests might be amused by professional dancers, jugglers, and contortionists, who helped to while away the merry hours. The symposium was in the charge of a toastmaster selected by the guests. He directed the amount of wine to be drunk, and the other features of the evening, and upon him depended to a great degree the character of the entertainment. The symposium was an expression of the social and intellectual culture of the Greek people.

IV. AMUSEMENTS AND ATHLETIC GAMES

The Greek Fondness for Amusements. — If we should visit Athens at the time of Pericles we should find that the life of the average citizen was a life of comparative leisure. He had slaves to do all his ordinary work, while he sought diversion and recreation. It was not regarded as the correct thing for a gentleman to engage in a trade or even in commercial business. The poorer classes either engaged in farming outside the city, or loitered about the courts waiting to be drawn on a jury. But there was no man, high or low, who did not enjoy " a good time." Even the great religious festivals devoted to the worship of the gods, afforded an opportunity for human pleasures. Such days were not merely holydays but holidays. All the people — men, women, and children, and even the slaves — were expected to drop their ordinary work, whatever it might be, and join in the crowd of pleasure seekers. It was on such occasions that the theater was open and the men of Athens gathered to be entertained by the tragedies of Sophocles or amused by the comedies of Aristophanes.

The Gymnasium and Athletic Sports. — As we have already visited the Acropolis, with its wonderful buildings, and the theater, with its stirring plays, and of course the Agora, which was the " civic center " of Athens, let us now go to the Lyceum, the Academy, or some other place for exercise, outside the walls. Such a place was called a "gymnasium," but we find that it was not, as we might expect, a room filled with exercising machines of various kinds. It was a large, open area, shaded with trees and surrounded with a beautiful colonnade and seats for visitors.

The gymnasium was at first simply a school for physical education. Here boys and young men were taught by an experienced instructor how to develop symmetrical bodies. Exercise in the open air under the rays of the sun, without clothing, gave them the ruddy glow of health and well-developed muscles. Among the exercises were contests in running, jumping, wrestling, and so forth. These became interesting, and men from the city with nothing else to do, came to watch the boys' games. The gymnasium, open every day as it was, came to be a place of public resort. The sophists came there to find pupils. Other teachers and philosophers came there and gave lectures to any who desired to hear them. And so the gymnasia rivaled the Agora as centers of everyday life; the gymnasium was a sort of popular university as well as a place of public amusement.

The Stadium and Public Exhibitions. — We can see that the great interest shown in athletic sports would require a special place in which to give public exhibitions. And so the "stadium" was built for this purpose. We must keep in mind the fact that what we are learning about Athens was true of nearly every other Greek city. Every important city had its stadium. It was laid out on a level piece of ground, if possible near a sloping hillside with terraces upon which the spectators could sit. If there was no convenient hill for this purpose, an earthen embankment would be thrown up. In front of the spectators was the athletic field, which was made long enough for the chief foot race — a dash of about 200 yards, or 600 feet. It was also wide enough to accommodate a number of runners without interference. Lines were drawn for the start and the finish. In the longer foot races the competitors ran back and forth between the starting and finishing lines — each around his own post and not

all around an oval end, as was the case in much later times.
The longer races ranged from six to twenty-four laps, — that
is, from about three quarters of a mile to nearly three miles.
Sometimes the races were run in armor — each man wearing a
helmet and carrying a shield upon his left arm.　The stadium

STADIUM AT ATHENS (Rebuilt in 1896–1906)

was used not simply for foot racing, but for all the athletic events
which made up the public exhibitions during the time of the great
festivals.

The Five Athletic Events. — In every public exhibition
which took place in the stadium one of the most important features was what was called the "pentath'lon." This was a
series of five contests which took place on the same day
between the same contestants — the winner of three out of
five being declared the victor. It consisted of the following
events:

(1) *Running*. The Greeks always regarded the foot race as a very important feature of athletics (picture, p. 122). We are not told which kind of foot race formed a part of this series; but it was probably the 200-yard dash.

(2) *Jumping*. The Greeks had what we call the long jump, — either the standing or running jump. In their contests they did not have the high jump or the pole jump, as we do. But they did use either stone or metal weights, as we to-day use the dumb-bells to as-sist in jumping. There is a record that a certain Greek athlete once jumped 55 feet. But as this is a physical impossibility, it is supposed to mean a "hop, step, and jump," with which we are familiar. In other public contests, how-ever, the jump was prob-ably the standing long jump.

"Discobolus" of Myron

(3) *Discus throwing*. The discus was a circular piece of stone or bronze, which required the utmost strength of the athlete to throw to a distance. Each contestant was required to use a discus of the same size and weight as the others, and the winner was judged by the distance covered, which was determined by a measuring rod.

(4) *Javelin throwing*. The javelin was a simple pole or rod, eight or ten feet long, with a leather thong or loop near the center,

into which the fingers might be inserted to prevent the hand from slipping. The contest was decided by the distance covered rather than by the accuracy of aim.

(5) *Wrestling.* There were two kinds of wrestling, — the "upright" and the "ground." In the upright wrestle the contestants stood face to face, and each tried in any way to seize his opponent and throw him fairly to the ground. In the ground wrestle the combatants struggled with each other after the throw, to compel one or the other to "give up," — that is, to acknowledge that he was beaten. It was only the upright wrestling which formed a part of the pentathlon.[1] The final victor in these athletic games received as a trophy an olive wreath; this was regarded as more honorable than any royal crown.

THE WRESTLERS — GROUND WRESTLE

The Hippodrome: Horse and Chariot Racing. — Athletic games took place in the stadium. Besides these games there was another kind of contest, which was given in the "hippodrome," consisting of horse and chariot racing. The hippodrome in different cities might be near the stadium, or at a distance. It was simply a race course laid out upon a level piece of ground, and would remind us of the race track at one of our country fairs. If possible it was placed near a hillside upon which the spectators might stand. At either end of the track was a pillar to mark the place where the horses and chariots turned. The distance around the track was little less than a mile. Women were not

[1] Boxing was regarded by the Greeks as a brutal sport, fit only for professional pugilists, and was excluded from the public exhibitions.

present at the hippodrome races, but they were allowed to enter their horses in them.

In the horse races, then as now, the horses were ridden by trained jockeys who were paid for their services. The chariot races were more important and afforded the greatest excitement to the spectators. They were of two kinds, the one with two-horse chariots and the other with four. The two-horse chariots ran eight times around the course, and the four-horse chariots ran twelve times around. These were the most exciting because they were the most dangerous. The crowd watched with intense eagerness, especially when the drivers were rounding the turning posts, expecting to see a chariot

FOUR-HORSE CHARIOT
(Coin of Syracuse)

overturned by striking against the pillar or colliding with other chariots.

The Pan-Athenian Festival. — The greatest and most splendid holiday, or rather series of holidays, celebrated by the Athenians was the Pan-Athenian Festival. This was given in honor of their most revered and guardian deity, Athena. It occurred once in four years, in the month of July. It extended over several days, and attracted visitors from the whole Ægean world. It was the occasion when the festive life of Athens reached its highest expression.

The festival opened with competitions in poetry and music, which lasted for three days. They were given in the new music hall—the Ode'um—built by Pericles for this purpose, near the theater of Dionysus, at the east end of the Acropolis (map, p. 190). Here were given recitations from the Homeric poems, as they had recently been collected by Pisistratus (p. 131). The recitations were given in a singing tone, and accompanied by the lyre or the flute. Such recitations appealed to the new spirit of patriotism which, as we have seen, followed the Persian wars (p. 188). This part of the festival program was relieved by competitions between trained musicians, who played upon the lyre and the flute. We can readily see that such exercises were inspiring, and a fit opening to the great festival.

The next two or three days were of a more festive character, and devoted to the exhibition of the popular games that have already been described. They were now witnessed not simply by the residents of the city and the outlying towns of Attica, but by the crowds that had flocked to Athens from the neighboring states and from the islands of the Ægean. The crowds first gathered in the stadium to witness the athletic sports and to compare the skill of the boys and men of Athens with that of their own athletes whom they had left at home. At the close of the athletic games, which lasted for two days, the people repaired on the next day in still greater crowds to the hippodrome to see the jockeys compete with their riding horses, and the more exciting contests in the chariot races. Besides the usual prize, the victor in the athletic and equestrian events of the Pan-Athenian festival received "a richly decorated amphora,"

PAN-ATHENIAN VASE
(6th century B.C.)

or vase. On one side of this vase was a figure of Athena brandishing her shield and spear.

On the next day after the horse races — this being the seventh day of the festival — there were some exhibitions that would appear quite strange to us. These were chiefly war dances and a military competition. The most celebrated war dance was called the Pyrrhic dance. Its orgin is unknown, but it had probably descended from barbarous times, when such a dance was a signal for actual warfare — as among our American Indians. At Athens it was performed by men in armor, imitating

PYRRHIC DANCE

the positions and quick motions of persons actually engaged in battle. The military competition was a sort of sham fight between two squadrons of cavalry drawn from different tribes. The day closed with the torch race, which took place at night. The runners, boys or young men, started from a point outside the city with torches lighted, and raced to a finishing point within the city. The game was to reach the finish line first, with the torch still lighted. The race might be made between single competitors or between teams. In the latter case each team would be arranged in relays, the torch being passed on from one member to another. The effort of the runners to keep their torches lighted while racing at full speed was the cause of great amusement among the spectators.

But the most important day of the whole festival was that of the great Pan-Athenian procession. We have some idea of the character and splendor of this procession from the frieze of the Parthenon (p. 194). Its object was to convey to the temple of Athena, as an offering to the goddess, her new robe (*peplos*), embroidered by certain selected maidens of Athens. It contained the finest needlework capable of being produced by feminine hands, interwoven with scenes representing the victories of the goddess over her enemies. It was regarded as especially sacred; it was carried in the procession not by the hands of men, but suspended from the mast of a ship, the most conspicuous object of an admiring populace. In the procession the whole population of Athens was represented, not only that of the city but that of the Athenian colonies and allies, who sent their official deputies, bringing their offerings to the goddess. The long line of the procession started from near the Dipylon gate (map, p. 190) and passed through the streets of the city to the Acropolis, where the robe was carried into the Parthenon and placed upon the statue of Athena.

Selections for Reading

Knowlton, Topic A 10, "Age of Pericles; Life of the Athenians" (1).[1]

Mahaffy, Old Greek Life, Ch. 4, "Public Life of the Greek Citizen" (11).

—— Social Life, Chs. 6–8, "Greeks of the Attic Age" (11).

Gulick, Ch. 3, "Dwelling Houses"; Ch. 7, "Occupations of Young Men"; Ch. 14, "Social Life and Entertainments" (11).

Abbott, Pericles, Ch. 18, "Athens of Pericles; Manners and Society" (27).

Blümner, Ch. 4, "Marriage and Women" (11).

Guhl and Koner, pp. 115–118, "The Hippodrome"; pp. 159–183, "Dress"; pp. 272–275, "The Dance" (11).

Tucker, Ch. 8, "Woman's Life and Fashions"; Ch. 12, "Festivals and the Theater" (11).

Becker, Scene the First, "The Friends of Youth"; Scene the Sixth, "The Banquet" (11).

Gardiner, Greek Athletic Sports, Ch. 11, "Athletic Festivals at Athens"; Ch. 12, "The Stadium"; Ch. 21, "The Hippodrome" (11).

Whibley, Companion, Ch. 7, "Private Antiquities" (11).

Special Study

THE GREEK HOUSE AND HOME LIFE. — Mahaffy, "Old Greek Life," Ch. 3 (11); Tucker, Ch. 5 (11); Gulick, Ch. 3 (11); Blümner, Ch. 5 (11); Guhl and Koner, pp. 78–84 (11); Harper's Dictionary, "Domus" (11).

[1] The figure in parenthesis refers to the number of the topic in the Appendix, where a fuller title of the book will be found.

CHAPTER XVI

THE DECLINE OF THE GREEK STATES

Synopsis

I. The Peloponnesian War (431–404 B.C.). — Beginning of the War. — The War under Pericles: his Funeral Oration. — The Plague and the Death of Pericles. — The War and Peace Parties. — Alcibiades and the Sicilian Expedition. — Alcibiades and His Intrigues with Persia. — Last Years of the War. — The Fall of Athens.

II. The Supremacy of Sparta (404–379 B.C.). — The Despotic Rule of Sparta. — Persia and the "March of the Ten Thousand." — War between Persia and Sparta. — The Corinthian War: Peace of Antalcidas.

III. The Ascendancy of Thebes (379–362 B.C.). — The Revolution at Thebes. — Overthrow of the Spartan Power: Battle of Leuctra. —Temporary Supremacy of Thebes. — Failure of the Grecian States System.

I. The Peloponnesian War (431–404 B.C.)

Beginning of the War. — The peace that Pericles had made with Sparta was expected to last for thirty years (p. 176). But it really lasted for less than half that time. Sparta and her allies were again becoming jealous of Athens. They saw her now at the head of a wide empire that extended over the Ægean. They saw her ships controlling the commerce of every sea. They saw her magnificent buildings rising on the Acropolis, her artists and writers receiving the highest honor, her statesmen taking the lead in Grecian affairs, and her treasury overflowing with gold. But Sparta too had been growing strong. She had gathered about her the cities of the Peloponnesus, and had taken from Athens many of the cities of central Greece. Sparta prided herself on the best disciplined army in the world. It needed but a spark to light this jealousy into a flame. The spark was furnished by Corinth, a member of the Peloponnesian

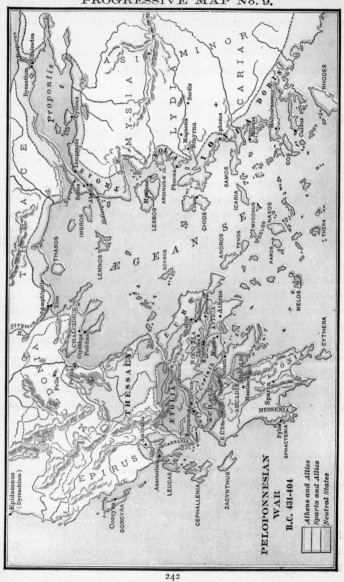

PELOPONNESIAN
WAR
B.C. 431-404

Athens and Allies
Sparta and Allies
Neutral States

League. Corinth complained to Sparta that Athens was med-
dling with some of the Corinthian colonies, and that Athens
had thus broken the Thirty Years' Peace. A meeting of the
Peloponnesian states was called at Corinth. It was there decided to take the part of Corinth and declare war upon Athens.
Thus began the so-called Peloponnesian War, which lasted,
with some intermissions, for twenty-seven years.

The War under Pericles : his Funeral Oration. — Pericles
was about sixty years of age when the war began ; but the
policy that he recommended was approved by the people. He
saw that the Athenian army could not cope with the Spartan
army in the open field, and so the people of Attica were called
upon to find a safe retreat within the walls of the city. It was
a sore distress for them to watch from the city walls their burning homes. To counteract the Spartan invasion in Attica Pericles
sent the Athenian fleet from the harbor to destroy the towns
along the Peloponnesian coast. Thus the war was carried on —
a series of attacks by land and counter attacks by sea. One of
the most interesting features of the early part of the war was
the celebration in honor of the soldiers who had fallen in battle.
This might remind us of our own " Memorial Day." Pericles
was chosen as the orator. His speech is reported by Thucydides.
It is a description of the greatness of Athens, and a eulogy upon
the heroic men who had given up their lives for their country.
We are reminded of Lincoln's Gettysburg Address by these
eloquent words :

"I would have you day by day fix your eyes upon the greatness of Athens,
until you become filled with the love of her. . . . Bear in mind that this
empire has been acquired by men who knew their duty and had the courage
to do it, and who in the hour of conflict feared to perform a dishonorable
act. . . . Remember that the whole earth is a sepulcher of honorable
men. Not only are they commemorated by columns and inscriptions in
their own country, but in foreign lands there remains an unwritten memorial
of them, graven not on stone, but in the hearts of men. Make them your
examples, and esteeming courage to be freedom, and freedom to be happiness, do not shun the perils of war."

The Plague and the Death of Pericles. — While the Athenians were trying to carry out the policy of Pericles, the city was visited by a terrible pestilence. It is said that this plague was brought from Egypt. But it was especially severe in Athens on account of the unsanitary way in which the people were living. The city was crowded with people who had fled for refuge from the neighboring towns. They quartered themselves as best they could — in tents, and on the roofs of houses, in the open squares, under the fortifications, on the sides of the road leading to the Piræus — living under the most unhealthful conditions, with a scarcity of water supply. The plague struck the city in the middle of the summer, and spread like wildfire. Thucydides has given a vivid description of the horrible condition of the city at this time. The victims of the epidemic were seized with despair. Persons refused to minister to the sufferings of their nearest relatives, and left them to perish. It was said that nearly one fourth of the population was carried away.

The most distinguished victim of the plague was Pericles. It had already taken from him his two sons, his sister, and most of his intimate friends. In his death Athens lost her greatest statesman. He was a man born to rule. He was distinguished for his calm and noble presence. His friends spoke of him as having the majesty of Zeus. His father was Xanthippus, who won the naval battle at Mycale (p. 164). His mother was the niece of the great political reformer, Clisthenes. He received the best education the time afforded; and one of his teachers was the noted philosopher Anaxagoras, who inspired him with high moral aims. He was a patriot, and devoted his whole life to promote the interests of his native state. Although a noble by birth he took up the cause of the people. He strengthened the Athenian democracy, while he maintained the authority of Athens over her maritime empire. He was a great soldier, a great orator, and a great statesman. But even more than this, he was the great patron of Athenian culture. It was due to him more than to any other one man that Athens became not only the " school of Hellas," as he wished it to be, but, in a certain sense, the teacher of the world in philosophy, literature, and art.

The War and Peace Parties. — After the death of Pericles Athens became the prey of demagogues. There were those who wished to carry on the war to the bitter end. There were others who wished to forsake it altogether. The great body of the people swayed back and forth, drifting from one leader to another according to their passing whims. The man who aspired to the position of Pericles as the leader of the " war party " was Cleon, a coarse leather dealer, a bold demagogue, and a loud orator. Opposed to him, as leader of the " peace party," was Nicias (nĭsh'ĭ-as), a well-bred man, a conservative leader, but over-cautious and devoid of energy.

The war between the states was carried on with merciless cruelty. This was true both of the Athenians and of the Spartans. The capture of a town was the signal for a general slaughter. Women and children were reduced to slavery. When the inhabitants of Mitylene, on the island of Lesbos (map, p. 242), revolted from Athens, a decree was passed at the instigation of Cleon that every one should be put to death, and a ship was dispatched to put the decree into effect. On the next day the decree was changed to apply only to the leaders, and another ship with the swiftest rowers was sent to overtake the first and carry the second order. But under the last order over a thousand persons were put to death. The terrible war dragged on. In a battle at Amphip'olis, in Chalcidice (map, p. 242), the Athenian general, Cleon, and the Spartan general, Bras'idas, were both killed. The leader of the peace party, Nicias, now came forward and made a new treaty with Sparta, called the " Peace of Nicias." This lasted but a short time.

Alcibiades and the Sicilian Expedition. — At this time appeared one of the most brilliant and unprincipled characters that Athens ever produced, namely, Alcibi'ades. He united in his character the ability of a statesman and the conscience of a traitor. His early life was a life of dissipation. Fascinating in person, descended from a noble family, a kinsman of

ALCIBIADES

Pericles, a pupil of Socrates, he became the worst kind of political adventurer, — selfish, cunning, and treacherous. Under his influence the Athenians were lured into an expedition which proved the most disastrous in their history.

The dazzling scheme which this new war champion held up before the eyes of the Athenians was the conquest of Syracuse, in Sicily.

Syracuse was at war with another city of Sicily, which had asked Athens for aid. The conquest of Syracuse would open the way for a new empire in the West. "It is impossible for us," said Alcibiades to the Assembly, "to mark out the limits of our dominion; and as our policy compels us to continue the plan of reducing others, let us make this expedition and humble the pride of Sparta and the allies, by showing that we care not for the present treaty; at any rate, let us conquer the Syracusans if we do not extend our rule over the whole of Hellas" (Thucydides, VI., 16–18). By such flattering words the scheme of Alcibiades became the policy of Athens. An immense fleet was prepared under the command of three generals, one of whom was Alcibiades himself. No sooner had the fleet begun its operations against Syracuse, than an order came from Athens commanding Alcibiades to return to answer the charge of sacrilege. In one night before the sailing of the fleet it was found that numerous pillars of Hermes set up in different parts

PILLAR OF
HERMES

of the city as a protection against evil, had been mutilated — an act charged against Alcibiades. He did not dare to face the charge, but fled to Sparta and lent his aid in conducting the war against his own country.

After two years, the expedition of the Athenians against Syracuse proved a most disastrous failure. Their fleet was destroyed in the harbor of Syracuse. Their army was annihilated in a desperate attempt to retreat by land. Their generals were condemned to death. "Thus ended," says Thucydides, "the greatest undertaking of this war, and the most disastrous for the Athenians; for they suffered no common defeat, but were absolutely annihilated — army, fleet, and all — and of the many thousands who went away, only a handful ever saw their homes again" (VII., 87).

Alcibiades and his Intrigues with Persia. — But the arch-traitor had not yet finished his treacherous career. He tried now to stir up a revolt among the Athenian cities on the Asiatic coast. He induced the Persians to assist these cities in their revolt against Athens. The Athenian empire was now threatened with ruin through the united efforts of Sparta and Persia. In face of this combined opposition the Athenians struggled to maintain their authority. They sent their fleets across the Ægean Sea, where they were obliged to meet the strong fleets of Persia, their ancient enemy.

Alcibiades now began to be tired of the simple life of the Spartans, which offered too small a field for his depraved tastes. The Spartans at last became suspicious of his loyalty, and brought charges against him, which he had no desire to face. Fearing for his life, this man who had already turned traitor to his native country, now turned traitor to his adopted country, and fled from Sparta. He took up his residence at the luxurious court of Tissapher'nes, the Persian governor at Sardis (map, p. 242). For a time at least he seemed to be a loyal friend of Persia. He assured the governor that it would be for the interests of Persia not to take sides with either Sparta or Athens, but let them wear each other out. The Persian authority might then be extended over all the Greek cities.

Last Years of the War. — But the strangest part of this strange story was the effort of Alcibiades to return once more as a citizen to Athens. He was now under sentence of death. He induced the Athenians to change their form of government, putting it under a " Council of Four Hundred," which might revoke the sentence against him. He desired to do some service to Athens that would entitle him to return. He got into the good graces of the generals of the fleet and was appointed its commander. He now turned traitor to Persia, and gained some notable victories over the Persian and Spartan fleets. But on an unfortunate day, during his temporary absence, the Athenian fleet was defeated by the new Spartan admiral, Lysan'der. For this failure Alcibiades was deposed from his command. Some years after, this remarkable and treacherous man was assassinated by his enemies. The last battle of the Peloponnesian War was fought (405 B.C.) in the Hellespont near the mouth of a little river called Ægospot'ami (" Goat's Streams "). A new Spartan fleet had been built with the aid of Persian gold furnished by the younger Cyrus, the new Persian governor in Asia Minor. With the new armament Lysander captured the entire Athenian fleet, and this event destroyed the maritime power of Athens. Lysander followed up his victory by reducing the cities on the Hellespont and Bosporus. The Athenian allies fell away, and nothing was now left for Sparta to do but to reduce the city of Athens itself.

The Fall of Athens (404 B.C.). — After a short time Lysander blockaded the Piræus; and the Spartan army encamped before the walls of the city. Without money, ships, allies, or food supply, Athens refused to surrender. It was only starvation that brought the city to terms. Corinth and Thebes demanded that the city be totally destroyed. But Sparta refused to destroy a city that had done so much for Greece in the past. Athens was, however, required to destroy the Long Walls and the fortifications of the Piræus, and to become a subject ally of Sparta. Accepting these conditions, Athens opened her gates to the enemy, and the Athenian empire was no more.

Thus ended the Peloponnesian war, which had lasted for twenty-seven years. It had desolated nearly every part of the Greek world ; and, in spite of the courage displayed, it had revealed some of the weakest and worst phases of the Greek character — political jealousy, local self-interest, deceit, and cruelty.

II. The Supremacy of Sparta (404–379 B.C.)

The Despotic Rule of Sparta. — Sparta now succeeded for a time to the empire which Athens was compelled to give up. The cities of Greece had been called upon to revolt against Athens in order to obtain their liberties. But they soon found that the tyranny of Athens was light compared with the despotism of Sparta. As Sparta was the patron of oligarchy, she compelled the cities to give up their democratic governments. A military governor, called a " harmost," was placed over most of them ; and whatever civil authority there was to be exercised was placed in a board of ten persons, called a " dec'archy." Under such a government the property and lives of the people could not be safe. The imperial policy of Sparta was determined largely by the influence of Lysander, who, on account of his recent victories, was now the leading man in the Spartan state.

In Athens there was established a board of thirty oligarchs — who have received the name of the " Thirty Tyrants " (404–403 B.C.). Under their leader, Crit'ias, their rule was harsh and oppressive and resulted in anarchy and a reign of terror. Citizens were put to death, and property was confiscated without mercy. It was only by a popular revolution led by the patriot Thrasybu'lus that the Thirty were deposed and a democratic form of government reëstablished. This was sufficient to show that the imperial rule of Sparta would not long be tolerated by the cities of Greece.

Persia and the " March of the Ten Thousand." — While Sparta was trying to establish her authority over the cities in

Greece and Asia Minor, Cyrus the Younger, the Persian governor of Asia Minor, aspired to place himself on the Persian throne in place of his brother, Artaxerx'es. He enlisted in his service about ten or twelve thousand Asiatic Greeks, besides a large number of native troops. With these he pushed his way through Asia Minor, Syria, and Mesopotamia toward the

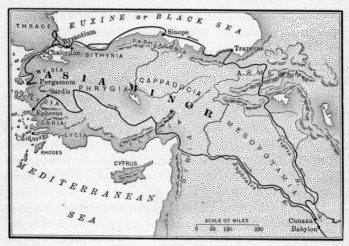

MARCH OF THE TEN THOUSAND

Persian capital at Susa. He met Artaxerxes in a battle at Cunax'a, near Babylon. The Greek forces defeated the great army of the king; but Cyrus, their commander, was killed, and the other leaders were entrapped and put to death. The Greeks then chose new leaders, chief among whom was Xenophon, the historian. They retreated up the banks of the Tigris River, harassed by the Persian army, — through the snows of Armenia, suffering from cold and hunger, — and finally along the shores of the Euxine to the friendly city of Chalcedon (kal-sē'don) and so to the Ægean Sea. This famous " March of the Ten Thousand," described by Xenophon in his " Anabasis," revealed the weakness of the Persian empire.

It also showed the superiority of the Greek soldiers, and led directly to a conflict between Persia and Sparta.

War between Persia and Sparta. — The rebellious attempt of Cyrus, assisted as it was by Greeks, aroused the wrath of the Persian king. He therefore appointed his faithful general, Tissaphernes, governor of Asia Minor, with orders to reduce all the Grecian cities on the coast. Sparta now regarded herself as the protector of the Greeks, and answered their call for help. The war against Persia which followed was carried on for six years, — at first under inferior generals, but finally under the able Spartan king Agesila'us. This commander defeated Tissaphernes, recovered the Asiatic cities, carried the war into the enemy's country, and threatened to overthrow the empire itself. To relieve his empire from the presence of the Spartan army, the Persian monarch sent an emissary to Greece with bags of gold to stir up a revolt among the subjects of Sparta. The dangers at home compelled the Spartans to recall Agesilaus from Asia, and the conquest of Persia was delayed for more than half a century.

The Corinthian War : Peace of Antalcidas. — When Agesilaus reached Sparta, he found a large number of Greek cities united in an attempt to throw off the Spartan yoke. Thebes, Corinth, Athens, and Argos had formed a league to free themselves from Spartan rule. The war which ensued is called the " Corinthian war," because it was waged mostly in the vicinity of the isthmus. Besides many engagements fought on land, a decisive naval battle was fought near Cnidus on the southwest coast of Asia Minor (map, p. 250). In this battle the Greek allies, under the Athenian general Conon, and now assisted by the Persians, practically destroyed the maritime power of Sparta. Conon freed the cities on the Asiatic coasts from the Spartan power, and then sailed to Athens. Under his direction, the fortifications of the Piræus and the Long Walls, which had been razed after the Peloponnesian war, were rebuilt.

The stress of the war was so great that Sparta was willing

to come to terms with Persia. She accordingly sent an ambassador, named Antal'cidas, to the Persian court with the request that the king settle the affairs of Greece. The king willingly accepted this office, and dictated the terms of peace — namely, (1) that all the Greek cities of Asia Minor should be turned over to Persia; (2) that the central islands of the Ægean, — Imbros, Lemnos, Scyros (map, p. 242), — should remain as heretofore under Athens; and (3) that all the states of Greece proper should not form alliances with one another, but should remain " free and independent." This was the so-called " Peace of Antalcidas " (387 B.C.). It was, in fact, a humiliating submission to the dictation of Persia.

Now that the alliances against her had been broken up, Sparta once more began her aggressive policy. She even seized the citadel of Thebes, and placed within it a Spartan garrison. Such acts of aggression led, as we shall soon see, to the uprising of Thebes, with other states, and to the overthrow of the Spartan supremacy.

III. THE ASCENDANCY OF THEBES (379–362 B.C.)

The Revolution at Thebes (379 B.C.). — The story of the revolution which resulted in freeing Thebes and the rest of Greece from Spartan rule, centers about the names of two great Theban patriots — Pelop'idas and Epaminon'das. These men had been boon companions from their youth. Epaminondas had once saved the life of his friend. It was Pelopidas who ventured upon the dangerous task of freeing his native city. He knew that this could be done only by means of some stratagem. He was now an exile living in Athens. Here he found six other brave Theban exiles who were willing to risk their lives with him. Disguised as peasants they stole into Thebes, and found refuge at the house of a friend.

One night the Spartan officers were holding a lively banquet, where the wine flowed freely and the air was filled with rollicking songs. In the midst of their hilarity, it was proposed to receive a party of beautiful young women who would add to the merriment of the feast. The women, decked with flowing robes and adorned with richly embroidered veils, mingled freely with the drunken banqueters. But when the Spartan officers ventured to lift their veils to gaze upon their lovely faces, they were met by dagger thrusts — for the party of beautiful women proved to be Pelopidas and his fellow-conspirators in disguise. The morning found the people in a revolution. Proclamations were issued, announcing that Thebes was free. The Spartan garrison was driven from the city. The conspirators were crowned with wreaths, and Pelopidas became one of the chief men of the state.

Under the guidance of Epaminondas the other cities of Bœotia gained their independence, and formed a new Bœotian confederacy to withstand the power of Sparta.

Overthrow of the Spartan Power : Battle of Leuctra (371 B.C.). — Sparta was alarmed at the rising power of Thebes. She therefore sent an army into Bœotia to destroy the newly formed confederacy, but was defeated in the memorable battle at Leuctra, near Thebes. The ruling spirit in Bœotia was Epaminondas, the great Theban patriot, whose name is one of the most distinguished among Grecian statesmen and generals. To him is due the new arrangement of the Grecian phalanx which won the battle of Leuctra. He seems to have discovered one of the great principles of successful warfare — that is, to be stronger than the enemy at the point of contact. The old Greek phalanx was arranged in lines eight men deep. The Spartan army was so formed at Leuctra. Epaminondas also arranged the main part of his line in the same way. But on his left wing, which he intended to be the point of contact,

BATTLE OF LEUCTRA

he arranged the phalanx in the form of an irresistible column fifty men deep, guarded on the extreme left by an invincible body of cavalry, known as the "Sacred Band." In this way he crushed the Spartan right wing; and the rest of his army was pushed forward to complete the victory. The battle of Leuctra had two important effects: first, it introduced a new feature into ancient warfare, which was afterward employed by the Macedonians; second, it overthrew the Spartan power and insured for the time being the ascendancy of Thebes.

Temporary Supremacy of Thebes (371–362 B.C.). — The policy of Epaminondas was to make Thebes the supreme power in Greece. He completely alienated Athens by attempting to establish the Theban power over the Athenian allies; and he even called upon Persia to aid him in his purpose. To extend Theban influence into the Peloponnesus, Epaminondas invaded this territory, and delivered several states from Spartan control.

While Thebes was thus extending her power to the south under Epaminondas, she was also extending her power to the north under Pelopidas. She brought Thessaly under her authority, and even gained some influence with Macedonia. It was not long before troubles arose again in the Peloponnesus. Epaminondas again invaded the country and met the Spartans and their allies at Mantine'a (362 B.C.), where he gained a victory; but at this battle Epaminondas was killed. As the Thebans, without their leader, were unable to follow up their victory, peace was established. With the decline of the Theban power, Athens was once more regarded as the leading city of Greece.

Failure of the Grecian States System. — If we look back over the history of Greece for the last hundred years, we must be impressed by two great facts — on the one hand, the wonderful progress that was made in her intellectual life, in her art, her literature, and philosophy; on the other hand, the pitiful failure that was made in the development of a national state. In one sense, indeed, the Greeks formed a single nation. They all had practically the same language, the same religion, the same customs, the same ideas of physical perfection, the same love of liberty. But they did not possess a great capacity for political organization. It is true that they were able to develop a city state with a certain amount of self-government, far in advance of the Oriental world. But when they attempted to organize these cities under a common government they failed.

Their various leagues failed, because under the predominance of one city the rights of the others were not respected. Athens had failed to respect the equal rights of her allies. Sparta had ruled her subjects with despotic authority. With all their love of liberty the Greeks failed to recognize that other principle of a stable and peaceful government — the respect for a higher law based upon the common welfare.

Selections for Reading

Knowlton, Topic A 11, "The Peloponnesian War" (1).[1]

Seignobos, pp. 156–159, "Strife among the Greek States" (1).

Shuckburgh, Ch. 16, "The Peloponnesian War to the Peace of Nicias"; Ch. 17, "The Sicilian Expedition and Fall of Athens" (10).

Smith, Wm., Ch. 25, "Causes of the Peloponnesian War"; Ch. 10, "The Supremacy of Thebes" (10).

Oman, Ch. 26, "Outbreak of the Peloponnesian War and its Causes"; Ch. 32, "Expedition of the Athenians to Syracuse" (10).

Bury, Ch. 11, "Decline and Downfall of the Athenian Empire" (10).

Allcroft, Vol. III., Ch. 1, "Introductory" (comparison of Athens and Sparta); Ch. 6, "Brasidas and Cleon" (10).

Curtius, Vol. III., Vol. IV., Ch. 1, "Athens under the Thirty" (10).

Harper's Dictionary, "Exercitus" (military system of the Greeks) (11).

Plutarch, "Alcibiades," "Lysander," "Nicias," "Agesilaus," "Pelopidas," (26).

Thucydides, Bk. II., Chs. 35–46 (funeral oration of Pericles); Bks. VI., VII. (account of the Sicilian expedition) (17).

Special Study

THE "MARCH OF THE TEN THOUSAND." — Smith, Wm., Ch. 36 (10); Oman, pp. 417–420 (10); Bury, Ch. 12, § 2 (10); Allcroft, Vol. III., Ch. 2 (10); Curtius, Vol. IV., pp. 185–192 (10); Holm, Vol. III., pp. 2–6 (10).

[1] The figure in parenthesis refers to the number of the topic in the Appendix, where a fuller title of the book will be found.

CHAPTER XVII

THE MACEDONIANS AND ALEXANDER'S EMPIRE

Synopsis

I. THE RISE OF MACEDONIA UNDER PHILIP (359–336 B.C.). — The New Epoch in Greek History. — Macedonia and the Greeks. — Philip II. and his "War-Machine." — Philip of Macedon as a Statesman. — The Interference of Philip in Grecian Affairs. — Demosthenes and Philip. — Battle of Chæronea: the End of Greek Freedom. — The Congress of Corinth; Death of Philip.

II. THE EMPIRE OF ALEXANDER (336–323 B.C.). — Beginning of Alexander's Career. — Asia Minor; Battle of the Granicus. — Syria; Battle of Issus and Siege of Tyre. — Egypt; Founding of Alexandria. — Central Persia; Battle of Arbela. — The Far East; Battle of the Hydaspes. — Death and Character of Alexander. — The Civilizing Work of Alexander.

III. DISSOLUTION OF ALEXANDER'S EMPIRE (323–301 B.C.). — The Wars of Succession. — Kingdom of the Seleucidæ; Syria. — Kingdom of the Ptolemies; Egypt. — Kingdoms in Asia Minor. — Macedonia and the Greek Federations. — Constitution of the Achæan League. — The Struggle of the Leagues. — The Intervention of Rome.

I. THE RISE OF MACEDONIA UNDER PHILIP (359–336 B.C.)

The New Epoch in Greek History. — The failure of the Greek states to develop a national government led to the final overthrow of the very liberties which they were so anxious to preserve. The supremacy which they were unwilling to give to Athens, to Sparta, or to Thebes, they were at last obliged to yield to Macedonia. The rise of Macedonia, and the interference of this new power in the internal affairs of Greece, therefore, marks a new epoch in the history of the Grecian states.

But we shall see that Macedonia established her supremacy not only over the states of Greece, but also over the countries of western Asia; so that Greece and the Orient became united

in a common world-empire. The importance of this new
period lies not only in the establishment of a common political
authority over the countries of the ancient world, but also
in the union of Greece and the Orient in a wider civilization,
which we may call " Græco-Oriental." But first let us see
how this union was accomplished, under the supremacy of
Macedonia and the leadership of Philip II. and Alexander the
Great.

Macedonia and the Greeks. — Macedonia was a country
lying to the north of Thessaly, beyond the Cambu′nian Mountains. The people were remotely related to the Greeks. But
they were still, for the most part, in a semi-barbarous condition,
although they were capable of becoming a strong nation. They
were a hardy race, and had in them the making of good soldiers.
In the highlands they were separated into many tribes, each
under its own chief. But in the lowlands, near the sea, they
had come into contact with the Greek colonies, and had begun
to be more civilized and to have something like a united government. At the time of the Theban supremacy, Macedonia
became so strong and threatening that Pelopidas invaded the
country, checked the ambition of its ruler, and brought the
young prince Philip back to Thebes as a hostage. Philip,
while in bondage, became versed in the civilized arts of Greece,
and especially in the military system of Epaminondas, and thus
became fitted for his future work as the king of Macedonia.

Philip II. and his " War-Machine." — On his return to
Macedonia, Philip was appointed regent of the kingdom at
the age of twenty-three, and in a short time he had himself
proclaimed king. He proved to be a man of wonderful ability,
versed in the best as well as the worst arts of statecraft. He
possessed unusual powers of organization. He was able as a
warrior, and still more able as a wily diplomatist. Like every
other great soldier, Philip knew that military success depends
upon possessing the two great " sinews of war " — a strong
army and a plentiful supply of money.

In forming his army he collected his subjects from all parts of his little kingdom, and placed them under the strictest discipline. He organized them into divisions and subdivisions. He inspired them with his own ambitious spirit. His battle line was formed upon the plan of the Greek phalanx (p. 123); but he strengthened it as Epaminondas had done before him, by making the line sixteen instead of eight men deep. The men were heavy-armed, like the Greek hoplite (p. 123), but

MACEDONIA BEFORE AND AFTER PHILIP II.

the lances of some of the ranks were eighteen feet long. The front of the phalanx presented a projecting forest of bristling spears. Such a body of infantry came to be known the world over as the " Macedonian phalanx." Philip also organized a magnificent body of heavy-armed cavalry made up of the best men of the kingdom. He was especially partial to this branch of the army. The name *Philip* means a " lover of horses." He honored this select body of cavalrymen by calling them his " Companions." In action they became the right arm of his battle line. Moreover, Philip had in his army men who used heavier weapons, which we might call " artillery," for attacking fortified places, — implements for throwing heavy missiles, such as stones and large arrows, to a great distance.

With such a " war-machine," made up of infantry, cavalry, and artillery, Philip was furnished with one of the sinews of war. The other source of military strength is money. This might be used both to equip and supply the army — and also sometimes to conciliate the enemy by bribes. To obtain the money necessary to carry on his campaigns, Philip took possession of the rich gold mines

PHILIP II. (Coin)

in the Thracian mountains. These mines yielded an annual income of about a thousand talents (nearly $1,200,000). Near them he founded a new city, calling it after his own name, Philip'pi.

Philip of Macedon as a Statesman. — Philip began his work by consolidating his own kingdom. At his accession to the throne, Macedonia was an unpretentious little state. It occupied a small strip of territory between the Haliacmon and Axius rivers, with a bit of seacoast on the Thermaic Gulf (map, p. 258). Its capital was a small town, called Pella, near the Greek colonies of Chalcidice. It was threatened on the north by the barbarous tribes of Pæonia and Thrace, on the west by the Illyrians, and on the south by the Greeks through Thessaly. He pushed back the barbarians on the north and west, and conciliated the Greeks by claiming to be their friend and making a treaty with them.

But the great ambition of Philip was to make himself master of Greece. We need not suppose, however, that this was a purely selfish ambition. Philip had a great love and admiration for Greek culture. He entertained Greek artists and Greek philosophers at his court. He had no reason to hate Greece or the Greeks. On the contrary, he looked upon Greece as the seat of the highest culture of the world. But the land of culture which he admired was now distracted by civil wars. It was torn in pieces by mutual hatred and distrust. Was this always to last? He looked back over the past history of Greece, and saw that such had been practically the case for more than a hundred years — in fact, ever since Athens and Sparta had once united to repel the Persians. Ever since that time Greece had been a disunited country. How could it be united? Only by some strong power, able to repress their local differences. Philip believed that it was his mission to bring the cities of Greece under a common authority. This was the vision of a statesman.

But more than this, Philip looked beyond the sea. He saw that the real enemy of Greece was Persia — Persia with its different civilization. It was Persia that was the great foe of Greek culture. It was Persia that was continually fomenting discord among the Greek states. With Greece united, the old-time enemy in Asia might be destroyed. Greek culture, instead of being repressed, might be extended over the East. And then, perhaps, it might advance the civilization of the world. It was such ideas that made Philip of Macedon one of the great world statesmen. We may perhaps hesitate to believe that a mere Macedonian king could have such broad statesmanlike views. Let us then watch his future career, and the inspiration that he gave to his more distinguished son, Alexander. It is possible that this vision of the future did not dawn upon Philip's mind all at once; but there is no doubt that it was clearly defined before his death.

The Interference of Philip in Grecian Affairs. — If we look at the map (p. 258) we see to the east of the old kingdom of Macedonia a remarkable three-pronged peninsula, called then, as it is called to-day, Chalcidice. Philip looked with envy upon this coast line, lying between his little kingdom and the sea. The cities of the peninsula were grouped together in a confederacy with Olyn'thus as their capital. Philip had already taken possession of Amphip'olis on his way to open the gold mines near his new town of Philippi. He now wished to get possession of Olynthus. This would open the way to the whole of Chalcidice, and give him an admirable seaboard.

Before this was accomplished, however, Philip suddenly received a call from Greece to help settle a dispute between certain Greek cities. This was what he desired more than anything else — to interfere in Grecian affairs. The trouble, it seems, was concerning the sacred oracle of Apollo at Delphi, situated in Phocis (map, p. 84). The Phocians had seized certain fields near the temple and used them for raising crops. This was regarded as a terrible sacrilege. The Phocians were summoned before the Amphictyonic council (p. 138), and were fined. They refused to pay the fine, and replied by seizing the treasures of the temple itself. Such a crime should be punished. Thebes, who had no love for the Phocians, took the lead in making war upon them. This was called a " Sacred War." Nearly all the states of Greece were drawn into it. Athens joined the Phocians, and Thebes called upon the Thessalians for help, and the Thessalians in turn called upon Philip. Welcoming the golden opportunity, Philip appeared as the ally of the Greek city of Thebes, and the champion of the Greek god, Apollo. He caused his soldiers to wear laurel wreaths in honor of the god. He became master of Thessaly, and pressed on toward Phocis. But he found the pass of Thermopylæ blocked by an Athenian force. Instead of exposing his own army to slaughter, he deemed it more prudent to retire, and finish his campaigns in the north.

Demosthenes and Philip. — The one great man who now appeared as the defender of Greece against Philip was Demosthenes (p. 214). He had already made a reputation as an orator, and he now assumed the rôle of a statesman. To arouse Greece to a sense of her danger, he delivered the first of a series of famous orations known as " Philippics." Philip was busy in the north, trying to get possession of Olynthus. That city appealed to Athens for aid, and Demosthenes delivered his "Olynthiac orations" to urge the people to make

DEMOSTHENES

war upon Philip and to save the Chalcidian city. His earnest efforts induced the Athenians to declare war, but failed to save the beleaguered town. Olynthus fell (348 B.C.), and with it the whole Chalcidian peninsula. The towns were obliged to pull down their walls, and the inhabitants were reduced to slavery. The kingdom of Philip now extended nearly to the Hellespont on the east, and to the pass of Thermopylæ on the south.

To allay the fears which had been inspired by Demosthenes, Philip consented to a peace with Athens — the Peace of Philoc'-rates (346 B.C.) — in which each party professed friendship for the other and each agreed to respect the other's possessions. Having conciliated Athens, Philip marched to Delphi, dismantled the Phocian towns, scattered their inhabitants in small villages, and received himself the two votes in the Amphictyonic council that hitherto had belonged to Phocis. To extend his influence in Greece, he then formed friendly alliances with a number of the states in the Peloponnesus.

Battle of Chæronea; the End of Greek Freedom (338 B.C.). — Athens was still suspicious of the designs of the Macedonian king. She saw that Philip was threatening to make further aggressions in northern and central Greece. Through the influence of Demosthenes, Athens and Thebes now joined in a final effort to crush the king. But at Chærone'a, in Bœotia, Philip defeated the combined forces of the Grecian allies, and destroyed the last opposition to his power. This battle is generally regarded as marking the loss of Grecian independence. But we can see that the independence of Greece had been gradually declining since the first interference of Philip in Grecian affairs. Greece fell before Macedonia on account of her incapacity to form a united state, like that which Philip had created for his own people.

The Congress of Corinth; Death of Philip. — Philip now proceeded to do for Greece what Greece had failed to do for herself. He called together at Corinth a congress of all the states. This congress is said to have been the most representative body that the Hellenic world had ever seen — Sparta only standing aloof. The king gave to the Greeks a constitution which formed a kind of federal state. Every city was to be free, and to manage its own affairs, and not to be subject to any tribute. The Amphictyonic council was to be the supreme arbiter in the settlement of disputes between the different states. The king was to be the president, and to have the power to declare war and peace. At this congress Philip also revealed his greatest project, which was nothing less than the conquest of Persia, in which Greeks and Macedonians would unite in avenging the wrongs done to Greece since the days of Xerxes. The proposals of the king were accepted, and he was appointed commander in chief of the armies which were to invade the Persian empire. But while making plans for this expedition, Philip was assassinated (336 B.C.), and the completion of his work was left to his son, Alexander the Great.

II. The Empire of Alexander (336–323 B.C.)

Beginning of Alexander's Career. — It is said that the Greek artist Apel'les drew a picture of the young Alexander with a thunderbolt in his hand. This probably expressed the popular idea of the fiery, impetuous youth. The people had heard the story of his taming the wild steed Buceph'alus, which no one else could mount. They had heard of his fierce cavalry charge against the Theban phalanx at the battle of Chæronea. They knew that his mother was a half-barbarian princess, with a fitful temper and a dash of superstition. They had no

doubt heard that the boy had been taught to believe that he was a descendant of Achilles, the hero of the Trojan War. But perhaps they did not know that since he was thirteen years old he had been a faithful pupil of Aristotle, the soundest of the Greek philosophers. The chief credit that the people could give to this young man was that he was the son of their great king, Philip.

At the age of twenty Alexander ascended his father's throne. His first work was to quell the spirit of revolt which seemed everywhere to show itself with the news of his father's death. He put out of the way his possible rivals. He entered Greece and had himself proclaimed commander in chief, as his father had done. He punished the tribes of the north and west which threatened the frontiers of his kingdom. Angered by a Grecian revolt led by Thebes, he wiped that city from the earth, sparing only the temples and the house of the poet Pindar. Having pacified his kingdom in Europe, he was ready to enter upon the conquest of Asia.

ALEXANDER

Asia Minor; Battle of the Granicus (334 B.C.). — The first country to be brought under his control was Asia Minor. He crossed the Hellespont with a small but well-trained army, consisting of thirty thousand infantry and five thousand cavalry. He first visited the plains of Troy, already hallowed in his imagination by the tales of Homer; here he offered a sacrifice to Athena, and paid homage to the tomb of Achilles. His first battle was fought at the Grani'cus (p. 266), a small stream flowing into the Propontis. Here he practically destroyed the whole Persian army, with but a small loss on his own part. The victory at the Granicus was followed by the speedy submission of the cities in Asia Minor. Alexander then moved north to Gordium, the old capital of Phrygia, where he quartered his army for the winter, and

BATTLE OF GRANICUS

a, Macedonian phalanx; *b*, allied cavalry; *c*, companion cavalry; *d*, light infantry; *e*, archers and javelin throwers

according to the well-known story "cut the Gordian knot."

Syria; Battle of Issus and Siege of Tyre (333 B.C.). — The

BATTLE OF ISSUS
(For letters, see map above)

next country to be conquered was Syria. Alexander marched from Gordium southward into the open plains of Syria, where he expected to meet the armies of the Persian king, Darius III. In the meantime, Darius had assembled a vast horde of six hundred thousand men and moved to the north and to the rear of Alexander's army, hoping to cut off its retreat. Alexander marched back and attacked Darius in his chosen position, near Issus. After a severe conflict, a large part of the Persian army was destroyed and the rest put to flight. Alexander then continued his march southward through Sidon and reached Tyre. At this place he met the most serious resistance that he encountered in all his campaigns. The new city of Tyre was situated on an island, about half a mile from the coast. Having no fleet at hand, Alexander could reach the city only by building an immense mole, or causeway, through the

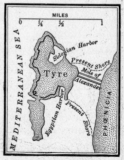

SIEGE OF TYRE

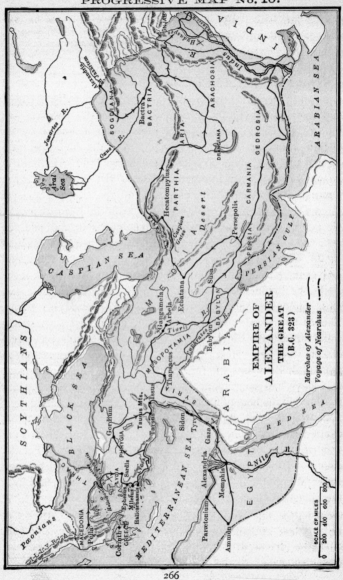

EMPIRE OF
ALEXANDER
THE GREAT
(B.C. 323)

Marches of Alexander
Voyage of Nearchus

SCALE OF MILES
0   200   400   600   800

sea to the walls. By this stupendous piece of work he was able to storm and capture the city. The overtures for peace which the Persian king now felt disposed to offer him, were scornfully rejected.

Egypt; Founding of Alexandria (332 B.C.). — There remained only one more province on the Mediterranean to be secured, and that was Egypt. The march to the south, however, was blocked at Gaza, a strongly fortified town defended by its faithful governor, Batis. To assault its walls Alexander performed another great feat of engineering skill. He built a mound of earth, two hundred and fifty feet high and twelve hundred feet broad at the base, around the entire city. Although repulsed three times, he finally took the town by storm. He put to death what remained of the garrison, and sold the women and children into slavery. The way was now open to Egypt, where the people welcomed Alexander as one who would deliver them from the power of Persia. On the coast west of the Delta, he founded the new city of Alexan'dria, the first and most famous of many towns which perpetuated his name. Thence he moved westward along the coast, and then southward through the Libyan desert to the noted temple and oracle of Zeus Ammon. Here, it is said, the oracle addressed him as the son of Zeus and the future conqueror of the world. This may have had some influence upon Alexander, in leading him to claim divine honors for himself.

Central Persia; Battle of Arbela (331 B.C.). — Having organized the government of Egypt, Alexander returned to Tyre and made his preparations to pierce the heart of the Persian empire. He crossed the Euphrates River and passed through upper Mesopotamia beyond the Tigris. In a broad plain near the village of Gaugame'la, and thirty miles west of Arbe'la, he came face to face with the army of the Great King. Here was to be fought the battle which was to decide the fate of Persia. Since his defeat at Issus, Darius had gathered an immense armament which rivaled that of Xerxes, — a million infantry, forty thousand cavalry, two hundred scythed chariots, and fifteen elephants. To meet this host Alexander had now an

BATTLE OF "ARBELA"

(For letters, see p. 265)

army of forty thousand infantry and seven thousand cavalry. His attack began with a cavalry charge toward the enemy's left; and this he suddenly changed and directed in the form of a wedge against the center, where Darius himself was urging on his troops. The frightened king fled, his army became demoralized, while the rest of Alexander's troops pressed forward and gained a complete victory. The battle at Gaugamela — usually called the " battle of Arbela " — sealed the doom of the empire. Alexander then moved south to Babylon, which surrendered to him; next to the Persian capital Susa, which also opened its gates; and then to Persepolis, which was taken after a feeble resistance. These three cities were the richest in the world, and by their capture Alexander came into possession of immense treasures. He proclaimed himself the monarch of Persia, but he disgraced his name by wantonly firing with his own hand the magnificent palace at Persepolis.

The Far East; Battle of the Hydaspes (326 B.C.). — Alexander had now traversed the western and central provinces of the Persian empire. There remained the far eastern provinces, which were speedily reduced to his authority. It was during this period that Alexander blackened his name by two of his most infamous crimes. The one was the assassination of his faithful general, Parme′nio, on the charge of conspiracy; the other was the murder, in a fit of drunken frenzy, of his dearest friend, Clitus, who had saved his life at the battle of the Granicus. Of these dastardly crimes, it can only be said to his credit that he bitterly repented of them.

Not satisfied with the conquest of Persia, Alexander crossed the Indus, and proceeded through the Punjab to the river Hydas'pes. Here, after a severe engagement, he gained a victory over the armies of India, led by Porus, the most able king of the Far East. Struck by the royal bearing of Porus, Alexander made him viceroy of his new Indian province. The Macedonian soldiers, now wearied with years of marching and fighting, refused to go farther into unknown lands, and Alexander was obliged to return. Down the Indus and then westward through the sands of the desert, his army marched back to Persepolis and Susa; while his fleet under Nearchus (near'kus) explored anew the ancient water route from the Indus to the Euphrates. Alexander repaired to Babylon, now the capital of his newly conquered world.

Death and Character of Alexander. — On his return to Babylon Alexander did not rest. He hoped to push his conquests into Arabia, and to give a firmer organization to his Græco-Oriental empire. But in a short time he was stricken down by a fever, and died (323 B.C.) at the age of thirty-two years and eight months. His last words were a request that the empire be given "to the most worthy." His body was carried to Egypt, and was buried at Alexandria with divine honors.

What shall be thought of Alexander? This is a question which has provoked much difference of opinion. When we try to answer such a question as this we sometimes fail to distinguish between the personal qualities of a man, and the character of the work that he has accomplished.

If we look at the personal qualities of Alexander we shall see many things that we cannot admire. In the first place, he had an ungovernable temper. He would sometimes indulge in paroxysms of rage that were shocking to behold. Such fits of passion are inconsistent with the highest type of manhood. The English poet Pope calls him "The youth who all else but himself subdued." In the next place, he had an inordinate love of drink. He was given to excessive dissipation. It was in a drunken fit that he murdered his dearest friend and foster-brother, Clitus. Even when entering upon a laborious campaign he often burdened his body and brain with artificial stimulants. His death was no doubt hastened by the drunken carousals that attended his attack of fever. Moreover, Alexander was the victim of the most excessive vanity. He at first compared himself with the godlike heroes of Homer. After conquering Persia and assuming the dignity of the Great King, he claimed to possess divine attributes — insisted that he should be looked up to as a god. At one time he formally demanded that the Greeks recognize his divinity. Of course, sensible men could hardly comply with such a demand. Sparta is said to have made the indifferent reply : " We allow Alexander to call himself a god, if he likes."

Such glaring defects of character would convince us that instead of being divine, he was pitifully human. But still he possessed some moral qualities of a high order, especially generosity and magnanimity. When in his normal state of mind he was generous to a fault. His possessions he willingly shared with others. With one or two exceptions, he never practiced the cruelty toward his enemies that marked the wars between the Greek cities. He never devastated the country and wantonly destroyed property. The only exception was the destruction of the palace at Persepolis, and this was done in a fit of drunken frenzy. He had no race hatred, but considered one people as good as another. Such inconsistencies of character belonged to the man whom we call " Great "; but his title of greatness depends upon something else than upon his personal qualities.

The Civilizing Work of Alexander. — Some of the older historians used to look upon Alexander as scarcely more than an ambitious soldier who, having subdued Persia, " sighed for more worlds to conquer." Other more recent historians have looked upon him as having done more for the world's civilization than any other human being. These, of course, are extreme views. That he was an ambitious soldier, there is no doubt. That his work resulted in advancing the world's civilization, there is no doubt. But we can hardly believe that Alexander had clearly in his own mind all the untold benefits that resulted from his conquests. He was carrying out the ideas of his father, Philip; but he must be given credit for doing what his father was not permitted to do.

In the first place, he was successful in conquering Persia, which his father had planned; but this alone might have been of no benefit to the world. In the next place, he carried with him wherever he went the culture of Greece. This gave a new life to the decaying civilization of the East. He was a great colonizer. He planted new cities in the train of his army, and encouraged their settlement by Greeks and
Macedonians. Greek cul-
ture thus came to be the
culture of the Eastern
world. It is said that
he planted seventy such
cities, many of them

COIN OF ALEXANDER

named after himself, like the famous city in Egypt. Moreover, he broke down the distinction between different races. To him there was no distinction between the Greeks and the barbarians, between the people of the West and the people of the East. He encouraged the intermarriage of races. He himself married a Persian princess, and induced his soldiers to take Oriental wives. We might perhaps call Alexander the first great "cosmopolitan," — a citizen of the world. His real greatness rests upon the fact that he brought the two parts of the world together — Greece and the Orient. With all our modern criticism, perhaps there has been no finer tribute to the work of Alexander than that of Plutarch:

"Blending together as in a festal cup, laws, customs, races, and rational affections, he taught men to consider the whole earth as their native land, all honest men as their family, and only the wicked as strangers."

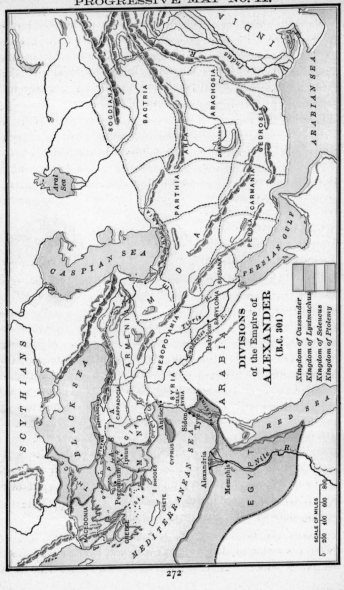

DIVISIONS
of the Empire of
ALEXANDER
(B.C. 301)

Kingdom of Cassander
Kingdom of Lysimachus
Kingdom of Seleucus
Kingdom of Ptolemy

SCALE OF MILES
0 200 400 600 800

We may notice other incidental results of his conquests. He benefited trade and commerce by throwing into circulation the vast treasures of gold and silver hoarded by Oriental monarchs. It is said that he took from the royal vaults at Persepolis 120,000 talents (about $144,000,000). The naval expedition by Nearchus from the Indus to the Euphrates opened to the world a new commercial route from India to Europe. A great stimulus to science resulted from the explorations made by Alexander and his followers in the East.

But still it remains true that the great world empire which he carved out with his sword fell to pieces almost immediately after his death.

III. Dissolution of Alexander's Empire (323–301 B.C.)

The Wars of Succession. — The years which followed the death of Alexander were years of intrigue and war between his different generals, who were trying to get control of the empire that Alexander had left. Various attempts were made to keep the empire together. At first one of the generals, Perdic'cas, tried to rule, and divided the provinces between himself and the other chieftains; but they refused to recognize his authority. Afterward another general, Antig'onus, aspired to the position of the Great King; but he was opposed by the other generals, who were themselves getting control of various provinces. After years of bitter strife, Antigonus was defeated and slain at the battle of Ipsus in Phrygia (301 B.C.), and the victorious generals divided among themselves the fragments of the empire that Alexander had established (map, p. 272).

SELEUCUS (Coin)

Kingdom of the Seleucidæ; Syria. — Seleu'cus was the general who had already taken possession of Babylon, together with a large part of the eastern provinces. He now received in addition Mesopotamia,

Syria, and the eastern part of Asia Minor. He removed his capital from Babylon to An'tioch in Syria; but in this way he also weakened his hold upon his eastern provinces. He divided his whole territory into seventy-two satrapies, ruled not by natives but by Greeks and Macedonians. The eastern provinces were intrusted to his son Anti'ochus, who afterward succeeded to his father's throne (280 B.C.). This extensive empire was known as Syria, or the "Kingdom of the Seleu'cidæ," and remained the greatest power in Asia until the Roman conquest (64 B.C.).

Kingdom of the Ptolemies; Egypt. — Ptolemy I. (tol'e-my) was one of Alexander's generals who was put in possession of Egypt directly after the death of the conqueror, and maintained himself there during the wars of succession. He afterward added to his kingdom Palestine, lower Syria, and Cyprus. Under his administration and that of his successors Egypt rose to prosperity and greatness. The first Ptolemy organized the kingdom into provinces based upon the ancient divisions of the country; but the civil and military authority was placed in the hands of Greeks and Macedonians. Alexandria became the great commercial emporium of the Mediterranean, and the center of the world's learning. Egypt remained the land of commerce and of culture until it was absorbed by the Roman empire (30 B.C.).

Kingdoms in Asia Minor. — No part of Alexander's empire was so completely broken up after his death as was Asia Minor. Here. after some years, we find the new kingdoms of Per'gamum, Bithyn'ia, and other smaller states, as well as the island republic of Rhodes, which included some of the cities on the adjacent coast. Of these several states the kingdom of Pergamum was the most important, and under its kings Eu'menes I. and At'talus I. rose to a position of considerable power and influence.

Macedonia and the Greek Federations. — After the death of Alexander the Greeks made a fresh attempt to throw off the power of Macedonia. This unsuccessful revolt, which is known as the " Lamian war " (323–321 B.C.), was inspired chiefly by Demosthenes, who after its disastrous close fled from Athens and took his own life by poison. After the battle of Ipsus, Macedonia remained in the hands of Cassander, who secured it as his share of Alexander's empire.

While weak successors of Cassander were trying to maintain their authority in Greece, there grew up two confederations which were the most important factors in later Greek politics. In the course of time they came to include the most important states of Greece, except Athens and Sparta. One of these confederations was the Ætolian League. This was originally a union of warlike mountain tribes in Ætolia, but it gradually extended its power so as to include nearly all the states of central Greece, and also Elis in the Peloponnesus.

A body quite similar to the Ætolian League in its organization, but far superior in its character, was the Achæan League, which comprised most of the states in the Peloponnesus. The power and greatness of the Achæan League were due to the famous leader Ara'tus, who for a time appeared as the deliverer of Greece from Macedonian rule. In a few years the whole Peloponnesus, except Laconia and Elis, was combined (229 B.C.) in a single federal state — the most advanced political organization that had ever existed in Greece.

Constitution of the Achæan League. — The Achæan League is often referred to as the most striking example of a federal republic existing in the ancient world, and is sometimes likened to our own government. In the first place, each city retained its equality and independence — having its own government, electing its own officers, and managing its own local affairs. In the next place, the general powers of the league were vested in a central or federal government. This consisted of (1) a general (or president), and a council or cabinet of ten persons who exercised administrative powers; (2) a boulé, or senate, of about one hundred and twenty persons, which prepared

THE ÆTOLIAN AND ACHÆAN LEAGUES, ABOUT 229 B.C.

measures for the assembly and managed foreign affairs; and (3) an assembly of the whole people, in which the citizens of each city possessed one vote. The assembly passed all federal laws, and elected all federal officers. As the federal assembly was not a representative body, and as all the citizens would not be disposed to attend its meetings, there was a tendency for the league, although democratic in theory, to become aristocratic in fact, and also for the " general " to exercise a great influence in shaping its policy.

The Struggle of the Leagues. — The two leagues — Ætolian and Achæan — had been formed to maintain their independence against Macedonia. The only state in the Peloponnesus that had not joined either was Sparta. Sparta was jealous of the growing power of the Achæans, and made war upon them. They called upon Macedonia for help, which was given. Sparta was defeated. But the Achæans, as a result of their alliance with Macedonia, were obliged thereafter to recognize the authority of the Macedonian king. The Ætolians now thought it was their turn to become the supreme power in Greece. Accordingly, they tried, with the aid of Sparta, to bring the Achæan league under their authority. The Macedonian king — now the young prince Philip V. — interfered and brought them almost to the point of submission. But in the midst of his successful campaigns, Philip suddenly received news that Hannibal, a great Carthaginian general, was in Italy, making war on Rome. He therefore concluded a peace with the Greeks, and formed an alliance with Hannibal.

PHILIP V.

The Intervention of Rome. — During this period in which the Grecian leagues were striving to resist the encroachments of Macedonia, events were taking place which finally led to the supremacy of a new foreign power in Greece. The new power was Rome, which was beginning to make its influence felt beyond the coast of Italy. It was the interference of the Macedonian king, Philip V., in the war between Rome and Hannibal, that led, as we shall hereafter see, to the interference of Rome in the affairs of Macedonia and Greece. From this time the history of Greece becomes a part of the history of Rome. But before we begin to study the rise and extension of the Roman power and the development of its new world empire, we must first get some idea of that new culture which the ancient world received through Alexander's conquests and the work of his successors.

Selections for Reading

Knowlton, Topic A 13, "Alexander and his World Empire " (1).[1]

Seignobos, Ch. 15, "The Greeks in the Orient" (1).

Shuckburgh, Ch. 19, "The Macedonian Period"; Ch. 20, "Alexander the Great" (10).

Oman, Ch. 42, "Philip and Demosthenes"; Ch. 43, "The End of Grecian Freedom"; Ch. 44, "Alexander the Great" (10).

Bury, Ch. 16, "The Rise of Macedonia"; Ch. 17, "The Conquest of Persia" (10).

Wheeler, Alexander, Ch. 12, "The Persian Empire"; Ch. 31, "Death of Alexander" (27).

[1] The figure in parenthesis refers to the number of the topic in the Appendix, where a fuller title of the book will be found.

Mahaffy, Survey, Ch. 8, "Alexander and his Successors" (10).

—— Greek Life, Ch. 18 (Hellenism, society, literature, art) (10).

Curtius, Vol. V., Bk. VII., Ch. 3, "Athens and Philip" (10).

Holm, Vol. III., Ch. 26, "Concluding Years of Alexander's Reign"; Index, "Ætolian League," "Achæan League" (10).

Dodge, Alexander, Ch. 12 (military system of Philip and Alexander); Ch. 48, "The Man and the Soldier" (27).

Freeman, Historical Essays, "Alexander the Great" (3).

Plutarch, "Demosthenes," "Alexander" (26).

Demosthenes, Orations, "The First Olynthiac," "The First Philippic" (17).

Special Study

THE CHARACTER OF ALEXANDER. — Smith, Wm., pp. 552, 553 (10); Goodspeed, Anc. World, pp. 218–221 (1); Oman, Ch. 44 (10); Curtius, Ch. 17 (10); Allcroft, Vol. V., pp. 155–158 (10); Holm, Vol. III., Ch. 27 (10); Wheeler, "Alexander," Ch. 31 (27); Freeman, Essays, 2d series, pp. 161–206 (3); Dodge, "Alexander," Ch. 48 (27); Plutarch, "Alexander" (26).

SARCOPHAGUS OF ALEXANDER (So-called)

CHAPTER XVIII

THE GRÆCO–ORIENTAL, OR HELLENISTIC, CULTURE

Synopsis

I. HELLENIC AND HELLENISTIC CULTURE. — Hellenic Culture in Greece. — Post-Aristotelian Philosophy: Epicureanism and Stoicism. — Examples of Pure Hellenic Art. — Meaning of Hellenistic Culture.

II. HELLENISTIC CULTURE IN ASIA MINOR. — Pergamum as a Center of Culture. — Architecture and Sculpture of Pergamum. — Literature and Science of Pergamum. — The School of Rhodes.

III. HELLENISTIC CULTURE IN SYRIA. — The Civilization of the Seleucidæ. — Antioch as a Center of Culture. — Attempt to Hellenize the Jews.

IV. HELLENISTIC CULTURE IN EGYPT. — Alexandria as a Center of Culture. — Museum and Library of Alexandria. — The Literature and Scholarship of Alexandria. — The Cultivation of the Sciences at Alexandria. — The Medical School at Cos. — The Commerce of Alexandria. — The Gifts of Greece to Civilization.

I. HELLENIC AND HELLENISTIC CULTURE

Hellenic Culture in Greece. — We generally call the period that followed the death of Alexander the " Hellenistic " period. It was then that the culture of the world was made up largely of both Greek and Oriental elements. But we must remember that in Hellas proper the old culture of Greece still remained. We may call this purer form of Greek culture " Hellenic," to distinguish it from the mixed or " Hellenistic " form of culture that grew up in the countries of the Orient. In Greece we still see the influence of the pure Hellenic spirit. The Greek language was still spoken by the people and used by all orators. The old Greek literature and art were still held up as models of taste. Athens remained an intellectual center where were taught the principles of Greek rhetoric, oratory, and philosophy.

MENANDER

There were many pure Greek writers of this period, of whom the greatest was Menan'der. A native of Athens, he was a writer of comedy, and a worthy successor of Aristophanes. As politics was now excluded from the stage, he directed his satire upon the manners and customs of the people. From the fragments that remain of his works we know that Menander possessed keen wit and used elegant and refined language. His works were the favorite comedies of the later Greeks, and were afterward the models of the Roman writers Plautus and Terence. Here is a fragment of Menander on the use of riches:

"Abundance is a blessing to the wise;
The use of riches in discretion lies.
Learn this, ye men of wealth — a heavy purse
In a fool's pocket is a heavy curse."

Post-Aristotelian Philosophy: Epicureanism and Stoicism. — The later Greek philosophy must be regarded as Hellenic rather than Hellenistic, because it followed the schools of Socrates, Plato, and Aristotle and was not affected by Oriental ideas. It dwelt much upon Ethics, or the philosophy of life. The question as to the best way to live — what is the highest good — was the subject discussed by the greatest thinkers.

The Epicure'an school of philosophers took its name from Epicu'rus, who was born at Samos and had taught in the cities of Asia Minor before he came to Athens. Epicurus tried to rescue men from the influence of superstition and the old mythological ideas concerning the gods. He taught that men should be influenced, not by the fear of the gods, but by the desire to obtain the highest happiness — not the passing pleasure of the hour, but the permanent happiness of a lifetime.

The Stoic philosophy, which was a higher system than the Epicurean, was founded by Zeno. He taught at Athens in a *Sto'a*, or porch, on the Agora, from which his school received its name. Like Epicurus, he rejected the prevailing mythological notions. He believed that the world is governed by a Universal Reason which is revealed in the

EPICURUS

laws of nature. According to Zeno, men should live, not to appease the gods, but to conform to the highest " law of nature."

ZENO

He also sympathized with the broader ideas of the age, and believed that men's duties should not be limited to their own city or even to Greece, but should extend to all mankind.

Of these two schools it is easy to see that the doctrines of Epicurus would be the more likely to be perverted. Men living solely for pleasure, for self-gratification, would justify themselves by saying, We are followers of Epicurus. In this way "Epicureanism" would come to mean something far different from what Epicurus intended. But Stoicism taught that men should do right, without regard to pleasure or pain.

Examples of Pure Hellenic Art. — We may also see that the high ideals that marked the days of Phidias and Praxiteles still inspired the painter and the sculptor. The most celebrated painter of this time was Apelles, a native of Col'ophon, a Greek city on the coast of Asia Minor (map, p. 179). He painted portraits of Philip of Macedon, and the famous one of

APHRODITE OF MELOS

Alexander wielding the thunderbolt (p. 263). He was a great artist, who was willing to receive criticism. The story is told that one day he placed a picture in the public square to hear the remarks of those who passed by. A cobbler pointed out a fault in a shoe on one of the figures, and Apelles immediately corrected it. The next day the cobbler, elated by his previous success, ventured to criticize the legs, when Apelles rebuked him with the remark, " Let the cobbler stick to his last." Apelles was noted for his accuracy of drawing and fine coloring.

Sculpture was the finest of the Greek arts; and during this Hellenistic period some statues were produced that show the pure Hellenic spirit. If we should ask a group of art critics what they regarded as the finest statue in the world, they would probably answer the " Aphrodite of Melos " — often called " Venus de Milo." It was found in Melos, an island in the Ægean Sea, and is now in the Louvre at Paris. Who was the sculptor and when it was made, nobody knows. But it is generally assigned to the Hellenistic period. It has, however, the same exquisite beauty and the same perfection of form that are seen in the works of Phidias and Praxiteles. The graceful outlines and elegant pose have never been surpassed. It has lost the arms, and no modern sculptor has been able to restore them. It is one of the choicest legacies of Greece to the modern world.

Another famous statue assigned to this period is the Apollo Belvedere. This has been regarded as the beau ideal of manly beauty. So nearly does it approach the pure Hellenic style that it has been said that in it " we see Lysippus in the form and Praxiteles in the face." (Perry.)

HEAD OF APOLLO BELVEDERE

To this period also belongs the magnificent statue of the " Winged Victory of Samothrace " — a small island near the Thracian coast. This figure of victory was erected as a trophy of a naval triumph. She was originally represented as standing upon the prow of a ship with a trumpet at her lips. Although now mutilated, the figure illustrates the finest style of Greek art.

Meaning of Hellenistic Culture. — We have thus seen that there were examples of pure Hellenic art in Greece after the conquests of Alexander. But there is one important point that we should keep in mind. This is the fact that the culture which had been developed by the Greeks themselves was considerably modified by being taken up by the people of foreign countries. For example, the Greek language, when spoken by a Syrian, a Jew, or an Egyptian, would no longer remain the pure language of Sophocles or Plato, but would acquire features

WINGED VICTORY OF SAMOTHRACE

foreign to the Attic tongue. So the architecture and sculpture of Greece would have impressed upon them a certain Oriental character and spirit, which would distinguish them from the more refined art of Phidias and Praxiteles. To this Greek culture as modified by Oriental influences we apply the term " Hellenistic." The Hellenistic culture, then, means the language and civilization of the peoples of the East which arose from the planting of Greek colonies among those peoples by Alexander and his successors. It might be described, in short, as the Orientalized form of Hellenism. The Greek influence extended into central Asia and as far east as the Indus; but the chief seats of the Hellenistic culture were the countries on the eastern shores of the Mediterranean — Asia Minor, Syria, and Egypt.

II. Hellenistic Culture in Asia Minor

Pergamum as a Center of Culture. —The chief seat of the new civilization in Asia Minor was the city of Pergamum — the capital of the kingdom of the same name (map, p. 272). The kings of this country came to be wealthy and somewhat powerful monarchs. They gained an enviable reputation by putting a stop to a disastrous invasion of the Gauls — a barbarian people

The Great Altar at Pergamum (Restoration)

who came from the West in the third century B.C. and invaded Greece and Asia Minor, and who were finally settled in the province of Gala'tia, in the interior of Asia Minor. This victory over the Gauls was the heroic event in the history of Pergamum, and was commemorated in many works of art.

THE DYING GAUL

Architecture and Sculpture of Pergamum. — The kings of Pergamum adorned their capital with splendid buildings, which rivaled the architecture of Athens. The central architectural feature of the city was a vast altar dedicated to Zeus Soter (the Savior). This was built to commemorate the victory over the barbarian Gauls, and the divine assistance then given. The altar was situated on the summit of the Pergame'an acropolis, said to have been more than eight hundred feet above the level of the sea. It was adorned with elaborate sculptures and especially with a gigantic frieze, on which was represented the battle between the gods and the barbarian giants. This altar with its decorations was regarded as one of the marvels of the ancient world. We have preserved to us a valuable relic of the Pergamean art, and also of the Gallic invasion, in the well-known copy of the "Dying Gaul" (usually called the "Dying Gladiator"; p. 285). This is worth our careful study as a specimen of Hellenistic art, showing a departure from the purest Greek models, in the realistic representation of a wounded barbarian warrior.

Literature and Science of Pergamum. — The city of Pergamum was a center not only of art, but also of learning. Although it made no important contributions to literature, it was distinguished for a remarkable collection of literary works — a library of two hundred thousand volumes, — that is, long rolls of manuscript, — which rivaled the more renowned

LAOCOÖN AND HIS SONS

collection at Alexandria. Such "books" had previously been written upon Egyptian papyrus. But as the exportation of this material was prohibited by the Ptolemies, the kings of Pergamum adopted in its place the skins of animals (called *Pergamenæ chartæ*, from which comes our word "parchment"). The city of Pergamum also became the home of many scientific men, — grammarians, mathematicians, natural philosophers, and physicians, — of whom many acquired great renown, as Cra'tes in philology and Galen in medicine.

The School of Rhodes. — Another important center of Hellenistic culture in Asia Minor was Rhodes, famous for its school of rhetoric and its code of maritime law. The art of

Rhodes reveals the same Oriental influences that appeared at Pergamum. This is seen in the taste for colossal figures and impressive groups of statuary. The famous Colossus of Rhodes, a statue one hundred and fifty feet high, was reckoned as one of the "seven wonders of the world." The most noted example of Rhodian sculpture that remains to us is the group of Laoc'oön, a priest of Apollo, and his sons, who were destroyed by serpents sent by Athena. The agony depicted upon the face of the priest, though wonderfully expressive, is far removed from the calm repose which marks the purer Hellenic art.

III. Hellenistic Culture in Syria

The Civilization of the Seleucidæ. — The Seleucidæ were the most zealous followers of Alexander in the founding of new cities. These new towns, which numbered more than seventy, became the active centers of Greek influence. They were colonized by Greeks. In them the Greek language was spoken, Greek methods of city government were adopted, the commercial spirit of the Greeks was present, and Greek buildings were erected. But these Greek towns, springing up by the side of the older Asiatic cities, felt the influence of Oriental customs and ideas. The Greeks absorbed the Oriental love of wealth and passion for luxury, and developed a form of life which was neither purely Greek nor purely Eastern, but a mingling of the two — a composite culture in which the Oriental features were improved and the Hellenic features debased.

Antioch as a Center of Culture. — The city which presented the most conspicuous type of this Græco-Oriental or Hellenistic culture in Syria was Antioch, the capital of the kingdom. The original city was founded by Seleucus I. and named in honor of his father Antiochus. Here were gathered people of many nations; but the prevailing form of culture was Greek, imbued with the Oriental taste for magnificence. The buildings glistened with precious stones and ornaments of gold. The broad, regular streets were lined with the most splendid porticoes, colonnades, and statues. Beyond the walls of the city was the cypress grove of Daphne, said to be one of the most attractive places in the world. It contained the tree of Daphne, into which this nymph, according to tradition, was changed when fleeing from Apollo. The grove was reached by a road passing through beautiful villas and gardens enlivened with fountains and medicinal springs. It was adorned with stately temples, baths, and places of amusement. In the temple of Apollo was a colossal statue of that god, said to rival the Zeus of Phidias. All this fondness for luxury shows that the Greeks, while exercising a powerful influence upon the East, were themselves coming under the spell of Orientalism.

Attempt to Hellenize the Jews. — The only opposition to the Hellenizing movement in western Asia appeared in Palestine. Here the people were attached to their ancient language and religion. It is said that Alexander offered strong inducements for the Jews to settle in Alexandria, where they could retain their religion unmolested. Many of them took advantage of this offer; but while preserving their own religion, they could not help imbibing much of the Hellenistic spirit. In Palestine itself, however, the Jews succeeded in resisting these foreign influences. It is true that they sometimes affected the Greek culture by learning to speak the Greek language and adopting Greek names; but the mass of the people clung to their Hebrew language and customs. When Palestine passed from the control of Egypt to that of Syria, a systematic attempt was made by the Syrian king, Antiochus IV. (Epiph'anes), to force upon the Jews the Greek language and customs, including the Greek religion. This was accompanied by a most unjust and bitter persecution. It aroused a national revolt, which ended only with the establishment of the independence of the Jewish nation. The attempt to Hellenize the Jews thus proved a failure; and the Jews remained practically free from Syrian control until the Roman conquest (63 B.C.).

IV. Hellenistic Culture in Egypt

Alexandria as a Center of Culture. — In Egypt we find the most important intellectual center of the Hellenistic world. The Ptolemies did not, like the Seleucidæ, attempt to bring the whole kingdom under Greek influence by the erection of many new cities. They rather attempted to concentrate into a single city the various elements of Greek culture. This city was Alexandria, which was founded by the great conqueror himself. It was, first of all, a commercial center, taking the place of Tyre as the important emporium of the Mediterranean. It came to be the most cosmopolitan city of the world, with a population of nearly a million inhabitants, made up of Egyptians, Greeks, Macedonians, Jews, and people from nearly every Asiatic country. The ideas of various people found here a common meeting place. The Ptolemies respected the religion of the Egyptians and that of the Jews, while clinging to their own Grecian gods. And these various religions were often mingled with one another. The Greco-Egyptian god Sera'pis, for example, was a combination of qualities that made him an acceptable object of worship to both Greeks and Egyptians. Though the country surrounding Alexandria was not attractive, the architecture of the city united Greek taste with Oriental splendor. There were many public buildings, such as theaters, race courses, and sanctuaries; but the most imposing of these was the Serape'um, the temple of the common god Serapis.

Museum and Library of Alexandria. — Alexandria obtained its highest renown as the home of scholars. In this city we find blended the Greek and the Egyptian taste for philosophy and science. The most famous work of the Ptolemies was the establishment of the Museum and the Library. The Museum was a collection of buildings dedicated to the Muses, and might not inaptly be called a "University." Here were gathered philosophers, scholars, and students from all countries — Greece, Asia Minor, Judea, Babylon, and even India. It is said that at one time as many as fourteen thousand students found a home in Alexandria. In connection with the Museum were botanical and zoölogical gardens, dissecting rooms, and astronomical observatories. But the most famous of these buildings was the great Alexandrian Library, containing over five hundred thousand manuscripts. It was the desire of the Ptolemies to possess an authentic copy of every existing work of Greek literature. This library was the most extensive collection of manuscripts in the ancient world.

The Literature and Scholarship of Alexandria. — The literature which was produced at this time was for the most part lyric poetry and scientific writings. One poet of this period holds a high rank among the pastoral poets of the world; this was Theoc′ritus. Although born at Syracuse, he lived at Alexandria. His " idylls," describing the beauties of nature, have been admired by all people, and perhaps approach more nearly than any other literature of this period to the pure æsthetic spirit of the early Greeks. Here is a little fragment in which the poet praises his friend Ptolemy Philadelphus:

> "What is his noble trait? — A royal spirit
> To point out genius and encourage merit;
> The poet's friend, humane, and good, and kind;
> Of manners gentle, and of generous mind.
> He marks his friend, but more he marks his foe;
> His hand is ever ready to bestow;
> Request with reason, and he'll grant the thing,
> And what he gives, he gives it like a king."

History was cultivated by Manetho, an Egyptian priest, who wrote the " Chronicles of Egypt," while the Babylonian Berosus was doing a similar kind of work for Babylonian history. But the most thorough literary scholarship of Alexandria was devoted to the careful study of the ancient Greek writers. Aristar′chus, the grammarian, gained a reputation for his edition of the poems of Homer. Translations of important works of literature also formed a part of the work of these Alexandrian scholars. The most noted of these translations was the Sep'tuagint, a Greek version of the Jewish Scriptures.

The Cultivation of the Sciences at Alexandria. — Alexandria was also a meeting place for Greek and Oriental science; and a great impulse was given in the direction of a more strictly scientific method. There are many famous names of scientists connected with this seat of ancient learning. The chief sciences cultivated at this time were mathematics, astronomy, geography, and physics. It is enough for us to notice a few of the chief names connected with these different branches of sciences.

The chief mathematician was Euclid, who opened a school of geometry at Alexandria. He is called the "Father of Geometry." We know scarcely anything about his life; but there is a little story about him that is often repeated. The king Ptolemy was one of his pupils. Being tired of the study of angles and triangles, he asked Euclid if there was not an easier way for a king to master the subject, and Euclid replied, "There is no royal road to geometry." It is interesting for us to know that the geometry we study to-day is based upon the "Elements of Geometry," written by Euclid.

The most noted astronomer of the ancient world was Hipparchus. He has been called by one modern writer the "patriarch of astronomy." He made his observations partly at Alexandria and partly from the island of Rhodes. He studied the heavens not as the old Babylonians had done, — to find out the will of the gods, and to foretell human events, — but to discover the nature and motions of the heavenly bodies. He was the first to discover the slow motion which astronomers now call the "precession of the equinoxes." He made a catalogue of more than a thousand of the fixed stars. The work of Hipparchus was later carried on by another noted astronomer, Claudius Ptolemy. The system of astronomy which he explained is called the "Ptolema'ic System," in which the earth is regarded as the center of the solar system, and which was not corrected until modern times by Copernicus.

The name that we most closely associate with geography is that of Eratos'thenes. He was the librarian of the Alexandrian library. He studied all the known sciences and was regarded as the most learned man of his age; but he is especially famous for his work in geography. At the time of Homer it was supposed that the earth was flat. Aristotle had proved that it is round. But nobody had any idea of its size. It was Eratosthenes who first adopted a scientific method of measuring its circumference. His method was correct, and with better instruments of observation his result would doubtless have been correct. He lived to be eighty years old. Threatened with blindness and tired of life, he refused to take food and died of starvation.

The man who made the most remarkable discoveries in physics was Archime'des. He was also distinguished as a mathematician. A native of Syracuse in Sicily, he spent some time in Alexandria. Many stories are told about this remarkable man. It is said that King Hi'ero of Syracuse, suspecting that a certain goldsmith had mixed a lighter alloy with the gold in a crown he had been ordered to make, applied to Archimedes to detect the fraud without injuring the crown. The solution occurred to him while taking a bath in a brimming tub of water and observing that the amount of water displaced was equal in volume to that of his own body. This principle, he reasoned, would apply to the crown; and elated with the discovery he rushed into the

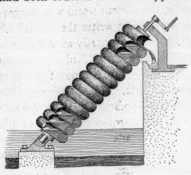

THE ARCHIMEDES SCREW

street crying, "Eureka" ("I have found it"). He discovered the law of the lever and fulcrum, and said to the king, "Give me a place to stand and I will move the world." He invented a method of raising water by means of a screw. While the city of Syracuse was besieged by a hostile Roman fleet, it is said that he invented powerful machines to attack the vessels and succeeded in burning some of the ships by means of powerful mirrors. But these stories can give little idea of the great discoveries he made, both in mathematics and in physics.

The Medical School at Cos. — It is interesting to know, in connection with the wonderful growth of science at Alexandria, that there grew up not far away a scientific school which was celebrated by another great name of antiquity. This was the medical school at Cos, an island near Rhodes (map, p. 242). It was regarded as a branch of the " University " of Alexandria. To this place the Ptolemies used to send their sons to be educated. The most celebrated teacher of this school was Hippoc'rates, who is known the world over as the " Father of Medicine." He was the first to free medicine from superstition, and to regard the office of the physician as distinct from that of the priest. He believed that the body is governed by natural laws; that health is due to the observance of these laws; and that disease is due, not to the anger of the gods, but to the failure of men to observe the laws of health. With all our advancement in modern science we have not outgrown the fundamental ideas of Hippocrates.

Cos and the neighboring regions were once ruled by a prince named Mauso'lus, who was a patron of learning. It was not, however, on account of his love of learning that he became celebrated, but on account of the magnificent tomb that his wife had built in his honor at the city of Halicarnassus. This tomb received the name of " Mausole'um " — a word adopted into the English language — and was numbered among the " seven wonders of the world."

The Commerce of Alexandria. — Alexandria under the Ptolemies became the greatest trade center of the world. Its situation at the mouth of the Nile opened to it the commerce of the Mediterranean. On the little island of Pharos near the harbor of Alexandria, Ptolemy I. built a magnificent light-house. This was included among the " seven wonders of the

PHAROS LIGHTHOUSE (Coin)

world." [1] A canal which connected the Nile with the Red Sea brought Alexandria into relation with Babylon and the great cities of the East. Alexander had been specially interested in bringing the cities of the world into commercial relations. He had improved the landing stations at Babylon and dredged the Euphrates; and he had even planned a great commercial city at the mouth of the Euphrates, and another at the mouth of the Indus. There was a trade route from India up the Persian Gulf, across the desert to Antioch. But this was a tedious route, and goods had to be transported a long distance on the backs of camels. The one thing that quickened the commerce of the East more than anything else was the vast hoards of money that Alexander had let loose from the royal vaults of Persia. Before his time, commerce had been mostly by barter; that is, the exchange of goods for goods. Now money came to be a common medium of exchange. It helped the merchant to trade between distant points. But Alexandria was the chief center of all this new commercial life. Her merchants brought spices from Arabia, pearls from India, and even silks from China, and distributed them to the people living on the Mediterranean.

The Gifts of Greece to Civilization. — As we look back over the history of Greece we may perhaps get some idea of the important place this country occupied in the ancient world. It is true that Greece may at first have been the heir of the Orient.

[1] The "seven wonders of the world" were: (1) the pyramids of Egypt; (2) the hanging gardens at Babylon; (3) the statue of Zeus at Olympia; (4) the temple of Artemis (Diana) at Ephesus; (5) the Mausoleum at Halicarnassus; (6) the Colossus at Rhodes; and (7) the Pharos (lighthouse) at Alexandria.

She got some of her early ideas, no doubt, from the East.   She received her letters and inherited her commerce from Phœnicia ; and perhaps obtained some ideas of architecture and religion from Egypt.   But in spite of this the Greeks were by far the most original people of the ancient world.

In the first place, Greece was the first civilized nation to develop a form of popular government.   This country may be called the "home of liberty."   The people had a large share in the affairs of the state.   The greatest Greek statesmen, such as Solon and Clisthenes and Pericles, worked out a political system which rested upon the whole body of citizens.   The Athenian city-state was, in fact, a "government of the people, by the people, and for the people."

In the next place, Greece developed a body of literature which as a whole surpassed that of any other people of antiquity. We need only to be reminded of the poems of Homer, the songs of Alcæus and Sappho, the great tragedies of Æschylus and Sophocles and Euripides, the histories of Herodotus and Thucydides, and the orations of Pericles and Demosthenes, to be convinced of the preëminence of the Greeks in literary composition.

Again, the Greeks surpassed all the peoples of antiquity in their philosophical ideas.   Anaxagoras had taught that the world is governed by a supreme Intelligence.   Socrates had taught men how to think for themselves and to discover the true principles of human conduct.   Plato had exalted the higher ideals of life and showed that these ideals are embodied in the true, the beautiful, and the good.   Aristotle was the first to show that facts form the true basis of a sound philosophy.   From such ideas sprang new schools of philosophy which touched nearly every phase of human thought.

Moreover, the Greeks had a transcendent genius for art.   The Egyptians and the Babylonians, or any other people of the Orient, had nothing to be compared with the supreme beauty of the Grecian art.   The names of Myron, of Phidias, of Polygnotus, of Praxiteles, of Scopas, of Lysippus, are sufficient to remind us of the great accomplishments of the Greeks in the domain of sculpture.

But more than this, and much more important to us, is the fact that the surpassing culture of the Greeks has become the heritage of the world. We have seen Greece, even in her political decline and fall, still preserving her intellectual supremacy, and after the conquests of Alexander scattering the fruits of her culture among the various peoples with whom she came into contact. We should also remember that this beneficent influence was not confined to the old world, but has continued down to our own day. Whatever flaws we may have discovered in the old Greek character, we should not fail to appreciate that political, intellectual, and æsthetic type of culture which was developed by the people of Hellas, and which forms one of the great gifts of antiquity to modern civilization.

Selections for Reading

Seignobos, Ch. 15, "The Greeks in the Orient" (1).[1]
Ducoudray, Ch. 10, "The Diffusion of the Greek Genius" (1).
Felton, Vol. II., pp. 275–278, "Spread of Hellenism" (10).
Mahaffy, Survey, Ch. 9, "The Hellenistic World" (10).
—— Greek Life, Ch. 9, "Alexandria and its Rivals" (10).
—— Alexander's Empire, Ch. 10, "The Golden Age of Hellenism"; Ch. 20, "Commerce and Culture of Pergamum and Rhodes" (10).
Holm, Vol. IV., Ch. 14, "Culture of the Greek World, 300–220 B.C." (10).
Gardner, P., Ch. 15, "Successors of Alexander and Greek Civilization" (10).
Gardner, E. A., Handbook, Ch. 5, "The Hellenistic Age" (12).
Freeman, Essay, "The Macedonian Period" (3).
Tarbell, Ch. 10, "Hellenistic Period of Greek Sculpture" (12).
Butcher, pp. 1–40, "What We Owe to the Greeks" (10).

Special Study

THE ALEXANDRIAN SCHOOL. — Seignobos, pp. 184–186 (1); Ducoudray, pp. 203–204 (1); Mahaffy, Survey, pp. 282–288 (10); Encyclopedias, "Alexandrian School," "Alexandrian Age," and names of Alexandrian scientists.

[1] The figure in parenthesis refers to the number of the topic in the Appendix, where a fuller title of the book will be found.

THE ROMAN PEOPLE

CHAPTER XIX

ITALY AND THE TRADITIONAL ORIGIN OF ROME

Synopsis

I. THE GEOGRAPHY OF ITALY. — Transition to Roman History. — The Italian Peninsula. — Climate and Products. — Phases of Roman History.

II. THE PEOPLES OF ITALY. — The Settlement of Italy. — Latium and the Latins. — Etruria and the Etruscans. — The Greeks in Magna Græcia. — Central Italy; the Sabines and Samnites.

III. THE EARLY LEGENDS OF ROME. — Legends regarding the Founding of the City. — Legends of the Early Kings. — Legends of the Later Kings. — Legends of the Early Republic. — Significance of the Roman Legends.

1. THE GEOGRAPHY OF ITALY

Transition to Roman History. — If we had been living in Greece a few years after the death of Alexander the Great we should have seen some wonderful changes taking place in the world. We could not help noticing the new life that was springing up in the East. The old empire of Persia was now dotted with new cities settled by Macedonians and Greeks. It seemed as if the whole Eastern world which had been conquered by Alexander was now to be a Greek world under his successors. But if we turned our eyes to the West we should see a different state of things. Here the Greeks had long ago planted cities which had become the seats of Hellenic culture. Many Greek colonies had been established in Sicily and southern Italy (p. 114). But now all these colonies had fallen under the dominion of a new power that had conquered the whole of Italy. If we

had been Greeks at this time we should no doubt have thought
that this rising power in the West ought to be crushed, and not
allowed to overrun the rest of the Greek world. This is precisely what Philip V. of Macedon thought when he suddenly
dropped his quarrel in Greece and decided to join Hannibal
in his war against Rome (p. 277).

MOUNTAINS,
    RIVERS, AND
    DIVISIONS OF
    ITALY

We are now brought
face to face with Rome,
the mistress of the Italian
peninsula. The Greek and the
Roman world now touched each
other. We may well wonder how it
came to pass that an obscure, half-civilized people, living on a
little group of hills on the Tiber, had grown to be the ruling
power in Italy. Was there anything in the land where they
lived that favored the growth of such a great power? Were
there any people already in Italy from whom they could get

some ideas of a more civilized life? If we look at the geography and early peoples of Italy, we may get some idea as to how the Romans came to be a strong nation.

The Italian Peninsula. — As we look at the map of the Italian peninsula the first thing that strikes us is the fact that it is not broken up by an intricate network of small mountain chains and little valleys, as was the case with the Grecian peninsula (compare maps, pp. 84 and 298). In Italy we see one long chain of mountains, the Apennines, running from one end of the peninsula to the other. This divided Italy into two large and quite distinct parts. In the eastern part, on the Adriatic Sea, the mountain chain runs near the coast, making the shores abrupt, watered only by small streams, and having no good harbors. In the western part, however, on the Tyrrhe'nian Sea, we notice that the mountain chain runs farther away from the coast. This gives more extensive lands, broader plains, larger rivers, more fertile fields, and more good harbors. It has been said that Italy has her back to the East. We shall no doubt be convinced that the part of the peninsula most favorable to a civilized life and to a united country would be the broad lands west of the Apennines, — the lands comprising Latium (lā'shǐ-um) in the center, Etru'ria on the north, and Campa'nia and other provinces on the south. Notice that the Tiber is the principal river in the center of this section.

Climate and Products. — The climate of Italy varies greatly, as we pass from the north to the south. In the valley of the Po the winters are often severe, and the air is chilled by the neighboring snows of the Alps. In central Italy the climate is mild and agreeable, snow being rarely seen south of the Tiber, except on the ranges of the Apennines; while in southern Italy we approach a climate almost tropical, the land being often swept by the hot south wind, the *sirocco*, from the plains of Africa.

The soil of Italy is generally fertile, especially in the plains of the Po and the fields of Campania. The staple products in ancient times were wheat, the olive, and the vine. For a long time Italy led all the countries of the world in the production of olive oil and wine. The production of wheat declined when Rome, by her conquests, came into commercial relation with more fertile countries, such as Sicily and Egypt.

Phases of Roman History. — As we approach the study of Roman history, we shall find that we can look at it from different points of view; and it will present to us different phases.

In the first place, we may look at the external growth of Rome. We shall then see her territory gradually expanding from a small spot on the Tiber, until it takes in the whole peninsula of Italy, and finally all the countries on the Mediterranean Sea. Our attention will then be directed to her generals, her armies, her battles, her conquests. We may trace on the map the new lands which she gradually brought under her sway. Looked at from this point of view, Rome will appear to us as the great *conquering* nation of the world.

Again, we may look at the way in which Rome ruled her subjects, the way in which she built up, from the various lands and peoples that she conquered, a great state, with its wonderful system of government and law. We shall then see the work of her statesmen and lawgivers, her magistrates, her senate, and her assemblies. From this point of view she will seem to us the great *governing* nation of the world.

Finally, we may look at the way in which the Romans were themselves improved in their manners and customs, as they came into contact with other peoples — how they learned lessons even from those whom they conquered, and were gradually changed from a rude, barbarous people to a highly civilized and cultivated nation. We shall see the straw-thatched huts of early times giving place to magnificent temples and theaters and other splendid buildings. We shall see the rude speech of the early Romans growing into a noble language, capable of expressing fine, poetic feeling and lofty sentiments of patriotism. We shall also see Rome giving the fruits of her cul-

ture to the less favored peoples whom she takes under her
control; and when she passes away, we shall see her bequeath-
ing her treasures to future generations. From this point of
view Rome will appear to us as the great *civilizing* nation of
the world.

In order to understand the Romans well, we should look at
them in all these phases; we should study their conquests,
their government, and their civilization.

II. The Peoples of Italy

The Settlement of Italy. — Long before Rome was founded,
every part of Italy was already peopled. Many of the peoples living there came from the north, around the head of
the Adriatic, pushing their way toward the south into different parts of the peninsula. Others came from Greece by
way of the sea, settling upon the southern coast. It is of
course impossible for us to say precisely how Italy was settled. It is enough for us at present to know that most of the
earlier settlers spoke an Indo-European, or Aryan, language,
and that when they first appeared in Italy they were scarcely
civilized, living upon their flocks and herds and just beginning
to cultivate the soil.

Latium and the Latins. — The people that we are the most
interested in at present are the Latins, because the early Romans
were Latins. Their country was Latium, just south of the
Tiber — a very small country, scarcely larger than one of our
counties. The earliest inhabitants, so far as we know, were
half-civilized people — shepherds, living upon their flocks and
herds, gathered in little villages about the hills, and dwelling in
rude straw-thatched huts. About the eighth century B.C. there
were said to be thirty of these villages, or so-called " cities."
To protect themselves from their warlike neighbors, they were
united in a league, something like the leagues of Greece. Their
chief town was Alba Longa (Long White City; map, p. 309)

A TEMPORARY VILLAGE OF STRAW HUTS IN MODERN ITALY — SUPPOSED TO BE
LIKE AN ANCIENT LATIN VILLAGE

near which rose the highest peak in Latium, the Alban Mount.
Here the people gathered each year for a festival in honor of
their common god, the Latin Jupiter.

Etruria and the Etruscans. — The people of Latium might
perhaps have remained a barbarous people had they not lived
near more civilized neighbors. Among the most important
of these neighbors were the Etrus'cans. In some respects the
Etruscans were the most mysterious people of the ancient world,
for the simple reason that their language has never been deciphered. No one has been able to tell where they came from,
or how they came into Italy. When Rome was founded they
occupied the fertile fields of Etruria, north of the Tiber; but
before that time they were spread over a large part of Italy
— in the valley of the Po and the plains of Campania.

The people of Etruria were, next to the Greeks, the most
civilized people of Italy. Their prosperity was due not simply
to agriculture but also to commerce. We know that they came
into commercial relations with Carthage and Greece, and even
with Egypt and Phœnicia. They had the use of gold, bronze,

and iron. In their tombs we find decorated vases, paintings on the walls, and numberless ornaments, showing that the Etruscan women were fond of finger rings, earrings, breastpins and bracelets. The Etruscans built strongly fortified cities. They used the arch in their sewers and in their city gates. Their religion was a gloomy and weird superstition. Their priests, or augurs, were supposed to discover the will of the gods and to predict the future, by observing the entrails of sacrificed animals and the flight of birds. Their sports were cruel, including gladiatorial shows. The Romans derived many of their customs from them.

PART OF ETRUSCAN TOMB

The Greeks in Magna Græcia. — But the most civilized and cultivated people in Italy were the Greeks. They planted their colonies at Taren'tum, and on the western coast as far as the Bay of Naples (map, p. 114). The earliest of these colonies was Cumæ, near Naples, said to have been founded as far back as 1000 B.C. or earlier. The Greeks also, as we have seen, held the eastern and southern coasts of Sicily, while the Carthaginians were encroaching on the western coast of the island. In all the Greek colonies there were the evidences of Greek culture and refinement. Here we might see Greek temples, Greek theaters, Greek statues. We might find the people reading Greek poetry and Greek philosophy. But in very early times the people of Latium did not feel the influence of the Greeks as they did that of the Etruscans.

Central Italy: the Sabines and Samnites. — The central part of Italy is a mountainous country. Here lived a warlike, pastoral people, who could not cultivate the rocky soil; and so they got their living from their herds which they pastured upon the mountain sides. One tribe of these people was the Sabines. There is a story that once upon a time the Sabines, being hard pressed in a war, vowed to Mars, their god of war, that everything born the following spring (the so-called Sacred Spring) should be sent wherever the god might direct; and so the children born that spring, when they were grown up, were sent away led by an ox, the sacred animal of Mars. Where the animal stopped in its wanderings, they founded Bovia'num (the City of the Ox; map, p. 345). From this colony, it was said, sprang the Samnite nation. This people became a hardy race. They were the most warlike nation in Italy; and in later times they became the bitterest enemies of Rome.

III. The Early Legends of Rome

Legends regarding the Founding of the City. — The ancient Romans knew as little as we do regarding the way in which Italy was first peopled. But they fancied that they had in their legends the true story of the settlement of Latium and the founding of their own city. These legends

ÆNEAS (Coin)

tell of the flight of Æne'as from the flames of Troy (p. 90), bearing on his shoulders his father Anchises and leading by the hand his boy Asca'nius; of his landing upon the shores of Latium; of the founding of the city of Lavin'ium and later of Alba Longa. These legends also tell of the miraculous birth of the twin children Rom'ulus and Remus, whose reputed father was Mars, the god of war; of their being thrown into the Tiber and of their being rescued by a wolf, near the foot of the Pal'atine hill (map, p. 310); of their desire afterward to found a new city on the spot of their deliverance; of their quarrel, which resulted in the death of Remus, leaving Romulus as the surviving founder of the city.   The date of the founding of the city, according to Roman reckoning, was 753 B.C.

Legends of the Early Kings. — According to the old legends Rome was at first a kingdom, and the first king was Romulus.   To people his new city he opened an asylum for refugees, and he captured wives from the neighboring

BRONZE WOLF AT THE CAPITOL, ROME

Sabines.   He divided the people into tribes, curies, and clans. He formed an alliance between the Romans and the Sabines, who agreed to live peacefully together as citizens of one town. After a reign of thirty-seven years he was translated to heaven and worshiped under the name of Quiri′nus.

The second king was Numa Pompil′ius, a Sabine, who was elected by the people, after an interregnum of a year.   He was a peaceful ruler, was said to hold communication with the gods, and with the nymph Egeria, and was regarded as the founder of the religious institutions of Rome, as Romulus was regarded as the founder of the political institutions.

During the reign of the third king, Tullus Hostil′ius, a war was carried on with Alba Longa.   The issue of this war was decided, so the story goes, by a combat between the three Hora′-tii, champions of the Romans, and the three Curia′tii, champions of Alba — resulting in the triumph of the Romans and the submission of Alba to the Roman power.

The fourth king, Ancus Marcius, was a Sabine, the grandson of Numa.   He too was a man of peace, but was drawn into a war with several of the Latin cities. Having subdued them, he transferred their inhabitants to the Av'entine hill (map, p. 310).

Legends of the Later Kings. — The three later kings of Rome are said to have been Etruscans. The first of these was Tarquin'ius Priscus, who migrated to Rome from the Etruscan city of Tarquinii. He strengthened his position as king by adopting the royal insignia of the Etruscans — a crown of gold, a scepter, an ivory chair, and twelve attendants called *lictors*, each carrying a bundle of rods (*fasces*) containing an ax, the symbol of absolute power. He carried on war with the Latins and Sabines, drained the city, laid out the Forum, and dedicated a temple to Jupiter on the Cap'itoline hill.

The next of the later kings was Servius Tullius, the son of a slave woman of the king's household. He united Rome and the Latin cities in a league; reorganized the government; and erected a new wall inclosing the seven hills.

THE ELDER BRUTUS

The last king was Tarquinius Superbus, who ruled as a despot, and was at last driven from the throne by the elder Brutus and his friend Collati'nus (510 B.C.).

Legends of the Early Republic. — The legends contain many stories relating not only to the overthrow of the kingdom but also to the early years of the republic. It is said that after the last Tarquin was expelled, the people elected in his stead Brutus and Collatinus to rule them for a year; that Brutus condemned his own sons to death for conspiring to restore the Tarquins; that the Etruscans under a prince called Lars Porsen'na (or Por'sena) lent their aid to the

Tarquins, and that their armies were prevented from entering Rome by the heroic defense of the wooden bridge by Horatius Cocles. It is related that the cause of the banished king was then espoused by the Latins and that their armies were defeated at the battle of Lake Regil'lus (not far from Alba Longa) by the aid of the twin gods Castor and Pollux.

HORATIUS COCLES

(Medallion)

Significance of the Roman Legends. — Such were some of the stories which, embellished with many miraculous incidents, the Romans were proud to relate, as explaining the origin of their city and the beginning of their institutions. Like all other legends these stories have little value as evidence of what actually took place. They contain many improbable details. They refer to particular persons as the creators of their institutions, although these must have been the result of a slow process of growth. Some of the stories were borrowed from the Greeks, and used by the Romans for their own purpose. So incredible are some of these legends that the whole body of this traditional history is sometimes set aside as unworthy of belief or even of serious consideration.

But while their credibility may be questioned, the significance of these traditions should not be overlooked. While they may not indicate what actually occurred, they show what the people really believed. They show that the Romans took pride in their political institutions, that they honored the virtues of courage and patriotism, and that they believed their destiny was in the hands of the gods. They continued to be an inspiration to the Roman people — in their wars, in their political life, in their literature and art. While we may not regard these legends as history, it is yet true that, without a knowledge of them, there is much in Roman history that we could not understand.

Selections for Reading

Knowlton, Topic A 16, "The Land of Italy" (1).[1]

Seignobos, Ch. 17, "Ancient Peoples of Italy" (1).

Goodspeed, Ancient World, pp. 240–258 (geography and peoples of Italy) (1).

Liddell, Bk. I., "Rome under the Kings" (18).

Merivale, General History, Ch. 3, "The Earliest Legends" (18).

Pelham, Bk. I., Ch. 1, "The Traditions" (18).

How and Leigh, Ch. 2, "The Peoples of Italy"; Ch. 3 (legends of the kings) (18).

Mommsen, Vol. I., Bk. I., Ch. 9, "The Etruscans"; Ch. 10, "The Hellenes in Italy" (18).

Livy, Bk. I. (legends of the kings) (25).

Vergil, Bk. I. (wanderings of Æneas) (25).

Munro, Source Book, Part I., "Italy — Rome" (25).

Special Study

THE ETRUSCANS. — Smith, Wm., Smaller History, pp. 3–4 (18); Liddell, 16–17 (18); How and Leigh, pp. 12–14 (18); Mommsen, Vol. I., Bk. I., Ch. 9 (18); Encyclopedias, Article "Etruria."

[1] The figure in parenthesis refers to the number of the topic in the Appendix, where a fuller title of the book will be found.

CHAPTER XX

THE EARLY CITY STATE: ITS ORIGIN AND GROWTH

Synopsis

I. ORIGIN OF THE ROMAN CITY. — The Site and Hills of Rome. — The Latin Settlement on the Palatine. — The Sabine Settlement on the Quirinal. — Union of the Romans and the Sabines. — The Third Settlement, on the Cælian.

II. THE ELEMENTS OF THE EARLY CITY STATE. — The Early Roman Family : the Family Worship. — The Roman Gens. — The Roman Curia. — The Early Roman Government. — Changes in the Early City State. — Growth of the Roman City. — Conquests in Latium.

III. LIFE AND CUSTOMS OF THE EARLY ROMANS. — The Early Roman Religion : the Gods. — Religious Ceremonies and Officials. — The Early Roman Law. — Occupations of the People.

I. ORIGIN OF THE ROMAN CITY

The Site and Hills of Rome. — By studying the situation of Rome itself we may perhaps get a clearer idea of the probable origin of the city than we can get from the traditional stories. The city was located on the southeast bank of the river Tiber, about eighteen miles from the sea. To the south of this locality was Latium, or the country of the Latins ; to the northeast was the country of the

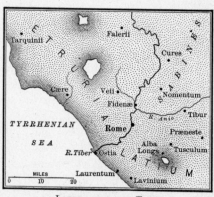

LANDS ABOUT THE TIBER

Sabines; and to the northwest, across the Tiber, was the land of the Etruscans. The city thus grew up at the point of contact between three different peoples, who exercised a great influence upon the early development of the state.

If we look more closely at this locality, we shall see that it contained a group of seven hills which could be occupied and defended against the attack of enemies. Of these hills three lay to the northeast — the Quir'inal, the Vim'inal, and the Es'quiline; three lay to the south — the Palatine, the Cælian, and the Aventine; while between these two minor groups rose the small and rugged elevation of the Capitoline. The most important of the hills were the Quirinal in the first group, and the Palatine in the second. These two were the large hills best fitted for defense, and hence for occupation by settlers. If we compare them, it is evident that the Palatine occupies the most central and commanding position, and its settlers, as we shall see, became the controlling people of the seven-hilled city.

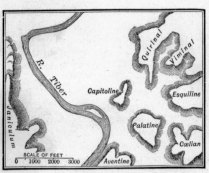

THE HILLS OF ROME

The Latin Settlement on the Palatine. — So far as we know, the first people to get a foothold upon the site of Rome were the Latins, who formed a settlement upon and about the Palatine hill. This Latin settlement was at first a small village. It consisted of a few farmers and shepherds who were sent out from Latium (perhaps from Alba Longa) as a sort of outpost, both to protect the Latin frontier and to trade with the neighboring tribes. The people who formed this settlement were called *Ramnes*. They dwelt in their rude straw huts on the slopes of the Palatine, and on the lower lands in the direction of the Aventine and the Cælian. The outlying lands furnished the fields which they tilled and used for pasturage. For protection against attacks, the sides of the Palatine hill were strengthened by a wall built of rude but solid masonry. This fortified place was called *Roma Quadra'ta*, or "Square Rome." It formed the citadel of the colony, into which the settlers could drive their cattle and conduct their families when attacked

HUT-SHAPED URN

by hostile neighbors. What some persons suppose to be the primitive wall of the Palatine city, known as the "Wall of Romulus," has in recent years been uncovered, so that we can see its general character.

"WALL OF ROMULUS"

The Sabine Settlement on the Quirinal. — Opposite the Palatine settlement there grew up a settlement on the Quirinal hill. This Quirinal settlement seems to have been an outpost or colony of the Sabine people, just as the Palatine settlement was a Latin colony. The Sabines were pushing southward from beyond the river A'nio. The settlers on the Quirinal were called

Tit'i-es; their colony formed a second hill-town, similar in character and nearly equal in extent to the Palatine town.

Union of the Romans and the Sabines. — The two hill-towns which thus faced each other naturally became rivals for the possession of the lands near the Tiber; but being so nearly of equal strength, neither could conquer the other. They therefore formed an alliance, were united by a permanent league, and really became a single city — or perhaps we might better call it a double city. To celebrate this union, the intervening

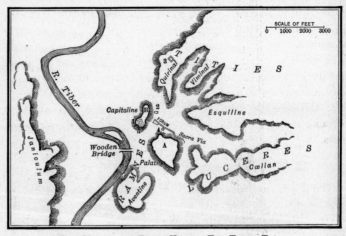

THE CITY OF THE EARLY KINGS — THE THREE TRIBES

A, Roma Quadrata. B, Arx, or Citadel
Temples, Altars, etc.: 1, Jupiter Capitolinus; 2, Janus; 3, Quirinus; 4, Vesta;
5, Tarpeian Rock

space was dedicated to the two-faced god, Janus, who watched the approaches of both towns. The Capitoline hill was chosen as the common citadel. The space between the two towns was used as a common market place (*forum*), and also as a place for the common meeting of the people (*comitium*). This union of the Palatine and Quirinal towns into one community, with a common religion and government, was an event of great importance. It was, in fact, the first step in the process of " incorporation " which afterward made Rome the most powerful city of Latium, of Italy, and finally of the world.

The Third Settlement, on the Cælian. — The union of the Romans (*Ramnes*) and the Sabines (*Tities*) was followed by the introduction of a third people, called the *Lu'ceres*. This people was probably a body of Latins who had been conquered and settled upon the Cælian hill — although they are sometimes regarded as having been Etruscans. Whatever may have been their origin, it is quite certain that they soon came to be incorporated as a part of the whole city community. The city of the early Roman kings thus came to be made up of three divisions, " tribes " (*tribus*, a third part, from *tres*, three). The evidence of this threefold origin was preserved in many institutions of later times. The three settlements were gradually united into a single city state with common social, political, and religious institutions. By this union, the new city became strong and able to compete successfully with its neighbors.

II. THE ELEMENTS OF THE EARLY CITY STATE

The Early Roman Family: the Family Worship. — Let us look in upon this little city state that had grown up about the seven hills near the Tiber. We should see scattered about, here and there, groups of low thatched houses. We should find each house occupied by a single family. But we should find this family to be quite different from the modern family. Instead of its being composed simply of a man and his wife with their children, there would be also the sons' wives and the grandchildren, perhaps for two or three generations — all under the absolute power of the household father (*paterfamilias*).

We should find the father to be a very religious man. He believed that the spirits of his ancestors hovered about the house, protecting the members from evil. He believed that these revered spirits should be worshiped: and each day he

wculd gather the family around the domestic altar, where the
fire was kept continually burning, and share with them the daily
meal. The father was thus a sort of priest in the family. He
derived his authority from the ancestral gods. He was said to
have the power of "life and death" — which simply means
that no one could interfere in his control of his own family. He
might expose the new-born infant, if he thought it ought not to
live. He was subject to no law, except the law of custom; that
is, the usages approved by public opinion. Marriage was a
sacred ceremony by which the wife became initiated into the
worship of her husband. If a daughter married into another
family, she became subject to the father of that family and
shared in its religion. When a father died, the sons became
the heads of new families, and the guardians of the unmarried
daughters and infant children. But we must not suppose that,
because the father was supreme, he was necessarily a cruel despot. Indeed, he had great regard for the preservation of his
family. It was a great calamity for the family and its worship
to become extinct. To prevent this the father might adopt a
son to carry on the family worship.

The Roman Gens. — In the process of time the families
which were descended from a common ancestor would come
to form a large group of family relatives — as we sometimes
see in our large family reunions. This larger family group
had frequent meetings, and kept up a common religious
worship in honor of their oldest ancestor. They all bore his
name. They also had a common burying ground, and had
common lands upon which they raised their crops, or pastured
their flocks and herds. When they were obliged to go to war
they fought together under their common leader; and this
leader was the one who conducted their common worship and
settled disputes between members of the different families.
He was thus a war chief, a priest, and a judge. Such a group of
family relatives, bound together by a common name and a common worship, formed a clan, — or as the Romans called it, a

gens. The tribes which formed the early Roman state were made up of many such clans, or *gen'tes.*

The Roman Curia. — Sometimes it would be necessary for the chief of a tribe or the king to call the people together to approve of some plan of his — for example, to say whether they would follow him to war. But instead of calling all the people together in one place to vote, as they did at Athens, a part of a tribe — consisting of several neighboring gentes — would meet in one place and cast its vote, another part in another place and cast its vote, and the majority of such votes would decide the will of the people. Such a division of the tribe for the purpose of voting was called a *curia.* There were ten such *curiæ* in each tribe, and a meeting of the people voting by curiæ was called the *comi'tia curia'ta.* When the people came to meet all together in one place, as in the Forum, they still continued to vote separately by curiæ.

The Early Roman Government. — We can now see how the early Roman government was formed. Each tribe had a chief, or king, a council of one hundred members, and an assembly of ten curiæ. With the union of the first two tribes, their governments also were united so as to form a single government. Thus their two kings were replaced by one king chosen alternately from each tribe. Their councils and assemblies were also united so as to form single bodies. And when the third tribe is added, we have a single king, a single council of three hundred members, and a single assembly (*comitia curiata*) of thirty curiæ.

(1) The Roman *king* (*rex*) was the chief of the whole people. He was elected, or at least approved, by the people, and inaugurated under the sanction of the gods. He was in a sense the father of the whole nation — their chief priest, commander in war, and supreme judge. Like the father in the household, he had the power of life and death over all his subjects.

(2) The Roman *senate*, or council of elders, was composed of the chief men of the gentes, who were chosen by the king to assist him with their advice. Upon the death of the king

they might choose a temporary king (*interrex*) to act as ruler. until the regular successor was chosen.

(3) The *comitia curiata* was the assembly of all the people capable of bearing arms, arranged by curiæ. Each curia had a single vote, and the will of the assembly was determined by a majority of such votes. In a certain sense the assembly was the highest authority in the state. It approved the nomination of the king by the senate, and passed a law (*lex curiata de imperio*) conferring upon him his power. To the assembly the king submitted important questions, such as those regarding peace or war. The early city state may therefore be described as a democratic monarchy, in which the king derived his power from the people.

Changes in the Early City State. — We haye seen how the earliest Roman state grew up from the union of the three tribes; we have also seen how these tribes were in turn made up of the old Roman families and *gentes*. It was only the members of these old families and *gentes* who had anything to do with the early Roman government. It was they only who could vote in the assembly and could serve in the army. In this early period the number of slaves was small; but in the course of time there grew up around the city a large new body of free persons, made up of refugees from the outlying towns and other immigrants, and perhaps of captives taken in war. Now this new class of persons had at first no right in the state, and no social standing. They could not vote in the assembly. They could not intermarry with Roman citizens. But they might hold property and carry on trade under the protection of a citizen, called their "patron." Many of them attached themselves to some Roman citizen as their patron, and were called his "clients," or dependents.[1]

[1] The relation between patron and client was quite close: the patron assumed the duty of defending the interests of his client, and the client was bound to pay a certain respect to his patron. In the course of time it came to be regarded as an honor for a Roman citizen to have many clients.

This new population came to be known as "plebe′ians ";
while the body of old Roman citizens were known as "patricians."
But the patricians soon found out that these dependent people
could fight as well as anybody, and that some way was needed
in which they could be enrolled in the army. This led to the
formation of new tribes, a new army, and a new assembly.

(1) *The New Local Tribes.* — The Romans now made a new
division of the people, based not upon blood like the old tribes,
but upon locality; that is, upon the place where people lived.
The whole city and surrounding country was divided into thirty
local districts, — four for the city (like our wards) and twenty-
six for the country (like our townships). These districts were
known as " local tribes." All persons living in one of these districts, whether patricians or plebeians, were now liable to military service.

(2) *The New Army; the Centuries.* — The new army was
arranged in companies of 100 men each, called " centuries."

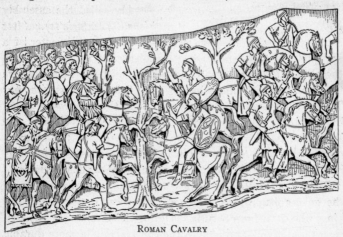

ROMAN CAVALRY

Now in ancient times every man was obliged to furnish his own
weapons or equipment. The wealthiest men, who were able to
furnish a horse, formed the cavalry (or *eq′uites*); of these there

were eighteen centuries. Then came the infantry, arranged in five classes, according to the weight of armor the men could furnish. The first class, with the heaviest armor, comprised eighty centuries, the second, third, and fourth classes twenty centuries each, and the fifth class thirty centuries. The new Roman army thus comprised nearly twenty thousand men, made up of both patricians and plebeians.

SOLDIER WITH FULL ARMOR

(3) *The New Assembly; the Comitia Centuriata.* — There was every reason why the important questions relating to war which had been left to the old body of men capable of bearing arms should now be left to the new body of armed men. As a matter of fact, the new fighting body became a new voting body; and there arose a new assembly called the assembly of the centuries (*comitia centuria'ta*). After a time the *comitia centuriata* came to have the character of a real political and legislative body, of greater importance than the old *comitia curiata*. It did not meet in the Forum where the old assembly met, but in the field of Mars (*campus Martius*) outside the city. In this body the votes were taken by centuries. But as the cavalry and the first class of the infantry had 98 century votes, and the rest of the infantry classes had only 90 votes, it is evident that this assembly was really an aristocratic body, governed by the wealthier classes.

Growth of the Roman City. — It is said that these changes in the government which we have just noticed were made by the kings who came from Etruria. During this time we see the city growing in population, and in the construction of more durable buildings. The Etruscans were great builders, and their cities were well fortified. Previous to this time the Romans had a wall only about the Palatine hill. But now one of these Etruscan kings, Servius Tullius, encircled all the seven hills with a strong fortification, making a circuit of about five miles. This so-called "Servian wall" continued to be the only fortification

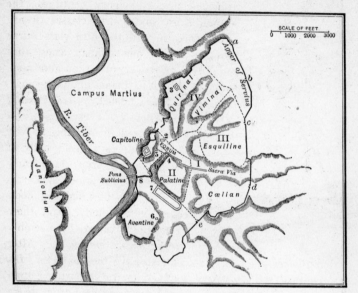

THE CITY OF THE LATER KINGS — WALLS OF SERVIUS

The four Servian regions: I., Suburana; II., Palatina; III., Esquilina; IV., Collina.

The chief gates of Rome: a, Collina; b, Viminalis; c, Esquilina; d, Querquetu-lana; e, Capena; f, Ratumena.

The chief buildings, etc.: 1, Temple of Jupiter Capitolinus; 2, Janus; 3, Quirinus; 4, Vesta; 5, Saturn; 6, Diana; 7, Circus Maximus; 8, Cloaca Maxima; 9, Vicus Tuscus.

about the city for many centuries, and remains of it are seen at the present day. More durable temples also were built — one to Jupiter on the summit of the Capitoline hill, one to Saturn at the foot of the Capitoline, and one to Diana on the Aventine. The *Circus Maximus*, a place for chariot racing, was laid out between the Palatine and the Aventine, for the amusement of the

Falerii

Sutrium

Nepete

SABINI

ETRUSCANS

Cures

Cære

Veii

R. Cremera

Fidenæ

R. Alia

Nomentum

Mons Sacer

R. Anio

Tibur

Rome

R. Tiber

Pedum

Praeneste

Tusculum

Alba Longa

Mt. Algidus

HERNICI

Ostia

Aricia

Laurentum

Lavinium

Lanuvium

Velitrae

Signia

Ardea

Norba

Antium

VOLSCI

Setia

TYRRHENIAN SEA

AEQUI

ROMAN DOMINION
At the End of the Kingdom
B.C. 510

Roman domain (ager Romanus)
Subject territory in Latium

Pontine Marshes

Tarracina or Anxur

Circeii

SCALE OF MILES
0   5   10   15   20   25   30

people. A great arched sewer, the *Cloa'ca Maxima*, was opened to drain the marshy lands about the Forum; it emptied into the Tiber. So well constructed was this drain that it is used to-day as one of the sewers of the city. All these public works show the great influence that the Etruscans had upon the early Roman city.

END OF THE CLOACA MAXIMA

Conquests in Latium. — While Rome was thus becoming strong, and her people were becoming more united and better organized, she was also gaining power over the neighboring lands. The people with whom she first came into contact were the Latins. A number of Latin towns were conquered or otherwise brought under her power, and some of the conquered territory was added to the Roman domain (*ager Roma'nus*). She also pushed her conquests across the Anio into the Sabine country, and across the Tiber into Etruria. So that before the fall of the kingdom, Rome had begun to be a conquering power.

III. LIFE AND CUSTOMS OF THE EARLY ROMANS

The Early Roman Religion: the Gods. — We have no written records that go back to the time of the kings, but scholars have been able, from recent excavations and other means, to find out many things about the life of the early Romans. We know their religion was derived mostly from the Latins, the Sabines and the Etruscans. Their religion was very practical, like the people themselves. They had no beautiful mythology, no finely spun stories about the gods, like the Greeks; neither did they attempt at first to carve images of the gods, like the Greeks. They worshiped their gods at shrines and public altars placed about the city; these were their first temples.

One of the earliest deities of Rome was Vesta, the goddess of the domestic hearth; for her the sacred fire was kept burning.

STATUE OF A VESTAL VIRGIN

And since the state was regarded as a great family, a city altar was erected to her upon which the fire was kept burning. This fire was constantly watched by six chosen maidens, called the "Vestal Virgins." As the state grew, the people began to worship state gods. To lead them in war they worshiped Mars, the god of war. To protect them from storms and thunderbolts they worshiped Jupiter, the god of the heavens. To obtain bountiful harvests, they worshiped Saturn, the god of the seed-time; Ce′res, the goddess of the fields; Minerva, of olives; Flora, of flowers; Liber, the god of wine. There was a god for almost everything. Janus, their god of beginnings and entrances, was two-faced, looking into the past and the future. In January, the month of Janus, a Roman citizen was expected to look into his past and make good resolutions for the future — as we sometimes do to-day. It is impossible to mention all of the deities of early Rome; but the people were very willing to admit into their divine circle the gods of other peoples.

Religious Ceremonies and Officials. — The early Romans believed that the favor of the gods was to be kept by observing certain ceremonies, and that these had to be carefully performed

according to set rules.   Hence they looked up to their priests, —
pontiffs and augurs, — who were acquainted with the proper
forms.   These men were public officials, appointed by the
king; for religion was a part of the state.   Their duty was to
see that all the rites were properly observed.   If a public prayer
was to be made, the suppliant
had to follow the words pronounced by the priest.   If a
sacrifice was made, the priest
saw to it that the proper kind
of animal was selected, of proper
color and age, whether ox or
sheep or swine.   There were
special bodies of priests, or
pontiffs, to look after particular
religious duties; such as the
dancing priests (*Salii*) to watch
over the shield of Mars, which
was supposed to have fallen from

A ROMAN SACRIFICE

heaven; the Arval Brothers, to make an annual sacrifice to
insure the fertility of fields.

A peculiar part of the early Roman religion was the method
used to find out the will of the gods, — a custom which the
Romans obtained from the Etruscans.   This was called " taking
the auspices."   The body of augurs were supposed to be specially
versed in interpreting the divine will.   If any great enterprise
was under consideration, such as going into battle, it was
necessary to know whether it would be successful.   The taking
of the auspices was done by watching the flight of birds, their
number and in what part of the heavens they appeared.   It was
done by examining the entrails of animals slain in the sacrifice,
whether they were found to be in a perfect condition or not.
The will of the gods might be indicated by some natural phe-
nomenon, as an eclipse, or the appearance of a comet, which
might be interpreted as a bad " omen."   If an assembly were

interrupted by a sudden peal of thunder, it would be a bad omen, and the assembly would be dissolved. All this shows that the early Romans were a very superstitious people.

The Early Roman Law. — When two men have a quarrel, they sometimes settle their dispute by coming to blows; and the one who is the stronger thinks he is in the right. This is the way in which uncivilized men often settle their disputes, that is, by " self redress." But the Romans soon learned that such a mode of settling disputes was bad in every way. It disturbed the public peace; and also men in a passion lose their sense of justice. If a man disturbed the peace or injured his neighbor, it would be better to have his case settled by a public officer, such as the king. If he had committed a great crime, such as treason or murder, the king condemned him to death — to be hurled from the high rock on the Capitoline hill (the Tarpe'ian rock), or thrown into the Tiber. For lesser crimes he was fined to pay a certain number of cattle or sheep. If he had injured his neighbor, by not paying a debt, the injured party might compel him to go before the king, who listened to what the parties had to say and, if the facts warranted, condemned the debtor to pay the debt. If the debtor still refused or was unable to pay, the creditor could then keep him bound in chains and fed on bread and water for sixty days. The creditor, however, was obliged to give him a chance on three successive market days to find some one willing to guarantee the payment of the debt. If no one offered to do this, the poor debtor might be bound to the creditor as a bondman or sold into slavery.

In early times property consisted chiefly of slaves, cattle, and farming implements. Such pieces of property might be exchanged one thing for another, that is, by barter; or for so many cattle or sheep, — which was the first kind of money at Rome. When the Romans began to have copper and before they had learned how to coin it into money, they might sell a piece of property for a piece of copper weighed out with a hand-balance. When a father died the family property was divided equally among the legal heirs — the wife, the sons, and unmarried daughters. In the early Roman law, women were never legally independent, but held their property under the guardianship of some male relative.

Occupations of the People. — The early Roman people were, for the most part, a nation of farmers or shepherds. The land was owned and cultivated in common by the clans; and at harvest time the products of the soil were distributed among the several households. It was not long, however, before the arable land was divided among the several families, each family receiving a little farm of about twenty *iu′-*

ROMAN FARMER

gera (twelve and a half acres). The farmer and his sons cultivated this plot of ground, raising grain, vegetables, olives, and figs. They rested from their labors on the great festival days devoted to the gods, when no kind of work was allowed.

While farming was the chief occupation of the early Romans, there were persons who were engaged in several trades. Indeed, it is said that Numa, the second king of Rome, established eight guilds, or trade unions. Among these were goldsmiths, coppersmiths, carpenters, fullers, and shoemakers. There were no bakers or weavers, because the baking of bread and the weaving of cloth were done by the women of the household. The early Romans also carried on commerce with their neighbors. They held an annual fair, when people from all the villages of Latium came together and exchanged goods. Recent excavations in Rome and Latium show that in very early times the Latins, as well as the Etruscans, came into relation with Carthage and Greece, from which countries they obtained decorated vases and other wares.

Selections for Reading

Seignobos, Ch. 18, "Roman Religion " (1).[1]

Smith, Wm., Smaller History, Ch. 2, "The Early Kings "; Ch. 3, "The Later Kings" (18).

Shuckburgh, Ch. 5, "The Regal Period " (18).

Pelham, Bk. I., Ch. 2, "Origin of the City and Commonwealth "; Ch. 3, "Rome under the Kings " (18).

How and Leigh, Ch. 4, "The Regal Period " (18).

Ihne, Early Rome, Ch. 9, "People of the Regal Period" (18).

Abbott, Ch. 1, "Rome under the Kings "; Ch. 2, "Monarchical Institutions " (22).

Granrud, First Period, Ch. 1, "Original Constitution of Rome"; Ch. 2, "Later Royal Constitution " (22).

Mommsen, Vol. I., Bk. I., Ch. 4, "Beginnings of Rome"; Ch. 5, "Original Constitution of Rome"; Ch. 6, "The Non-Burgesses and the Reformed Constitution " (18).

—— Abridged, Ch. 3, "Rome's Original Constitution"; Ch. 4, "Reforms of Servius Tullius" (18).

Greenidge, Public Life, Ch. 1, "Earliest Constitution of Rome"; pp. 9–33 (the Roman family) (22).

Parker, Ch. 2, "Roma Quadrata"; Ch. 5, "The City of the Seven Hills" (20).

Munro, Source Book, Part II., "Religion" (25).

Special Study

ATTEMPTS TO RESTORE THE TARQUINS. — Smith, Wm., Smaller History, pp. 30–34 (18); Liddell, Ch. 4 (18); How and Leigh, pp. 32–34 (18).

[1] The figure in parenthesis refers to the number of the topic in the Appendix where a fuller title of the book will be found.

CHAPTER XXI

THE STRUGGLES OF THE PEOPLE FOR EQUAL RIGHTS

Synopsis

I. THE REPUBLICAN REVOLUTION. — Establishment of the Consulate. — The Dictatorship. — The New Senators. — The Two Popular Assemblies. — The Valerian Laws.

II. THE STRUGGLE FOR ECONOMIC RIGHTS. — Relation of the Patricians to the Plebeians. — Economic Distress of the Plebeians. — First Secession of the Plebeians. — The Tribunes of the People. — The New Assembly: the *Comitia Tributa*.

III. THE STRUGGLE FOR EQUAL LAWS. — The Demand for a Written Code. — The Decemvirs and the XII. Tables. — The Second Secession and Overthrow of the Decemvirate. — The Valerio-Horatian Laws. — The Right of Intermarriage.

IV. THE STRUGGLE FOR POLITICAL EQUALITY. — Progress of the Plebeians. — The Consular Tribunes. — The Censorship and the New Quæstors. — The Destruction of the City by the Gauls. — The Licinian Legislation. — Final Equalization of the Orders. — Summary of the Republican Constitution.

I. THE REPUBLICAN REVOLUTION

Establishment of the Consulate. — The Roman legends tell exciting stories of the people's revolt against the last king, Tarquinius Superbus (Tarquin the Proud). The last Tarquin, like the other Etruscan kings, had been a strong ruler; but he had used his power in a despotic manner. His family was corrupt, and had committed crimes that the Roman people could not tolerate. The people, therefore, banished him and his family from the city, and decreed that there should henceforth be no king at Rome.

Three times the banished king strove to recover his lost power. In the midst of the last memorable battle — at Lake Regillus —

the Romans said that there appeared two gigantic youths riding upon snow-white horses, and equipped in splendid armor. Through their aid the victory was turned in favor of the Romans. The people recognized in these brilliant warriors the twin gods, Castor and Pollux; and they built in the Forum a temple in commemoration of this, their final deliverance from the power of the Tarquins.

According to the legends, the revolt against the king was managed by two leaders, Brutus and Collatinus, who were chosen by the people to rule over them for a year. However that may be, we know that the highest office of the Roman republic was put into the hands of two men — at first called "prætors," or leaders, and afterwards "consuls." These new officers were elected annually by the *comitia centuriata*. They had the royal insignia (p. 306); but each consul was a restraint on the other, and the two together had smaller powers than those of the former king. The consuls exercised the power of life and death outside of the city, but not in it; when in Rome itself, the ax was withdrawn from the *fasces*. The consuls commanded the army, but the control of the finances was given to two other officers elected by the assembly, called "quæstors."

LICTORS, WITH FASCES

The Dictatorship. — The Romans saw that in times of great danger the power of the consuls might not be strong enough to protect the state. To meet such an emergency it was provided that a *dictator* should be appointed, who was to be a sort of temporary king. He was to have entire control of the city and the army. He was even given the power of life and death over citizens; and his lictors (attendants) retained the ax in the *fasces*. But this extraordinary power could be held for only six months, after which time the consuls resumed their regular authority as chief magistrates. With the dictator there was generally appointed another officer, who was second in authority, called the master of horse; but over him, as over every one else, the dictator was supreme.

The New Senators. — When the consuls were elected, the legends say that one of their first acts was to fill up the senate to the number of three hundred members. The last king had practically ruled without the senate, and he had no reason to fill the vacancies when they occurred. But the new consuls wished the help of the senate, and therefore desired to keep its numbers complete. From this time the senate came to have more and more power; for its members were appointed for life. It claimed the right to ratify or reject all laws passed by the *comitia centuriata;* it had the supervision of the state religion and of the state treasury; and it disposed of the public lands conquered from the enemy.

The Two Popular Assemblies. — With the establishment of the republic, the two assemblies with which we are already acquainted, the *comitia curiata* and the *comitia centuriata*, both remained. But the former lost a great deal of its old power, which became transferred to the latter. The assembly of the centuries was thus the body in which the people generally expressed their will. Here they elected the officers, and passed the most important laws. It was this assembly which became the chief legislative body during the early republic.

The Valerian Laws. — The legends say that after the death of Brutus, his colleague Valerius (who had succeeded Collatinus) did not call an assembly to elect another consul. This aroused the fear that Valerius wished to make himself king. But it was soon found that instead of aiming to be king, he was preparing a set of laws which would prevent any one from becoming king, and would also protect the people from the arbitrary power of their magistrates. One of these laws declared that any person who assumed the chief power without the people's consent should be condemned as a traitor. Another law provided that any citizen who was condemned for a capital crime should have the right of an appeal to the people assembled in the *comitia centuriata*. These laws, known as the Valerian laws, may be called the "first charter of Roman liberty," because they protected the people from the exercise of arbitrary power. So highly honored was Valerius that he was surnamed Poplic'ola, or the People's Friend.

II. The Struggle for Economic Rights

Relation of the Patricians to the Plebeians. — The patricians and plebeians had united in their efforts to drive out the kings; but when the struggle against the kingship was ended, the chief fruits of the victory fell to the patricians. The plebeians could, it is true, still vote in the *comitia centuriata;* but they could not hold any of the new offices, nor could they sit in the senate. Rome became a republic, but it was an aristocratic, and not a democratic republic; that is, the chief power rested not in the whole people, but in a particular class. The plebeians might perhaps have submitted to the government of the patricians, if it had not been exercised in a selfish and oppressive manner. But the patrician rule proved to be as despotic as that of the kings; and a long and fierce struggle ensued between the two orders.

Economic Distress of the Plebeians. — The sorest burden which now rested upon the plebeians was the harsh law of debt. Having lost their property by the misfortunes of war, they were obliged to borrow money of the rich patricians; and they were thus reduced to the condition of a debtor class. But a debtor in the early days of Rome was especially wretched. If he could not pay his debt, he was liable to be arrested, thrown into a dungeon, and made the slave of his creditor. His lot was chains, stripes, and slavery.

Another cause which kept the plebeians in a state of poverty was the unjust distribution of the public land (*ager publicus*) which had been acquired in war. This land properly belonged to all the people, and might have been used to relieve the distress of the poor. But the government was in the hands of the patricians, and they disposed of this land for their own benefit; they allowed it to be "occupied," at a nominal rent, by members of their own order. As long as the land remained public, it could not be sold by the occupants; but the longer the rich patricians retained the occupation of this land, the more they would look upon it as their own property, and ignore the fact that it belonged to the whole Roman people. Thus the common people were deprived of their just share of the land which they had helped to conquer.

First Secession of the Plebeians. — It was the hard law of debt which first drove the plebeians to revolt. As there was no legal way to redress their wrongs, they decided that they would no longer serve in the army, but leave the patricians to fight their own battles. They therefore deserted their general, marched in full array to a hill beyond the Anio, which they called the Sacred Mount, and proposed to form an independent city. The patricians saw that the loss of the plebeian army would be the destruction of Rome. They were therefore compelled to agree that the debts of all insolvent persons should be canceled, and that those imprisoned on account of debt should be released.

The Tribunes of the People. — But the most important result of this first secession was the creation of a new office, that of 'tribune of the people." In order to protect the plebeians from any further oppressive acts on the part of the patrician magistrates, it was agreed to appoint two tribunes from among the plebeians themselves. These new officers were given the power to "veto" — that is, to forbid — the act of any magistrate which bore unjustly upon any citizen. In order that the tribunes might exercise their authority without hindrance, their persons were made "inviolable" — which means that they could not be arrested, and that any one who interfered with them in the exercise of their lawful duty could be put to death. The tribune could not leave the city during his year of office. His house had to be kept open day and night, so that any plebeian might find a safe refuge. There were also appointed two plebeian *æ'diles*, to take charge of the public buildings and to perform police duty.

The New Assembly: the Comitia Tributa. — We can see that the establishment of the tribunate was an important step in protecting the rights of the plebeians. Another step was due to the growth of a new assembly. This assembly was made up of all the people — patricians as well as plebeians — living in the different " local tribes " (p. 317). It voted by tribes and was hence called the *comitia tribu'ta*. But as there were twenty-six tribes in the country where most of the plebeians lived, and only four tribes in the city where most of the patricians lived, the plebeians could outvote the patricians. Hence the new assembly of the tribes was essentially a plebeian body, while that of the centuries was controlled by the patricians. The new tribal assembly was presided over by the tribunes of the people, and elected the plebeian officers — the tribunes and the ædiles; while the older assembly of the centuries was presided over by the consuls and elected the patrician officers — the consuls and quæstors. A few years later, as we shall see, the laws passed by the *comitia tributa* were made binding upon the whole people; and thus became a means for bringing about an equality between the two orders.

III. The Struggle for Equal Laws

The Demand for a Written Code. — The plebeians were at a great disadvantage during all this time, because the law was administered solely by the patricians. The laws had never been written down or published. The patricians could therefore administer them as they saw fit. Accordingly one of the tribunes

Gaius Terentil'ius Harsa, proposed that a commission be appointed to codify the law and to publish it to the whole people. This proposal, though both fair and just, was bitterly opposed by the patricians, and was followed by ten years of strife and dissension. It was finally agreed that a commission of ten men, called " decem'virs," should be elected, by the *comitia centuriata*, to draw up the law, and that this law should be published and be binding upon patricians and plebeians alike. It was also agreed that the commissioners should have entire control of the government while compiling the laws. Thus for a time the patricians were to give up their consuls and quæstors, and the plebeians were to give up their tribunes and ædiles. Both parties were to cease their quarreling and await the work of the decemvirs.

The Decemvirs and the XII. Tables (450 B.C.). — The body of ten commissioners, called the First Decem'virate, entered upon the work assigned to it, gathered together the law which had hitherto been kept secret, and inscribed it on ten tables of brass. These tables were erected in the Forum, where they could be seen by every one, and were declared binding on all the people. At the close of the year, a Second Decemvirate was appointed to complete the code, and two more tables were added. This whole body of law was called the Twelve Tables, and formed the basis of the most remarkable system of law that the world has ever seen. There was nothing strange, however, in the XII. Tables themselves. They contained nothing especially new. The old law of debt remained as it was, and the distinction between patricians and plebeians was not destroyed. The XII. Tables were important because they put the law before the eyes of the people; and plebeians, as well as patricians, could know what were their rights.

The Second Secession and Overthrow of the Decemvirate. — While the decemvirs were engaged in codifying the laws, the old republican officers were temporarily suspended. It was expected that the decemvirs would lay aside their exceptional authority when their work was accomplished. But it seems that the second body of decemvirs refused to resign, and threatened to establish a permanent despotic government in place of the old consulate. It is said that the leader of this movement was Appius Claudius.[1] However this may be, the people, fearing that their liberties were in danger, once more seceded from the city. The Roman state seemed again on the point of ruin, and the decemvirs were forced to resign. The old government was restored, with newly elected consuls friendly to the plebeians. These were Lucius Valerius and Marcus Horatius.

The Valerio-Horatian Laws (448 B.C.). — The second secession of the plebeians resulted not only in the overthrow of the decemvirate and the restoration of the consulate; it resulted also in the passage of certain important laws, which received the name of the new consuls:

(1) The right of appeal in capital cases (p. 330) was reaffirmed, and this applied to plebeians as well as to patricians.

(2) The power of the plebeian tribunes was sanctioned by the declaration that he who raised his hand against them should be accursed.

(3) The authority of the plebeian assembly was made clear by the provision that its acts should be binding upon the whole people — patricians as well as plebeians. This provision made the *comitia tributa* a real legislative body for the whole state.

These laws made definite and clear the constitutional rights of the people, and secured to them the privileges they had already claimed. They may be called " the second charter of Roman liberty " (for the first charter, see p. 330).

The Right of Intermarriage. — The XII. Tables had preserved the old customary law prohibiting intermarriage be-

---

[1] With this movement is connected the traditional story of Virginia: that she was the beautiful daughter of a plebeian soldier and was killed by her father to prevent her from falling into the hands of Appius Claudius. Some authorities, however, are inclined to believe that Appius Claudius was really the friend of the people, and that this story was invented by the patricians to bring his name into dishonor.

tween patricians and plebeians. But soon after the overthrow
of the decemvirate this was superseded by a new law (*lex Ca-
nuleia*, 445 B.C.) which granted the right of intermarriage between the two orders. This insured their social and civil equality, and paved the way for their political equality, and finally
their union into a harmonious people.

IV. The Struggle for Political Equality

Progress of the Plebeians. — In order that we may keep
in mind a little more clearly just what progress the plebeians
had made up to this time, and what they still demanded, let us
look for a moment at the following table, which contains a
list of the general rights possessed by a full Roman citizen:

The rights of citizenship (*civitas*)	Public rights (*iura publica*).	Right of holding office (*honores*).
		Right of voting (*suffragium*).
	Private rights (*iura privata*).	Right of intermarriage (*connubium*).
		Right of property and contract (*commercium*).

The plebeians now possessed the lowest right, the *commercium;* they could hold property and carry on trade just
like any other Roman citizens. They had just now obtained
the *connubium*, or the right of contracting a legal marriage
with a patrician. They had also the *suffragium*, or the right
of voting in the assemblies of the centuries and of the tribes.
As regards the *honores*, or the right of holding office, they
could be elected to the lower offices, that is, could be chosen
tribunes of the people and ædiles; but could not be elected
to the higher offices, that is, could not be chosen consuls and
quæstors. What the plebeians now wanted was a share in the
higher offices, especially in the consulship.

The Consular Tribunes (444 B.C.). — Instead of allowing
the plebeians a direct share in the consulship, the patricians
agreed to the appointment of certain new officers, who should
have the same power but not the same honor as the consuls,

and who could be elected from either the patrician or the plebeian class. These new officers were called "military tribunes with consular power," sometimes known as "consular tribunes." It was provided, however, that the senate might in any given year determine whether consuls or consular tribunes should be elected. As a matter of fact, the senate for many years after this time decided in favor of the election of consuls. But later, as the plebeians grew in political influence, the election of consular tribunes became the rule.

The Consorship and the New Quæstors. — As the patricians saw that the plebeians were growing stronger, they resorted to a new plan to keep as much power as possible in their own hands. To do this, they created another new office, the censorship, and transferred to the two censors some of the most important powers hitherto exercised by the consuls. The censors were to draw up the census, that is, to make an estimate of every man's property, to assign each man to a proper class in the centuries, whether he belonged to the cavalry or the infantry, and to designate who was entitled to sit in the senate. The censors came to have a general supervision of public morals; for improper conduct they could expel a member from the senate or deprive a citizen of his vote. By the exercise of this extraordinary power, the censorship came to be the most influential office in the Roman state. The censors were elected every five years, from the patrician class. But to offset this advantage, the patricians agreed that there should be two new quæstors (421 B.C.), to be elected from the plebeians.

The Destruction of the City by the Gauls (390 B.C.). — The reforms in favor of the plebeians made them willing to fight side by side with the patricians. The Roman armies were now gaining victories over their neighbors on the outskirts of Latium — the Volscians,[1] the Hernicians, and the Æquians (map, p. 320).

[1] The history of the Volscian wars is made interesting by the story of Coriola'nus, which tells us that this young patrician incurred the hatred of the common people, fled to the Volscians, and led an army against his native city; that ! is mother and

They had also obtained a stronghold in Etruria by the capture of the fortified city of Ve'ii. As the siege of this city lasted for nearly ten years (405–396 B.C.), and as the soldiers could not go home and cultivate their farms, they now received for the first time pay for their services.

But no sooner was Veii captured than the Romans were startled by the approach of a savage people from the north. These people were the Gauls, who had come from beyond the Alps, had overrun the valley of the Po and Etruria, and were now within a few miles of Rome at the little river Allia. They were men the like of whom the Romans had never seen before — with their gigantic bodies, their long yellow hair, their flashing blue eyes, and their heavy swords and battle-axes. The Romans sent an army to meet them and suffered a terrible defeat. The Gauls pressed on to Rome, and captured the city. Only the Capitoline hill with its strong fortifications remained untaken. The grave senators, the story goes, took their seats in the Forum, resolved to meet calmly their fate,

GALLIC SWORDS

hoping that for their sacrifice the gods might save the city. The Gauls were at first awestruck at the sight of these venerable men sitting unarmed in their sacred robes, like fearless messengers from heaven. At length a Gallic chief ventured to stroke the long beard of one of the senators; the old hero raised his ivory staff and smote the offender; whereupon the barbarian slew him and his companions. The whole city was now plundered and burned, and the Gauls laid siege to the Capitol, which could be approached only by steep cliffs.

his wife went to the Volscian camp and pleaded with him to cease his wars; and that Rome was thus saved. The memory of the Æquian wars is preserved in the story of the Roman patriot Cincinna'tus, who was called from his country home to rescue the Roman army from a defile where it was surrounded by the Æquians and threatened with destruction; and who with great speed and skill conquered the Æquian army and returned the next evening to Rome in triumph.

One night while the Gauls were attempting, one by one, to scale the cliff, the consul Manlius was awakened by the cackling of the sacred geese, and slew the assailants as they approached. For this he was called the " Savior of the Capitol." One story relates that the Gauls left the city on receiving a thousand pounds of gold. Another story says that the dictator Camillus appeared and drove off the barbarians, exclaiming, " Rome is ransomed with steel, not with gold."

The Roman city was now in ashes. Every man was in haste to rebuild his own home. No common plan was adopted, and the new city became a network of narrow and irregular streets. The destruction of Rome by the Gauls was a disaster not only to Rome, but to the world, because the records of the ancient city perished, leaving much of the early history dark and obscure.

The Licinian Legislation (367 B.C.). — The recent wars had resulted in turning the attention of the people away from political questions. They had also resulted in reducing the common people again to a condition of poverty and distress. Their fields had been wasted by invading armies. They were again obliged to borrow money. The oppressive laws of debt had not been changed. Their lands had been taken up by the richer landlords. This brought economic questions again to the front. The new reformers were called upon not simply to continue the work in the direction of political equality, but to devise some methods to relieve their fellow-citizens impoverished by the recent wars. The cause of the people was at last taken up by two able leaders, the tribunes Gaius Licin'ius Stolo and Lucius Sextius. These men brought forward the following proposals :

(1) To relieve debtors, it was proposed to apply the interest already paid on a debt to the reduction of the principal and to allow a period of three years in which to pay the rest of the debt.

(2) To improve the condition of the poorer citizens, it was provided that the occupation of the public lands should be

open to all; that no person should be allowed to hold more than five hundred *iugera* (about 300 acres); and that the number of slaves on any estate should be limited, so that free laborers should have an opportunity to work for wages.

(3) To settle the political strife between the classes it was proposed that the consular tribunes should be done away with, and that consuls only should henceforth be elected, one of whom must be a plebeian.

After some years of strife these proposals became laws; and one of their authors, L. Sextius, was elected the first plebeian consul. On account of the importance of this body of laws we may call it " the third charter of Roman liberty."

Final Equalization of the Orders. — When the Licinian laws were finally passed, their economic provisions were soon forgotten, but the political struggle for the offices still continued. With the loss of the consulate, the patricians succeeded in taking away its judicial power and conferring it upon a new officer called the prætor (367 B.C.), who had to be a patrician. It was also provided that there should be two patrician ædiles (called curule ædiles) to offset the plebeian ædiles. But it

CURULE CHAIR
(Coin)

was not many years before all the offices retained by the patricians were opened to the plebeians, and political equality was fully established between the two orders.[1] The old Roman aristocracy based upon blood no longer possessed any political importance. The union of patricians and plebeians into one compact body of citizens was a great step in the growth of that principle of " incorporation " which finally made the Romans the strongest people and gave them the best-organized government of the ancient world.

[1] The distinction between the plebeian and the curule ædileship gradually passed away. The dictatorship was opened to the plebeians in 356 B.C.; the censorship in 351 B.C.; and the prætorship in 337 B.C. The independent legislative power of the *comitia tributa* was confirmed by the Hortensian law in 286 B.C.

Summary of the Republican Constitution. — Following is a brief outline of the constitution of the Roman republic:

I. THE SENATE — three hundred members, chosen by the censor, having control of the religion and the finances, of the provinces and of foreign affairs, and generally the approval or rejection of laws passed by the assemblies (*auctoritas patrum*).

II. THE POPULAR ASSEMBLIES.
   1. The *Comitia Curiata* — assembly of the curies, with, generally speaking, no power except formally to confer the *imperium*.
   2. The *Comitia Centuriata* — assembly of the centuries, presided over by an officer having the *imperium* (consul, prætor, or dictator); having the power to elect the consuls, censors, and prætors, to declare war, to act upon laws submitted to it, and to decide on appeals in capital cases.
   3. The *Comitia Tributa* — assembly of the tribes, presided over by a tribune, or other high magistrate; having power to elect the tribunes, ædiles, and quæstors, and to pass laws submitted to it.

III. THE MAGISTRATES.
   1. *The Curule Magistrates.*
       (1) The Consuls — two, who presided alternately over the senate, proposed laws to the *comitia centuriata*, and commanded the armies.
       (2) The Dictator — one, having supreme power for not more than six months; appointed by the consul when directed by the senate; assisted by the Master of Horse (*Magister Equitum*).
       (3) The Prætor — at first one, *prætor urbanus*, to judge in cases between citizens; afterward a second, *prætor peregrinus*, to judge between foreigners or between citizens and foreigners.
       (4) The Censors — two, with power to make the census, assess the property, classify the people, revise the senatorial list, and supervise the public morals.
       (5) The Curule Ædiles — two, having charge of the public works and the public records.
   2. *The Non-Curule Magistrates.*
       (1) The Plebeian Ædiles — two, having powers like the curule ædiles.
       (2) The Tribunes — two, afterward ten, with power of veto and intercession, and of proposing laws to the *comitia tributa*.
       (3) The Quæstors — two, afterward eight, having charge of the treasury and public accounts.

All these magistrates were elected annually, except (1) the censors, who were elected every five years to hold office for a year and a half, and (2) the dictator, who was appointed only as occasion required.

References for Reading

Knowlton, Topic A 17, "The Struggle in Rome for Equal Rights" (1).[1]

Seignobos, pp. 227–232, "The Government of the Republic" (1).

Smith, Wm., Smaller History, Ch. 5, "The Decemvirate" (18).

Shuckburgh, Ch. 8, "Constitutional History from 509 to 390 B.C." (18).

Pelham, Bk. I., Ch. 1, "The Foundation of the Republic and the Struggle between the Orders" (18).

How and Leigh, Ch. 5, "Institutions of the New Republic"; Ch. 12, "The Licinian Laws and the Equalization of the Orders" (18).

Taylor, Chs. 3–5, "Struggle between the Orders" (22).

Ihne, Early Rome, Ch. 13, "Tribunes of the People" (18).

Granrud, Second Period, "The Equalization of the Orders" (22).

Greenidge, Public Life, Ch. 2, "Growth of the Republican Constitution" (22).

Mommsen, Vol. I., Bk. II., Ch. 1, "Changes of the Constitution"; Ch. 2, "The Tribunate of the Plebs"; Ch. 3, "Equalization of the Orders" (18).

Livy, Bk. II., Chs. 27–33 (first secession of the plebeians); Bk. III., Chs. 33–34 (the decemvirate) (25).

Plutarch, "Publicola" (26).

Special Study

THE TWELVE TABLES. — Shuckburgh, pp. 101–104 (18); Liddell, Ch. 11 (18); How and Leigh, p. 70 (18); Mommsen, Vol. I., pp. 363–368 (18); Morey, "Roman Law," Ch. 3 (22); Harper's Dictionary, "Twelve Tables" (19).

[1] The figure in parenthesis refers to the number of the topic in the Appendix, where a fuller title of the book will be found.

CHAPTER XXII

THE CONQUEST AND ORGANIZATION OF ITALY

Synopsis

I. CONQUEST OF THE ITALIAN PENINSULA (340–275 B.C.). — The Reduction of Latium. — The Conquest of Central Italy. — The Absorption of Magna Græcia: War with Pyrrhus.

II. POLITICAL ORGANIZATION OF ITALY. — The Roman Policy of Government. — The Roman State: Ager Romanus. — The Roman Municipalities. — The Roman and Latin Colonies. — The Italian Allies.

III. THE MILITARY SYSTEM. — The Roman Army. — Divisions of the Army. — Order of Battle. — Armor and Weapons. — Military Rewards and Honors. — Military Roads.

IV. LIFE IN THE OLD ROMAN REPUBLIC. — The Old Roman Character. — The Public Life of the Citizen. — The Old Family Life. — Dwellings, Dress, and Food. — The Economic Condition of the People.

I. CONQUEST OF THE ITALIAN PENINSULA (340–275 B.C.)

The Reduction of Latium (340–338 B.C.). — To those living in Rome about 340 B.C., everything seemed to indicate a period of prosperity. The plebeians had gained their rights. The people were united and patriotic. The army was strong and well-organized. A temple of Concord was built to commemorate the union of the two orders. The Romans had already made successful wars against the Volscians and Æquians on the borders of Latium.

When the Latins saw the success of the plebeians, they believed that they also should have a share in the Roman government. They therefore sent deputies to Rome proposing that one of the consuls should be a Latin, and that the senate should be enlarged by the admission of Latin members. When the consul heard of this proposal he exclaimed in anger, " If a Latin ever dares to cross the sacred threshold of the senate house, I will slay him with my own hand." And so the league between the Latins and the Romans was broken and a war followed.

In their wars the Romans maintained the strictest discipline over their soldiers. A story is told of Titus Manlius, son of the consul commanding the Roman army. The young Manlius, contrary to his father's orders, left the ranks to fight a single combat with one of the enemy's champions. The enemy was slain, and Manlius carried the spoils in triumph to his father. But the father, instead of congratulating the son on his success, condemned him to death for disobedience of orders. The words " Manlian orders " came to mean the commands that must be obeyed at all hazards.

Another story of this war illustrates the devotion of the true Roman soldier. The consul Decius Mus was warned in a dream that that army would be victorious whose commander sacrificed himself in battle. When he saw his own lines giving way he mounted his horse and plunged into the ranks of the enemy to seek death for himself and victory for his country. The day was saved ; and the name of Decius was ever after honored as an example of patriotic devotion.

The Latin war closed in the same year (338 B.C.) in which Philip of Macedon defeated the Greeks at the battle of Chæronea (p. 262). So that at the same time that Macedonia was completing the conquest of Greece, Rome was beginning the conquest of Italy. The Latin league was broken up. No Latin city could henceforth have any relation with any other Latin city. Every city was made directly subject to Rome. Rome was now the mistress of Latium.

The people of Latium did not get what they had demanded at the outset — that is, a share in the Roman government. But they were allowed the private rights of Roman citizens — the *connubium* or the right of intermarriage, and the *commercium* or the right of carrying on commercial relations with Rome under the protection of the Roman law.

The Conquest of Central Italy (338–290 B.C.). — In extending their territory to the south the Romans came into contact with the Samnites, the most warlike people in central Italy. The Samnites were now trying to get possession of Campania. The Romans protested, and war followed. During this war the Roman army suffered a most humiliating disaster. The army was entrapped in a defile, called the Caudine Forks, in the hills separating Samnium from Campania. Surrounded on all sides by the Samnite forces, the Romans had no chance of escape. Nothing was left but to surrender. Every soldier was deprived of his armor, and the whole army with bowed heads was obliged to pass " under the yoke " — that is, under a spear placed across two other upright spears fastened in the ground. The commanding consuls were compelled to sign a treaty of peace, giving up all the territory they had conquered. Under these conditions the army was allowed to return to Rome. To hide their disgrace, the soldiers stole into the city under cover of night. The senate was shocked, and refused to accept a treaty made without its approval. All the officers of the defeated army were sent back in chains to the enemy. But the Samnite general demanded that the treaty must be kept, or that the whole army must be sent back to the defile where they had surrendered. The senate refused to do either — and the war went on.

The Samnites were now joined by other nations, until it seemed that all Italy had united to destroy the Roman power. The Romans showed a grim determination to meet the host of foes by whom they were surrounded on the north and the south. The decisive battle of the war was fought at Senti'num, a hundred miles north of Rome, beyond the Apennines (map, p. 354). Here, when the Roman lines were wavering, the consul Decius Mus, the son of the old hero of the Latin war, following his father's example, devoted himself to death. As the soldiers saw their leader charging upon the spears of the enemy, they were inflamed with new courage and gained a great victory for Rome. The rest of Italy, including the Samnites, was soon subdued. Rome now ruled supreme from Cisalpine Gaul to the borders of Magna Græcia. The new territory was held in subjection by the planting of military colonies over many of the conquered cities.

The Absorption of Magna Græcia: War with Pyrrhus (280–272 B.C.). — We have had our attention called more than once to the Greek colonies in southern Italy, which came to be known

MAGNA GRÆCIA — THE WAR WITH PYRRHUS

as Magna Græcia. Many of these cities had been in existence for hundreds of years. They were now falling into decay. They were frequently at strife with one another and harassed by the neighboring mountaineers — such as the Lucanians.

They were generally willing to accept the protection of Rome. By taking their part Rome gradually absorbed all the Greek cities except Tarentum, now the most vigorous and prosperous of them all. Tarentum was determined to maintain her independence even against Rome.

One day the people of Tarentum were sitting in their theater on the hillside overlooking the sea. They saw a Roman squadron approaching their shores. This was in violation of an existing treaty. The enraged people rushed down from the theater, manned their ships and gained an easy victory over the small Roman squadron. The Roman senate dispatched an envoy to Tarentum to demand satisfaction. The people of Tarentum were just then engaged in a rollicking festival in honor of the

PYRRHUS

Grecian wine god, Dionysus (p. 203). In the midst of a laughing crowd a drunken clown ran up and threw a handful of dirt upon the white toga of the Roman envoy. "Ah," shouted the envoy, " you laugh now, but this stain will be washed out with your best blood." An insult to a Roman ambassador was an insult to Rome; and war was declared against the insolent city. Tarentum immediately sent to Greece for help, and Pyrrhus, king of Epirus, responded to the call.

Pyrrhus was the ablest Greek general since the days of Alexander the Great. He hoped now to found a Greek empire in the West. He brought with him an army of twenty-five thousand men and twenty elephants. On the plains of Heracle'a, not far from Tarentum, the Roman legion first met the Greek phalanx. After a severe battle the Roman lines gave way before the monstrous elephants. But the army of Pyrrhus suffered a great loss. He wondered at the bravery of the Romans, and he exclaimed, "With such an army I could conquer the world." From this time a victory attended with great loss has been called a "Pyrrhic victory."

A WAR ELEPHANT

Pyrrhus was convinced that Rome could not be conquered, and he sent his trusted minister, Cin'eas, — who was said to have conquered more nations with his tongue than Pyrrhus had done with his sword, — to sue for an honorable peace from the Roman senate. The persuasive speech of Cineas was broken by the stern words of Appius Claudius, the blind old censor : "Let the senate never make peace with an enemy on Italian soil." Cineas returned to his master with the report that the "Roman senate was an assembly of kings." Pyrrhus soon went over to Sicily, hoping to rescue the Greek cities which were then subject to Carthage. But he did not meet with the success that he expected. He engaged in another battle with the Romans at Beneventum. Here his army suffered a severe defeat ; the great losses of Pyrrhus prevented him from following out his plans. Discouraged by his futile campaigns in Italy, he retired to Greece. Tarentum, the last Greek city of Magna Græcia, was now absorbed into the Roman dominion. Within the next few years the spirit of revolt which lingered in Etruria and other parts of Italy was suppressed ; and the Roman authority was completely established from Cisalpine Gaul to the Sicilian strait (map, p. 360). Rome was now the mistress of Italy.

By the absorption of Magna Græcia, the Romans came under the influence of Greek culture. After this time we begin to see a greater taste for literature, philosophy, art, and the refinements of life.

II. Political Organization of Italy

The Roman Policy of Government. — To understand how Rome conquered the peoples of Italy is less important than to understand how she governed these peoples after they were conquered. From the time that she broke up the Latin league until she brought Italy under her control, she was gradually developing that remarkable capacity for political organization which finally made her the greatest governing power of the ancient world. We must not suppose that she had from the first a completely formed policy of government. On the contrary, this policy was growing with her growth, and becoming more clearly defined with her increasing dominion. So far as we are able to define her general method of governing we might say that it included three important features : (1) *isolation*, or the separation of the subject communities from one another so as to prevent the possibility of united resistance; (2) *local government*, or the granting to each community the right to manage its own local affairs so far as this was consistent with Roman supremacy; (3) *gradual incorporation*, or the conferring upon different communities, to a greater or less extent, of the rights of citizenship.

The Roman State : Ager Romanus. — When we come to consider the way in which Rome governed her subject populations scattered throughout Italy, we must remember, first of all, that she did not treat them all just alike. To some she gave more rights, to others less. To some she gave the full rights of Roman citizenship ; to others she gave only a part of these rights ; and to others she gave none at all. All that territory to which she gave the full rights of citizenship was called the Roman domain (*ager Roma'nus*). The cities in this territory had the right of local self government, and regulated their own affairs. The people in this territory were, generally speaking, full Roman citizens. They had the right of intermarriage with Romans and the right to trade, to hold property, to make contracts under the protection of the Roman law. They also had the right to vote and hold office. This whole territory was now divided into thirty-three " local tribes," and the people enrolled in these tribes could go to Rome if they wished to and vote in the *comitia tributa*. But the people in the outlying country districts would find it inconvenient to travel so far to cast a vote, and as Rome had no system of representation, the right of suffrage was rarely exercised by these people.

The Roman Municipalities. — There were certain cities whose inhabitants, though Roman citizens, were not enrolled in the thirty-three local tribes. They had not therefore the right to vote. They were citizens without the suffrage (*cives sine suffragio*). They had, however, the right to govern themselves, and had the private rights of Roman citizens, that is, the right of trade and intermarriage. Such cities were called *municipia*. In later times the inhabitants of these municipalities received all the rights, public and private, of full Roman citizens. Roman life was centered in the cities, so that it has been said : " Rome was a city governing cities." The Roman municipality as a self-governing community incorporated into the state was one of the most advanced features of the Roman system of government. It is one of the features of government that Rome has bequeathed to modern times.

The Roman and Latin Colonies. — One of the ways in which Rome governed the subject population was by the sending out of colonies. But we should notice the difference between the Roman colonies and the Latin colonies. The Roman colonies were made up of full Roman citizens, sent out in early times to garrison the towns along the coasts of Latium and Campania. They are hence sometimes called maritime colonies. The men of such Roman colonies retained all the rights, public and private, of full Roman citizens. The Latin colonies,[1] on the other hand,

---

[1] Important Latin colonies were Luceria and Venusia in Apulia, Beneventum in Samnium, Pæstum in Lucania, Hadria in Picenum, and Arim'inum in Umbria (maps, pp. 354, 410).

were made up of persons who did not retain the full rights of citizens. They retained only the *commercium*, that is, the right to trade and make contracts under the protection of the Roman law. They had not the right of intermarriage with Roman citizens, nor the right to vote. But all these colonies were garrisons, sent out to keep in subjection a conquered city or territory. They were generally made up of veteran soldiers, or sometimes of poor Roman citizens, to whom was allotted a portion of the conquered land. The colonies carried everywhere the Roman language and the Roman spirit, and were thus an important means of extending Roman institutions.

The Italian Allies. — The largest part of the subject communities comprised the Italian cities which were conquered and left free to govern themselves, but were bound to Rome by special treaties. They were obliged to recognize the sovereign power of Rome. They were not subject to the land tax which fell upon Roman citizens, but were obliged to furnish troops for the Roman army in times of war. These cities of Italy, thus held in subjection to Rome by special treaties, were known as federated cities (*civitates fœderatæ*), or simply as allies (*socii*); they formed the most important part of the Italian population not incorporated into the Roman state.[1]

III. THE MILITARY SYSTEM

The Roman Army. — The conquest of Italy was due, in great measure, to the efficiency of the Roman army. The strength of the Roman government, too, depended upon the army, which was the real support of the civil power. By their conquests the Romans became a nation of warriors. Every citizen between the ages of seventeen and forty-five was obliged to serve in the army when the public service required it. In early times the wars lasted only for a short period, and consisted in ravaging the fields of the enemy; and the soldiers' re-

[1] This organization of Italy continued substantially until the Social war (90 B.C.).

ward was the booty which he was able to capture. But after
the siege of Veii, the term of service became longer, and it became necessary to give to the soldiers regular pay. This pay,

SOLDIERS AND THEIR BOOTY

with the prospect of plunder and of a share in the allotment of
conquered land, furnished a strong motive to render faithful
service.

Divisions of the Army. — In case of war it was customary to raise four legions, two for each consul. Each legion
contained thirty maniples, or companies, of heavy-armed
troops, — twenty maniples consisting of one hundred and
twenty men each, and ten maniples of sixty men each, — making in all three thousand heavy-armed troops. There were also
twelve hundred light-armed troops, not organized in maniples.
The whole number of men in a legion was therefore forty-two
hundred. To each legion was usually joined a body of cavalry,
numbering three hundred men. After the reduction of Latium
and Italy, the allied cities were also obliged to furnish a certain
number of men. These men were called *auxiliaries*, and served
on the wings of the legion.

Order of Battle. — In ancient times the Romans fought in
the manner of the Greek phalanx, in a solid square. This arrangement was well suited to withstand an attack on a level

plain, but was not adapted to other kinds of warfare. About the time of the conquest of Veii, the Romans introduced the more open order of "maniples." When drawn up in order of battle, the legion was arranged in three lines: first, the *hasta'ti*, made up of young men; second, the *prin'cipes*, composed of the more experienced soldiers; and, third, the *tria'rii*, which comprised the veterans, capable of supporting the other two lines. Each line was composed of ten maniples, those of the first two lines consisting of one hundred and twenty men each, and those of the third line consisting of sixty men each; the maniples, or companies, in each line were so arranged that they were opposite the spaces in the next line, as follows:

1. *Hastati*   ▬   ▬   ▬   ▬   ▬   ▬   ▬
2. *Principes*   ▬   ▬   ▬   ▬   ▬   ▬   ▬
3. *Triarii*   ▬   ▬   ▬   ▬   ▬   ▬   ▬

This arrangement enabled the companies in front to retreat into the spaces in the rear, or the companies in the rear to advance to the spaces in front.

Behind the third line usually fought the light-armed and less experienced soldiers. Each maniple carried its own ensign; and the legion carried a standard surmounted with a silver eagle.

ROMAN STANDARDS

Armor and Weapons. — The defensive armor of all the three lines was alike — a coat of mail for the breast, a brass helmet for the head, greaves for the legs, and a large oblong shield carried upon the left arm. For offensive weapons, each man carried a short sword, which could be used for cutting or thrusting. The soldiers in the first two lines each had also two javelins, to be hurled at the enemy before coming into close quarters; and those of the third line each had a long lance, which could be used for piercing. It was with such arms as these that the Roman soldiers conquered Italy.

Military Rewards and Honors. — The Romans encouraged the soldiers with rewards for their bravery. These were bestowed by the general in the presence of the whole army. The highest individual reward was the " civic crown," made of oak leaves, given to him who had saved the life of a fellow-citizen on the battlefield. Other suitable rewards, such as golden crowns, banners of different colors, and ornaments, were bestowed for singular bravery. The highest military honor which the Roman state could bestow was a " triumph " — a solemn procession, decreed by the senate, in which the victorious general, with his army, marched through the city to the Capitol, bearing in his train the trophies of war. The usual condition which entitled a general to a triumph was that he must have gained a great victory in which at least five thousand of the enemy had been slain.

The day of a triumph was a gala day in the city of Rome. The streets leading to the Forum and the Capitol were lined with people ready to welcome the returning soldiers. At the head of the procession marched the senators and the magistrates : then came the chariots loaded with the booty taken from the enemy, and the captives in chains; next the triumphal car drawn by four horses and bearing the victorious general crowned with a laurel wreath and clothed in a purple robe embroidered with gold; and finally the soldiers with laurel branches in their hands and singing a triumphal song. The procession ascended to the Capitol, and the general laid his crown on the knees of Jupiter and returned thanks for the victory.

Military Roads. — An important part of the military system of Rome was the network of military roads by which her armies and munitions of war could be sent into every part of Italy. The first military road was the Appian Way (*via Appia*), which was built by Appius Claudius during the Samnite wars. It connected Rome and Capua, and was afterward extended to

PRINCIPAL ROMAN ROADS

Venusia, and finally as far as Brundisium. This furnished
a model for the roads which were subsequently laid out to
other points in Italy. Among the other roads were the Flamin-
ian way, which ran north to Arim'inum, and thence afterward
to Placentia; and the Aurelian way which ran north along the
coasts of Etruria to the borders of Cisalpine Gaul. Although
we read of roads in Persia (p. 72) and in other ancient countries,
the Romans were probably the first people to reduce road-
making to an art. They spared no labor and expense to make
these highways straight, smooth, and durable. The roads
were laid out upon the most direct and level course from city

to city, without regard to natural obstacles, piercing mountains and spanning morasses and rivers. The surface of the road was a pavement constructed of slabs of hard rock, nicely fitted together; and this was supported by strata of stones and gravel laid in cement to the depth of two feet or more, and having a width of about fifteen feet. So durable were these highways that the remains of many of them exist to the present day. After a time they came to be used by the Romans not merely for the movement of troops, but as pathways of trade and also as lines of communication, or post-roads. The Roman roads were thus a means of binding together the different parts of the Roman state, securing the dominion of Rome and extending her civilization.

IV. LIFE IN THE OLD ROMAN REPUBLIC

The Old Roman Character. — The old Romans were accustomed to look back to this period as the golden age of the Republic. It was now that the simple and stern virtues of the old Roman character were most clearly seen. The men of this day were men of strong wills and rigid morals. They cared little for the elegancies of life. They were trained to rule themselves and hence could rule others. Their greatest ambition was to serve the state, and to sacrifice themselves for their country. They held up as examples such men as Cincinnatus, who left his plow in the furrow to answer his country's call; or Decius Mus, who devoted his life to save the Roman army. They lived a plain, simple life, and had not yet become corrupted by wealth and luxury.

The Public Life of the Citizen. — The severe virtues that the old Roman cultivated in his private life marked his public life as well. He was a patriotic citizen. But it was only those people who lived rather near the Roman city who could engage very much in public affairs. Here we see again the difficulty in not having some kind of representation at Rome. Those who lived at a great distance would find it inconvenient to go to Rome either to vote or to run for office. Still on important occasions many people would flock to Rome from the outlying districts to vote for a popular candidate, or for some desirable law. The *comitia tributa* was now held in the Campus Martius, where the *comitia centuriata* had been held from the first. These assemblies voted by groups — either by centuries or tribes — and there was no opportunity for public discussion, the people voting simply *Yes* or *No* upon the question submitted to them. These meetings were held in an orderly way by men who believed they were performing a public duty.

The man who desired a public office sought it because he thought he could be of some service to the state, and not merely to benefit himself. He showed that he was a candidate by assuming a white robe (*candidatus*), and going about shaking hands with his friends and soliciting their votes. Both patricians and plebeians were now eligible for office. No person could, however, be reëlected to the same office except after an interval of ten years. At this time plebeians could be senators and thus occupy the most dignified position in the state. It was a high-minded censor who determined a man's qualifications for the position of senator.

The Old Family Life. — The foundation of the old Roman character was found in the family. The family of the old Romans was the most sacred of institutions. It was bound together by religious rites in which the dead and the living both shared. The father watched over his children with the greatest care, that they might become worthy citizens of the Republic, and might preserve the family worship for the future. Marriage was a religious institution and was looked upon as a lifelong union. The mother of the family occupied a very important position. She was the companion of her husband and was in every sense socially his equal. She managed the household, trained her children, was honored in public, and could be present at public festivals. It has been said that woman occupied in the old Roman family " a position unattained by the women of any other nation in the ancient world." The boys, after seven years of age, were sent to school, where they were taught the Twelve Tables and the duties of citizenship, while the girls were kept at home and taught their domestic duties. At the age of seventeen the boy assumed the manly gown (*toga virilis*), became subject to military service, and entered upon the duties of life. Under such a training the old Roman Republic produced women of virtue and discretion and men of integrity and honor.

Dwellings, Dress, and Food. — The houses of this period were very simple. They were beginning to be covered with shingles instead of roofs thatched with straw. The ordinary house consisted of a single large room, or hall (*atrium*), surrounded by a few small bed-chambers. This hall was the living room and contained the images of the household gods, and the sacred hearth upon which the fire was kept smoldering. A couch, some stools, and a table comprised the furniture. At meal time the family sat on stools about the table, and had not yet adopted the Greek custom of reclining on couches.

Dinner was served in the middle of the day. The food was simple, the chief dish being coarse flour boiled with water. The principal meat was pork. There were also flat, round cakes of wheat or barley; vegetables, such as onions, beans, and turnips; fruits, such as figs and olives. Milk was an important article of diet. With such a frugal fare as this the old Romans were able to develop a strong physical manhood.

Their dress was equally simple. It consisted of an undergarment, over which was drawn a short-sleeved woolen tunic reaching to the knees. To this was added for the street a blanket of white wool called the *toga*. The dress of the women was like that of the men, except in being longer and more flowing.

TOGA

Neither sex wore hats. The feet were protected not by shoes, but by sandals. The men wore both hair and beard long; the razor had not come into common use.

SANDALS

Every form of luxury was avoided; it is said that a censor struck off from the roll of the senators an ex-consul whose offense was in having ten pounds of silver plate in his house.

The Economic Condition of the People. — The old Romans of this age were chiefly an agricultural people. They were still a nation of farmers, as they always had been. But they were now far better off than they were in the old days, when they were struggling with the patricians for their rights. They were not bound down by the distressing law of debt. New lands had been opened up for them by the conquests in Italy. Colonies of the poorer citizens had been sent out to these lands, where they could obtain better means of living. Money was becoming more plentiful by which they could stock their farms. The small plots of ground which they received were adequate to support their families. The product of the farm was chiefly wheat and barley; but vegetables and fruit were also raised, and the olive was widely cultivated. On market days the farmer went to town to dispose of his produce. The wealthy people lived in the cities, but they were dependent upon the farmer for their means of living, so that agriculture came to be the most honorable of occupations, and contributed much to the prosperity of the Roman Republic during this golden age.

During the early period of the Republic and before the great conquests, the number of slaves at Rome was comparatively small. They were obtained chiefly from the captives taken in the wars with the neighboring tribes in Italy. We are told that when the Romans captured Veii (p. 337) the freemen of that city were sold at auction. Slaves had been furnished from those unhappy citizens who were sold into slavery to satisfy the claims of their creditors. But we read of a law passed just before the Great Latin War which prevented the debtor from being put into chains, and made him liable only to the extent of his goods. Slaves were not harshly treated at this time. They might often be seen working side by side with the farmer and his sons tilling the soil. Of course the number of slaves was gradually increasing with the reduction of Italy; but it was not until after the great foreign conquests that slavery began seriously to affect the life of the Roman people.

Selections for Reading

Knowlton, Topic A 18, "The Conquest of Italy" (1).[1]

Smith, Wm., Smaller Hist., pp. 81–83, "Organization of Italy" (18).

Liddell, Ch. 27, "Final Reduction and Settlement of Italy" (18).

Pelham, Bk. II., Ch. 2, "The Conquest of Italy" (18).

How and Leigh, Ch. 13, "Subjugation of Latium and Campania"; Ch. 16, "War with Tarentum and Pyrrhus" (18).

Merivale, General History, Ch. 16, "Summary of Roman Institutions" (18).

Mommsen, Vol. I., Bk. II., Ch. 7, "Struggle between Pyrrhus and Rome and Union of Italy" (18).

Taylor, Ch. 6, "Rome and Italy" (22).

Granrud, pp. 98–101, "Conquest and Organization of Central and Southern Italy" (22).

Smith, Dictionary, "Colonia" (the Roman colonial system); "Viæ" (Roman road-making); "Exercitus" (the Roman army) (19).

Munro, Source Book, Part IV., "The Constitution of the Republic" (25).

Livy, Bk. IX., Chs. 1–6 (battle of Caudine Pass) (25).

Special Study

ROMAN AND LATIN COLONIES. — Pelham, pp. 102–106 (18); Shuckburgh, p. 104, note (18); Liddell, pp. 254–257 (18); Harper's Dictionary, "Colonia" (19).

---

[1] The figure in parenthesis refers to the number of the topic in the Appendix, where a fuller title of the book will be found.

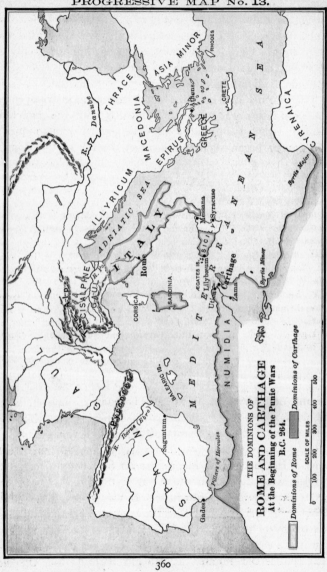

R. Danube

THRACE

ASIA MINOR

RHODES

MACEDONIA

ILLYRICUM

EPIRUS

GREECE

Athens

CRETE

CYRENAICA

ADRIATIC SEA

ITALY

Rome

Messana

SICILY

Syracuse

M E D I T E R R A N E A N   S E A

Syrtis Major

Syrtis Minor

ALPS

CISALPINE

GAUL R. Po

CORSICA

SARDINIA

ÆGATES IS.

Lilybaeum

Utica

Carthage

Zama

NUMIDIA

BALEARIC IS.

G A U L

PYRENEES

R. Iberus (Ebro)

Saguntum

Pillars of Hercules

Gades

S P A I N

THE DOMINIONS OF
ROME AND CARTHAGE
At the Beginning of the Punic Wars
B.C. 264.

SCALE OF MILES

0   100   200   300   400   500   600

Dominions of Rome   *Dominions of Carthage*

CHAPTER XXIII

THE CONQUEST OF THE MEDITERRANEAN WORLD

Synopsis

I. THE FIRST PUNIC WAR (264–241 B.C.). — Rome and Carthage. — The New Roman Navy: Victory at Mylæ. — Invasion of Africa by Regulus. — Progress of the War in Sicily. — Victory at the Ægates Islands. — Interval between the Wars.

II. THE SECOND PUNIC WAR (218–201 B.C.). — Hannibal and Rome. — Hannibal's Invasion of Italy: his Early Victories. — Battle of Cannæ. — The Turning of the Tide. — Battle of the Metaurus. — Publius Scipio Africanus. — Battle of Zama, and End of the War.

III. WARS WITH MACEDONIA AND SYRIA (200–168 B.C.). — The War with Macedonia. — The Liberation of Greece. — War with Antiochus of Syria. — The New Macedonian War.

IV. REDUCTION OF THE ROMAN CONQUESTS (168–133 B.C.). — Change of the Roman Policy. — Reduction of Macedonia and Illyricum. — Destruction of Corinth and Reduction of Greece. — The Destruction of Carthage and Reduction of Africa. — Revolt and Subjugation of Spain. — The Servile War in Sicily. — Pergamum, the first Asiatic Province.

I. THE FIRST PUNIC WAR (264–241 B.C.)

Rome and Carthage. — Rome was now a compact, well-organized state. Her citizens covered nearly one third of Italy. Her colonies were sent out to repress any signs of disorder. Her allies were loyal to her and willing to support her armies. But across the Mediterranean Sea, on the coasts of Africa, was another power which was destined to be her deadly rival. This power was Carthage. It was in fact a far older power than Rome. It had centuries before been established as a colony of the old city of Tyre in Phœnicia. It brought with it the commercial spirit of Phœnicia, and had built up a great commercial empire. It brought with it, too, the old

Oriental civilization of Phœnicia, with many of its corrupting ideas of religion. The Carthaginians worshiped the god Baal, and sacrificed human victims to their brazen god Moloch. Carthage was governed by two chief men, and by a senate of one hundred members; but the people had no share in the government as they had at Rome. The empire was governed entirely by the senate, which was made up of rich merchants, who ruled for their own interests. The army was made up of hired foreign soldiers — black Libyans armed with spears, expert Numidian horsemen, slingers from the Balear'ic isles. The strength of Carthage lay in her splendid fleet of quinqueremes, or ships with five banks of oars. Although Carthage seemed strong, it yet represented a decaying civilization; and the conflict between Rome and Carthage was a struggle between the rising power of the West and the declining power of the East.

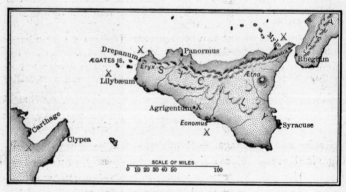

SICILY — THE FIRST PUNIC WAR

For a long time before 264 B.C. Carthage had been trying to get control of Sicily. She had got possession of the western part of this island, and was pushing her way to the eastern part. But the Roman people determined that she should be driven entirely from the island. Thus began the first Punic war — so called because the Latin word for Carthaginian is

Punicus. In Sicily town after town fell before the Roman army, and the important city of Agrigen'tum was captured after a siege of seven months.

The New Roman Navy: Victory at Mylae. — But when the enemy's fleet appeared off the coasts of Sicily, the Romans saw that Carthage, to be overcome, must be met upon the sea as well as upon the land. Taking as a model a Carthaginian vessel which had been wrecked on the Italian shore, they constructed, it is said, a hundred vessels like it in sixty days. In the meantime their soldiers were trained into sailors by practicing the art of rowing upon rude benches built upon the land and arranged like the banks of a real vessel. The Romans knew that their soldiers were better than the Carthaginians in a hand-to-hand encounter. To make use of this advantage, they provided their ships with drawbridges which could be used in boarding the enemy's vessels. Thus equipped with a fleet, Rome ventured upon the sea as a rival of the first naval power of the world. The new navy was placed under command of the consul Duil'ius, who gained a decisive victory off the northern coast of Sicily near Mylæ. The Romans thus had fought and won their first great battle upon the sea. Duilius was given a magnificent triumph, and to commemorate the victory a column was erected in the Forum, adorned with the beaks of the captured vessels (*Colum'na Rostra'ta*).

COLUMN OF DUILIUS

Invasion of Africa by Regulus (256 B.C.). — Elated by this success, the Romans felt prepared to carry the war into Africa. With a still larger fleet, they defeated the Carthaginian squadron which attempted to bar their way on the southern coast of Sicily, off the promontory of Ec'nomus. Two legions, one of which was under Reg'ulus, landed on the coast of Africa east of Carthage, and laid waste the country. So easily was this accomplished that the Romans decided that one consul,

REGULUS (Coin)

with his army, would be enough to finish the work in Africa. The other consul was therefore recalled, and Regulus remained. The Carthaginians attempted in vain to make peace. They then placed their army in the hands of a Spartan soldier named Xanthip'-pus. He defeated the Roman legions with great slaughter, and made Regulus a prisoner. A fleet was then sent from Italy to rescue the survivors, but this fleet on its return was wrecked in a storm. Thus ingloriously closed the war in Africa.

Progress of the War in Sicily (255–241 B.C.). — For several years after this, the war languished in Sicily. The long series of Roman disasters was relieved by the capture of Panormus on the northern coast, which was soon followed by a second victory over the Carthaginians, at the same place. It is said that the Carthaginians, after this second defeat, desired an exchange of prisoners, and sent Regulus to the Roman senate to advocate their cause, under the promise that he would return if unsuccessful. But Regulus, it is said, persuaded the senate not to accept the offer of the Carthaginians; and then, in spite of the tears and entreaties of his friends, went back to Carthage. Whether this story is true or not, it illustrates the honor and patriotism of the true Roman.

After the Roman victories at Panormus, the Carthaginians were pushed into the extreme western part of the island. The consul Publius Claudius determined to destroy the enemy's fleet lying near Drep'anum; but he was defeated with the loss of over ninety ships. The superstitious Romans believed that this defeat was due to the fact that Claudius had impiously disregarded the auguries; when the sacred chickens had refused to eat, he had in a fit of passion thrown them into the sea. The consul was hence recalled by the senate, and a dictator was appointed in his place. After the loss of other fleets by storms, and after fruitless campaigns against the great Carthaginian soldier, Hamil'car Barca, the Roman cause seemed a failure.

Victory at the Ægates Islands (241 B.C.). — It is in the midst of such discouraging times as these that we are able to see the strong elements of the Roman character — patriotism, fortitude, and steadfast perseverance. With a loss of one sixth of their population and a vast amount of treasure, they still persisted in the attempt to conquer Sicily. Wealthy citizens advanced their money to build a new fleet. In this way two hundred ships were built, and a decisive victory was gained at the Æga'tes Islands, off the western extremity of Sicily.

The Carthaginians were unprepared for the terrible defeat that they suffered, and now sued for peace. They were obliged to give up Sicily, release all the Roman prisoners without ransom, and pay to the Romans 3200 talents (about $4,000,000), within ten years. Thus ended the first Punic war, which had lasted for twenty-three years. During

CARTHAGINIAN COIN

this time Rome had shown her ability to fight upon the sea, and had fairly entered the lists as one of the great powers of the world. But this first contest with Carthage, severe as it was, was merely a preparation for the more terrible struggle which was yet to come.

Interval between the Wars (241–218 B.C.). — Both parties knew that the peace would be nothing but a truce; and that they must prepare for a more bitter conflict in the future. Carthage spent her time in extending her empire in Spain.

Rome organized her new territory in Sicily as her first "province" — which means a conquered territory outside of Italy under the control of a Roman governor. She also captured the islands of Sardinia and Corsica and erected them into a second province. She then cleared the Adriatic Sea of a nest of pirates which were infesting the coast of Greece, and came into friendly relations with the Grecian cities. She finally conquered the barbarians in Cisalpine Gaul. The conquered territory was now secured by new colonies, and Rome was practically supreme to the Alps. Her people were made more devoted to her by the share they received in the new lands. Her dominions were now so well organized and her authority so secure that she felt prepared for another contest with Carthage.

II. The Second Punic War (218–201 b.c.)

Hannibal and Rome. — The first Punic war had been a struggle with the greatest naval power of the Mediterranean;

HANNIBAL

the second Punic war was to be a conflict with one of the greatest soldiers that the world has ever seen. While yet a boy, Han'nibal became inured to camp life. His father, Hamilcar, took him to Spain that he might become accustomed to the hardships of a soldier's life. In after years Hannibal used to tell the story of how he came to go to Spain and how he came to be an enemy of Rome. "When I was nine years old," he said, "I was standing near the altar as my father was making a sacrifice. After the ceremony he ordered his servants to withdraw, called me to his side, and caressing me asked me if I would not like to follow him to Spain. Eagerly I begged him to take me. He took me by the hand and led me to the altar, and standing over the victims he said, 'Swear by these victims that you will always be an enemy to Rome.'" Hannibal never forgot this oath. In camp he learned the lessons of war. He became the idol of the soldiers, and they looked up to him as a model of military discipline. When his father died he became the commander in chief of the Carthaginian army. He felt that his mission was now come.

A CARTHAGINIAN GOD (BAAL)

There was a town in Spain by the name of Sagun'tum; the Romans claimed that it was their ally. Hannibal attacked it, and after a siege of eight months captured it. The Romans sent an embassy to the Carthaginian senate to demand the surrender of Hannibal. The chief Roman envoy, it is said, lifted up a fold in his toga and said, " Here we bring you peace or war; which do you choose?" " Give us either," was the reply. " Then I offer you war," said the envoy. " And this we accept," shouted the Carthaginians. Thus was begun one of the most memorable wars of ancient times.

Hannibal's Invasion of Italy: his Early Victories. — Even at the beginning of the war Hannibal showed his great genius as a soldier. When the Romans prepared to attack Spain and Africa, Hannibal decided that the best way to defend them would be to invade Italy and threaten Rome. Leaving his brother Has'drubal to protect Spain, he crossed the Pyrenees with fifty thousand infantry, nine thousand cavalry, and a number of elephants. At the Rhone the barbarians blocked his

way; he turned to the north and crossed the river without opposition. He came to the Alps, the mountain wall of Italy. To
cross these lofty mountains with his army, in the face of hostile
natives, with scarcely any roads to guide his march, was a task
that required almost superhuman effort. He began the ascent.
The mountaineers attacked him. From the higher ground they
rolled down huge rocks upon his struggling men and horses. In
the face of such perils, in nine days he reached the top of the
mountains, and the plains of the Po valley were spread out before him. He now aroused the flagging spirit of his soldiers

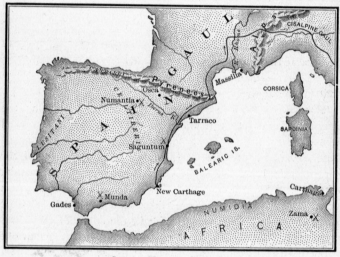

SPAIN — HANNIBAL'S ROUTE

with such words as these: "Here on the summit of the Alps we
hold the citadel of Italy; below us on the south are our friends,
the Gauls, who will supply us with provisions from their bountiful lands and will help us against their foes; and yonder in the
distance lies Rome."

If the ascent of the mountain had been tedious, the descent
was even more difficult. Autumn was coming on and heavy

snows had fallen, which hindered the army's progress. Men
and animals slipped and fell over precipices. At one place the
soldiers worked for three days to prepare a road over which the
elephants might pass. After such discouraging difficulties and
dangers Hannibal descended into the valley of the Po, having lost
half of his army. Here he recruited his ranks from the Gauls, who
eagerly joined his cause against the Romans. He first defeated
the Roman cavalry on the north of the Po, near the little stream
Tici'nus. He then moved south of the Po, and on the banks
of the Trebia gained a victory over a large Roman army.

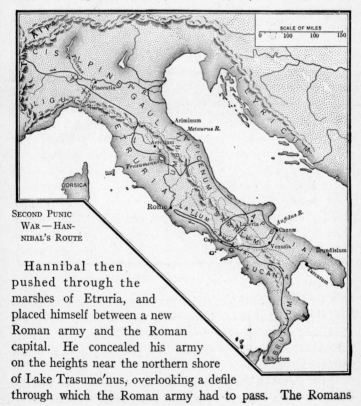

SECOND PUNIC
WAR — HAN-
NIBAL'S ROUTE

   Hannibal then
pushed through the
marshes of Etruria, and
placed himself between a new
Roman army and the Roman
capital. He concealed his army
on the heights near the northern shore
of Lake Trasume'nus, overlooking a defile
through which the Roman army had to pass. The Romans

entered this defile, not suspecting the terrible doom that awaited them. At a given signal the soldiers of Hannibal rushed to the attack. The Romans were overwhelmed on every side, and those who escaped the fierce Gauls and the dreaded onslaught of the Numidian cavalry were drowned in the waters of the lake. Fifteen thousand Romans and Italians fell on that fateful day, with Flamin'ius, their leader. " We have lost a great battle, our army is destroyed, Flaminius is killed," was the simple announcement that the prætor made to the Roman senate.

Battle of Cannæ (216 B.C.). — The frightful disaster at Lake Trasumenus led to the appointment of a dictator, Q. Fabius Maximus, who on account of his cautious policy was called "Cuncta'tor," or the Delayer. New armies were raised and the city was put into a state of defense. The Romans soon grew tired of the cautious and indecisive movements of Fabius; and two new consuls were elected to take his place, who were expected to pursue a more vigorous policy. These were Terentius Varro and Æmilius Paullus. Hannibal's army was now in Apu'lia, near the little town of Cannæ on the Au'fidus River. To this place the consuls led their new forces, consisting of eighty thousand infantry and six thousand cavalry — the largest army that the Romans had, up to that time, ever gathered on a single battlefield. Hannibal's army consisted of forty thousand infantry and ten thousand cavalry. But the brain of Hannibal was more than a match for the extra thirty-six thousand Romans. As this was Hannibal's greatest battle, we may learn something of his wonderful skill by looking at its plan.

The Romans drew up their heavy infantry in solid columns, facing to the south, to attack the center of Hannibal's line. In front of the heavy-armed troops were the light-armed soldiers, to act as skirmishers. On the Roman right, near the river, were two thousand of the Roman cavalry, and on the left wing were four thousand cavalry of the allies. With their army thus arranged, the Romans hoped to defeat Hannibal.

But Hannibal laid his plan not simply to defeat the Roman army, but to draw it into such a position that it could be entirely destroyed. He therefore placed his weakest troops, the Spanish and Gallic infantry, in the center opposite the heavy infantry of the Romans, and pushed them forward in the form of a crescent, with the expectation that they would be driven back and pursued by the Romans. On either flank he placed his heavy infantry of African troops, his best and most trusted soldiers, drawn back in long, solid columns, so that they could fall upon the Romans when the center had been driven in. On

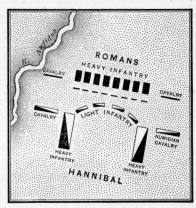

BATTLE OF CANNÆ

his left wing, next to the river, were placed four thousand Spanish and Gallic cavalry, and on the right wing his superb body of six thousand Numidian cavalry, which was to swing around and attack the Roman army in the rear, when it had become engaged with the African troops upon the right and left.

The description of this plan is almost a description of the battle itself. When the Romans had pressed back the weak center of Hannibal's line, they found themselves ingulfed in the midst of the Carthaginian forces. Attacked on all sides, the Roman army became a confused mass of struggling men, and the battle became a butchery. Seventy thousand Roman soldiers are said to have been slain, among whom were eighty senators and the consul Æmilius. The small remnant of survivors fled to the neighboring towns, and Varro, with seventy horsemen, took refuge in Venusia. This was the most terrible day that Rome had seen since the destruction of the city by the Gauls, nearly two centuries before. Every house in Rome was in mourning.

The Turning of the Tide. — During the period which followed the battle of Cannæ, the Roman character was put to its severest test. The people feared the worst. Many of their allies were turning against them. Capua, the most important city in Italy, after Rome, opened her gates to Hannibal; and Tarentum, which held a Roman garrison, was betrayed into his hands. Syracuse transferred her allegiance from Rome to Carthage, and many other cities in Sicily threatened to revolt. It was at this time that Philip V., the king of Macedonia, also made his alliance with Hannibal (see p. 277), and threatened to invade Italy to assist him. In the face of all these discouragements, the Roman people, supported by the faithful Latin towns and colonies, remained firm, and with fixed resolution determined to prosecute the war with greater vigor than ever before.

It was not long before the tide began to turn, and the energetic efforts of the Romans began to be rewarded. Syracuse was recaptured (212 B.C.) by Marcellus, the able governor of the province of Sicily. Capua also was retaken (211 B.C.), in spite of the efforts of Hannibal to draw away the Roman army from besieging that city, by marching to the gates of Rome. Moreover, Tarentum was recaptured (209 B.C.) by Fabius Cunctator, his last service in the field. Besides, the Romans, by forming an alliance with the cities of Greece, were able to prevent the Macedonian king from invading Italy.

Battle of the Metaurus (207 B.C.). — While Hannibal had been engaged in Italy, his brother Hasdrubal had been kept in Spain by the vigorous campaign which the Romans had conducted in that peninsula under two brothers named Scipio (sĭp'ĭ-o). Upon the death of these generals, the younger Publius Cornelius Scipio was sent to Spain and earned a great name by his victories. But Hasdrubal was determined to go to the rescue of his brother in Italy. He followed Hannibal's path over the Alps into the valley of the Po. Hannibal had moved into Apulia, where he was awaiting news from Hasdrubal. There were now two enemies in Italy, instead of one. One Roman army under Claudius Nero was therefore sent to oppose Hannibal in Apulia, and another army under Livius Salina'tor was sent to meet Hasdrubal, who had just crossed the river Metau'rus.

It was necessary that Hasdrubal should be crushed before Hannibal was informed of his arrival in Italy. The consul Claudius Nero therefore left his main army in Apulia, and with eight thousand picked soldiers hurried to the aid of his colleague in the north. The battle which took place at the Metaurus was decisive, and really determined the issue of the second Punic war. The army of Hasdrubal was entirely destroyed, and he himself was slain. The first news which Hannibal received of this disaster was from the lifeless lips of his own brother, whose head was thrown by the Romans into the Carthaginian camp. Hannibal saw that the death of his brother was the doom of Carthage; and he sadly exclaimed, " O Carthage, I see thy fate!" Hannibal retired to the southern end of Italy; and the Roman consuls received the first triumph that had been given since the beginning of this disastrous war.

PUBLIUS SCIPIO AFRICANUS

Publius Scipio Africanus. — Of all the men produced by Rome during the Punic wars, Publius Cornelius Scipio (afterward called Africa'nus) came the nearest to being a military

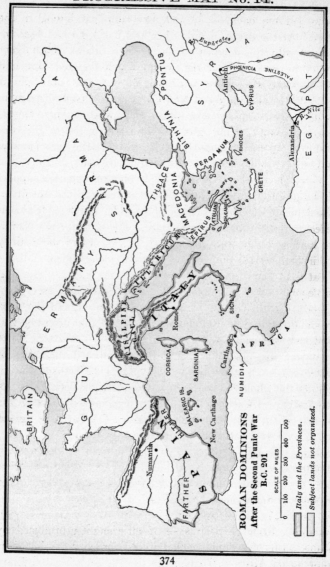

ROMAN DOMINIONS
After the Second Punic War
B.C. 201

SCALE OF MILES

0 100 200 300 400 500

Italy and the Provinces.

Subject lands not organized.

genius. From boyhood he had, like Hannibal, served in the
army. At the death of his father and uncle, he had been intrusted with the conduct of the war in Spain. With great
ability he had defeated the armies which opposed him, and
had regained the entire peninsula, after it had been almost
lost. With his conquest of New Carthage and Gades (see map,
p. 368), Spain was brought under the Roman power. On his
return to Rome, Scipio was unanimously elected to the consulship. He then proposed his plan for ending the war; namely,
to keep Hannibal shut up in the southern part of Italy, and
to carry the war into Africa. This plan received the support
of the people; and Scipio proceeded to carry it into execution.
When her armies in Africa were defeated, Carthage felt compelled to recall Hannibal from Italy. For fifteen years Hannibal had carried on the war in Italy, laying waste the country
and inflicting upon the Romans a loss of 300,000 men.

Battle of Zama, and End of the War (201 B.C.). — The final
battle of the war was fought (202 B.C.) near Zama (see map,
p. 368). In this battle Hannibal was defeated, and the Carthaginian army was annihilated. It is said that twenty thousand men were slain, and as many more taken prisoners. The
great war was now ended, and Scipio imposed the terms of
peace (201 B.C.), which were as follows: (1) Carthage was to
give up the whole of Spain and all the islands between Africa
and Italy; (2) Carthage was to pay an annual tribute of 200
talents (about $250,000) for fifty years; (3) Carthage agreed
not to wage any war without the consent of Rome.

Rome was thus recognized as the mistress of the western
Mediterranean. Carthage, although not reduced to a province, became a dependent state. Syracuse was added to the
province of Sicily, and the territory of Spain was divided into
two provinces, Hither and Farther Spain, each under a Roman
governor. Rome had, moreover, been brought into hostile relations with Macedonia, which paved the way for her conquests in the East.

III. Wars with Macedonia and Syria (200–168 B.C.)

The War with Macedonia (200–197 B.C.). — When the second Punic war was fairly ended, Rome felt free to deal with Philip V. of Macedonia, and to take a firm hand in settling the affairs of the East.   Philip had annoyed her, not only by making an alliance with Hannibal, but afterward by sending a force to assist him at the battle of Zama.   And now the ambitious

SEAT OF THE MACEDONIAN AND SYRIAN WARS

schemes of Philip were not at all to her liking.   For instance, he was overrunning the coasts of the Ægean Sea, and was threatening Pergamum and Rhodes, as well as the cities of Greece. When an appeal came to Rome from these states for protection, she espoused their cause, and declared war against Macedonia. The great hero of this war was Flamini'nus; and the decisive battle was fought (197 B.C.) near a hill in Thessaly called Cynosceph'alæ (Dog's Heads). Here Philip was completely defeated, and his army was destroyed. Macedonia was thus humbled, and there was now no power in Europe which could successfully dispute the supremacy of Rome.

The Liberation of Greece (196 B.C.). — To complete her work in eastern Europe, and to justify her position as defender of the Greek cities, Rome withdrew her garrisons and announced the independence of Greece. This was proclaimed by Flamininus at the Isthmian games, amid wild enthusiasm and unbounded expressions of gratitude. Rome was hailed as " the nation which, at its own expense, with its own labor, and at its own risk, waged war for the liberty of others, and which had crossed the sea that justice, right, and law should everywhere have sovereign sway " (Livy, xxxiii., 33).

War with Antiochus of Syria (192–189 B.C.). — The cities of Greece generally seemed contented with their treatment at the hands of the Romans — except the members of the Ætolian League. This restless people desired to be free from the protection of Rome, and appealed for aid to the king of Syria, Antiochus III. In response to this appeal the Syrian king landed in Greece with a small army of 10,000. He was speedily defeated and driven back into Asia Minor. The Roman armies followed him, and fought their first battle upon Asiatic soil at Magnesia (190 B.C.) — which proved a decisive victory. Much of the

ANTIOCHUS III. (Coin)

territory conquered from Antiochus was turned over to Pergamum and Rhodes. The Romans then subdued the revolted Ætolians and pacified the cities of Greece.

One of the conditions of the peace with Antiochus was the surrender of Hannibal, who had actively aided the king in the late war. But Hannibal fled from Syria; and being pursued by the Romans, this great soldier and enemy of Rome took his own life by poison.

The New Macedonian War (171–168 B.C.). — Macedonia had been an ally of Rome during the late war with Antiochus; and at its close Philip was disappointed that he had not received some share of the conquered lands. But it was Rome's policy to strengthen the weak, and to weaken the strong. At the death of Philip V. his son Perseus came to the throne of Macedonia. The ambitious schemes of Perseus led to another war between his country and Rome. The Roman armies under Æmilius Paullus (son of the consul slain at Cannæ) gained a decisive victory near Pydna (168 B.C.). Here the Macedonian phalanx fought its last great battle, and the Roman legions gave a new evidence of their superior strength. Macedonia was now broken up into four separate districts, which were to be governed by their own officers, but which were forbidden to have any relations with one another.

All the chief men of Greece who had given any aid to the Macedonian king were transported to Italy, where they could not stir up a revolt in their native country. Among the Achæan captives was the historian Polyb'ius, who now gathered the materials of his great work on Roman history.

IV. REDUCTION OF THE ROMAN CONQUESTS (168–133 B.C.)

Change of the Roman Policy. — We sometimes think that Rome started out upon her great career of conquest with a definite purpose to subdue the world, and with clear ideas as to how it should be governed. But nothing could be farther from the truth. She had been drawn on from one war to another, often against her own will. When she first crossed the narrow strait into Sicily at the beginning of the first Punic war, she little thought that in a hundred years her armies would be fighting in Asia; and when in earlier times she was compelled to find some way of keeping peace and order in Latium, she could not have known that she would, sooner or later, be compelled to devise a way to preserve the peace and order of the world. But Rome was ever growing and ever learning. She learned how to conquer before she learned how to govern. It was only after the late Macedonian war that Rome became convinced that her method of governing the conquered lands was not strong enough to preserve peace and maintain her own authority. She had heretofore left the conquered states to a certain extent free and independent. But now, either excited by jealousy or irritated by the intrigues and disturbances of the conquered peoples, she was determined to reduce them to a more complete state of submission.

Reduction of Macedonia and Illyricum. — She was especially convinced of the need of a new policy by the continued troubles in Macedonia. The experiment which she had tried, of cutting up the kingdom into four separate states, had not been entirely successful. The time had now come for Rome to adopt her new policy in respect to Macedonia. The four previous divisions of the kingdom were abolished, and each city or community was made directly responsible to a governor sent from Rome. By this new arrangement, Macedonia became a Roman province (146 B.C.).

About this time — perhaps a little earlier — the king of Illyricum was accused of favoring the cause of Macedonia, and of having formed a secret alliance with Perseus. The country was hence invaded by a Roman army; its king was deposed and a Roman governor appointed in his place. Thus Macedonia and Illyricum became the first two Roman provinces east of the Adriatic Sea.

Destruction of Corinth and Reduction of Greece. — The Achæan League, the capital city of which was Corinth, was now the only important independent state in the Hellenic peninsula. This league was trying to exercise authority over all the cities of the Peloponnesus. But Sparta resisted, and appealed to Rome for protection. The commissioners sent by Rome to settle this difficulty were grossly insulted by the Achæan assembly sitting at Corinth. The Romans were now determined to break up the league. Corinth was ruthlessly destroyed (146 B.C.), and its art treasures were sent to Rome. The destruction of Corinth was a barbarous act of war, such

RUINS AT CORINTH

as no civilized nation has ever approved. Rome now applied to Greece her policy of isolation, and forbade all confederations among the cities. A few cities — such as Athens and Sparta — were allowed to retain their freedom, while the rest were placed under the authority of the Roman governor of Macedonia. In later times Greece became a separate province called Acha'ia.

The Destruction of Carthage and Reduction of Africa. — Another example of the severe policy which Rome was now adopting is seen in the destruction of Carthage. This city had been growing in prosperity since the second Punic war, and seemed to excite the envy, if not the fear, of Rome. The bitter jealousy of Rome was expressed by Cato the Censor, who ended every speech in the senate with the words — " Carthage must be destroyed." Rome waited for a pretext to destroy the prosperity of her old and hated rival. This she soon found in the fact that Carthage had taken up arms against the neighboring kingdom of Numidia, which was an ally of Rome. Rome interfered and demanded that Carthage must, to insure peace, give up three hundred of her youths as hostages; then, that she must give up her arms and munitions of war; finally, that the city of Carthage itself must be abandoned. With this last unjust demand the Carthaginians refused to comply. Whereupon Rome invaded Africa with an army under Scipio Æmilia'-nus — the adopted grandson of the great Scipio Africanus who had defeated the Carthaginians at Zama. History records no more heroic defense than that offered by the Carthaginians

SITE OF CARTHAGE

to the Roman armies. To make weapons of war the temples were turned into workshops; and it is said the women cut off their long hair to be twisted into bowstrings. At last Carthage fell, and by command of the Roman senate the city was consigned to the flames and its surviving inhabitants were carried away as captives. The destruction of Carthage took place in the same year (146 B.C.) in which Corinth was destroyed. The terrible punishment inflicted upon these two cities in Greece and Africa was an evidence of Rome's grim policy to be absolutely supreme everywhere. Like Macedonia, the territory of Carthage, called " Africa," was reduced to the form of a province under a Roman governor. It soon became a Romanized country. Its commerce passed into the hands of Roman merchants, the Roman manners and customs were introduced, and the Latin language became the language of the people. The destruction of Carthage is usually called the " third Punic war." But it occurred nearly seventy years after the second Punic war; and its chief significance is due to the fact that it illustrates the new policy adopted by Rome in dealing with her subject territory.

Revolt and Subjugation of Spain. — While the Romans were engaged in creating the new provinces of Macedonia and Africa, they were called upon to maintain their authority in the old provinces of Spain and Sicily. We remember that, after the second Punic war, Spain was divided into two provinces, each under a Roman governor (see p. 375). But the Roman authority was not well established in Spain, except upon the eastern coast. The tribes in the interior and on the western coast were nearly always in a state of revolt. The most rebellious of these tribes were the Lusitanians in the west, in what is now Portugal; and the Celtibe'rians (see map, p. 368) in the interior, south of the Ibe'rus River.

The war against the Celtiberians centered about their chief stronghold, Numantia, a town south of the headwaters of the Iberus. The defense of Numantia, like that of Carthage, was heroic and desperate. Its fate was also like that of Carthage. It was compelled to surrender (133 B.C.) to the same Scipio Æmilianus. Its people were sold into slavery, and the town itself was blotted from the earth.

The Servile War in Sicily. — While Spain was being pacified, a more terrible war broke out in the province of Sicily.

This was an insurrection of the slaves of the island. One of the worst results of the Roman conquests was the growth of the slave system. Immense numbers of the captives taken in war were thrown upon the market. One hundred and fifty thousand slaves had been sold by Æmilius Paullus; fifty thousand captives had been sent home from Carthage. Italy and Sicily swarmed with a servile population. It was in Sicily that this system bore its first terrible fruit. Maltreated by their masters, the slaves rose in rebellion under a leader, called Eunus, who defied the Roman power for three years. Nearly two hundred thousand insurgents gathered about his standard. Four Roman armies were defeated and Rome herself was thrown into consternation. After the most desperate resistance, the rebellion was finally quelled and the island was pacified (132 B.C.).

Pergamum, the First Asiatic Province. — This long period of war and conquest outside of Italy — the period from 264 B.C. to 133 B.C. — was closed by the almost peaceful acquisition of a new province. The little kingdom of Pergamum, in Asia Minor, had maintained, for the most part, a friendly relation to Rome. When the last king, Attalus III., died (133 B.C.), having no legal heirs, he bequeathed his kingdom to the Roman people. This newly acquired territory was organized as a province under the name of

ROME MISTRESS OF THE WORLD

"Asia." The smaller states of Asia Minor, and Egypt, still retained their peaceful and subordinate relation as dependencies. The supreme authority of Rome, at home and abroad, was firmly established. Rome was now the mistress of the Mediterranean.

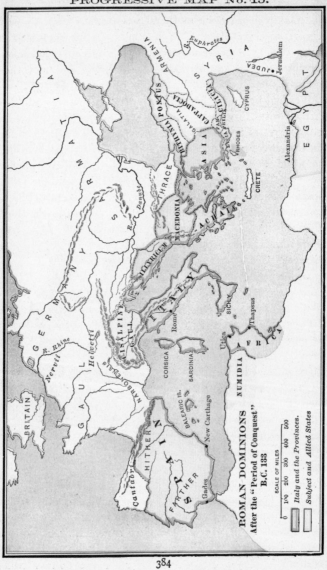

ROMAN DOMINIONS
After the "Period of Conquest"
B.C. 133

SCALE OF MILES
0   100   200   300   400   500

Italy and the Provinces.
Subject and Allied States

Selections for Reading

Knowlton, Topic A 19, "The Acquisition by Rome of a World Empire" (1).[1]

Seignobos, pp. 238–258 (Roman conquests in the West and East) (1).

Goodspeed, pp. 300–307, "The Struggle with Carthage" (1).

Shuckburgh, Ch. 17, "Rome and Carthage" (18).

Pelham, Bk. III., Ch. 1, "Rome and Carthage" (18).

Smith and Greenidge, Ch. 15, "Wars in the East" (18).

Munro, Source Book, Part IV., "The Punic Wars" (25).

Liddell, Bk. V., "Rome and the Conquest of the World" (18).

How and Leigh, Chs. 23–27, "Fifty Years of Conquest" (18).

Plutarch, "Marcellus," "Fabius," "Flamininus" (26).

Livy, Bk. XXI., Chs. 6–15 (siege of Saguntum); Chs. 32–38 (Hannibal's passage of the Alps); Chs. 44–52 (Battle of Cannæ) (25).

Polybius, Bk. I., Chs. 22–23 (the victory of Duilius); Ch. 59 (the fleet built by private subscription); Bk. VI., Chs. 19–42 (the Roman Army) (25).

Special Study

TAXATION OF THE PROVINCES. — Pelham, pp. 185–187 (18); Liddell, pp. 389–393 (18); Ramsay and Lanciani, Ch. 8 (19); Arnold, Prov. Admin., pp. 179–187 (22); Harper's Dictionary, "Stipendium," "Publicani," "Vectigalia" (19).

[1] The figure in parenthesis refers to the number of the topic in the Appendix, where a fuller title of the book will be found.

CHAPTER XXIV

THE ROMAN PEOPLE AFTER THE CONQUESTS

Synopsis

I. THE NEW ROMAN GOVERNMENT. — General Decay of Patriotism. — The New Nobility. — The Nobility and the Senate. — The Decline of the Assemblies.

II. ROME AND THE PROVINCES. — Organization of the Provinces. — The Provincial Governor. — The Towns of the Province. — The Administration of Justice. — The Collection of Taxes.

III. THE NEW CIVILIZATION. — Foreign Influences: Hellenism. — Changes in the Roman Religion. — Beginnings of Roman Literature. — Græco-Roman Art. — Roman Manners and Morals. — Cato the Censor.

IV. ECONOMIC EFFECTS OF THE CONQUESTS. — Growth of Wealth and Luxury. — The Rule of Money. — Growth of Large Landed Estates. — Decay of Agriculture and Ruin of the Peasantry. — The City Populace. — Roman Slavery.

I. THE NEW ROMAN GOVERNMENT

General Decay of Patriotism. — We may well wonder what would be the effect of the conquests upon the Roman people — upon their government, upon their civilization, and upon their economic life. For about a hundred and thirty years (264–133 B.C.) the Romans had been carrying on wars with foreign nations. Their dominions now comprised nearly all the coasts of the Mediterranean Sea. But these wars had resulted in transforming and in debasing, in many respects, the character of the Roman people. By plundering foreign countries, they had come to be avaricious, to love wealth more than honor, to indulge in luxury, and to despise the simplicity of their fathers. One of the great evils which began to show itself at this time was the general decay of patriotism. While the wars may have been regarded by some as a means to glorify the Roman people, they were too often looked at as a means to gratify personal ambition, and to afford an opportunity to appropriate the spoils of conquest. The men who carried on these wars and who ruled the conquered lands, were more anxious to enrich themselves than to promote the common good. Those who were intrusted with official duties were more devoted to their own interests than to the welfare of the whole people. With the loss of a patriotic spirit the Romans lost those higher qualities and stern virtues they once possessed.

The New Nobility. — During the whole period that we are now studying, the Roman government was a republic. But it would not be correct to think of Rome at any time as a democratic republic. When the old kingdom was overthrown, the new republican government passed into the hands of the patrician class. And when the political distinction between patricians and plebeians was broken down, there was soon developed a new aristocracy, made up of the richest and most influential men of both orders, which got control of the government. This new nobility was not based upon birth, like the old patriciate, but upon office holding; and it was only the superior, or so-called " curule offices " — those of consul, dictator, prætor, censor, and curule ædile — that conferred distinction. All those who could boast of an ancestor that had held such an office were regarded as nobles (*nobiles*); and their superior distinction consisted in the right to set up in their homes the ancestral images (*jus imaginis*). It is true that any full Roman citizen had the legal right to be elected to a curule office; but, as a matter of fact, the noble families were able by their wealth to influence the elections so as practically to retain these offices in their own hands.

The Nobility and the Senate. — But it was not simply the holding of the curule offices that gave to the new nobility their great political power. It was the fact that the curule offices opened the way to the senate. The members of the senate were chosen by the censor, who was obliged to place upon his list, first of all, those who had held a curule office. On this account, the nobles had the first claim to a seat in the senate; and, consequently, they came to form the great body of its members. When a person was once chosen senator he remained a senator for life, unless disgraced for gross misconduct. In this way the nobles gained possession of the senate, which became, in fact, the most permanent and powerful branch of the Roman government. It managed the finances of the state; controlled the erection of public works; directed the foreign policy; administered the provinces; determined largely the character of legislation; and was, in fact, the real sovereign of the Roman state.

The Decline of the Assemblies. — As the power of the senate increased, that of the popular assemblies declined. The old patrician assembly of the curies (*comitia curiata*) had long since been reduced to a mere shadow. The other two assemblies — especially that of the centuries (*comitia centuriata*) — still held an important place as legislative bodies. But there were two reasons why they declined in influence. The first reason was their unwieldy character. As they grew in size and could only say *Yes* or *No* to the questions submitted to them, they were made subject to the influence of demagogues, and lost their independent position. The second reason for their decline was due to a provision (Publilian law, 339 B.C.) that no law could be passed by the centuries unless it had first received the approval of the senate. Thus the senate could control largely the character of the laws.

II. ROME AND THE PROVINCES

Organization of the Provinces. — The most important feature of the new Roman government was the organization of the provinces. There were now eight of these provinces (p. 384): (1) Sicily, acquired as the result of the first Punic war; (2) Sardinia and Corsica, obtained during the interval between the first and second Punic wars; (3) Hither Spain and (4) Farther Spain, acquired in the second Punic war; (5) Illyricum, reduced after the third Macedonian war; (6) Macedonia (to which Achaia was attached), reduced with the destruction of Corinth; (7) Africa, organized after the third Punic war; and (8) Asia, bequeathed by Attalus III., the last king of Pergamum.

The method of organizing these provinces was in some respects similar to that which had been adopted for governing the cities in Italy. Rome saw clearly that to control these newly conquered cities and communities, they must, like the cities of Italy, be isolated, that is, separated entirely from one another, so that they could not combine in any effort to resist her authority. Every city was made directly responsible to Rome. The great difference between the Italian and the provincial town was the fact that the chief burden of the Italian town was to furnish military aid — soldiers and ships; while that of the provincial town was to furnish tribute — money and grain. Another difference was that Italian land was generally free from taxes, while provincial land was subject to taxation.

THE CAPTIVE PROVINCE

The Provincial Governor. — A province might be defined as a group of conquered cities, outside of Italy, under the control of a governor sent from Rome. At first these governors were prætors, who were elected by the people. Afterward they were proprætors or proconsuls — that is, persons who had already served as prætors or consuls at Rome. The governor held his office for one year; and during this time was the supreme military and civil ruler of the province. He was commander in chief

of the army, and was expected to preserve his territory from
internal disorders and from foreign invasion. He also administered justice between the provincials of different cities. Although the governor was responsible to the senate, the welfare
or misery of the provincials depended largely upon his own
disposition and will. Sometimes he was a real despot, increasing his own fortune at the expense of his subjects.

The Towns of the Province. — All the towns of the province
were subject to Rome; but it was Rome's policy not to treat
them all in exactly the same way. Like the cities of Italy,
they were graded according to their merit. Some were favored,
like Ga'des (in Spain) and Athens, and were treated as allied
towns (*civitates fœderatæ*); others also, such as Utica (in Africa),
were free from tribute (*immunes*), though under strict control;
but the great majority of them were considered as tributary
(*stipendiariæ*). But all these towns alike possessed local self-
government, so far as this was consistent with the supremacy
of Rome; that is, they retained their own laws, assemblies,
and magistrates.

The Administration of Justice. — In civil matters, the citizens of every town were judged by their own magistrates. But
when a dispute arose between citizens of different towns, it
was the duty of the governor to judge between them. At the
beginning of his term of office, he generally issued an edict,
setting forth the rules upon which he would decide such differences. Each succeeding governor reissued the rules of his
predecessor, with the additions which he saw fit to make. In
this way there grew up a body of common law which applied
to the whole province and was intended to afford justice in
cases not reached by the existing town laws. The people of
the province were thus united under a common judicial system,
and their rights were generally well protected in their dealings
with one another.

The Collection of Taxes. — The Roman revenue was mainly
derived from the new provinces. But instead of raising these

taxes directly through her own officers, Rome let out the business of collecting the revenue to a set of money dealers, called *publica'ni*. These persons agreed to pay into the treasury a certain sum for the right of collecting taxes in a certain province. Whatever they collected above this sum, they appropriated to themselves. This rude mode of collecting taxes, called "farming" the revenues, was unworthy of a great state like Rome, and was the chief cause of the oppression of the provincials. The governors, it is true, had the power to protect the people from being plundered. But as they themselves received no pay for their services, except what they could get out of the provinces, they were too busy in making their own fortunes to watch closely the methods of the taxgatherers.

III. The New Civilization

Foreign Influences: Hellenism. — When we think of the conquests of Rome, we usually think of the battles that she fought, of the armies that she defeated, and the lands that she subdued. But these were not the only conquests which she made. She appropriated not only foreign lands, but also foreign ideas. While she was plundering foreign temples, she was obtaining new ideas of religion and art. The educated and civilized people whom she captured in war and of whom she made slaves, often became the teachers of her children and the writers of her books. In such ways as these Rome came under the influence of foreign ideas. The most powerful of these foreign influences was that of Greece. The conquest of Greece led to the introduction of Hellenism into Rome. We might say that when Greece was conquered by Rome, Rome was civilized by Greece. The foreign influences were seen in her new ideas of religion, in her literature and her art, and in her manners.

Changes in the Roman Religion. — As Rome came into contact with other people, we can see how her religion was affected by foreign influences. The worship of the family remained

much the same; but the religion of the state became considerably changed. It is said that the entire Greek Olympus was
introduced into Italy. The Greek deities came to receive
Latin names. The Latin Jupiter was identified with the Greek
Zeus, the god of the heavens; Minerva with Athena, the goddess
of wisdom; Mars with Ares, the god of war; Venus with Aphrodite, the goddess of love; and so on. The Romans adopted the
Greek ideas and stories regarding the gods; and their worship
became more showy and elaborate. Even some of the superstitions and fantastic rites of Asia found their way into Rome.
These changes did not improve the religion. On the contrary,
they made it more corrupt. The Roman religion, by absorbing
the various ideas of other people, became a world-wide and
composite form of paganism. One of its redeeming features

TEMPLES OF LOYALTY, JUNO, AND HOPE

was the worship of exalted qualities, such as Honor and Virtue;
for example, alongside of the temple to Juno, temples were
also erected to Loyalty and Hope.

Beginnings of Roman Literature. — Before the Romans came
into contact with the Greeks, they did not have anything which
can properly be called a literature. They had, it is true, certain
crude verses and ballads; but it was the Greeks who first
taught them how to write. It was not until the close of the

first Punic war, when the Greek influence became strong, that we begin to find the names of any Latin authors. The first author, Androni'cus, who is said to have been a Greek slave, wrote a Latin poem in imitation of Homer. Then came Nævius, who combined a Greek taste with a Roman spirit, and who wrote a poem on the first Punic war; and after him, Ennius, who taught Greek to the Romans, and wrote a great poem on the history of Rome, called the " Annals." The Greek influence is also seen in Plautus and Terence, the greatest writers of Roman comedy. Plautus was a man of humble origin and wrote for the common people; his comedies are full of life and bustle, with unexpected situations and coarse jesting, such as would appeal to the crowd. Terence was a more accomplished writer and far superior to Plautus in elegance of language and refinement of taste.

Græco-Roman Art. — As the Romans were a practical people, their earliest art was shown in their buildings. From the Etruscans they had learned to use the arch and to build strong and massive structures. But the more refined features of art they obtained from the Greeks. While the Romans could never hope to acquire the pure æsthetic spirit of the Greeks, they were inspired with a passion for collecting Greek works of art, and for adorning their buildings with Greek ornaments. They imitated the Greek models and professed to admire the Greek taste; they came to be, in fact, the preservers of Greek art. Around the Forum arose public porticoes like those about the Agora at Athens.

But this professed admiration for Greek art was often a mere pretense. Rich people vied with one another in having the largest number of Greek statues in their houses. How little the Romans really appreciated the real beauty of Grecian art is shown by the story of the Roman general, Mummius, at the destruction of Corinth. In packing off a shipload of works of art to be sent to Rome, he warned the sailors that if they destroyed or injured any of the Greek statues or pictures on the voyage, " they must replace them with others of equal value ! "

Roman Manners and Morals. — It is difficult for us to think of a nation of warriors as a nation of refined people. The brutalities of war seem inconsistent with the finer arts of living. But as the Romans obtained wealth from their wars, they affected the refinement of their more cultivated neighbors. Some men, such as Scipio Africanus, looked with favor upon the introduction of Greek ideas and manners; but others, such as Cato the Censor, were bitterly opposed to it. When the Romans lost the simplicity of the earlier times, they came to indulge in luxuries and to be lovers of pomp and show. They loaded their tables with rich services of plate; they ransacked the land and the sea for delicacies with which to please their palates. Roman culture was often more artificial than real. The survival of the barbarous spirit of the Romans in the midst of their professed refinement is seen in their amusements, especially the gladiatorial shows, in which men were forced to fight with wild beasts and with one another to entertain the people.

Cato the Censor. — There was one noted man who stood out against the spirit of the new age. This was Cato the Censor, a Sabine farmer who rose from the plow to the highest honors of the Republic. Entering the army at seventeen, he had fought in all the campaigns against Hannibal, with courage and success. For thirty-five years he was the most influential man in Rome. Before his death he had passed through the whole course of political honors — quæstor, ædile, prætor, consul, and censor. He wrote a book on Agriculture; another on the Origins of the Roman People. But he gained his great distinction by his opposition to the new Hellenic culture. He was the type of the old Roman, and was attached to the " customs of the fathers." Like the Romans of the old republican days, he believed that the family was the foundation of the state; and that the occupation of a farmer was the most worthy of a citizen. In his office of censor he revised the lists of senators, and erased the names of those men whom he regarded as unworthy of the honor. He set his face against all forms of extravagance. He wrote many speeches, the most of them directed against the new ideas, which he believed were undermining the old Roman character.

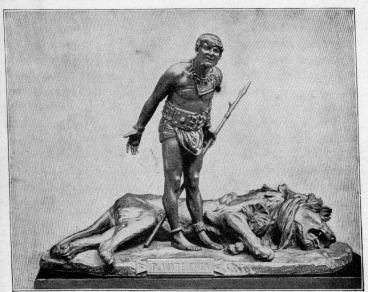

THE GLADIATOR

IV. ECONOMIC EFFECTS OF THE CONQUESTS

Growth of Wealth and Luxury. — The Roman conquests brought about a great change in the manner of living. By their wars the Romans had acquired vast sums of wealth from the conquered people. The conquered lands formed a part of the Roman domain. Much of the property of the conquered people was confiscated and brought to Rome. These are the words with which the people surrendered themselves to the Roman conqueror: " We surrender to you the people, the town, the fields, the waters, the gods of the boundaries, and movable property; all things which belong to gods and to men we deliver to the power of the Roman people." Rome became the richest city in the world. The wealth of Carthage, of Macedonia, of Greece, and of the Orient was used to swell the estates of Roman aristocrats. The old simplicity gave way to luxury. Rich villas increased in number; immense gardens, magnificent baths, sumptuous feasts, became common.

If one of us could go into a Roman house of this day, he would see that a great change had taken place since the time before the conquests. He would see that the house had been enlarged by the addition of a great court, surrounded by Greek columns and opening to the sky. He would see the walls decorated with elaborate frescoes, costly pieces of furniture in place of the old couch and table, the people dressed in richer costumes, and many slaves to perform the menial duties of the household. He would see that the simple life of the past had departed — at least for those who were able to appropriate the spoils of other lands.

The Rule of Money. — Money now came to be the god of the Roman world. Silver and gold taken from the conquered provinces poured into Rome; and there came to be a class of moneyed men. These were the so-called " knights," or *equites*. In the early Roman army the wealthiest men were *equites* because they belonged to the cavalry (p. 317). Now the word had lost its military meaning and was applied to the wealthier class of citizens, not including the senators. As there was a law preventing the senators from engaging in any kind of business, all the large business enterprises of Rome fell into the hands of the *equites*. These " knights " were the capitalists of Rome. They obtained possession of much money, and used it to make more money. The people of the provinces had to borrow money of the Roman knights, and pay them a high rate of interest. The knights were the money changers; they carried on a sort of banking business at stalls in the public squares, where they grew rich by speculation. They were the contractors, making contracts for public works, for public buildings and roads, even for collecting the revenues from the provinces. In short, they held the purse strings of the Roman people; and every one who was in need of money was their victim.

Growth of Large Landed Estates. — In the " golden days " of the Republic Italy was a land of many small farms. It was a provision of the Licinian law that no one should hold more than 300 acres (p. 339). Upon a much smaller plot of ground the farmer could raise enough wheat and barley, figs and olives, to support his family. But by this time the old Licinian law had become a dead letter. During the foreign wars the farmer had been obliged to leave his plow in the furrow and take up his sword. As the campaigns were frequently long his land remained uncultivated, or fell into the hands of rich landlords. Many of the landlords were senators, who were prevented by law from engaging in commercial pursuits. They would not cultivate these lands themselves, but would rent them out, or place them under the charge of superintendents. In this way most of the small farms disappeared, and in their place arose great landed estates. Moreover, many great estates were no longer devoted to the raising of grain, but were turned into sheep pastures and cattle ranges. The work of the farmer and of the free laborer was no longer needed; the cheaper labor of slaves was sufficient. The evils of this system were afterward pointed out by the Roman writer Pliny, who said it was the great landed estates that destroyed Italy.

Decay of Agriculture and Ruin of the Peasantry. — The rich landlords took up not only the Italian land but much of the conquered land in the provinces. This was regarded as the public domain, which cost the state nothing. It was won by the sword. Such lands in Sicily, in Africa, in Macedonia, were let out by the state at a very small rent. As they cost the landlords very little for rent, grain could be raised there at a small expense. Grain thus raised on the confiscated land in the provinces was hence cheaper than the grain raised on Italian soil; and it flooded the markets of Rome and Italy. In this way the agriculture of Italy was made profitless; and this was another reason why the old farms were used for the grazing of flocks and herds. The poor farmer himself was left without any means of support. He had no way to gain a livelihood but to go into the army. But when the wars were over, he was deprived of this resource. Many an Italian peasant, who was once able to own and work his own farm, was now turned into a vagabond. He could work neither for himself nor for anybody else; for the landlords had deprived him of his land, and slaves had deprived him of the demand for his free labor.

The City Populace. — These poor country people, deprived of every honest means of support, flocked to the towns, especially to the city of Rome. Here, with little work to be found, they formed the dregs of the city population, an ill-fed mob, craving for something to eat at the public granary. It came to be a

ROMAN GRANARY — LARGE EARTHEN JARS BURIED IN THE GROUND

great public problem how to feed this mass of human beings. Grain was often doled out to them at the public expense. It came to be another great problem how to amuse them and keep them from brooding over crimes. Accordingly, spectacular games at the circus were given for their entertainment.

But this mob of people had the right to vote, and their suffrage was sought by every office-seeker. Elections were carried by every sort of bribery. The man would stand the best chance of election who would promise to reduce the price of grain, or who would give the greatest show at the circus. " Bread and the circus " came to be the cry of the Roman populace. They looked with envy upon those who were better off. They attributed their misery to the policy of the government and especially to the senatorial order. They looked upon the rich as their enemies. They wished for a general ruin, that every one might obtain a share in the hoarded wealth of the city and make a fortune through plunder.

Roman Slavery. — According to the ancient custom, the Romans reduced to slavery all captives taken in war, and frequently the inhabitants of captured towns. The number of slaves increased vastly as the result of the great wars of conquest. As a general rule the slaves were sold at auction by the ædiles ; but at the time of great victories the slaves were sold on the spot to slave dealers who followed the armies. The slave belonged to the master like any other chattel. He had no rights, and was expected to obey his master in every respect.

The slaves were engaged in every kind of occupation, from the most honorable to the most menial. There were public slaves, owned by the state, — from scribes to caretakers of public buildings. There were professional slaves, — teachers, musicians, actors, physicians. There were household slaves, — cooks, waiters, slaves in charge of the wardrobe, the bath, the silver plate. There were artisan slaves, — shoemakers, carpenters, tailors. Rich families took a pride in the number of their slaves. But the most degraded of this class of persons were the rustic slaves, who worked upon the country estates. These were often ill-fed and cruelly treated, working in chains by day and shut up at night in underground prisons. They were the persons who engaged in terrible revolts, such as the servile war in Sicily (p. 382).

One of the evil results of Roman slavery was the fact that it tended to destroy the value of all free labor and to reduce the common freeman to a condition of helplessness.

Selections for Reading

Pelham, Bk. III., Ch. 3, "The Roman State and People" (18).[1]

How and Leigh, Chs. 28–30, "Internal History" (266–146 B.C.) (18).

Merivale, General History, Chs. 26, 27, "Rome after the Conquests" (18).

Liddell, Chs. 49, 50, "Rome at the Close of the Conquests" (18).

Mommsen, Vol. II., Bk. III., Ch. 11, "The Government and the Governed"; pp. 470–491 (the new Hellenism and introduction of foreign luxuries); pp. 500–518 (the Roman drama) (18).

Abbott, Ch. 5, "The Supremacy of the Nobilitas" (22).

Harper's Dictionary, "Provincia," "Stipendium," "Publicani," "Vectigalia" (19).

Granrud, Third Period, "The Supremacy of the Senate" (22).

Taylor, pp. 212–234 (the supremacy of the senate) (22).

Arnold, Ch. 1, "What a Province Was"; Ch. 2, "Period of the Republic"; Ch. 6, "Towns in the Provinces" (22).

Friedländer, pp. 21–30 (the classes in the towns); pp. 30–43 (the finances in the towns) (19).

Munro, Source Book, Part VII., "Results of Foreign Wars" (25).

Plutarch, "Cato the Censor" (26).

Special Study

CATO THE CENSOR AND THE GREEK INFLUENCE. — Liddell, pp. 450–455 (18); How and Leigh, pp. 302–305, see also index "Hellenism" (18); Shuckburgh, pp. 405, 406, 518–521 (18); Cruttwell, pp. 91–98 (23); Pelham, pp. 192–198 (18); Mommsen, Vol. II., pp. 413–423, 557–567 (18); Plutarch, "Cato the Censor" (26).

---

[1] The figure in parenthesis refers to the number of the topic in the Appendix, where a fuller title of the book will be found.

CHAPTER XXV

THE BEGINNING OF THE GREAT REVOLUTION

Synopsis

I. THE ATTEMPTED REFORMS OF THE GRACCHI. — The Crisis at Rome.
— Appearance of Tiberius Gracchus. — His Proposed Reforms. — Failure
and Death of Tiberius Gracchus. — The Rise of Gaius Gracchus. — His
Effort to Weaken the Senate. — His Effort to Enfranchise the Italians.
— His Death and the Restoration of the Senate.

II. THE RISE AND FAILURE OF MARIUS. — Marius as a Military Leader.
— Marius and the Popular Party. — The Social War and the Incorporation
of Italy. — Rivalry of Marius and Sulla. — Occupation of Rome by Sulla.
— The Flight of Marius. — The Marian Massacres and Death of Marius.

III. THE TRIUMPH AND DICTATORSHIP OF SULLA. — Sulla and the First
Mithridatic War. — Sulla's War with the Marian Party. — The Sullan
Proscriptions. — The Dictatorship and Constitution of Sulla.

I. THE ATTEMPTED REFORMS OF THE GRACCHI

The Crisis at Rome. — In 133 B.C. there were perhaps a
few men in Rome who realized that they were on the eve of a
great revolution. The great wars were just over; and the
people were already beginning to reap the bitter fruits of these
wars. The people had become divided into two great classes
— the rich and the poor. The aristocratic senators, who were
ruling the state for their own interest, evidently believed that
the country was safe so long as they could hold the power.
The knights (*equites*) were satisfied with their ill-gotten wealth.
But the rest of the people were broken down under the yoke of
misgovernment.

The great mass of the city population were suffering for want
of enough food. The poor country farmers — what there were
left of them — were struggling to maintain a living from the

fields which had not yet fallen into the hands of the rich land-lords. The Latin colonists and Italian allies, scattered through-out Italy, were no better off than the country farmers. The people of the provinces were subject to a heavy tribute. A vast body of slaves formed the lowest and most helpless part of the population. We could hardly believe that this condition of things would last forever. Something evidently needed to be done to relieve the people from their burdens. Rome had reached a great crisis in her history.

Appearance of Tiberius Gracchus. — The first serious attempt to remedy the existing evils was made by Tibe′rius Gracchus.

THE GRACCHI

He was the elder of two brothers who sacrificed their lives in efforts to benefit their fellow-citizens. Their mother was the noble-minded Cornelia, the daughter of the great Scipio Africanus. It is said that one day she was in a company of high-born ladies, who were showing her their jewels, and asked her to show them hers. She sent for her two boys and, pointing to them, said: " These are my jewels." Tiberius when a young man served in the Spanish army under Scipio Æmilianus, the distinguished Roman who conquered Carthage and Numantia. It is said that when Tiberius Gracchus passed through Etruria, on his way to and from Spain, he was shocked to see the fertile fields cultivated by gangs of slaves, while thousands of free citizens were living in idleness and poverty. In horror he exclaimed: " The wild beasts of Italy have their dens, but the men who have shed their blood for Italy have only the light and air they breathe; they wander houseless, homeless, with their wives and children." Tiberius was a man of refined nature and a deep sense of justice, and he determined to do what he could to remedy these evils.

His Proposed Reforms. — Tiberius Gracchus was elected tribune and began his work of reform in 133 B.C. He believed that the wretched condition of the Roman people was due chiefly to the unequal division of the public land, and especially to the failure to enforce the Licinian laws (p. 338). He therefore proposed to revive these laws; to limit the holding of public land to five hundred *iugera* (about 300 acres) for each person; to pay the present holders for any improvements they had made; and then to rent the land thus taken up to the poorer class of citizens. This seemed fair enough; for the state was the real owner of the public land, and could do what it wished with its own. But the rich landlords, who had held possession of this land for so many years, looked upon the measure as the same thing as taking away their own property; and there immediately arose a fierce conflict between the old senatorial party and the followers of Tiberius.

Failure and Death of Tiberius Gracchus. — Tiberius determined to pass his law in the assembly, without the approval of the senate. The senate, on the other hand, was equally determined that the law should not be passed. Accordingly, the senators induced one of the tribunes, whose name was Marcus Octa'vius, to put his veto (p. 331) upon the passage of the law. This act of Octavius was entirely legal, for he did what the law gave him the right to do. Tiberius, on the other hand, in order to outdo his opponent, had recourse to a high-handed measure. Instead of waiting a year for the election of new tribunes who might be devoted to the people's cause, he called upon the people to deprive Octavius of his office. This was an illegal act, because there was no law which authorized such a proceeding. But the people did as Tiberius desired, and Octavius was deposed. The law of Tiberius was then passed in the assembly of the tribes, and three commissioners were chosen to carry it into effect.

The law of Tiberius and the method which he had used to pass it increased the bitterness between the aristocratic party and the popular party. Contrary to law, Tiberius announced himself as a candidate for reëlection. The day appointed for the election came. Two tribes had already voted for the reelection of Tiberius, when a band of senators appeared in the Forum armed with sticks and clubs; and in the riot which ensued Tiberius Gracchus and three hundred of his followers were slain. This was the first blood shed in the civil wars of Rome. The killing of a tribune by the senators was as much an illegal act as was the deposition of Octavius. Both parties had disregarded the law, and the revolution was begun.

The Rise of Gaius Gracchus. — After the death of Tiberius his law was for a time carried into execution. The commissioners proceeded with their work of redividing the land. But the people were for a time without a real leader. After the lapse of ten years the cause of reform was again taken up by Gaius Gracchus, the brother of Tiberius, and the conflict was renewed. Gaius had served as quæstor in Sicily. When he returned to Rome and was called to account, he replied, " I have spent none of the people's money. Others have taken out casks of wine and brought them back filled with gold. The purse I took with me I have brought back empty."

Gaius Gracchus was in many respects an abler man than Tiberius. No more sincere and patriotic, he was yet a broader statesman and took a wider view of the situation. When he obtained the position of tribune (123 B.C.) his influence for a time was all-powerful. He was eloquent and persuasive, and practically had the control of the government. First of all, he tried to help the people by a law which was really the most mischievous of all his measures. This was his famous "corn law." It was intended to benefit the poor population in the city, which was at that time troublesome and not easy to control. The law provided that any Roman citizen could receive grain from the public storehouses for about half its usual price. Gaius may not have known what evil effect this law was destined to produce; he may not have realized that this was the way to increase the number of paupers. But it insured his popularity with the lower classes. He then renewed the agrarian laws, that is, the land laws of his brother; and also provided for sending out colonies of poor citizens into different parts of Italy, and even into the provinces.

His Effort to Weaken the Senate. — But Gaius believed that such measures as these would afford only temporary relief, so long as the senate retained its great power. It was, of course, impossible to overthrow the senate. But it was possible to take from it some of the powers which it possessed. From the senators had hitherto been selected the jurors (*iu'dices*) before whom were tried cases of extortion and other crimes. By a law Gaius took away from the senate this right to furnish jurors in criminal cases, and gave it to the Roman knights, that is, the wealthy class outside of the senate (p. 396). This gave to the knights a more important political position, and drew them over to the support of Gaius, and thus tended to split the aristocratic classes in two. The senate was thus deprived not only of its right to furnish jurors, but also of the support of the wealthy men who had previously been friendly to it. This was a great triumph for the popular party; and Gaius looked forward to another victory.

His Effort to Enfranchise the Italians. — When he was re-elected to the tribunate Gaius Gracchus came forward with his grand scheme of extending the Roman franchise to the people of Italy. This was the wisest of all his measures, but the one which cost him his popularity and influence. It aroused the jealousy of the poorer citizens, who did not wish to share their rights with foreigners. The senators took advantage of the unpopularity of Gaius, and now posed as the friends of the people. They induced one of the tribunes, by the name of Drusus, to play the part of a demagogue. Drusus proposed to found twelve new colonies at once, each with three thousand Roman citizens, and thus to put all the reforms of Gaius Gracchus into the shade. The people were deceived by this stratagem, and the attempt of Gaius to enfranchise the Italians was defeated.

His Death and the Restoration of the Senate. — Gaius did not succeed, as he desired, in being elected tribune for the third time. A great part of the people soon abandoned him, and the first attempts at reform came to naught. It was not long before a new law was passed which prevented any further distribution of the public land. Gaius lost his life in a tumult in which three thousand citizens were slain. Thus in a similar way perished the two Gracchi, who had attempted to rescue the Roman people from the evils of a corrupt government.

The Gracchi had failed. The senate and the aristocracy were too strongly intrenched to be overthrown by the tribunes, even though supported by the popular assembly. Hence with the death of these reformers the senate was restored to its previous position as the chief ruling body of the state. The government became more corrupt than ever before. The senators ruled to enrich themselves, while the real interests of the people were forgotten. On the other hand, the people had no capable leaders, and their cause for a time seemed lost. It is true that the people had learned something from the revolutionary attempts of the Gracchi. They had learned that they could pass laws, even without the approval of the senate; and that they could obstruct, if they could not overthrow, the policy of the nobles.

II. The Rise and Failure of Marius

Marius as a Military Leader. — In referring to the death of Gaius Gracchus, the French orator Mirabeau once said, " When dying, the last of the Gracchi threw a handful of dust toward heaven as though to invoke an avenger; from this dust Marius arose." Marius was a son of the soil. His father was a poor farmer living among the hills of Latium. Without education he worked his way up until he was tribune two years after the death of Gaius Gracchus. But it was not so much his political skill as his military genius that brought him to the front. He had already served with the great Scipio Æmilianus at the siege of Numantia (p. 382). Under the

MARIUS (So-called)

control of the senate Rome was now carrying on a war in Africa with Jugurtha, an unprincipled usurper who was trying to get control of the kingdom of Numidia. Jugurtha was able to prolong this war by the liberal use of gold; and he expressed his opinion of Rome by calling it " a venal city ready to perish whenever it could find a purchaser." The people became tired of the way in which the senate was conducting this war, and elected Marius as consul to finish it. Marius fulfilled all the expectations of the people; he defeated the enemy, and Jugurtha was brought back a prisoner to Rome. A triumph (p. 353) was given to the conqueror, in which the captive king was led in chains; and Marius became the people's hero.

But a greater glory now awaited Marius. While he was absent in Africa, Rome was threatened by a deluge of barbarians from the north — the Cimbri and Teu'tones. This invasion called to mind the terrible days when the Gauls had invaded Italy and destroyed Rome. Already the Roman armies had been defeated; in the great battle at Arausio sixty thousand Romans are said to have perished. All eyes were turned toward Marius as the only man who could save Rome. He was reëlected to the consulship and assigned to his new command. He gained one

SEAT OF THE CIMBRIC WAR

great victory over the Teutones at Aquæ Sextiæ in Southern Gaul; and another the next year over the Cimbri at Vercellæ in northern Italy. In these two battles the barbarian armies were annihilated. Marius was now saluted as the "savior of Rome," and received another magnificent triumph.

Marius and the Popular Party. — On account of his humble origin Marius was by nature in sympathy with the cause of the people. During his military career, he had already broken down the class distinctions in the army, and had placed the rich and the poor, the Romans and the Italians, side by side in the ranks. The popular leaders now sought the support of his great name and his military prestige in their war against the senate. The chief leaders of the popular party, since the death of the Gracchi, were Saturni'nus and Glaucia — men of no great ability. Marius now threw himself into the hands of these leaders, and was again elected to the consulship — the sixth time he had held that office. With all his great military skill Marius had no plan of reform; he was simply the tool of others. Certain radical laws were passed in spite of the violent opposition of the senate, and the cause of the people for the moment seemed victorious. Saturninus then proposed his own reëlection as tribune, and attempted to overawe the assembly by an armed force. A riot followed, and the senate called upon Marius, as consul, to put down the insurrection and save the republic. He reluctantly obeyed, and in the ensuing conflict his colleagues, Saturninus and Glaucia, were killed. Marius himself showed no capacity as a party leader. He fell into disrepute and retired from Rome. The senate again assumed the reins of government, and this first attempt to support the people's cause by the aid of a military commander proved a failure.

The Social War and the Incorporation of Italy (90–88 B.C.). — The Italian allies had long been clamoring for the rights of citizenship. Their complaints finally broke out into an open war. This war of the allies (*socii*) is known as the "Social war." It was really a war of secession. Its purpose was to found a new Italian state, "Italica," with its capital at Corfin'ium. The parties at Rome now ceased from their quarreling and united to preserve the republic. Even Marius returned to serve in the Roman army. A hundred thousand men took the field against an equal number raised by the allies. In the first year the war was unfavorable to Rome. In the second year (89 B.C.) new preparations were made and new commanders were appointed. Marius, on account of his age, was not continued in his command; while Lucius Cornelius Sulla, who was

once a subordinate of Marius, was made chief commander in Campania. The great credit of bringing this war to a close was due chiefly to Sulla. The Social war was a great affliction to Italy. It is roughly estimated that three hundred thousand men, Romans and Italians, lost their lives in this struggle.

Although Rome was victorious in the field, most of the Italians obtained what they had demanded before the war began, that is, the rights of Roman citizenship. The Romans granted the franchise (1) to all Latins and Italians who had remained loyal during the war; and (2) to every Italian who should be enrolled by the prætor within sixty days. Every person to whom these provisions applied was now a Roman citizen. The policy of "incorporation," which had been discontinued for so long a time, was thus revived. The greater part of Italy was now joined to Rome; and Italy and Rome became practically one nation.

Rivalry of Marius and Sulla. — One important result of the Social war was to bring Sulla into prominence, and thus to give to the aristocratic party a military leader — a leader perhaps quite equal to Marius as a soldier, and far superior to him as a politician. The senate recognized him as the ablest general of the time, when it now appointed him to conduct a war in the East against the great enemy of Rome, Mithrida'tes, king of Pontus, who was encroaching upon the Roman territory in Asia Minor and Greece.

SULLA (So-called)

Marius had watched with envy the growing fame of Sulla during and after the Social war. His whole nature was now inflamed with revenge and the desire to displace and destroy his hated rival. To regain his influence with the people, he reëntered politics, and joined hands with the popular leader, the tribune Publius Sulpicius. Sulla had scarcely left Rome, when Marius and Sulpicius persuaded the people to pass some laws which contained a provision giving to Marius instead of Sulla the command of the Mithridatic war. This law reversed the decree of the senate which had already given the command to Sulla. It thus made a personal issue between Marius and Sulla. Two messengers were sent to Sulla with the order that he turn over his command to Marius.

Occupation of Rome by Sulla. — Sulla had not yet left Italy. His legions were still encamped in Campania. He appealed to them to support the honor and authority of their commander. They responded to his appeal, and Sulla at the head of his troops marched to Rome. For the first time the Roman legions fought in the streets of the capital. Marius and Sulpicius were driven from the city, and Sulla for the time was supreme. He called together the senate, and caused the leaders of the popular party to be declared outlaws. He then annulled the laws passed by Sulpicius, and gave back to the senate the power to approve or reject all laws before they should be submitted to the people. With the army at his back Sulla could do what he pleased. When he had placed the government securely in the hands of the senate, as he thought, he left Rome for the purpose of conducting the war against Mithridates in the East.

The Flight of Marius. — Marius was now an exile, a fugitive from the country which he had once saved. The pathetic story of his flight and wanderings is graphically told by Plutarch. He says that Marius set sail from Ostia, but was soon forced by a storm to land at Circe'ii (map, p. 410), where he wandered about in hunger and great suffering; that his courage was kept up by remembering that when a boy he had found an eagle's nest with seven young in it, which a soothsayer had interpreted as meaning that he would be consul seven times; that he was again taken on board a vessel and landed at Minturnæ, where he was captured and condemned to death; that the slave who was ordered to kill him dropped his sword as he heard the stern voice of his intended victim shouting, " Man, darest thou kill Gaius Marius? " that he was then released and wandered to Sicily, and then to Africa, where, a fallen hero, he sat amid the ruins of Carthage; that at last he found a safe retreat in a little island off the African coast, and waited for vengeance and the time of his seventh consulship.

The Marian Massacres and Death of Marius. — During the absence of Sulla Rome passed through a reign of terror. The popular party, now under the leadership of the demagogue Cinna, sought to regain control of the government. But in an armed conflict, in which ten thousand citizens are said to have lost their lives, Cinna was defeated and driven from the city. Cinna then, following the example of his enemy Sulla, appealed to the army for support. At the same time Marius, who had fled to Africa, returned with a body of Numidian cavalry. Uniting their forces, Marius and Cinna marched to Rome and took possession of the city. Then began that scene of carnage which is known as the " Marian massacres," in which the ene- mies of Marius were everywhere cut down without mercy. The man who had once been saluted as the " savior of Rome " for- ever blackened his name by the most revolting deeds of a despot. This spasm of slaughter lasted for five days. Marius and Cinna then declared themselves to be consuls. But Marius held this, his seventh consulship, only a brief time, when he died — the " horror of Rome." Cinna continued to rule with absolute power. He declared himself consul each year, and named his own colleague. His incapacity is shown by the fact that during the three years of his supremacy he did nothing to strengthen the people's cause, of which he professed to be the leader. At last, hearing that Sulla was about to return from the East, Cinna led an army to prevent his landing in Italy; but he was killed in a mutiny of his own soldiers.

III. The Triumph and Dictatorship of Sulla

Sulla and the First Mithridatic War (88–84 B.C.). — While Rome was thus suffering from the massacres of Marius and the despotic rule of Cinna, Sulla was gathering fresh glories in the East. When he landed in Greece he found the eastern prov- inces in a wretched state. Mithridates, the king of Pontus (map, p. 384), had extended his power over a large part of Asia Minor. He had overrun the Roman province of Asia. He had induced the Greek cities on the coast, which had been brought under the Roman power, to revolt and join his cause. He had massacred over eighty thousand Italians living on the Asiatic coast. He had also sent his armies into Macedonia and Greece, and many of the cities there, including Athens, had de- clared in his favor. The Roman power in the East seemed well-nigh broken. It was at this time that Sulla showed his greatest ability as a soldier. Within four years he reëstablished the Roman power, and compelled Mithridates to sign a treaty of peace. He then returned to Italy to find his own party overthrown and himself an outlaw.

Sulla's War with the Marian Party. — Sulla landed in Italy (83 B.C.) with a victorious army of forty thousand men. He had restored the power of Rome against her enemies abroad; he now set to work to restore her authority against her enemies at home. The landing of Sulla in Italy without disbanding his army was the signal for civil war. Southern Italy declared in his favor, and many prominent men looked to him as the deliverer of Rome. The choicest of his new allies was a young man of twenty-three, whose future fame, as Pompey the Great, was destined to equal that of Sulla himself. Sulla marched to Campania and routed the forces of one consul, while troops of the other consul deserted to him in a body. A desperate battle was fought at Clusium, in Etruria, in which Sulla and Pompey defeated a third army. At last an army of Samnites which had joined the Marian cause was cut to pieces at the Colline gate (map, p. 319, gate *a*) under the very walls of Rome. Sulla showed what might be expected of him when he ordered six thousand Samnite prisoners to be massacred in cold blood.

The Sullan Proscriptions. — With Italy at his feet and a victorious army at his back, Sulla, the champion of the senate, was now the supreme ruler of Rome. Before entering upon the work of reconstructing the government, he determined first of all to complete the work of destroying his enemies. It is sometimes said that Sulla was not a man of vindictive nature. Let us see what he did. He first outlawed all civil and military officers who had taken part in the revolution against him, and offered a reward of two talents (about $2500) to the murderer of any of these men. He then posted a list (*proscriptio*) containing the names of those citizens whom he wished to have killed. He placed eighty names on the first list, two hundred and twenty more on the second, as many more on the third, and so on until nearly five thousand citizens had been put to death in Rome. If the proscriptions of Sulla were not inspired by the mad fury of revenge which led to the Marian massacres, they were yet prompted by the cool and merciless policy of a tyrant.

The Dictatorship and Constitution of Sulla. — When Sulla had destroyed his enemies, not only in Rome but throughout Italy, he turned to the work of reconstructing the government in the interests of the senate and aristocracy. Not relying upon the tribune's power which had been used by the Gracchi, nor upon the consular power which Marius had repeatedly held, he had himself appointed " perpetual dictator." This made him the absolute ruler of the state. As a support to his power he planted his veterans in military colonies in different parts of Italy, where they could be called upon in case of emergency. He then proceeded to frame his new constitution, the most important provisions of which were the following :

(1) He restored the senate to its previous position as the chief ruling body of the state, granting to it the right to initiate all legislation. That is, no law could be passed by the people unless it was first proposed by the senate.

(2) He still further weakened the power of the people by taking away from the *comitia tributa* the power of passing laws, transferring this power to the *comitia centuriata*, which was controlled by wealth.

(3) He reduced the power of the tribune to the mere right of " intercession," or the protection of a citizen from official injustice ; and forbade the tribune to propose laws.

(4) He reënacted the old law of succession to office, whereby no person could hold the same office a second time within a period of ten years.

(5) He organized a system of permanent criminal courts, and restored the jury list to the senate, as it had been before the days of the Gracchi.

The general tendency of Sulla's legislation was to annul all the principal changes which had grown out of the revolutionary attempts of the popular party and its leaders, and thus to reëstablish the government upon its old aristocratic basis.

After a reign of three years Sulla resigned his office as dictator. He retired to his country home on the Bay of Naples, and died in a few months, before he could know of the fate of his constitution. Upon his monument were inscribed the words: " No friend ever did him a kindness, and no enemy a wrong, without being fully repaid." The career of Sulla, like that of the Gracchi and of Marius, marks a stage in the decline of the republic and the establishment of the empire.

Selections for Reading

Knowlton, Topic A 20, "The Revolution: The Gracchi, Marius, Sulla" (1).[1]
Goodspeed, pp. 334–343 (From the Gracchi to Sulla) (1).
Liddell, Bk. VI., "First Period of the Civil War" (18).
Smith, Wm., Smaller Hist., Ch. 21, "The Gracchi"; Ch. 23, "The Cimbri and Teutones" (18).
Pelham, Bk. IV., Ch. 2, "From the Gracchi to Sulla" (18).
How and Leigh, Ch. 39, "The Social War"; Ch. 44, "The Sullan Constitution" (18).
Merivale, Gen. Hist., Ch. 32, "Rivalry of Marius and Sulla" (18).
Taylor, Ch. 11, "Cinna and Sulla" (22).
Shuckburgh, Ch. 38, "Mithridates in Asia and Greece" (18).
Mommsen, Vol. III., Bk. IV., Ch. 10, "The Sullan Constitution"; pp. 458–470 (character of Sulla) (18).
—— (Abridged), Ch. 22, "Marius as a Revolutionist" (18).
Freeman, Essay on "Sulla" (3).
Plutarch, "Marius," "Sulla" (26).

Special Study

THE ROMAN SENATE. — Pelham, pp. 159–167 (18); Shuckburgh, pp. 206–208, 397–399 (18); How and Leigh, p. 298 (18); Merivale, Gen. Hist., pp. 209–212 (18); Mommsen, Vol. I., pp. 406–412 (18); Ramsay and Lanciani, pp. 254–263 (19); Harper's Dictionary, " Senatus" (19).

[1] The figure in parenthesis refers to the number of the topic in the Appendix, where a fuller title of the book will be found.

CHAPTER XXVI

THE DEVELOPMENT OF ROMAN IMPERIALISM

Synopsis

I. THE RISE OF POMPEY AND CRASSUS. — The Drift of Roman Politics. — The Three Revolts: Lepidus, Sertorius, Spartacus. — The Consulship of Pompey and Crassus. — Overthrow of the Sullan Constitution. — The Military Supremacy of Pompey.

II. THE COALITION OF POMPEY, CRASSUS, AND CÆSAR. — The Rise of Julius Cæsar. — Cicero and the Catilinian Conspiracy. — Formation of the "First Triumvirate." — The Consulship of Cæsar. — Renewal of the Triumvirate at Lucca. — Cæsar and the Conquest of Gaul.

III. THE SUPREMACY OF CÆSAR. — Dissolution of the Triumvirate. — Alliance of Pompey with the Senate. — Rupture between the Senate and Cæsar. — Civil War between Pompey and Cæsar. — Cæsar's Triumphs and Titles. — Cæsar's Political Reforms. — Cæsar's Economic Reforms. — His Reform of the Provincial System. — His Other Reforms and Projects. — The Assassination of Cæsar.

I. THE RISE OF POMPEY AND CRASSUS

The Drift of Roman Politics. — From what we have seen of the political conflicts going on at Rome since the first appearance of the Gracchi, we might infer that no important results had been accomplished. The constitution of Sulla was evidently intended to put the government back where it was before the revolution began. The efforts of the people to overthrow the power of the senate and the aristocracy seemed to have come to nothing. The chiefs of the popular party had shown no great capacity for leadership, and had often degenerated into mere demagogues. But in spite of all these discouragements, there were two facts which seemed to show the drift of Roman politics. In the first place, there had been a growing tendency in the direction of a one-man power. This is shown in the tribunate of the Gracchi, in the successive consulships of Marius, in the absolute rule of Cinna, and in the dictatorship of Sulla. In other words, the Roman state was drifting toward imperialism. In the second place, the determined spirit of the people showed that the one-man power could not be permanently established upon an aristocratic basis like that of Sulla. The Roman people would evidently be satisfied only with a form of monarchy or imperialism which recognized the welfare of the whole Roman state. We are now to trace how such a form of imperialism came to be established.

The Three Revolts: Lepidus, Sertorius, Spartacus. — Sulla had hardly passed away when signs of discontent everywhere appeared. The evidence of this discontent is seen in three important revolts which took place at this time — the revolt of Lep'idus, the rebellion of Sertorius, and the insurrection led by Spar'tacus.

(1) The first attempt to oppose the new constitution was made by the consul Lepidus, a vain, ambitious man who aspired to be chief of the popular party, but who proved to be an incompetent leader, like many of his predecessors. He proposed to restore the tribunate, and to overthrow the whole Sullan régime. Failing in this, he raised an armed force, as Sulla and Cinna had done before him, to carry out his views. The senate placed in command of the army Pompey, one of Sulla's lieutenants. Pompey defeated Lepidus, and this feeble attempt at revolution failed (77 B.C.); but it served to bring Pompey to the front.

(2) A more serious attempt at revolution was made by Sertorius, a popular leader who had escaped to Spain during the Sullan proscriptions. Here he espoused the cause of the provincials, and attempted to establish in Spain an independent republic. Sertorius was himself a man of noble character, and also a very able soldier. Pompey was appointed proconsul, and was sent with a large army to put down this rebellion. The

war under Pompey was successfully carried on; but it was only after Sertorius had been treacherously slain by one of his own followers that the province was finally pacified (72 B.C.).

(3) Before the war in Spain was ended, the senate was called upon to meet a still more formidable danger in Italy. This was the revolt of the gladiators, under their renowned leader Spartacus. The gladiators were captives trained to

ROMAN GLADIATORS

fight one another in the arena for the amusement of the Roman populace. Seventy of these desperate men escaped from the training school at Capua, and gathered about them a motley horde of a hundred thousand slaves and outlaws. They defeated four Roman armies, and threatened to devastate the whole of Italy. In the absence of Pompey the senate selected Crassus—a wealthy aristocrat who had served as a soldier under Sulla — to put down this fearful insurrection. Spartacus was finally defeated (71 B.C.). A small remnant of his band fled to the north and fell in with Pompey on his return from Spain, and was destroyed. By this stroke of luck Pompey had the assurance to claim that, in addition to closing the war with Spain, he had also finished the war with the gladiators.

The Consulship of Pompey and Crassus (70 B.C.). — The senate had thus succeeded in maintaining its authority and putting down three attempts at revolution, with the aid of Pompey and Crassus. These generals now claimed the consulship as a reward for their service. But according to the Sullan laws they were not yet eligible to this office; and the senate was committed to the Sullan régime. Finding no hope of support from the senate, the two generals turned to the popular party. In return for the consulship they agreed to carry out the schemes of this party and annul the laws of Sulla. As a result of this bargain Pompey and Crassus joined hands, broke with the senate, became supporters of the popular party, and were elected to the consulship.

HEAD OF THE STATUE OF POMPEY
(So-called)

Overthrow of the Sullan Constitution. — True to their agreement, Pompey and Crassus proceeded, with the support of the people, to overthrow the constitution which Sulla expected would be lasting. The old power to propose laws was given back to the tribunes. The legislative power was restored to the tribal assembly, which now could pass laws without the approval of the senate. The exclusive right to furnish jurors in criminal cases was taken away from the senate. Also the power of the censors to revise the list of the senators, which Sulla had abolished, was restored; and as a result of this, sixty-four senators were expelled from the senate. By these measures the Sullan régime was practically destroyed, and the supremacy of the senate taken away. This was, in fact, the most decisive victory won by the popular party since the beginning of the revolution. It was also achieved without an armed conflict, simply by winning to the democratic cause the support of the two successful generals.

The Military Supremacy of Pompey. — Since the death of Sulla, the senators had taken comparatively little interest in the eastern provinces except as a source of wealth to themselves and to their supporters. As a result of this weak policy, the East was falling into a condition nearly as wretched as its condition before the campaigns of Sulla. The seas were infested with pirates, who cut off the grain supplies from Egypt; and the king of Pontus was still a menace to the Roman provinces. The people now determined to take into their own hands the management of eastern affairs. By two laws they raised their new leader, Pompey, to a position never before held by a Roman citizen — except perhaps by Sulla.

(1) *The Gabinian law* (67 B.C.). — To rid the sea of the pirates (who made their home in Cilicia and Crete) a law was proposed by the tribune Gabinius, giving to Pompey for three years supreme control over th Mediterranean Sea and its coasts for fifty miles inland. This law was passed, and Pompey was placed in command of a large fleet and army. Within ninety days he had swept the seas and cleared the coasts, and the Mediterranean was once more open to Roman commerce.

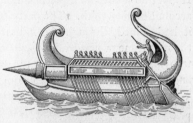

PIRATE VESSEL

(2) *The Manilian law* (66 B.C.). — In the next year a law was proposed by the tribune Manilius and supported by Rome's greatest orator, Cicero, giving to Pompey the entire control of the East until the tedious war now in progress against Mithridates should be brought to an end. The war had recently been conducted by Lucullus, a wealthy aristocratic general, who was charged with prolonging the war to enrich himself. Pompey now received the command. He defeated Mithridates and drove him out of his kingdom. He then invaded Syria and took possession of that country. He entered Palestine, — which the Romans called Jude'a, — and after a severe struggle succeeded in capturing Jerusalem (63 B.C.). All the eastern coasts of the Mediterranean were brought under his control. He organized the conquered territory into new

Roman provinces, and planted, it is said, thirty-nine new cities. Pompey was now looked upon as the most successful of Roman generals, and worthy of the title " the Great," once conferred upon him by Sulla.

II. The Coalition of Pompey, Crassus, and Cæsar

The Rise of Julius Cæsar. — During the absence of Pompey the popular party was under the professed leadership of Crassus. He had no ability as a politician, and was influential chiefly on account of his wealth. The party had, in fact, won what laurels it had gained, through the military prestige of Pompey. In the meantime, a new leader was coming to the front — a leader who was destined to become the greatest statesman of Rome, and to perform a work which no one else was able to accomplish.

CÆSAR

This man was Julius Cæsar. He was six years younger than Pompey. He was a nephew of Marius and the son-in-law of Cinna. He was, therefore, from the first well disposed toward the popular cause. He had tried to procure the franchise for the Latin colonies beyond the Po; and he had, while curule ædile, won the plaudits of the populace by the splendor of his games. Cæsar saw that the people's cause was in the ascendancy; and he aspired to become its leader, and to place himself at the head of the Roman state. This was a noble ambition on the part of Cæsar — to identify his own success with that of his fellow-citizens. But his ambition was checked for a brief time by the suspicion that he was implicated in the conspiracy of Cat'iline — a movement which aroused in the minds of all good citizens the most intense indignation.

Cicero and the Catilinian Conspiracy. — Catiline was a man of the stripe of Cinna. He professed to represent the cause of the people. He was like Cinna in not caring so much for the real interests of the people as for his own profit. He proved to be a demagogue and a desperado. He came to be feared by all the best citizens of Rome. He ran for the consulship and was defeated by the senatorial party, under the lead of Cicero. After a second failure to obtain the consulship, Catiline's true character was revealed. He adopted the desperate methods which had proved tempo-

CICERO

rarily successful in the days of Marius and Cinna. He determined to raise an army from all the lawless and discontented classes of Italy, to march upon Rome, seize the city, and destroy his enemies. This evil plan was discovered by Cicero, who had been elected consul. Catiline's army was defeated in Etruria. Catiline himself was killed in battle, and five of his fellow-conspirators were condemned to death by the senate; and Cicero put the judgment into execution.

Cicero seemed now to be the rising man of the state. Although not belonging to the senatorial order, he joined the cause of the senate. He had been from his youth an ardent student of the law, and had developed great powers as an orator. He was a man of pure motives and of the highest integrity. He had exposed the shocking misgovernment of the provinces by his impeachment of Verres, the corrupt governor of Sicily; and now he was hailed as the " Father of his Country." The senate regarded the suppression of the Catilinian conspiracy as its own victory. The popular leaders, although denying all connection with the conspiracy, fell into disrepute.

Formation of the " First Triumvirate " (60 B.C.). — The senate now supposed that the time had come again to assert its own authority. The only leaders of the people who seemed strong enough to oppose the senatorial policy were Pompey and Cæsar. The senate, therefore, determined first to humiliate Pompey, and next to embarrass Cæsar. In the first place, when Pompey returned from his victories, he expected that his arrangements in the East would be confirmed by the senate, and that his veterans would be rewarded with grants of land. The senate refused to do either. In the next place, when Cæsar returned from Spain — to which province he had been sent as propraetor and where he had won a military reputation — he wished to receive a triumph and to be elected to the consulship. The senate decided that he could not receive a triumph while in the city, and could not be elected to the consulship while outside the city. Cæsar accordingly gave up the triumph and entered the city. Here he found Pompey chafing against the senate; and the two generals agreed to unite in opposing the senatorial party. By its blundering policy, the senate had thus driven the two chieftains into a coalition, to which the wealthy Crassus was admitted. This " ring " is usually called the First Triumvirate, although it did not receive the approval of any law. It was composed of the most successful soldier, the ablest statesman, and the richest capitalist of Rome. These men united to advance their own interests in opposition to the senate. They were also, to all appearances at least, in sympathy with the popular party, and their success would no doubt advance the cause of the people.

The Consulship of Cæsar (59 B.C.). — According to the terms of the agreement Cæsar was elected to the consulship. He then went faithfully to work to fulfill his obligations to Pompey, and secured the passage of laws to strengthen the cause of the triumvirs. The acts of Pompey in the East were confirmed, and grants of land were made not only for Pompey's veterans but also for the needy citizens of Rome. Finally, a bill was passed by which Cæsar himself was assigned to the provinces of Cisalpine Gaul and Illyricum, to which was added Transalpine Gaul, or Narbonen'sis.

But before leaving for his provinces, Cæsar desired to cripple the power of the senate by depriving it of its chief leaders. These were Cicero and Cato the Younger. Cicero had restored the prestige of the senate by crushing the Catilinian conspiracy; and Cato, who was the grandson of Cato the Censor, was now the most conservative of the senatorial party. Cæsar's tool in this work was the tribune Clodius, a radical and unscrupulous politician, but a devoted friend of Cæsar. Through his influence, Cicero was banished on the charge of having put to death the Catilinian conspirators without giving them a regular trial. Cato was sent on a mission to Cyprus, where he would be removed from the politics of the capital. With this arrangement of affairs at Rome, Cæsar departed with his legions to Gaul.

CATO THE YOUNGER

Renewal of the Triumvirate at Lucca (56 B.C.). — If Cæsar made a mistake, it was in putting such a man as Clodius in charge of his interests at Rome. Clodius was by nature an adventurer and a demagogue, and by his rash acts he came near breaking up the triumvirate. He allied himself with the rabble of Rome; he paraded the streets with bands of armed ruffians, and the capital was threatened with mob rule. Pompey as well as the senate became disgusted with the régime of Clodius. They united their influence and obtained the recall of Cicero from his exile. At the same time Cato returned from his absence in Cyprus. With the return of the old senatorial leaders, and the discontent of Pompey, it looked as if the senate would once more regain its power, and the triumvirate would go to pieces.

But the watchful eye of Cæsar detected these symptoms of discontent, and a conference of the leaders took place at Lucca, a town in northern Italy, where a new arrangement was brought about. Cæsar was to be given an additional term of five years in Gaul, and to be elected consul at the end of that time; Pompey and Crassus were now to receive the consulship; and at the close of their term of office Pompey was to have the provinces of Spain and Africa, and the money-loving Crassus was to receive the rich province of Syria. In this way they would divide the Roman world among them. The terms of the agreement were apparently satisfactory to the parties concerned. Cæsar now felt that matters at Rome were safe, at least until he could complete his work in Gaul and fortify his own power with a devoted and invincible army.

Cæsar and the Conquest of Gaul (58–50 B.C.). — Within eight years Cæsar brought under his power all the territory bounded by the Pyrenees, the Alps, the Rhine, and the Atlantic Ocean, or about what corresponds to the modern countries of France, Belgium, and Holland. He at first conquered the Helve'tii, a tribe lying on the outskirts of his own province of Narbonensis. He then met and drove back a great invasion of Germans, who, under a prince called Ariovis'tus, had crossed the Rhine, and threatened to overrun the whole of Gaul. He then pushed into the northern parts of Gaul, and conquered the Nervii and the neighboring tribes. He overcame the Ven'eti on the Atlantic coast, and conquered Aquita'nia. He

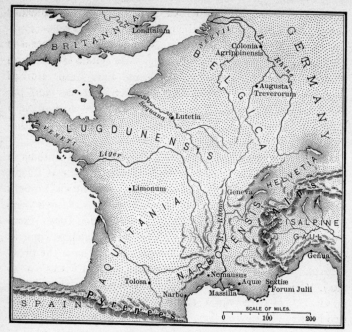

THE PROVINCE OF GAUL

also made two invasions into Britain (55, 54 B.C.), crossed the Rhine into Germany, and revealed to the Roman soldiers countries they had never seen before. After once subduing the various tribes of Gaul, he was finally called upon to suppress a general insurrection, led by a powerful leader called Vercinget'orix. The conquest of Gaul was then completed. A large part of the population had been either slain in war or reduced to slavery. The new territory was pacified by bestowing honors upon the Gallic chiefs, and self-government upon the surviving tribes. The Roman legions were distributed through the territory; but Cæsar established no military colonies like those of Sulla.

It would be difficult to overestimate the great benefits that resulted from Cæsar's conquest of Gaul. It gave a new barrier against the barbarians from the north. It afforded a new place for the sending out of colonies, thus affording a relief for the distressed population of Italy. It opened a new field of civilization, where the Latin language was spoken, the Roman literature flourished, the Roman law was practiced, and the foundation was laid for one of the great nations of modern times.

III. The Supremacy of Cæsar

Dissolution of the Triumvirate. — While Cæsar was absent in Gaul, the ties which bound the three leaders together were becoming weaker and weaker. The position of Crassus tended somewhat, as long as he was alive, to allay the growing suspicion between the two great rivals. But after Crassus took control of his province in Syria, he invaded Parthia, was badly defeated, lost the Roman standards, and was himself killed (53 B.C.). The death of Crassus reduced the triumvirate to a duumvirate, or partnership of two. But the relation between the two leaders was now no longer one of friendly support, but one of mutual distrust.

Alliance of Pompey with the Senate. — Pompey was not only drawing away from Cæsar; he was also coming into closer relations with the senate, which felt the need of some strong military support. The city was distracted by continual street fights between the armed bands of Clodius, the demagogue, and those of Milo, who professed to be defending the cause of the senate. In one of these broils Clodius was killed. His excited followers made his death the occasion of riotous proceedings. His body was burned in the Forum by the wild mob, and the senate house was destroyed by fire. In the anarchy which followed, the senate felt obliged to confer some extraordinary power upon Pompey. On the proposal of Cato, he was appointed " consul without a colleague." Under this unusual title Pompey restored order to the state, and was looked upon as " the savior of society." He became more and more closely bound to the cause of the senate; and the senate recognized its obligations to him by prolonging his command in Spain for five years.

Rupture between the Senate and Cæsar. — It was a part of the agreement made at the conference of Lucca, we remember (p. 426), that Cæsar was to receive the consulship at the close of his command in Gaul. He naturally wished to retain the control of his army until he had been elected to his new office. The senate was determined that he should not, but should present himself at Rome as a private citizen before his election. Cæsar well knew that he would be helpless as a private citizen in the presence of the enemies who were seeking to destroy him. Cato had already declared that he would prosecute him as soon as he ceased to be proconsul in Gaul. Cæsar promised, however, to give up his province and his army if Pompey would do the same, but Pompey refused. The senate then called upon Cæsar to give up two of his legions, on the plea that they were needed in the Parthian war. The legions were given up; but instead of being sent to the East they were stationed in Campania. Upon further demands, Cæsar agreed to give up eight legions of his army if he were allowed to retain two legions in Cisalpine Gaul until the time of his election. This the senate refused; and demanded that he must give up his province and his whole army by a certain day, or be declared a public enemy. The senate had offered him humiliation or war. He chose war, and crossed the Ru'bicon (49 B.C.), the stream which separated his province of Cisalpine Gaul from Italy (maps, pp. 298, 384).

Civil War between Pompey and Cæsar. — The contest was now reduced to a struggle between Pompey, the champion of the senate, and Cæsar, the champion of the people. Cæsar knew the value of time; at the instant when he decided upon war, he invaded Italy with a single legion. Pompey, unprepared for such a sudden move and not relying upon the two legions which the senate had taken from Cæsar, was obliged to withdraw to Brundisium (map, p. 345). Besieged in this place by Cæsar, he skillfully withdrew his forces to Greece, and left Cæsar master of Italy.

The campaigns of Cæsar against Pompey and his supporters may be summed up as follows: (1) He dispatched his Gallic legions across the Pyrenees into Spain (49 B.C.) and destroyed the armies of Pompey's lieutenants. (2) He crossed the Adriatic Sea into Greece, was defeated at Dyrra'chium (map, p. 376), but then in the decisive battle at Pharsa'lus (48 B.C.) defeated Pompey, who fled to Egypt and was treacherously slain by an Egyptian soldier. (3) He entered Egypt to quell a civil war between the young Egyptian prince, Ptolemy, and his sister, Cleopa'tra; defeated the army of Ptolemy, and placed Cleopatra on the Egyptian throne. (4) On his return to Italy by way of Asia Minor, he gained a victory (at Zela, 47 B.C.; map, p. 434) over Phar'naces, the king of Pontus and son of the great Mithridates, who was trying to stir up a revolt in the eastern provinces, — sending to the senate the famous dispatch, "*Veni, vidi, vici*," "I came, I saw, I conquered." (5) He passed over into Africa, and at the battle of Thapsus (46 B.C.) defeated the senatorial forces led by Cato, who committed suicide after the battle. (6) At the battle of Munda in Spain (45 B.C.) he crushed the last attempt at resistance, led by the sons of Pompey.

Cæsar's Triumphs and Titles. — When Cæsar returned to Rome, he came not as the servant of the senate, but as master of the world. He crowned his victories by four splendid triumphs, one for Gaul, one for Egypt, one for Pontus, and one for Africa. He made no reference to the civil war, and no citizens were led among his captives. His victory was attended by no massacres, no proscriptions, no confiscations. He was as generous in peace as he had been relentless in war. Cæsar was great enough to forgive his enemies. A general amnesty was proclaimed, and friend and foe were treated alike. During the period of his rule (49–44 B.C.) he exercised his power under various titles. He was consul, dictator, controller of public morals, tribune, chief priest (*pontifex maximus*), and chief of the senate (*princeps senatus*). He thus gathered up in his own person the powers which had been scattered among the various republican officers. The name of *impera'tor*, with which the soldiers had been accustomed to salute a victorious general, was now made an official title, and prefixed to his name. In Cæsar was thus embodied the one-man power which had been growing up during the civil wars.

JULIUS CÆSAR (Capitol)

Cæsar's Political Reforms. — Cæsar held his great power for only a short time. But the reforms which he made are enough to show us his policy, and to enable us to judge of him as a statesman. The first need of Rome was a stable government based on the interest of the whole people. The senate had failed to secure such a government. Cæsar believed that the only government suited to Rome was a democratic monarchy — a government in which the supreme power should be held permanently by a single man, and exercised, not for the benefit of any single class, but for the benefit of the whole state. Let us see how he accomplished this end.

In the first place, the senate was changed to meet this view. It had hitherto been a comparatively small body, drawn from a single class and ruling for its own interests. Cæsar increased the number to nine hundred members, and filled it up with representative men of all classes, not simply nobles, but also *ignobles* — Spaniards, Gauls, military officers, sons of freedmen, and others. It was to be not a legislative body, but an advisory body, to inform the chief of the condition and wants of Italy and the provinces. In the next place, he extended the Roman franchise to the inhabitants beyond the Po, and to many cities in the provinces. All his political changes tended to break down the distinction between nobles and commons, between Italians and the provincials, and to make of all the people of the empire one nation.

Cæsar's Economic Reforms. — The next great need of Rome was the improvement of the condition of the lower classes. Cæsar believed that the government ought not to encourage pauperism by helping those who ought to help themselves. There were 320,000 persons at Rome to whom grain was distributed. He reduced this number to 150,000. He provided means of employment for the idle by constructing new buildings in the city, and other public works, and also by enforcing the law that one third of the labor employed on landed estates should be free labor. He relieved the debtor class by a bankrupt law which permitted the insolvent debtor to escape imprisonment by turning over his property to his creditors. In such ways as these, while not pretending to abolish poverty, he afforded better means for the poorer classes to obtain a living.

His Reform of the Provincial System. — The despotism of the Roman republic was nowhere more severe and unjust than in the provinces. This was due to two things — the arbitrary authority of the governor, and the wretched system of farming the taxes (p. 391). The governor ruled the province not for the benefit of the provincials, but for the benefit of himself. It is said that the proconsul hoped to make three fortunes out of his province — one to pay his debts, one to bribe the jury if he were brought to trial, and one to keep himself. The tax collector also looked upon the property of the province as a harvest to be divided between the Roman treasury and himself. Cæsar put a check upon this system of robbery. The governor was now made a responsible agent of the emperor; and the collection of taxes was placed under a more rigid supervision. The provincials found in Cæsar a protector, because his policy involved the welfare of all his subjects.

His Other Reforms and Projects.—The most noted of Cæsar's other changes was the reform of the calendar, which has remained as he left it, with slight change, down to the present day. He also intended to codify the Roman law; to provide for the founding of public libraries; to improve the architecture of the city; to drain the Pontine Marshes for the improvement of the public health; to cut a channel through the Isthmus of Corinth; and to extend the empire to its natural limits, the Euphrates, the Danube, and the Rhine. These projects show the comprehensive mind of Cæsar.

The Assassination of Cæsar.—If Cæsar failed in anything, it was in not adjusting himself sufficiently to the conservative spirit of the time. There were still living at Rome men who were blindly attached to the old republican forms. To them the reforms of Cæsar looked like a work of destruction, rather than a work of creation. They saw in his projects a scheme for reviving the kingship. It was said that when Cæsar was offered a crown he looked at it wistfully; and that he had selected his nephew Octavius as his royal heir.

The men who hated Cæsar, and who conspired to kill him, were men who had themselves received special favors from him. The leading conspirators, Marcus Brutus and Gaius Cassius, had both served in Pompey's army, and had been pardoned by Cæsar and promoted to offices under his government. Brutus was especially beloved by Cæsar; but he was led to believe that by getting rid of Cæsar he would be following the example of his great ancestor, Brutus, who had expelled the Tarquins from Rome (p. 306). Joined by some fifty other conspirators, Brutus and Cassius formed a plot to kill Cæsar in the senate house. When the appointed day came, the Ides of March (March 15, 44 B.C.), Cæsar entered the senate chamber and took his seat. The band of conspirators gathered about him, as if to urge him to sign a petition that one of their number presented to him.

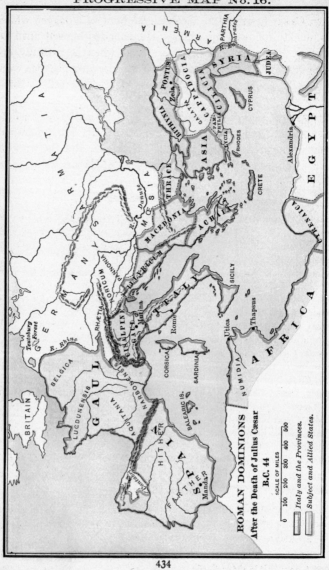

ROMAN DOMINIONS
After the Death of Julius Caesar
B.C. 44

SCALE OF MILES
0   100   200   300   400   500

Italy and the Provinces.
Subject and Allied States.

BRITAIN

GERMANY

Teutoburg Forest

R. Rhine

BELGICA

GAUL

LUCDUNENSIB

AQUITANIA

NARBONENSIS

HITHER

FARTHER

SPAIN

Munda

CORSICA

SARDINIA

BALEARIC IS.

SICILY

Thapsus

Utica

NUMIDIA

AFRICA

SARMATIA

PANNONIA

RHÆTIA

NORICUM

CISALPINE

GALLIA

Mutina

Rome

I T A L Y

R. Danube

MŒSIA

THRACE

MACEDONIA

ILLYRICUM

DALMATIA

ACHAIA

CRETE

RHODES

CYPRUS

ARMENIA

PONTUS

Zela

BITHYNIA

CAPPADOCIA

GALATIA

ASIA

PAM-
PHYLIA

LYCIA

CILICIA

SYRIA

R. Euphrates

PARTHIA

JUDEA

PHŒNICIA

Alexandria

EGYPT

When Cæsar hesitated he received the blow of a dagger, which was quickly followed by others. He defended himself until he saw that Brutus had drawn his sword, when he pitifully exclaimed, "And you too, Brutus!" — and drawing his toga over his head, he fell at the foot of Pompey's statue, pierced by three and twenty wounds.

It has been said that the murder of Cæsar was the most senseless act that the Romans ever committed. His death deprived Rome of the greatest man she ever produced. But the work of the conspirators did not destroy the work of Cæsar.

Selections for Reading

Knowlton, Topic A 21, "The Revolution: the Triumvirates" (1).[1]
Shuckburgh, Ch. 42, "Pompey in the East" (18).
How and Leigh, Ch. 47, "Cicero and Catiline" (18).
Pelham, Bk. V., Ch. 1, "The Dictatorship of Julius" (18).
Mommsen, Vol. IV., Bk. V., Ch. 11, "The Old Republic and the New Monarchy" (18).
—— (Abridged), Ch. 35, "Joint Rule of Pompey and Cæsar" (18).
Taylor, Ch. 15, "Cæsar" (22).
Abbott, Ch. 6, "Struggle between the Democracy and the Nobilitas" (22).
Granrud, Fourth Period, Ch. 7, "The Rule of Cæsar" (22).
Forsyth, Cicero, pp. 319–330 (character of Cicero) (27).
Oman, Seven Great Statesmen, Ch. 5, "Sulla"; Ch. 8, "Pompey"; Ch. 9, "Cæsar" (26).
Froude, Cæsar, Ch. 11, "Conspiracy of Catiline"; Ch. 28, "Character of Cæsar" (27).
Fowler, Cæsar, Ch. 18, "Cæsar's Use of Absolute Power" (27).
Munro, Source Book, Part VIII., "Last Century of the Republic" (25).
Shakespeare, "Julius Cæsar."
Plutarch, "Pompey," "Crassus," "Cato the Younger," "Cæsar," "Cicero."

Special Study

Cæsar's Campaigns in Gaul. — How and Leigh, Ch. 49 (18); Shuckburgh, Ch. 44 (18); Merivale, General Hist., Ch. 41 (18); Merivale, Empire, Chs. 5–12 (18); Dodge, "Julius Cæsar," Chs. 8–14 (27).

---

[1] The figure in parenthesis refers to the number of the topic in the Appendix, where a fuller title of the book will be found.

CHAPTER XXVII

THE CLOSING YEARS OF THE REPUBLIC

Synopsis

I. THE RIVALRY BETWEEN ANTONY AND OCTAVIUS. — The Confusion after Cæsar's Death. — Antony and Octavius. — The Second Triumvirate and the Death of Cicero. — War against the Liberators; Battle of Philippi. — Civil War between Antony and Octavius. — Battle of Actium. — Review of the Period of the Civil Wars.

II. ROMAN LITERATURE DURING THE CIVIL WARS. — The Greek Influence. — Varro, the Grammarian. — Cicero, the Orator and Philosopher. — The Historians, Cæsar and Sallust. — The Poets, Lucretius and Catullus.

III. ART AND LIFE UNDER THE LATER REPUBLIC. — Progress in Architecture. — The Old Roman Forum. — Holidays and Festivals. — Roman Education. — Daily Life of a Well-to-do Citizen. — Life among the Lower Classes. — Decay of Religion and Morals.

I. THE RIVALRY BETWEEN ANTONY AND OCTAVIUS

The Confusion after Cæsar's Death. — We need not be surprised that the death of Cæsar was followed by confusion and dismay. His murderers considered themselves as " liberators " of the republic. But their rash act gave to Rome another period of strife and civil war. They had killed Cæsar; but they had provided for no one to take his place. If they thought that the senate would be restored to its old position, they were grievously mistaken. The only leading man of the senate who had survived the last civil war was Cicero; but Cicero with all his learning and eloquence could not take the place of Cæsar. Soon there appeared new actors upon the scene, men struggling for the supreme power in the state — An′tony (Anto′nius), the friend of Cæsar and his fellow-consul; Octavius, his adopted son and heir; Lepidus, his master of horse; while Cicero still raised his voice in defense of what he regarded as his country's freedom.

Antony and Octavius. — The man who had stood nearest to Cæsar was Antony, his fellow-consul. He claimed that it was his duty to carry out the purpose of his murdered chief. He got possession of Cæsar's will and treasures, and influenced the senate to confirm all of Cæsar's acts. He called

ANTONY

upon the people to rise and avenge the death of their greatest friend. The liberators were obliged to flee from the city.

The only person who could well dispute the claims of Antony was Octavius — a young man of nineteen, who was Cæsar's grand-nephew and adopted heir. This young man assumed his adopted name Gaius Julius Cæsar Octavia'nus and disputed with Antony the right to act as Cæsar's representative. By his great generosity he won the favor of the people, who called him by the magic name of Cæsar. He now began to show that adroit skill for which he was afterward noted. His first purpose was to weaken An-

THE YOUNG OCTAVIUS

tony, who had deprived him of his inheritance. He therefore saw fit to unite his cause with that of the senate, which was already opposed to the ambitious schemes of Antony. By this piece of diplomacy Octavius gained the influence of Cicero, the leader of the senatorial party.

The hostility between Cicero and Antony grew to be bitter and relentless; and they were pitted against each other on the floor of the senate. But in a war of words Antony was no match for Cicero. By a series of famous speeches known as the " Philippics," the popularity of Antony was crushed; and he retired from Rome to seek for victory upon other fields.

The Second Triumvirate and the Death of Cicero (43 B.C.). — Octavius had no intention of supporting the cause of the senate. He therefore sought a reconciliation with his previous enemy, Antony. Antony was supported by Lepidus. A coalition was formed between these three leaders — Antony, Octavius, and Lepidus — usually called the Second Triumvirate. Unlike the First Triumvirate, this was sanctioned by a law of the tribal assembly. The leaders agreed to oppose the senate, to divide among themselves the western provinces, and then to make war upon the chief liberators, Brutus and Cassius, who held possession of the eastern provinces. They assumed a dictatorial power for five years, with the right of appointing all magistrates. Their decrees were to have the force of law without the approval of either the senate or the people.

It is to the eternal disgrace of these men who professed to espouse the cause of Cæsar, that they abandoned the humane policy of their great exemplar, and returned to the infamous policy of Marius and Sulla. Antony especially desired a proscription, as he was surrounded by thousands of personal enemies, chief among whom was Cicero, the author of the " Philippics." It is said that three hundred senators and two thousand knights were outlawed and their property was confiscated; besides, a large number of other persons were slain. The most distinguished victim of this horrible work was Cicero

When the old man was warned of his danger and urged to flee, he replied, " Let me die in my fatherland, which I have so often saved." He was slain, and his head was sent to Antony, whose wife, Fulvia, is said to have pierced the lifeless tongue with a needle in revenge for the words it had uttered against her husband.

War against the Liberators; Battle of Philippi (42 B.C.). — Having murdered their enemies at home, the triumvirs were now prepared to crush their enemies abroad. These were Brutus and Cassius, who had united their forces in the East. The hostile armies met near Philip′pi (42 B.C.), a town in Macedonia on the northern coast of the Ægean Sea (see map, p. 376). Octavius was opposed to Brutus, and Antony to Cassius. Octavius was driven back by Brutus, while Antony, more fortunate, drove back the wing commanded by Cassius. As Cassius saw his flying legions, he thought that

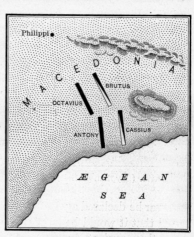

BATTLE OF PHILIPPI

all was lost, and stabbed himself with the same dagger, it is said, with which he struck Cæsar. This left Brutus in sole command of the opposing army; but he also was defeated in a second battle, and, following the example of Cassius, committed suicide.

The double battle at Philippi decided the fate of the republic. As Cicero was its last political champion, Brutus and Cassius were its last military defenders; with their death the republic was no more.

Civil War between Antony and Octavius. — The Roman world was now drifting fast toward an empire. It only remained to be seen who should be its first master, Antony or Octavius. Lepidus, the other triumvir, was too weak to receive much consideration. As the two powerful triumvirs could not rule together, Antony agreed to take the Eastern provinces and Octavius the Western. Octavius remained at Rome. He won the affections of the people, and tried to show them that peace and prosperity could come only through his influence. Antony went to Egypt and yielded to the fascinations of Cleopatra, "the serpent of the Nile." While Octavius was growing in popu-

CLEOPATRA (Egyptian portrait)

larity, Antony was becoming more and more an object of detestation. All doubt as to Antony's real character and purpose was settled when his will was found and published. In it he had made the sons of Cleopatra his heirs, and ordered his own body to be buried at Alexandria beside that of the Egyptian queen. This was looked upon as an insult to the majesty of Rome. The citizens were aroused. They demanded that war be declared against the hated triumvir. Octavius suggested that it would be more wise to declare war against Cleopatra than against Antony and the deluded citizens who had espoused his cause. Thus what was really a civil war between Octavius and Antony assumed the appearance of a foreign war between Rome and Egypt.

Battle of Actium (31 B.C.). — When war was declared, Antony and Cleopatra united their forces against Rome. Antony's main army was posted at Actium (see map, p. 376), south of the strait leading into the Gulf of Ambracia. His fleet was for the most part moored within the gulf. Octavius, with the aid of his trusted general Agrip'pa, succeeded in transporting an army to the coast of Epirus, and took up a position north of the strait and opposite the land forces of Antony. His fleet was stationed outside of the strait to await the approach of the enemy's vessels. Antony, on the advice of his ablest officers, desired that the battle should be waged with the land forces, but Cleopatra, proud of her navy, insisted that it should be

fought on the sea. The contest was therefore decided by a naval battle. As the fleet of Antony emerged from the strait, it was immediately attacked by Octavius and Agrippa. But scarcely had the battle begun, when Cleopatra with her squadron withdrew from the

BATTLE OF ACTIUM

line, and was quickly followed by Antony. Their sailors fought on until their fleet was destroyed. The battle of Actium closed the political career of Antony, and left Octavius the sole master of the Roman world.

Before returning to Rome Octavius restored order to the eastern provinces, and followed the fugitives to Egypt. Antony, defeated and ruined, committed suicide; and Cleopatra followed his example rather than be led a captive in a Roman triumph. Together this wretched pair were laid in the mausoleum of the Ptolemies. Egypt was annexed as a province of the new empire (30 B.C.). Octavius returned to Rome (29 B.C.), where he was given a triumph. The temple of Janus — the doors of which were always left open in time of war — was now closed for the first time since the second Punic war; and the Romans, tired of civil strife and bloodshed, looked upon the triumph of Octavius as the dawn of a new era of peace and prosperity.

Review of the Period of the Civil Wars. — There is no period of Roman history more eventful or instructive than that which we have just considered — extending from the time of the

Gracchi to the triumph of Octavius. If we look merely at the surface of events, it may perhaps seem to be hardly more than a period of strife, of turmoil, of revolution, and of civil war. But if we compare the wretched condition of things which Tiberius Gracchus first sought to remedy, with the new system which Julius Cæsar established and Octavius sought to make permanent, we must conclude that it was during this time that the Roman people were working out the greatest political problems of their history. In the midst of the greatest discouragements, and often under incompetent leaders, they continued to fight for justice, until they at last found a chieftain capable of defending their interests. The people learned that they could not secure their rights by means of unwieldy assemblies, which were often ruled by ambitious demagogues — and they had not discovered the modern principle of representation. If they could not obtain a government *by* the people, they could at least obtain a government *for* the people, under the control of an efficient magistrate devoted to their interests. With our advanced political ideas and experience, we may not believe that Roman imperialism is the best form of government; it was yet the highest and most successful form of government developed in the ancient world. By such a government, the Roman people secured political equality, and perhaps as much political freedom as was possible without representative institutions.

II. Roman Literature during the Civil Wars

The Greek Influence. — The triumph of Octavius took place just about a hundred years after the beginning of the great revolution under the Gracchi. To one who has followed the stormy conflicts of this period it seems hardly possible that the Romans could have been devoted to literature. But as a matter of fact, some of their greatest writers appeared during this time; and some of these writers were men who took an active part in Roman politics. While politics seemed to be their main business, they really had some appreciation of culture; and a great deal of this culture they obtained from Greece.

It is to the great credit of the Romans that they looked to the Greeks for their models in art and literature. It came to be the fashion to adorn their homes with Greek statues, to read the writings of Greek authors, and to present Greek plays in their theaters. It was at this time that the influence of Hellenism became very marked, and that under this influence Rome produced writers whose names belong to the literature of the world. The Latin language acquired some of the refinement of the Greek, and it gave to the Romans the capacity to develop a literature of their own which, though not equal to that of Greece, holds a worthy place by the side of it. Let us look at a few of the more important writers of this period.

Varro, the Grammarian. — The first great writer that comes before us is Varro, sometimes called the grammarian. He was born in the Sabine country and inherited the strong character that marked the old Roman. He went to Athens and studied philosophy. He found time to serve in the civil war under Pompey. But when Pompey was defeated Cæsar forgave him, and placed him over the library he intended for public use. After Cæsar's murder Varro was placed on the list of the proscribed by Antony; and the old man was obliged to lie concealed until after Antony's fury was spent. He was afterward allowed to live in peace at Rome until his death, which occurred in his eighty-eighth year. He wrote 490 books upon every variety of subject, from arithmetic and grammar to natural history, the history of Rome, and the knowledge of things divine.

Cicero, the Orator and Philosopher. — The greatest name in Roman literature, at least in prose literature, is that of Marcus Tullius Cicero. We have already met Cicero in the field of politics. He was what was called a " new man," that is, the first of his family to reach senatorial honor. It is remarkable that a man so active in politics should have gained such a reputation as a writer. But Cicero's ambition was to be an orator, and politics furnished the best field for oratory. In his education Cicero was first of all a Greek student. At school he spent his time largely in making translations from Greek authors. Afterward he studied Greek philosophy at Athens and Greek rhetoric at the school of Rhodes. His mind was inspired with the Hellenic spirit.

He was also an ardent student of the Roman law, and his first public appearance was as an advocate. His first great triumph was the prosecution of Verres, the robber-governor of Sicily. Cicero prepared no less than six orations against Verres, but after the delivery of the first the accused man was so stung with remorse that he fled into exile. Cicero ran the course of the Roman offices, from quæstor to consul. It was while he was consul that he pronounced the terrible invectives against Catiline. We have left to us fifty-seven of his orations, including the four against Catiline and the fourteen so-called " Philippics " against Antony. These place Cicero next to Demosthenes as one of the great orators of the world.

Cicero also wrote a number of philosophical works. Among these are the " Republic," the " Laws," the " Nature of the Gods," and two beautiful little essays on " Friendship " and " Old Age." These philosophical essays are not distinguished so much for originality as for their clear and excellent literary style.

The Letters of Cicero to his friends are among the most valuable of his writings. These are models of what true correspondence should be — sincere, honest, natural, and sympathetic. They deal with nearly every phase of his public and private life. The ancients paid more attention to letter writing than we do; they thought their friends worthy of their best thoughts expressed in the best style. But no other writer who has come down to us can be compared with Cicero for the grace and perfection of his letters.

The Historians, Cæsar and Sallust. — Cæsar was the foremost man of Rome. He was great as a soldier, great as a statesman, great as an orator, and great as a writer. As an orator he was said to rank next to Cicero, but unfortunately none of his orations have come down to us. The book with which we are most familiar is his " Commentaries on the Gallic War." This book is put into the hands of our students as a specimen of correct Latin. It is said to have been written by Cæsar as a report to the senate of his campaigns. It is hence written in a direct, businesslike way, telling exactly what took place, with no attempt at ornament. It set forth the life of the camp and the battlefield. It gives a clear description of military maneuvers, of engineering, of bridge building and other operations in which his army was engaged. He expresses great appreciation of the deeds of his soldiers, and lingers with delight over the exploits of his favorite tenth legion. Cæsar wrote other books, one on the " Auspices," one on " Divination," and one even on grammar. But all these books are overshadowed by the " Commentaries."

Another historical writer of this period was Sallust, a warm admirer and partisan of Cæsar. He was a man of great wealth and built a magnificent palace in the suburbs of Rome, surrounded by beautiful pleasure grounds, afterwards known as the " Gardens of Sallust." His two books which have come down to us are the " War of Jugurtha " and the " Conspiracy of Catiline." He lays bare the motives of these two despicable characters, and the depravity of the times in which they lived. Sallust took for his model the Greek historian, Thucydides. He believed that history should be written not simply to tell what took place, but to explain why it took place; that history should be the study not simply of facts but of principles. He wrote in a clear, vigorous style, and became a model for future historians.

The Poets, Lucretius and Catullus. — This period gave birth to one of the greatest philosophical poets of the world. This was Lucretius, who wrote a poem entitled the " Nature of Things." Lucretius was imbued with the spirit of Greek philosophy, and was especially attached to the philosophy of Epicurus. But he expounds this philosophy not to justify a life of pleasure, but to relieve the human mind from superstition. He believed that such a religion as that of the Romans tended to keep men continually in fear of the gods. He believed that they could find relief only in philosophy. But it is not as a book of philosophy that this work appeals to us, but as a sublime poem. He has given us wonderful descriptions of nature. The whole universe, which he seeks to explain, is set aglow by his imagination. He begins his whole poem with this address to Venus as his muse:

> "Delight of human kind, and gods above,
> Parent of Rome, propitious Queen of Love,
> Whose vital power, air, earth, and sea supplies,
> Inspires whate'er is born beneath the skies;
> Thee, Goddess, thee, the clouds and tempests fear,
> And at thy pleasing presence disappear;
> For thee the earth in fragrant flowers is dressed,
> For thee the ocean smiles and smoothes her breast,
> The heaven itself with more serene a light is blest."

Catullus was a poet of far different character from Lucretius. Lucretius was a serious man and stood aloof from the world. Catullus was a young man of pleasure, and fond of society. Lucretius dealt with some of the loftiest themes than can tax the human mind — the origin of the world, the nature of man, and the duties of life. Catullus treated of the gentler passions of the human heart — of love, its pleasures and its pains. Both of these poets drew their inspiration from Greece — Lucretius from the Greek philosophers, and Catullus from the Greek lyric poets. Catullus gave to the Latin language a grace and delicate refinement that it never before possessed. This little love-song reminds us of the Greek poetess, Sappho:

> "No nymph, amid the much-loved few,
> Is loved as thou art loved by me;
> No love was e'er so fond, so true,
> As my fond love, sweet one, for thee!

"Yes, e'en thy faults, bewitching dear!
    With such delights my soul possess,
That whether faithless or sincere,
    I cannot love thee more, nor less!"

III. Art and Life under the Later Republic

Progress in Architecture. — If we had walked along the streets of Rome about the time of the Gracchi we should have seen very few fine buildings. The early architecture of Rome was almost entirely derived from the Etruscan. This was solid but not beautiful. It was adapted for the construction of walls and sewers. The great bequest that the Romans received from the Etruscans was the use of the arch, which became a feature of Roman architecture. It was only after the Romans came into contact with the Greeks that they began to build finer structures. Many of the older buildings were destroyed by the riots that attended the civil wars, and they were replaced by others of a more artistic character. Many new temples were built — temples to Minerva, to Concord, to Honor, to

TEMPLE OF FORTUNE

Fortune, and others. The only one of these buildings that remains to us at present is the temple of Fortune. This has not the beauty of a Greek temple, but it shows something of the Greek influence by the row of columns that surround it. There were also built during the later republic new basilicas, or court-houses, the most notable being the Basilica Julia, which was commenced by Julius Cæsar. A new forum, the Forum Julii, was also laid out by Cæsar, and a new theater was constructed by Pompey. The great national temple of Jupiter Capitolinus, which was burned during the civil war of Marius and Sulla, was restored with great magnificence by Sulla, who adorned it with the columns of the temple of the Olympian Zeus brought from Athens. With the exception of the use of the arch, the general features of Roman architecture show the strong influence of Greek ideas — especially in the construction of temples, and in the use of columns, which the Romans generally surmounted with Corinthian capitals (p. 142).

With all their fine public buildings the streets of Rome did not present the appearance of the residential portions of our modern cities. They were so narrow and often so crowded that the pedestrian was jostled at every turn; so that a law was passed prohibiting wagon traffic in the daytime. The houses were built near together and to a great height. There was great danger from fires. There was no public system of street lighting, and people had to grope their way with the aid of a lantern or torch.

The Old Roman Forum. — The center of Roman public life was the Forum. This was the public square of the city. It was to Rome what the Agora was to Athens. It was situated in the center of the group of hills upon which the city was built. It was originally a swampy marsh, but it had been drained by the great sewer built by Servius Tullius. It was first used as a meeting place for the *comitia curiata*. It was also used as an athletic field for gladiatorial games. But in the time of the Republic it had come to be the " civic center " of Rome. Here was where public meetings were held, justice was administered, and goods were exposed for sale. It contained the senate house, where the senators met to transact their business. Facing the senate house was the elevated platform from which speakers addressed the people, adorned with the beaks of ships captured from the enemy, and hence called the *rostra*. From this platform Cicero delivered his second and third Catilinian orations, and it was the scene of some of the most important political struggles of the Republic. It is said that Gaius Gracchus in making his speeches, instead of facing the senate house, as was customary, faced the people to show that he regarded the people as the sovereign of Rome. By the time of Cicero and Julius Cæsar the Forum had come to be adorned with fine buildings, with temples, porticoes, and colonnades.

Holidays and Festivals. — The Romans were devoted to holidays. These days were originally religious in their character; they were dedicated to the gods, and no work was permitted and no public business was transacted. Even the slaves were allowed a day of rest. The holidays were days on which the Roman festivals occurred, when the people turned out to celebrate some great event or to do honor to some deity. One of the earliest of these festivals was the Lupercal, which is referred to in Shakespeare's play of Julius Cæsar. This was celebrated every year on the 15th of February, on the spot where Romulus and Remus were said to have been rescued by the wolf. It consisted of sacrifices in honor of the god of fertility, and was appropriate for a people made up of a body of shepherds, such as the Romans originally were.

In the time of the Republic these festivals were very numerous, and were accompanied by games in the Circus Maximus — such as horse and chariot racing and gladiatorial combats. The games began with a procession from the Capitoline hill, down through the Forum to the Great Circus, which lay between the Palatine and Aventine hills. Here the people were regaled with the spectacles prepared for them at the public expense or by some wealthy office seeker. The Great Circus was supposed to accommodate over 150,000 persons. In early times one festival occupied a single day, but before the end of the republic the entire number of days taken up with festivals was seventy-six.

The festivals were attended not only by shows in the circus, but also by plays in the theater. The theater never held at

Rome the dignified place that it held at Athens. The early Roman plays consisted simply of " mimes," or mimic actions or gestures, accompanied by the music of the flute. After the conquest of the Greek city of Tarentum imitations of the Greek comedy were introduced. The theaters themselves were temporary wooden structures, until Pompey erected the first stone structure, which was said to hold 40,000 people. The coarse ribaldry of the Roman plays never had a very elevating effect upon the morals of the people.

Roman Education. — The influence of Hellenism is especially seen in the increasing attention which the Romans paid to education. Roman education, like that of the Greeks, was intended to develop all the mental powers, and to train the young man for public life. Children — both boys and girls — began to attend school at six or seven years of age. The elementary studies were reading, writing, and arithmetic. The children were taught to write from a copy set upon their tablets, and to cipher by means of the counting board (*abacus*) and counters (*calculi*). After the conquests the children were placed under Greek teachers. They were taught the Greek language, and to read Homer and other Greek authors. The wealthy fathers

BOY WITH CALCULATING BOARD

sent their sons abroad to finish their education. They looked to the school of Athens and to the school of Rhodes in Asia Minor as their universities. To these schools the young men went to study rhetoric and oratory and philosophy. They brought back something of the Greek spirit, the Greek love of learning, and the Greek taste. An important part of education consisted in public recitals and declamations which were intended to train young men for the Forum, and were often held in the temples.

Daily Life of a Well-to-do Citizen. — In the earliest period the Romans had no method of reckoning time except by the position of the sun — the day extending from sunrise to sunset, and the night from sunset to sunrise. But about the time of the first Punic war sundials were introduced from Sicily. The day was now divided into twelve hours. The night was divided into four watches. These were the only divisions of time which seemed necessary for the Roman to regulate his daily life.

ROMAN SUNDIAL

It was customary for the master of the house to rise at sunrise, and offer a sacrifice with his family, including his slaves. After this he was accustomed to receive his clients (p. 316), and extend to them his morning salutations. At the third hour (nine o'clock) he took a slight repast of a roll of bread with a bit of honey or cheese. From the third to the sixth hour (that is, from 9 to 12 o'clock) he would devote himself to the more serious business of the day, — if he had any such serious business. This was the time for the meeting of the law courts in the Forum, and for attending to other legal matters. If he had no serious business, he would spend the time at public resorts, at the market places, or the shops, or in conversing with friends in the Forum, or killing time in gambling and other frivolous diversions. At the sixth hour (12 o'clock) the moderate mid-day meal was taken, and this was followed by a short siesta. The eighth and ninth hours (say 1:30 to 3:30 P.M.) were spent in taking exercise. The more active men went to the Campus Martius, where they indulged in running, jumping, wrestling, boxing, and spear-throwing. The older and less agile men engaged in ball-throwing, a favorite exercise with the Romans. This series of exercises, however, was preliminary to the bath, which in the late Republic had come to be regarded as an established institution. There were public baths where all persons were admitted for a small fee. The regular bath required the use of three rooms; the warm room (*tepidarium*), the hot room (*caldarium*), and the cold room (*frigidarium*).

After the bath came the principal meal of the day (about 4 o'clock). This consisted of three parts: a preliminary course to sharpen the appetite, with such viands as lettuce and shell-fish; the main part, consisting of a variety of meat courses, flesh, fish, and fowl, prepared by expert cooks; and a dessert usually of apples or some other kind of fruit and a flagon of wine. These repasts lasted into the evening and often into the small hours, closing the occupations of the day.

Life among the Lower Classes. — We may complain to-day of the great difference between the rich and the poor; but this difference is nothing compared to that which existed at Rome under the later republic. The well-to-do formed a comparatively small part of the population. A great mass of the people were living from hand to mouth, in the depths of poverty, almost on the verge of starvation. We have already seen how, after the great conquests, the Roman populace formed the materials of a mob, disposed to revolution and to riots. They were despised by the upper classes, and little attention is paid to them by the Roman writers. Their wretched condition is rarely even suggested by the historians we commonly read.

At Rome only the wealthy families lived in separate houses. The mass of the population lived, or rather ate and slept, in huge lodging-houses, called "islands" (*insulæ*). These were rudely constructed tenements, three or four stories high, built in the lower parts of the city, and often visited by fires. The ground floor was usually occupied by poor shops, kept perhaps by some of the lodgers. The inhabitants of these crowded tenements formed the riffraff of the city, using their rooms only for eating and sleeping, — prowling about the streets by day and night with more or less criminal intent. In such a life as this there could be no idea of home. The old sacredness of the family tie lost its hold upon the great mass of the people.

Decay of Religion and Morals. — While the Romans, during this period, showed many evidences of progress in their laws, their literature, and their art, they were evidently declining in their religious and moral sense. Their religion was diluted more and more with Oriental superstitions and degrading ceremonies. In their moral life they were suffering from the effects of their conquests, which had brought wealth and the passion for luxury and display. Ambition and avarice tended to corrupt the life of the Roman people. The only remedy for this condition of religious and moral decay was found in the philosophy of the Greeks, which, however, appealed only to the more educated classes.

Selections for Reading

Knowlton, Topic A 21, "The Revolution: the Triumvirates" (1).[1]

Seignobos, Ch. 23, "Fall of the Republic" (1).

Abbott, F. F., Ch. 7, "Period of Transition" (22).

Pelham, Bk. V., Ch. 2, "The Government of the Triumvirate" (18).

Taylor, Ch. 16, "The Struggle for the Crown" (22).

Merivale, General History, Ch. 48, "Octavius and Antony" (18).

Collins, Cicero, Ch. 9, "Cicero's Correspondence" (27).

Boissier, Cicero and his Friends, pp. 22–122, "Cicero in Public and Private Life" (27).

Preston and Dodge, Ch. 2, "The House and Everyday Life" (19).

Johnston, Ch. 4, "Children and Education" (19).

Sandys, pp. 200–208, "Daily Life" (19).

Shakespeare, "Antony and Cleopatra."

Plutarch, "Antony," "Brutus" (26).

Special Study

CHARACTER OF CICERO. — Forsyth, II., Ch. 25 (23); Merivale, Empire, Vol. III., pp. 148–153 (18); Mommsen, Vol. IV., pp. 724–726 (18); Plutarch, "Cicero" (26).

[1] The figure in parenthesis refers to the number of the topic in the Appendix, where a fuller title of the book will be found.

CHAPTER XXVIII

THE EARLY EMPIRE: AGE OF AUGUSTUS (31 B.C.–14 A.D.)

Synopsis

I. THE NEW IMPERIAL GOVERNMENT. — Beginning of the Empire. — Personality and Policy of Augustus. — Titles and Powers of Augustus. — Augustus and the Senate. — The Republican Assemblies and Magistrates. — The Imperial Army.

II. THE IMPERIAL ADMINISTRATION. — The Administration of Rome. — The Administration of Italy. — The Administration of the Provinces. — The Finances of the Empire. — The Frontiers of the Empire.

III. THE AGE OF AUGUSTUS. — The Advisers of Augustus. — Encouragement to Architecture. — Patronage of Literature. — Religious and Social Reforms. — Death and Character of Augustus.

I. THE NEW IMPERIAL GOVERNMENT

Beginning of the Empire. — We have taken the date of the battle of Actium (31 B.C.) to mark the beginning of the empire, because Octavius then became the sole and undisputed master of the Roman world. But it is not so important for us to fix upon a particular date for the beginning of the empire, as it is to see that some form of imperialism had come to be a necessity. During the whole period of the civil wars we have seen the gradual growth of the one-man power. We have seen it in the tribunate under the Gracchi; in the successive consulships of Marius; in the perpetual dictatorship of Sulla; in the sole consulship of Pompey; in the absolute rule of Julius Cæsar.

The name of " king " the Romans hated, because it brought to mind the memory of the last Tarquin. But the principle of monarchy they could not get rid of, because they had found no efficient form of government to take its place. The aristocratic government under the senate had proved corrupt, inefficient, and disastrous to the people. A popular government without representation had shown itself unwieldy, and had become a prey to demagogues. There was nothing left for the Romans to do but to accept some form of monarchy which would not suggest the hated name of king.

Personality and Policy of Augustus (31 B.C.–14 A.D.). — Since the death of Julius Cæsar Rome had passed through another civil war. Peace had come through the efforts of

THE EMPEROR AUGUSTUS

Octavius. It was now a question whether this peace would be lasting — whether Octavius would be able to do what Julius had failed to do. There was certainly no other man living so well fitted to put the new government into a permanent form as Octavius, — whom we may now call by his official title of Augustus. He had already shown himself to be a shrewd politician. It was to be seen whether he would prove a wise and successful statesman. He was attractive in person, and easily made friends. He lived a simple life, and disdained all show and pretense. He was a man of tact, and would not be likely to offend either of the old parties. He was unassuming in his manner, and would not give the impression that he was aiming at power. He was withal a broad-minded man, and would be likely to look after the interests of the whole people. His whole policy was a policy of conciliation. He wished to wipe out the hatreds of the civil war. He regarded himself as the chief of no party, but as the head of the whole state. He tried to reconcile the conservative and the progressive men of his time. All the cherished forms of the republic he therefore preserved;

and he exercised his powers under titles which were not hateful to the senate or the people.

Titles and Powers of Augustus. — Soon after returning to Rome, Augustus resigned the powers which he had hitherto exercised. He gave " back the commonwealth into the hands of the senate and the people " (27 B.C.). The first official title which he then received was the surname " Augustus," bestowed by the senate in recognition of his dignity and his service to the state. He then received the "proconsular power," which meant absolute authority over all the provinces that required the presence of an army. He had conferred upon himself the " tribunician power," which made his person sacred, and gave him the veto power over all the acts of the senate, the assemblies, and the magistrates. He moreover was made *pontifex maximus*, which gave him control over religious ceremonies. He also received the title of " Father of his Country." He occasionally exercised the power of censor, which gave him supervision over the manners and morals of the people, as well as over the choice of the senators. He still retained the title of " Imperator," which gave him the command of the army. But the title which Augustus chose to indicate his real position was that of *Princeps Civita'tis*, or " the first citizen of the state." The new " prince " thus desired to be looked upon as a magistrate rather than a monarch — a citizen who had received a trust rather than a ruler governing in his own name. But all real power was intrusted to his hands. He became, in fact, the ruler of the state.

Augustus and the Senate. — Augustus showed his conciliatory policy in fixing the position which the senate was to assume in the new government. He did not adopt fully the plan either of Sulla or of Julius Cæsar, but reconciled as far as possible their different ideas. He restored to the senate the dignity which it had in the time of Sulla. He did this by excluding the provincials and freedmen whom Cæsar had introduced into it, and by reducing its number from nine hundred to six hundred members. But still he did not confer upon it the great legislative power which Sulla intended it should have; he rather made it a kind of advisory body, according to Cæsar's idea. In theory the senate was to assist the emperor in matters of legislation, but in fact it was simply to approve the proposals which the emperor submitted to it.

The Republican Assemblies and Magistrates. — Augustus did not formally take away from the popular assemblies their legislative power, but occasionally submitted to them laws for their approval. The people in their present unwieldy assemblies, the emperor did not regard as able to decide upon important matters of state. Their duties were therefore practically restricted to the election of the magistrates, whose names he usually presented to them.

Augustus did not interfere with the old republican offices, but allowed them to remain as undisturbed as possible. The consuls, prætors, quæstors, and other officers continued to be elected just as they had been before. But the emperor did not use these magistrates to carry out the details of his administration. This was performed by other officers appointed by himself. The position of the old republican magistrates was one of honor rather than one of real authority.

The Imperial Army. — To support the imperial authority at home, and to maintain public order, Augustus organized a body of nine thousand men called the "prætorian guard," which force was stationed at different points outside of Rome. The emperor knew that his power must have also a strong military support in the provinces; but he was careful not to make the army a burden to the people. He therefore reduced the number of

PRÆTORIAN GUARDS

legions from fifty to twenty-five. As each legion contained not more than six thousand men, the whole army did not exceed one hundred and fifty thousand soldiers. These legions were distributed through the frontier provinces; the inner provinces and Italy were thus not burdened by the quartering of troops. The soldiers were no longer drafted into the army, as was the case under the republic, but were volunteers. They enlisted for twenty years, and thus formed a standing army, receiving regular pay. It was usually the poor citizens who became soldiers, adopting this occupation as a means of earning a living.

II. The Imperial Administration

The Administration of Rome. — We have read enough of the distracted condition of the Roman city during the last hundred years to see the need of some improvement in its government. Augustus met this need by creating certain new officers to keep the city under better control. He established a city police under the charge of a chief (*praefectus*), to preserve order and prevent the scenes of violence which had been of such frequent occurrence. He created a fire and detective department under the charge of another chief, to have jurisdiction over all incendiaries, burglars, and other night-prowlers. He placed the grain supply under a regular officer who was to superintend the transportation of grain from Egypt, and was held responsible for its proper distribution. Moreover, he broke up the secret clubs which had been hotbeds of disorder, and substituted in their place more orderly societies licensed by the government. Under these arrangements, life and property became more secure, and the populace became more orderly and law-abiding.

The Administration of Italy. — Italy now extended to the Alps, the province of Cisalpine Gaul having lately been joined to the peninsula. The whole of Italy was divided into eleven " regions," or administrative districts. In order to maintain the splendid system of roads which had been constructed during

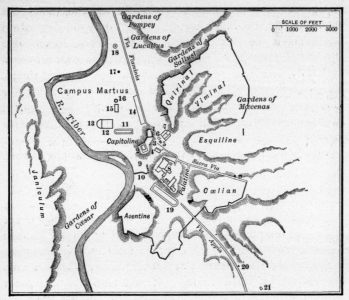

ROME UNDER AUGUSTUS

Chief Buildings: 1, Arx; 2, Capitolium; 3, Forum Romanum; 4, Basilica Julia; 5, Curia (senate house); 6, Forum of Julius; 7, Forum of Augustus; 8, Palace of the Cæsars; 9, Forum Boarium; 10, Cloaca Maxima; 11, Circus Flaminius; 12, Portico of Pompey; 13, Theater of Pompey; 14, Sæpta Julia (voting booths); 15, Baths of Agrippa; 16, Pantheon; 17, Solarium (obelisk); 18, Mausoleum of Augustus; 19, Circus Maximus; 20, Tomb of Scipio; 21, Temple of Mars.

the republican period, the emperor appointed a superintendent of highways to keep them in repair. He also established a post-system by which the different parts of the peninsula could be kept in communication with one another. He suppressed brigandage by establishing military patrols in the dangerous districts. It was his policy to encourage everywhere the growth of a more healthy life in the various cities of Italy. To relieve the poor people in Italy he continued the plan of Julius Cæsar in sending out colonies into the provinces, where there were better opportunities to make a living.

The Administration of the Provinces.— No people were more greatly benefited by the new government than those living in the provinces. We have seen the wretched condition of the people under the later republic, when they were robbed by the provincial governors and the taxgatherers. This system of extortion was now stopped. The provincials obtained a degree of freedom they had never enjoyed under the old senatorial rule. The provinces were thoroughly reorganized. They were first divided into two groups, — the *senatorial*, or those which remained under the control of the senate; and the *imperial*, or those which passed under the control of the emperor. The latter were generally those which required the presence of an army and a military governor. The governors of the imperial provinces were lieutenants, or so-called " legates " of the emperor. Appointed by him and strictly responsible to him, they were no longer permitted to prey upon their subjects, but were obliged to rule in the name of the emperor and for the welfare of the people. The senatorial provinces, on the other hand, were still under the control of proconsuls and proprætors appointed by the senate. But the condition of these provinces also was greatly improved. As the property of the provincials became more secure, their commerce revived, their cities became prosperous, and their lives were made more tolerable.

The Finances of the Empire. — With the division of the provinces, the administration of the finances was also divided between the senate and the emperor. The revenues of the senatorial provinces went into the treasury of the senate; while those of the imperial provinces passed into the treasury of the emperor. The old wretched system of " farming " the revenues, which had disgraced the republic and impoverished the provincials, was reformed. The collection of the taxes in the senatorial as well as the imperial provinces was placed in the charge of imperial officers. It was not long before the cities themselves were allowed to raise by their own officers the taxes due to the Roman government. Augustus also laid the foundation of a sound financial system by making careful estimates of the revenues and expenditures of the state; and by raising and expending the public money in the most economical and least burdensome manner. He was the first to make a general census in which the resources of the whole empire were carefully estimated.

The Frontiers of the Empire. — Under Augustus, the boundaries of the empire were extended, generally speaking, to the Rhine and the Danube on the north, to the Atlantic Ocean on the west, to the desert of Africa on the south, and nearly to the Euphrates on the east. The extension of the frontiers was intended not so much to increase the territory of the empire as to provide a proper barrier against the barbarians from the north. The new frontier provinces were Rhætia, Noricum, Pannonia, and Mœsia. The only two great frontier nations which threatened to disturb the peace of Rome were the Parthians on the east and the Germans on the north. The Parthians had retained the standards lost by Crassus, but Augustus by his skillful diplomacy was able to recover them without a battle. He abandoned, however, all design of conquering that Eastern people.

But his eyes looked longingly to the country of the Germans. He invaded their territory; and after a temporary success his general, Varus, was slain and three Roman legions were utterly destroyed by the great German chieftain, Arminius, in the Teutoburg forest (9 A.D.).

This great battle has ever since been celebrated by the Germans as marking the deliverance of their nation from the Roman power. But to Augustus it was a terrible disappointment. He could never think of it without crying, "Oh! Varus, Varus, give me back my legions." The attempt to conquer Germany having proved a failure, the frontiers remained for many years where they were fixed by Augustus; and he advised his successors to govern well the territory which he left to them rather than to increase its limits.

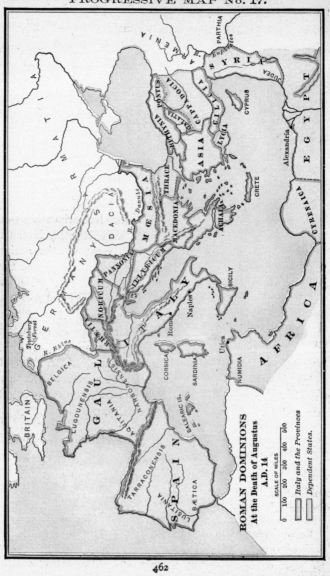

ROMAN DOMINIONS
At the Death of Augustus
A.D. 14

SCALE OF MILES
0 100 200 300 400 500

Italy and the Provinces
Dependent States.

III. The Age of Augustus

The Advisers of Augustus. — The remarkable prosperity that attended the reign of Augustus has caused this age to be called by his name. The glory of this period is largely due to the wise policy of Augustus himself; but in his work he was greatly assisted by two men whose names are closely linked to his own. These men were Agrippa and Mæce′nas.

Agrippa had been from boyhood one of the most intimate friends of Augustus, and during the trying times of the later republic had constantly aided him by his counsel and his sword. The victories of Augustus before and after he came to power were largely due to this able general. By his artistic ability Agrippa also contributed much to the architectural splendor of Rome.

The man who shared with Agrippa the favor and confidence of Augustus was Mæcenas, a wise statesman and patron of literature. It was by the advice of Mæcenas that many of the important reforms of Augustus were adopted and carried out. But the greatest honor is due to Mæcenas for encouraging those men whose writings made this period one of the " golden ages "

MÆCENAS

of the world's literature. It was chiefly the encouragement given to architecture and literature which made the reign of Augustus an epoch in civilization.

Encouragement to Architecture. — It is said that Augustus boasted that he " found Rome of brick and left it of marble." He restored many of the temples and other buildings which had either fallen into decay or been destroyed during the riots of the civil war. It is impossible to mention here all the buildings that were erected during his reign. On the Palatine hill he began the construction of the great imperial palace, which became the magnificent home of the Cæsars. He built a new temple of Vesta, where the sacred fire of the city was kept burning. He erected a new temple to Apollo, to which was attached a library of Greek and Latin authors; also temples to Jupiter Tonans and to the divine Julius. He claimed to have restored eighty-eight old temples, and to have built sixteen new ones.

THE PANTHEON (Restoration)

One of the noblest and most useful of the public works of the emperor was the new Forum of Augustus, near the old Roman Forum and the Forum of Julius. In this new forum was erected the temple of Mars the Avenger (*Mars Ultor*), which Augustus built to commemorate the war by which he had avenged the death of Cæsar. We must not forget to notice the massive Pantheon, the temple of all the gods, which is to-day the best preserved monument of the Augustan period. This is an immense circular building covered by a great dome with a span of a hundred and forty-five feet. It was built by Agrippa, in the early part of Augustus's reign, but was altered to the form shown on the opposite page by the emperor Ha'drian (second century A.D.). It is now occupied as a Christian church.

Patronage of Literature. — But more splendid and enduring than these temples of marble were the works of literature which this age produced. The greatest writers of this period were Vergil, Horace, and Liv'y. None of these writers were born at Rome; they came from the outlying towns in Italy, — Vergil from Mantua in Cisalpine Gaul, Horace from Venusia in southern Italy, and Livy from Padua near the banks of the Po. They early came to the capital and were received among the friends of Augustus and Mæcenas. They expressed the new ideals of life that Augustus was holding up to the Roman people.

Vergil wrote a collection of pastoral poems, called the "Eclogues," in which he sought to awaken a love for country life. He also wrote a series of beautiful poems called the "Georgics," in which he pictures in attractive verse the life of the farmer. By such means he hoped to arouse in the minds of the people a new taste for agricultural life — which was now sadly needed in Italy. For example, he writes:

> "When first young Zephyr melts the mountain snow,
> And Spring unbinds the mellowed soil below,
> Press the deep plow and urge the groaning team,
> Where the worn shares 'mid opening furrows gleam.
> Lands, o'er whose soil maturing time has rolled
> Twice summer's heat and twice the winter's cold,
> Profuse of wealth th' insatiate swain repay
> And crowd with bursting barns his long delay."

But the greatest of Vergil's poems is the world-renowned "Æne'id." In this he tells the thrilling story of Æneas and his wandering from Troy to Italy, and the miraculous origin of the Roman people. This was the great national poem of the Romans. It has received a high place in the world's literature.

If Vergil was the greatest national poet, Horace was the most original poet of Rome. His chief works were in the form of

" Satires," " Epistles," and " Odes."   His Satires deal with the
follies and foibles of society; they held something of the place
of the fashionable novel of our day.   His Epistles were addressed to his intimate friends, and show the genial good-fellow-
ship of their author.   But it is upon his inimitable Odes that his
fame chiefly rests.   These lyric poems have never been equaled
in beauty of sentiment and graceful rhythm.   They comprise
every variety of subject, from the praises showered upon Augustus and Mæcenas to the simplest joys and sorrows of everyday
life.   Horace was something of a philosopher, and believed in
the " golden mean."   For example, he says :

> "He that holds fast the golden mean,
>   And lives continually between
>   The little and the great,
>   Feels not the wants that pinch the poor,
>   Nor plagues that haunt the rich man's **door,**
>   Embittering all his state.
>
> " What if thine heaven be overcast,
>   The dark appearance will not last;
>   Expect a brighter sky.
>   The god that strings the silver bow
>   Awakes sometimes the muses too,
>   And lays his arrows by."

The greatest prose writer of this age was Livy, the historian.
The chief object of his work was to celebrate the glories of his
native country, and to reconcile the people to the rule of Augustus.   His history extended from the beginnings of Rome down
to his own day.   It was comprised in 142 books, of which only
35 have come down to us.   His " pictured pages " have been the
delight of all who love to read of noble deeds and great exploits.
His history is almost as much of a poem as Vergil's " Æneid."
In fact, it had almost the same purpose, — to excite the patriotism of the Roman people.   His desire to exalt Rome above everything else detracts somewhat from the value of his work as
an accurate history; but it may add to its attractiveness as a
picturesque narrative.

There were other noted writers of the Augustine age. Tibullus is called the father of the Roman elegy; he wrote pathetic verses of unrequited love in simple and graceful language. Propertius wrote poems similar to those of Tibullus, but with less delicacy and charm. Ovid wrote a series of love letters and a poem on " The Art of Love," besides a longer one entitled the " Metamorphosis," containing mythological stories in which heroes are represented as changed into other shapes; for example, the soul of Julius Cæsar is represented as translated into the form of a star. The whole literature of this period, whatever may have been its subjects, was imbued with a growing spirit of patriotism, and an appreciation of Rome as the great ruler of the world.

Religious and Social Reforms. — Besides encouraging art and literature, Augustus also tried to improve the religious and moral condition of the people. The old religion was falling into decay. With the restoration of the old temples, he hoped to bring the people back to the worship of the ancient gods. The worship of Juno, which had been neglected, was restored, and assigned to the care of his wife, Livia, as the representative of the matrons of Rome. Augustus tried to purify the Roman religion by discouraging the introduction of the foreign deities whose worship was corrupt. He believed that even a great Roman had better be worshiped than the degener-

LIVIA, WIFE OF AUGUSTUS

ate gods and goddesses of Syria and Egypt; and so the divine Julius was added to the number of the Roman gods to receive the worship of the people.

With the attempt to restore the old Roman religion, he also wished to revive the old morality and simple life of the past. He himself disdained luxurious living and foreign fashions. He tried to improve the lax customs which prevailed in respect to marriage and divorce, and to restrain the vices which were destroying the population of Rome.

Death and Character of Augustus. — Augustus lived to the age of seventy-five, and his reign covered a period of forty-five years. During this time he had been performing " the difficult part of ruling without appearing to rule, of being at once the autocrat of the civilized world and the first citizen of a free commonwealth." His last words are said to have been, " Have I not played my part well? " But it is not necessary for us to suppose that Augustus was a mere actor. The part which he had to perform in restoring peace to the world was a great and difficult task. In the midst of conflicting views which had distracted the republic for a century, he was called upon to perform a work of reconciliation. And it is doubtful whether any political leader every performed such a work with greater success. When he became the supreme ruler of Rome he was fully equal to the place, and brought order out of confusion. He was content with the substance of power and indifferent as to its form. Not so great as Julius Cæsar, he was yet more successful. He was one of the greatest examples of what we may call a constructive statesman. After his death Augustus was deified and given a rank among the Roman gods.

Selections for Reading

Knowlton, Topic A 22, "Augustus and his Age" (1).[1]
Goodspeed, Ancient World, pp. 359–373, "The World-Empire under the Principate" (1).
Capes, Early Empire, Ch. 1, "Augustus" (18).
Pelham, Bk. V., Ch. 2, "Foundation of the Principate" (18).
Taylor, Ch. 18, "The Princeps and the Government" (22).

[1] The figure in parenthesis refers to the number of the topic in the Appendix, where a fuller title of the book will be found.

Bury, Roman Empire, Ch. 2, "The Principate"; Chs. 6, 7, "Provincial Administration"; Ch. 10, "Rome under Augustus; His Buildings"; Ch. 11, "Literature of the Augustan Age" (18).

Abbott, Ch. 12, "The Establishment of the Empire" (22).

Merivale, General History, Ch. 51, "The Government as Organized by Augustus" (18).

—— Empire, Vol. III., Ch. 31, "The Imperial Authority"; Ch. 32, "The Imperial Administration"; Vol. IV., Ch. 34, "Organization of the Provinces by Augustus" (18).

Lanciani, Ruins, pp. 138–144, 302–307 (Augustus as a builder) (20).

Greenidge, Public Life, Ch. 10, "The Principate"; Ch. 11, "Italy and the Provinces under the Empire"; pp. 440–444 (the worship of the emperor) (22).

Shuckburgh, Augustus, pp. 265–293 (character of Augustus) (27).

Munro, Source Book, pp. 143–148 (Augustus) (25).

Special Study

THE WRITERS OF THE AUGUSTAN AGE. — Bury, "Roman Empire," Ch. 11 (18); Mackail, pp. 91–170 (23); Cruttwell, Part II. (23); See also Appendix (23) "Roman Literature."

TOMB OF AUGUSTUS (Restoration)

CHAPTER XXIX

THE EMPIRE UNDER THE SUCCESSORS OF AUGUSTUS

Synopsis

I. THE JULIAN EMPERORS (14–69 A.D.). — Tiberius and the Increase of the Monarchical Power. — Gaius, or Caligula, the Mad Prince. — Claudius, and the Beginning of the Conquest of Britain. — Nero, and the First Persecution of the Christians.

II. THE FLAVIAN EMPERORS (69–96 A.D.). — The Disputed Succession. — Vespasian, and the Destruction of Jerusalem. — Titus; the Destruction of Pompeii and Herculaneum. — Domitian, and the Extension of the Roman Power in Britain.

III. THE FIVE GOOD EMPERORS (96–180 A.D.). — Nerva, the Benevolent Prince. — Trajan and his Conquests in the East. — Hadrian and his Compilation of the Roman Law. — Antoninus Pius; the "Uneventful Reign." — Marcus Aurelius, the Philosopher on the Throne.

I. THE JULIAN EMPERORS (14–69 A.D.)

Tiberius and the Increase of the Monarchical Power (14–37 A.D.). — The first four successors of Augustus traced their descent from Julius Cæsar and Augustus, and hence are known as the Julian line. Augustus had made no permanent plan for the succession. But he had associated with him his stepson, Tibe′rius; and so Tiberius was accepted as his proper successor. In his personal character Tiberius presented a striking contrast to Augustus. Instead of being generous and conciliatory, he was sour and morose and often severe and cruel in his treatment of others. He was yet, in many respects, an able and vigorous ruler. He maintained the frontiers and managed the finances with skill and economy. Under his watchful care the provinces flourished, and were protected from the greed of their governors. His favorite maxim is said to have been, " A good shepherd should shear his sheep and not flay them."

He tried to follow the wise policy of Augustus; but being surrounded by those he could not trust, he sought to increase the monarchical power by adopting severe and tyrannical methods. In the first place he took away from the assemblies the power of electing their own officers, which had been left to them by Augustus, and transferred this power to the senate. In the next place, he changed the existing law of treason, so as to make it apply not only to offenses against the state, but also to offenses against the emperor himself. To carry out this law he instituted a class of informers, or detectives, to spy out his enemies. Moreover, he gathered together the prætorian guard in a single camp near Rome, where it would be better able to support his authority. His life at

TIBERIUS

CALIGULA

Rome was embittered by court jealousies and intrigues. He retired at last to the island of Capri in the Bay of Naples, where he spent his last days.

Gaius, or Caligula, the Mad Prince (37–41 A.D.). — Tiberius made no provision for a successor. The senate, therefore, chose as emperor a young favorite of the army, Gaius Cæsar. This prince is usually known as Calig′ula (meaning " Little Boots "), a nickname that was given him, when a boy, by the soldiers. His accession was hailed with joy, and he at first gave promise of a successful reign. But after a brief period, his mind, already diseased, gave way; and he indulged in all the wild freaks of an insane person. He imagined himself a god. He built a bridge from his residence on the Palatine hill to the Capitoline, that he might be " next-door neighbor of Jupiter." He nominated his horse for consul. Many other strange stories are told of this delirious young man. His brief reign of four years has little political significance, except to show that the empire might endure even with a mad prince on the throne.

RUINS OF THE PALACE OF CALIGULA

Claudius, and the Beginning of the Conquest of Britain (41–54 A.D.). — Claudius was the first emperor proclaimed by the army. When the senate hesitated to choose a successor, the prætorians, accidentally finding Claudius in the palace, assumed the right to name him as emperor. He was a man fifty years of age, of ungainly figure and awkward manners, and had been an object of contempt and ridicule. He is usually represented as a weak imbecile, but his reign stands out in refreshing contrast to the wild extravagances of Caligula. He is charged with having taken his freedmen into his counsels; but these freedmen were

educated Greeks and gave him excellent advice. He followed
the example of Julius Cæsar in extending the rights of citizenship
to the inhabitants of Gaul. He
followed the example of Augustus
in building works of public utility.
He constructed the Claudian aqueduct, which brought water to
the city from a distance of forty-
five miles.

But for us perhaps his most
memorable work was the beginning of the conquest of Britain.
Since the invasion of Julius Cæsar
the Romans had taken little interest in this island. With the
aid of his lieutenants, Claudius

CLAUDIUS

now effected a permanent landing in Britain, and succeeded in
subduing the southern part of the island. Britain was thus
opened to the benefits of Roman civilization.

RUINS OF THE CLAUDIAN AQUEDUCT

Nero, and the First Persecution of the Christians (54–68 A.D.).
— Claudius was followed by a ruler whose career proved to be

as disgraceful as that of Caligula, and far more criminal. This ruler was Nero. He was, like Claudius, proclaimed by the soldiers, and accepted by the senate. The early part of his reign was full of hope and promise. During this time he was under

NERO

the influence of the wise philosopher Sen'eca. After five years of beneficent rule he threw aside the counsels of Seneca and abandoned himself, not to a diseased mind, like Caligula, but to his own depraved nature. Then followed a career of wickedness, debauchery, extortion, and atrocious cruelty which it is not necessary to describe, but which has rendered his name a synonym for all that is vicious in human nature and despicable in a ruler. The world will never cease to abhor the name of Nero, because it was under him that occurred the first persecution of the Christians. It is in connection with this event that the name of the Christians is first mentioned by the Roman historians. The new religion had appeared in Judea about a generation before this time, and had made rapid progress in the eastern provinces. There was now a large community of Christians at Rome, made up of converted Jews and other persons. They were despised by the upper classes. A great fire at Rome furnished the occasion of the first persecution. The Roman historian Tacitus says that, in order to drown the rumor that Nero himself had caused this fire,

"Nero shifted the guilt on persons known as Christians, and punished them with exquisite tortures. Christus, from whom they derive their name, had been punished under Tiberius by the procurator Pontius Pilate. . . . In their deaths they were made the subjects of sport; for they were covered with the skins of wild beasts, worried to death by dogs, nailed to crosses, burned to serve for torches at night. Nero offered his own gardens for this spectacle." (Annals, Bk. XV., ch. 44.)

II. THE FLAVIAN EMPERORS (69–96 A.D.)

The Disputed Succession. — With the death of Nero the Julian line, which traced its descent from Julius and Augustus, became extinct. We may now discover one great defect of the imperial system — that is, the lack of any definite law of succession. In theory, the selection of a new emperor rested with the senate, with which he was supposed to share his power. But in fact, it depended upon the army. Since the time of Caligula, the choice of the prince had been assumed by the prætorian guards. But now the provincial armies also claimed the right to name the emperor's successor; so that it seemed evident, as Tacitus says, " that a prince could be made elsewhere than at Rome." But it was not so clear which of the armies had the greatest right to make this choice. The disputed claims led to a war of succession, which lasted about a year — the first civil war which had occurred within a century, or since the battle of Actium. After the other claimants had ruled in succession for brief terms, Vespa′sian, the commander of the army in Syria, was finally victorious and was accepted as emperor.

VESPASIAN

Vespasian, and the Destruction of Jerusalem (69–79 A.D.). — With Vespasian begins a new line of emperors, known as the Fla′vian line. The new emperor came from a Sabine family of humble origin. He proved to be an able prince, and his judicious rule brought in a new era of prosperity. He restored Rome from the disorders resulting from the reign of Nero and from the recent civil war. He constructed new buildings for the capital, the most noted of which was the great Flavian amphitheater, known as the Colosse′um (p. 501).

During his reign there was a revolt in Gaul, which was speedily put down. In no province of the empire did the civilization of Rome take a firmer hold. Gaul became a land of Roman colonies. Its cities were connected by Roman roads; the Latin language and literature, the Roman law, and Roman manners and art found there a congenial home. The ruins which we find in France to-day of the ancient buildings, — baths, aqueducts, and amphitheaters, — show how completely the province was Romanized.

But the most unfortunate event in the reign of Vespasian was the revolt of the Jews, which finally resulted in the destruction of

SPOILS OF JERUSALEM (From the Arch of Titus)

Jerusalem. There had been many changes in the government of Judea since its first conquest by Pompey. Some of these changes had been made to reconcile the Jews to the Roman sway. But there had been many things to awaken the opposition of the people; for example, the unreasonable prejudice against them at Rome, the insane attempt of Caligula to place his statue in their temple, as well as the harsh government of Nero. At last the Jews were provoked into a general rebellion. Vespasian was conducting the war against them when he was proclaimed emperor by his legions. The war was then left in the hands of his son Titus, who, in spite of desperate resistance, captured and destroyed the sacred city (70 A.D.). The Jews were left without a national home, and many of them became scattered in different parts of the empire. The representation of the seven-branched golden candlestick cut upon the arch of Titus is a striking memorial of this unfortunate war.

Titus; the Destruction of Pompeii and Herculaneum (79–81 A.D.). — Before Vespasian's death he had associated with him in the government his worthy son Titus. The new prince reigned only two years, but during this brief time he followed the generous policy of his father, and won from the people the title " the Delight of Mankind." The story is told of him that one evening with a party of friends he recalled the fact that he had granted no favor to any one since morning, and exclaimed to his friends, " I have lost a day." He dedicated the great

TITUS

amphitheater built by his father, with shows that lasted for a hundred days.

But the most memorable and unfortunate event of his reign was the great eruption of Vesu'vius (79 A.D.) which overwhelmed the two cities of Pompe'ii and Hercula'neum, situated on the Bay of Naples. The people had never suspected that this mountain was a sleeping volcano, although a few years before it had been shaken by an earthquake. The scenes which attended this eruption have been described by the younger Plin'y, whose uncle, the elder Pliny, lost his life while witnessing the great catastrophe. The buried city of Pompeii has been uncovered in modern times, and now one may see the relics that reveal in a vivid way the private life and customs of the ancient Roman people, who lived more than eighteen hundred years ago.

Domitian, and the Extension of the Roman Power in Britain
(81–96 A.D.). — The happy period begun by Vespasian and
Titus was interrupted by the exceptional tyranny of Domitian,
the younger brother of Titus. Domitian seemed to take for
his models Tiberius and Nero. He was guilty of confiscations
and extortions. He teased and irritated all classes. He persecuted the Jews and the Christians. Like Tiberius, he was

suspicious, and lived in perpetual
fear of assassination. His fears
were at last realized; a conspiracy
was organized against him, and he
was murdered by a freedman of
the palace.

The chief event of importance
in the reign of Domitian was the
extension of the Roman power
in Britain. The Roman general
Agric′ola had already been appointed governor of Britain by
Vespasian; but it was not until this
time that his arms were crowned

DOMITIAN

with marked success. The limits of the province were now
pushed to the north, and a new field was opened for the advance of civilization. Britain became dotted with Roman
colonies, united by great military roads. As in Gaul, the Roman
law and customs found a home, although they did not obtain
so enduring an influence as in the continental provinces.

III. THE FIVE GOOD EMPERORS (96–180 A.D.)

Nerva, the Benevolent Prince (96–98 A.D.). — With the death
of Domitian the empire came back into the hands of wise and
beneficent rulers. The period of prosperity which began with
Vespasian, was now continued for nearly a century. The
emperors of this period are known as " the five good emperors."

When we consider their uprightness of character, their political ability, and their uniform regard for the welfare of their subjects.

NERVA

we probably cannot find in the history of the world a like series of sovereigns, ruling with equal success for the same length of time. The first of these rulers was Nerva, whose mildness and tolerance contrasted strongly with the severe qualities of Domitian. Nerva was chosen neither by the prætorians nor by the legions, but by the senate. This fact shows that the empire was returning to the normal political system established by Augustus. Within his brief reign of two years he could do little except to remedy the wrongs of his predecessor. One of the noteworthy features of his short reign was his attempt to relieve the poor. He bought up large lots of land from the wealthy landlords, and let them out to needy citizens. He showed his interest in the cause of general education; he set apart a certain fund, the interest of which was used to educate the children of poor parents. He was universally beloved; and his wise and benevolent reign is praised by all ancient writers. Tacitus said of him, "He blended things once irreconcilable, princely power and liberty"—a statement that might apply to all these "good emperors."

TRAJAN

Trajan and his Conquests in the East (98–117 A.D.). — Trajan has the great distinction of being the first emperor who was not a native either of Rome or of Italy. He was a Spaniard by birth; and this fact shows that the dividing line between Roman and provincial was breaking down. Trajan was one of the greatest of the Roman sovereigns. He was a brave soldier, a wise statesman, and an able administrator. He had something of the conciliatory spirit of Augustus, and preserved the forms of the republic. He restored to the people the right of electing the

TRAJAN'S COLUMN, AND REMAINS OF TRAJAN'S FORUM, AT ROME

magistrates, which had been taken away by Tiberius. He respected the rights of the senate, and gave to it liberty of speech. He was also a liberal patron of literature and art.

While Trajan followed in the main the policy of Augustus, he departed from this policy in one particular. He did not restrict the frontiers within the limits that Augustus had intended. Under him the Romans became once more a conquering people. This warlike emperor pushed his conquests across the Danube and acquired the new province of Dacia. He also extended his arms into Asia, and as a result of a war with the Parthians brought into subjection Armenia, Mesopotamia, and Assyria. It was during the reign of Trajan that the Roman empire reached its greatest extent (see map, pp. 482, 483).

Hadrian and his Compilation of the Roman Law (117–138 A.D.). — The next emperor, Hā'drian, was proclaimed by the prætorians. But Hadrian did not regard this as a constitutional act, and requested to be formally elected by the senate. He differed from Trajan in not thinking that the greatness of Rome depended upon military glory. He therefore voluntarily gave up the extensive conquests which Trajan had made in the East, and once more made the Euphrates the frontier of the empire. Hadrian showed, if possible, a stronger sympathy with the provinces than any of his predecessors. To become acquainted with their condition, he spent a large part of his time in visiting them; and he is hence sometimes called " the Traveler." Of his long

HADRIAN

reign of twenty-one years he spent nearly two thirds outside of Italy. Hadrian also looked well to the defenses of the empire, especially against the barbarous tribes on the north. The most durable evidence of his defensive policy is seen in the extensive wall built on the northern frontier of the province of Britain, the remains of which exist at the present day and are known as " Hadrian's wall."

Perhaps the most important event in the reign of Hadrian was his compilation of the more liberal part of the Roman law. We remember that the ancient Roman law had been codified more than five hundred years before in the XII. Tables. Since that time there had grown up a new and far more liberal body of law, which recognized the rights of foreigners as well as

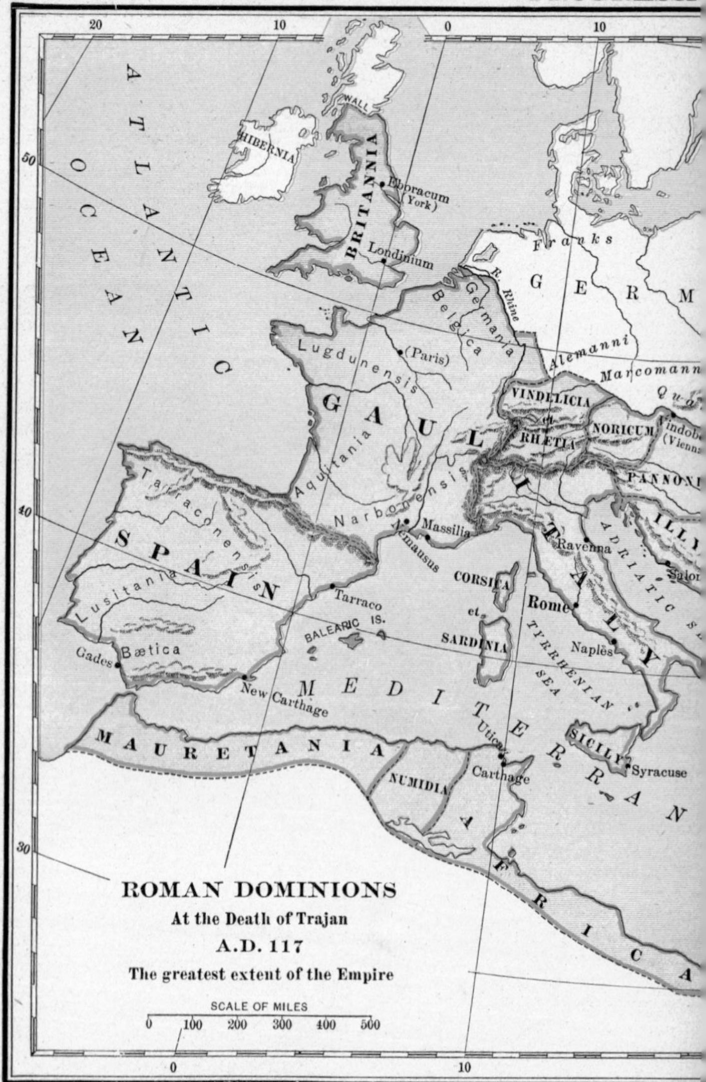

ATLANTIC OCEAN
HIBERNIA
WALL
BRITANNIA
Eboracum (York)
Londinium
Franks
R. Rhine
GERM
Germania
Belgica
Lugdunensis
(Paris)
GAUL
Aquitania
Narbonensis
Alemanni
Marcomanni
Qua
VINDELICIA
et
RHÆTIA
NORICUM
Vindob (Vienna)
PANNONI
ILLY
Salon
ADRIATIC SEA
SPAIN
Tarraconensis
Lusitania
Bætica
Gades
New Carthage
Tarraco
BALEARIC IS.
Massilia
Nemausus
CORSICA et SARDINIA
ITALY
Ravenna
Rome
Naples
TYRRHENIAN SEA
SICILY
Syracuse
MEDITERRANEAN
MAURETANIA
NUMIDIA
Utica
Carthage
AFRICA
ROMAN DOMINIONS
At the Death of Trajan
A.D. 117
The greatest extent of the Empire
SCALE OF MILES
0 100 200 300 400 500

citizens. Hadrian delegated to one of his jurists, Julia'nus, the task of collecting this new body of law, so that it could be used for the better administration of justice throughout the empire. This collection was called the "Perpetual Edict."

Antoninus Pius; the "Uneventful Reign" (138–161 A.D.).— If we desired to find in Roman history a more noble character

than that of Hadrian, we should find it in his adopted son and successor, Antoni'nus Pius. The emperors Antoninus and his son Marcus Aurelius are known as the "An'tonines." The description given of Antoninus by his son, Marcus Aurelius, is worthy to be read by the young people of all times. He says:

"In my father I saw mildness of manners, firmness of resolution, contempt of vain glory. He knew when to rest as well as to labor. He taught me to for-

ANTONINUS PIUS

bear from all improper indulgences, to conduct myself as an equal among equals, to lay on my friends no burden of servility. From him I learned to be resigned to every fortune and to bear myself calmly and serenely; to rise superior to vulgar applause, and to despise vulgar criticism; to worship the gods without superstition and to serve mankind without ambition. He was ever prudent and moderate; he looked to his duty only, and not to the opinions that might be formed of him. Such was the character of his life and manners — nothing harsh, nothing excessive, nothing rude, nothing which showed roughness and violence."

The reign of Antoninus, although a long one of twenty-three years, is known in history as the "uneventful reign." Since much that is usually called "eventful" in history is made up of wars, tumults, calamities, and discords, it is to the greatest credit of Antoninus that his reign is called uneventful. We read of no conquests, no insurrections, no proscriptions, no extortions, no cruelty.

Marcus Aurelius, the Philosopher on the Throne (161–180 A.D.). — Marcus Aurelius, who came to the throne at the death of Antoninus, was in his personal character one of the most remarkable men of antiquity. He was a philosopher as well as an emperor. He had studied in the school of the Stoics; and his "Meditations" — a book on the conduct of life — has been highly prized as a moral textbook by all subsequent generations. The history of the pagan world presented no higher example of uprightness and true manhood. But with all his personal worth, his reign was a period of misfortunes. It was now that Rome was afflicted with a deadly plague and famine, the most terrible in her history. In addition to this, the barbarians from the north were trying to break through the frontiers on the upper Rhine. But the emperor met these

MARCUS AURELIUS

dangers with courage and patience; and he died at his post of duty while resisting the enemies of Rome.

The only blot upon the memory of this noble prince is the fact that he was led to persecute the Christians. He was evidently mistaken as to their true character: and the people, superstitious as they were, believed that the Christians were the cause of all their calamities. We wonder the more at his making this terrible mistake when we read the noble sentiments that he expresses in his book; for example:

"From my mother I learned piety and to abstain not only from evil deeds, but from evil thoughts as well.

"The best way to avenge a wrong is not to be like the wrong-doer.

"Behave to all so that it may be said of you that you never wronged a man in deed or in word.

"Never value anything as profitable to yourself which shall compel you to break your promise, to lose your self-respect, to hate any man, to act the hypocrite, or to desire anything that needs walls or curtains.

"Await tranquilly your departure from life; there is naught else to do but to worship the gods, to do good to men, to be tolerant, and to practice self-restraint.

"Go through this brief span of life in harmony with Nature and come to your journey's end in contentment, just as the olive drops quietly to the ground when it is ripe."

Selections for Reading

Knowlton, Topic A 23, "The Successors of Augustus" (1).[1]

Pelham, Bk. V., Ch. 4, "The Julian Line"; Bk. VI., "The Antonines" (18).

Abbott, Ch. 13, "From Tiberius to Nero"; Ch. 14, "The Flavian Emperors" (22).

Capes, Early Empire, Ch. 2, "Tiberius"; Ch. 5, "Nero" Ch. 11, "Domitian"; Ch. 12, "The Position of the Emperor" (18).

Bury, Chs. 12, 13, "Principate of Tiberius"; Ch. 20, "Rebellions in Germany and Judea" (18).

Merivale, General History, Chs. 64-66 (the reigns from Nerva to Marcus Aurelius) (18).

Gibbon, Chs. 1-3 (the Roman empire from Augustus to Marcus Aurelius) (18).

Abbott, F. F., Roman Political Institutions, Part III., "Imperial Period" (22).

Munro, Source Book, Ch. 9, "The Early Empire" (25).

Special Study

THE CONQUEST OF BRITAIN. — Pelham, pp. 502-507, 544 (18); Merivale, General History, pp. 468, 499-502, 517 (18); Merivale, Empire, Vol. VI., pp. 16-51, Vol. VII., pp. 68-77, 342-348 (18); Bury, Ch. 16 (18).

[1] The figure in parenthesis refers to the number of the topic in the Appendix. where a fuller title of the book will be found.

CHAPTER XXX

THE ROMAN PEOPLE UNDER THE EARLY EMPIRE

Synopsis

I. General Condition of the Roman World. — The Culmination of the Empire. — The Imperial Government and the Loyalty of the People. — Condition of the Provinces. — Provincial Towns: Pompeii as a Typical Town. — Provincial Life, Travel, and Correspondence. — Industry and Commerce. — Improvement of the Roman Law.

II. Social and Domestic Life. — Classes of Roman Society. — Town Houses and Country Villas. — Furniture, Meals, and Clothing. — Social Life and Amusements. — Marriage and the Position of Women. — Funeral Ceremonies.

III. Art and Intellectual Life. — Roman Architecture. — The Literature of the Early Empire. — Roman Philosophy. — Books and Libraries.

IV. The Beginnings of Christianity. — Preparation for Christianity in the Empire. — Spread of Christianity. — Attitude of the People and the Government toward the Early Christians. — The Early Persecutions of the Christians.

I. General Condition of the Roman World

The Culmination of the Empire. — The death of Aurelius closed the most prosperous period of Roman history. It marks the culmination of the empire. When one looks at the general condition of the Roman world it will not be difficult to see that the fall of the Roman republic and the establishment of the empire were not an evil, but a great benefit to the Roman people. In place of a century of civil wars and discord which closed the republic, we see more than two centuries of internal peace and tranquillity. Instead of an oppressive treatment of the provincials, we see a treatment which is with few exceptions mild and generous. Instead of a government controlled by a proud and selfish oligarchy, we see a government controlled, generally speaking, by a wise and patriotic prince. From the accession of Augustus to the death of Marcus Aurelius (31 B.C. to 180 A.D.), a period of two hundred and eleven years, only three emperors who held power for any length of time — Tiberius, Nero, and Domitian — are known as tyrants; and their cruelty was confined almost entirely to the city, and to their own personal enemies. The establishment of the empire, we must therefore believe, marked a stage of progress and not of decline in the history of the Roman people. The Roman world reached its highest stage of development in the age of the Antonines, and this period has been called by Gibbon " the happiest in the history of mankind."

The Imperial Government and the Loyalty of the People. — The imperial government was a government, if not *by* the people, at least *for* the people. It furnished the highest example that the world has ever seen of what we may call a " paternal autocracy " — that is, a government in the hands of a single ruler, but exercised solely for the benefit of the people. In this respect the ideals of Julius and Augustus seem to have been completely realized. There was still a certain deference paid to the constitutional forms of the republic; but this deference to the past did not interfere with the emperor's real authority. The senate was treated with respect, but its members, being chosen by the emperor, were of course submissive to his will. There was no disposition to protest against the imperial authority, which received the cordial support of all citizens. Being thus subject to one government, the people felt more and more that they were one people. They felt bound together by a common feeling of loyalty. They felt that they were citizens not of Gaul or of Greece, but " citizens of the world," that is, of the whole empire.

Condition of the Provinces. — The provinces formed the great part of the empire. No doubt we may see a great deal in the early imperial system of which we in our day do not approve; still, the establishment of the empire was a great benefit to the Roman provinces. The government of the provinces remained very much as it had been established by Augustus. There were the *senatorial* provinces, each under officers appointed by the senate — the proconsul, or proprætor, who was the chief civil officer, and the quæstor, who looked after the finances. There were also the *imperial* provinces, under officers appointed by the emperor — the legate, who had command of the provincial army, and the procurator, who had charge of financial matters. The revenues of the empire were now based on the census, which was an enumeration of the inhabitants, with the property subject to taxation. The chief source of revenue was the tribute, or the tax upon land. The provincials were no longer plundered to support an avaricious class of nobles at Rome. Even Tiberius, who was tyrannical in many respects, was especially anxious concerning the welfare of the provinces. Claudius, also, and other emperors were generous in extending the rights of citizenship. It is true that the public or political right involved in citizenship had now no special importance; but it is also true that the private or civil rights were still a valuable possession for all Roman subjects. During this time, also, the provinces were extended so as to include Dacia, Thrace, Lycia in Asia Minor, Maureta'nia in Africa, and the southern part of Britain.

Provincial Towns: Pompeii as a Typical Town. — The provinces were made up of the towns. The people living in the country districts were supposed to belong to some neighboring town. In general the local government of the town was carried on by a town council, or *curia*, something like the senate at Rome, made up of the chief men of the town, the so-called *curia'les*. This council was presided over by two officers called *duum'viri*, who were the chief magistrates of the town. The tendency of all towns in the West was to conform to this model.

When we attempt to get an idea of the conditions of life in the various towns scattered over the empire, we find it difficult on account of the few references made to this life by the ancient writers. We find in general, however, that the cities of the eastern provinces remained to a great extent under the Græco-Oriental influence which followed the conquest of Alexander. On the other hand, the cities of the western provinces became more thoroughly Romanized. The western towns may, therefore, be regarded as reflections of the capital city on the Tiber.

The uncovered ruins of Pompeii enable us to judge somewhat of the character of a Roman town. Here we find the remains

PART OF POMPEII AS SEEN FROM AN AËROPLANE TO-DAY

of a city of small dimensions, of narrow streets, of houses of moderate size, but containing many features which we see in Rome itself — forums, theater, temples, as well as a basilica and an amphitheater. These monuments indicate a life quite similar to that of the metropolis. In some of the houses — such as the " House of Pansa " — we see the same taste for luxury, as is evident in the mosaic work, paintings, and other works of art. We also find some remarkable evidences of the ordinary life of the townsmen in the *graffiti*, or writings left upon the walls of buildings. Some of these hardly rise above the dignity of rude scribblings. They are most numerous upon the buildings in those places most frequented by the crowd. There are advertisements of public shows, of persons running for public office, memoranda of sales, cookery recipes, personal lampoons, sentimental love effusions, and hundreds of similar records of the ordinary life and thoughts of this ancient people.

Provincial Life, Travel, and Correspondence. — The general features that we see in Pompeii were no doubt repeated in the various towns throughout the provinces, especially in the West. There was evidently the same tendency in the cities of Gaul, Spain, and Africa to imitate the culture of the central city, to adopt the Roman language, art, and manners. But there were certain special features of provincial life which are worthy of notice.

With the overthrow of the old system of oppression that prevailed under the republic, there was a growing interest in public affairs on the part of the people. Each town vied with other towns in the improvement of the public works. The growing public spirit is shown in the buildings erected not only by the town itself, but by the generous contributions of wealthy private citizens.

The relations between the people of the provinces were also becoming closer by the improvement in the means of communication. The empire became covered with a network of roads, which were now used not merely for the transportation of armies, but for purposes of travel and correspondence. The great Appian Way (p. 353) was reconstructed during this period, and was the model for the other highways of the empire. The Romans traveled for business and for pleasure; and by some persons traveling by land or by sea was regarded as a part of one's education. It was a mark of culture to have spent some time in Greece, Asia Minor, or Egypt. Many of the Roman highways were used also as post-roads, over which letters might be sent by means of private runners or by government couriers. Foot-runners were accustomed to make a distance of twenty-five miles a day; while a mounted courier, with his relay of horses, might cover a hundred miles in the same time.

THE APPIAN WAY, NEAR ROME, BORDERED BY TOMBS (Reconstruction)

The postal system of Rome, although hardly to be compared with that of modern times, afforded a useful means for the transmission of official dispatches, and for the correspondence between private persons.

Industry and Commerce. — The two centuries following the triumph of Augustus may be considered the golden age of Roman industry and commerce. The old system of great landed estates was broken up, and the poor farmer had a better opportunity to make a living. The number of slaves was diminishing, owing to the cessation of wars and to the growing custom of manumission, or giving a slave his freedom. Free labor became more honorable, and better opportunities were given to those who were working at the different trades. At Rome many articles of luxury were produced, such as fine furniture, carvings, moldings, metal work, fine pottery, glass, and paper. The guilds, or associations, of workmen were reorganized under special licenses from the emperor; so that they became no longer centers of disturbance, but more like social and religious clubs for charitable work among their members. The towns in the provinces became more active industrial centers, exchanging their goods with one another. There thus grew up an extensive domestic trade.

Imports poured into Rome from all parts of the empire. From Spain came all kinds of minerals, gold, silver, copper, and iron, and various other products, such as wheat, wine, fruits, and honey. From Athens and other cities of Greece came marbles, bronzes, perfumes. From Asia Minor came woolen cloths, lead, copper, and iron. A foreign trade was also carried on with countries beyond the borders of the empire. From India, Persia, and China were imported silks, perfumes, precious stones, spices, and incense. There were three great commercial routes from the Far East — the first by way of the Indian Ocean and the Red Sea to Alexandria; the second by way of the Persian Gulf, the Euphrates River, and the Syrian desert to Antioch; and the third by way of the Caspian Sea, the Volga River and the Don to Olbia and Byzantium on the Black Sea (see map, p. 483).

Commerce was the most important industry during the imperial period. The mercantile pursuits — those of the merchant, the importer, the banker, the capitalist — were the most honored occupations.

Improvement of the Roman Law. — If we could have asked an intelligent person living in the provinces how he had received the greatest benefit from the Roman rule, he would doubtless have answered, from the improvement in the Roman law. He would tell us that the old code of the XII. Tables had been made, not for him, but for Roman citizens only; that he had received no advantage from that old law. The old prætor who had administered that law evidently believed that a foreigner had no rights that a Roman citizen was bound to respect. But in the process of time the Romans had found out that if they were to transact business with a foreigner they must respect his rights, and so they had appointed a new prætor, a so-called "foreign prætor," to settle disputes between Romans and foreigners, and between foreigners of different towns. The foreign prætor settled such cases according to what he believed was fair and right, without regard to the old XII. Tables. When the provinces came to be organized, the same kind of authority was given to the provincial governor; namely, to settle every case upon its own merits and according to his own sense of what was fair to both parties.

The foreign prætors and the provincial governors found they could settle disputes in the most satisfactory way by adopting certain common customs which were familiar to the parties concerned. These common customs became the basis of a new law, known as the law common to all nations, or simply the "law of nations." It recognized the rights of foreigners and protected them in their business relations with Romans and with one another. It thus proved of great benefit to all the provincials who were still regarded as foreigners. This new law was far more liberal and humane than the old law of the XII. Tables. It tended to break down the old distinctions between citizens and foreigners, between Romans and provincials. It became in fact a law for the whole empire.

Besides, there grew up in the time of the empire a body of trained jurists, who were authorized by the emperor to interpret the law according to their sense of justice and equity. These jurists were beginning to feel the influence of the Stoic philosophy and to recognize the truth of its high moral precepts. They were led to believe that law is a science founded upon the principles of justice, and that the law of the state must be so interpreted as to conform to these principles. The jurists also advised the emperor in the making of new laws. Laws were issued against the cruel treatment of slaves and against the arbitrary power of a father over his wife and children, as well as against other abusive customs. Thus it was that through the efforts of the prætors, the provincial governors, and the jurists the Roman law came to be the most admirable system of jurisprudence the world has ever seen.

II. Social and Domestic Life

Classes of Roman Society. — If we now look at the condition of society under the Flavian emperors and the Antonines, we shall notice that certain changes had taken place since the time of the republic. The general tendency was to create a greater degree of equality among the various classes. The wide distinctions which existed under the republic were breaking down. This will appear by considering the different classes of the Roman people:

(1) At the top of the social scale were the emperor and the imperial household. The position of the emperor was becoming more and more respected, but it was also evident that the position could be held by a man of humble origin, as in the case of Vespasian. Nearest the emperor were the so-called " friends of Cæsar," who made up his household and the circle of his selected guests. These persons were chosen from all classes and were often freedmen and provincials, whose honored position depended solely upon the favor of the prince.

(2) Next were the aristocratic classes, who still formed a sort of nobility — the senators and knights (*equites*). But the senatorial order was not now restricted, as formerly, to certain favored Roman families. On the contrary, the senators were selected by the emperor on account of their wealth, ability, or influence, and were chosen from persons from every part of the empire. The equestrian order (*equites*), also, was becoming less and less an exclusive body, and admission to it was a gift of the prince. It had no important political privileges, although it came to be customary for the emperor to select his officials from its members.

(3) The great body of the common people consisted of the professional classes, the lawyers, teachers, writers, physicians; the artisan classes, the smiths, weavers, fullers, bakers, etc.;

ROMAN MILL AND BAKERY (From frieze of a tomb)

and the agricultural classes, the farmers and free laborers. So far as their strictly civil rights were concerned — that is, the rights of person, of property, of inheritance, of contract, and of suing in a court of justice — all these people were on a plane of practical equality with the upper classes.

(4) The slaves were, of course, at the bottom of the social scale, and were deprived of civil rights. But their condition was far better than in the time of the republic. They were treated with more respect; their lives were protected; and there were increased facilities for manumission.

Town Houses and Country Villas. — To obtain a general idea of the life of the Roman people under the empire, we may first look at the Roman citizen in his own home, where he ruled as the head of his household. The best Roman houses were no longer the simple structures of the early republic, but were modeled after the most elaborate houses of the later Greeks, which had begun to show the effect of an Oriental taste. The excavations among the ruins of Pompeii have given us much knowledge of this domestic architecture. The principal room was the large reception room (*atrium*), entered from the street by a vestibule. It was supported by marble columns, and paved with mosaic. It was lavishly decorated with ivory, gold, and precious stones, and adorned with statues of bronze

ROMAN HOUSE, SHOWING THE ATRIUM IN THE FOREGROUND

and marble. On either side of the *atrium* were the library and the picture gallery, besides rooms for conversation. Leading to the rear was the peristyle, or open court, containing a garden and fountain, and surrounded by rows of columns. Beyond the peristyle were the dining room, the dormitories, the bathrooms, the kitchen, and the larder. With the exception of the rear rooms, the walls were frequently decorated with paintings, representing floating figures, and other designs.

The Romans were fond of the country; and the wealthy Roman sought a retreat from the dust and din of the city by having a country seat, or *villa*. The first condition of a desirable villa was a fine landscape view. This might be found near the mountains or near the seashore. Horace (p. 465) is continually talking about his Sabine farm, which was situated near the modern town of Tivoli (tē′vo-lē), near the Sabine hills. This was a favorite place of resort. Augustus and Mæcenas had villas here. The most extensive one was that of Hadrian, which occupied 160 acres. Another favorite resort was the shores of the Bay of Naples. Here were a large number of villas. But wherever they were situated, the villas were the centers of luxury and high living. They were adorned with marble porticoes, statues, mosaics, fountains — nothing was considered too splendid for them. They were more elaborate than the town houses. They had many dining rooms for the entertainment of friends at all seasons of the year. Many libraries, or studies, furnished a means for mental recreation. The villa represented the highest life of the well-to-do Roman citizen.

Furniture, Meals, and Clothing. — Judged by our modern standards, the Roman houses seem to have been scantily furnished. Carpets were unknown. The floors of the wealthy were covered with elaborate mosaic designs. The chief articles of furniture were beds, couches, cabinets, tables, chairs, and candela′bra or lamp-stands. They were made of choice wood, or of marble and bronze and were often of elegant designs. The splendid silver service found in some of the ruins show how magnificent was the plate used by many of the wealthy Romans. Common lamps were made of clay; the superior ones were of bronze and of fine workmanship.

ROMAN LAMPS

The custom of reclining at the evening meal, the Romans introduced from the Greeks, who adopted it from the Orientals. In the earliest times neither the Greeks nor the Romans reclined on couches, but sat on stools at their meals. In later times they reclined only at supper; there was no formality at other meals. Gener-ally the couches were arranged around the sides of a square or round table, an open side being left to the servants for passing the food. The guests re-clined on the left

DINING COUCHES (From a Pompeian fresco)

elbow, which rested on a cushion. In the elaborate preparation of their foods the rich Romans of the empire showed great fondness for display. Not satisfied with the simple meals of their ancestors, they vied with one another in obtaining the rarest delicacies from Italy and other lands. Fortunes were spent upon single feasts; and gluttony was reduced to what was supposed to be a fine art.

In very ancient times the Romans wore but a single garment, the tunic, made of wool. Afterward, the men adopted the *toga*, a loose garment thrown in ample folds about the person; and the women began to wear the *stola*, patterned after the Greek robe, together with the *palla*, or shawl, large enough to cover the whole figure. During the later republic and under the empire, the dress of the Romans became more expensive, being made of the richer materials of linen and silk imported from the East, and more elaborately trimmed; and a growing taste for expensive jewelry and other personal ornaments was developed among the Roman women.

Social Life and Amusements. — The social enjoyment of the Romans was in some respects like that of the Greeks, being found chiefly outside of the home. The Forum was to Rome

THE CIRCUS MAXIMUS (Restoration)

what the Agora was to Athens, a center of public and social life. But the ordinary Roman had not the Greek taste for intellectual companionship; he sought his chief recreation in the baths and in the crowds of the circus and the amphitheater.

(1) In their baths the Romans of the empire showed their growing appreciation of the luxuries of life. The private baths of the dwelling house no longer satisfied their needs. Public baths on an enormous scale were built by the emperors. These contained a large number of rooms, supported by columns of granite or marble, paved with mosaic, and adorned with works of art. They included not only bathing rooms, but gymnasia for exercising, gardens for lounging, galleries of statues and paintings, libraries for reading, and halls for conversation. The baths became centers of social life, where the rich and the poor, the emperor and the slave, met together — showing the democratic spirit of the life under the empire.

(2) The circus afforded a greater attraction for the people in general. The most important circus of Rome was the Circus Maximus. It was an inclosure about two thousand feet long and six hundred feet wide. Within it were arranged seats for different classes of citizens, a separate box being reserved for the imperial family. The games consisted chiefly of chariot races. The excitement was due to the reckless driving of the charioteers, each striving to win by upsetting his competitors. There were also athletic sports; running, leaping, boxing, wrestling, throwing the quoit, and hurling the javelin. Sometimes sham battles and sea fights took place.

(3) The Romans did not care so much for the theater; there were only three principal structures of this kind at Rome (p. 514). The theater was derived from the Greeks and was built in the form of a semicircle, the seats being apportioned, as in the circus, to different classes of persons. The shows consisted largely of coarse plays, mimes (p. 450), and dancing.

(4) The most popular and characteristic amusements of the Romans were the sports of the amphitheater. This building was in the form of a double theater, forming an entire circle or ellipse. Such structures were built in different cities of the empire, but none equaled the Colosseum, — the enormous am-

RUINS OF THE COLOSSEUM, OR FLAVIAN AMPHITHEATER

phitheater built by Vespasian (p. 475). The sports of the amphitheater were chiefly gladiatorial shows, the combats of wild
beasts, and sometimes sea-fights. On the occasion of the ded-
ication of the Colosseum by Titus, it is said there was a combat of gladiators, in which women took part, and five thousand
animals were slain. The arena was then filled with water and
a sea-fight took place, representing a battle in Greece, recorded
by the historian Thucydides.

The amusements of the Romans were largely sensational and
appealed to the brutal taste of the populace. Their influence
was almost always bad, and tended to degrade the morals of
the people.

Marriage and the Position of Women. — The marriage
customs comprised two ceremonies. There was first the
ceremony of betrothal, which included the consent of the bride's
father, and the announcement of the engagement in the form
of a festival, or the presentation of the betrothal ring. There
was, in the second place, the wedding ceremony. In the time
of the republic this might be a *religious* ceremony in which a
consecrated cake was eaten in the presence of the priest; or a
secular ceremony in which the father gave away his daughter
by the forms of a legal sale. In these cases, the bride passed
from the power of her father to that of her husband. In the
time of the empire it was customary for persons to be married
without these ceremonies, by their simple consent. In this
case, the bride remained under the power of her own father.

This custom tended to weaken the sacredness of the marriage
tie and of family life. As marriage was based on simple consent, divorce became easy and frequent. We are told that
there were women in Rome who counted their ages not by the
consuls, but by the number of their husbands. After marriage
the greatest liberty was allowed to the wife. Not being bound
to her husband by any legal tie, she was her own mistress. She
could go where she pleased, to public festivals, to the circus or
the amphitheater. In short she was subject to no restraint

except such as her own conscience might dictate. Under such conditions marriage became unpopular, and society became corrupt. But we should remember that, while these conditions may have prevailed among the upper classes and in the larger towns, the great mass of Roman women lived the simple, upright life of honorable wives.

Funeral Ceremonies. — The funeral customs of the Romans show the great respect which was paid to the dead. The nearest relative received the last breath of the dying person; and his hand closed the eyes and the mouth of the deceased. The body was prepared for burial by being anointed, clothed in garments suited to the rank of the deceased, and then placed upon a bier in the *atrium*, where the images of his ancestors were exhibited and where the body remained until the time for burial. A branch of cypress was hung at the door as a symbol of death. The funeral procession moved from the house, preceded by musicians and women hired to utter lamentations and to sing the funeral dirge. Then came those who impersonated the ancestors of the deceased, followed by the family and near relatives dressed in black; and then the bier carried on the shoulders of the bearers; and lastly the long train of mourning friends. If the deceased had been a person of high rank, the procession moved to the Forum, where a funeral oration was pronounced; and then continued its way to the place of burial, beyond the city walls.

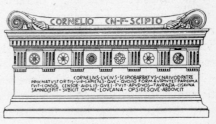

Tomb of Cornelius Scipio

In case the body was burned, the ashes were mingled with wine, milk, and costly perfumes, and placed in the family tomb. The tombs and monuments erected for the dead were often costly and imposing (p. 492). The greatest funeral ceremony among the Romans was the deification of the emperors, which took place on the Campus Martius. The image of the deceased emperor was burned upon a lofty funeral pile; an eagle was let loose bearing the soul to heaven, and to the name of the emperor was thereafter attached the title " the Divine."

TEMPLE OF JUPITER CAPITOLINUS (Restoration)

III. ART AND INTELLECTUAL LIFE

Roman Architecture. — It was during the period of the five good emperors, especially under Trajan and Hadrian, that the architecture of Rome reached its highest development. Roman architecture was still modeled, in certain respects, after that of the Greeks. But the Romans surpassed the Greeks in constructing buildings of massive strength and imposing dignity. By their splendid works they have taken rank among the world's greatest builders. We have already noticed the progress made in the age of Augustus. This progress was continued by his successors, and by the time of Hadrian Rome had become a city of magnificent public buildings. The architectural center of the city was the Roman Forum, with the additional Forums of Julius, Augustus, Vespasian, Nerva, and Trajan (see map, p. 514). Here were the buildings in which the gods were worshiped, the laws were enacted, and justice was administered. The most conspicuous buildings which would attract the eyes of one standing in the Forum were the splendid temples of Jupiter and Juno upon the Capitoline hill. Although it is true that the Romans obtained their chief ideas of architectural beauty from the Greeks, it is a question whether Athens, even in the time of Pericles, could have presented such a scene of imposing grandeur as did Rome in the time of Trajan and Hadrian, with its forums, temples, aqueducts, basilicas, palaces, porticoes, amphitheaters, theaters, circuses, baths, columns, triumphal arches, and tombs.

The Literature of the Early Empire. — The influence of the early emperors upon the intellectual life of Rome may be seen in the literature. The literary period which followed the brilliant age of Augustus has sometimes been called the " Silver Age." The despotic rule of the Julian emperors was not favorable to letters. Two names of that period, however, stand out with some prominence, those of Seneca and Lucan. Seneca was a distinguished Stoic philosopher who wrote instructive essays upon moral subjects; Lucan wrote a lengthy epic poem describing the civil war between Pompey and Cæsar. Under the patronage of the Flavian emperors there was a literary revival, marked by at least two distinguished writers, Pliny the Elder and Quintilian. Pliny, the most learned man of the day, wrote an extensive work on Natural History; while Quintilian, a native of Spain, was the author of an exhaustive treatise on Oratory. The revival which began under the Flavians culminated in the more vigorous literature of the time of the good emperors. Among the authors of that time were Pliny the Younger, the writer of epistles, and Suetonius, the biographer of the "Twelve Cæsars." But the two most distinguished Roman authors of the Flavian period were Tacitus, perhaps the greatest of Roman historians, and Ju'-venal, the greatest of Roman satirists. Juvenal thus reflects on the "approach of age":

> "Swift down the pathway of declining years,
> As on we journey through this vale of tears,
> Youth wastes away, and withers like a flower,
> The lovely phantom of a fleeting hour.
> 'Mid the light sallies of the joyous soul,
> The smile of beauty, and the social bowl,
> Inaudible, the foot of chilly age
> Steals on our joys, and drives us from the stage."

Roman Philosophy. — As the Romans were essentially a practical people, they had little taste for pure philosophy. They adopted, however, some of the philosophical systems of the Greeks, and paid special attention to the practical or moral side of these systems. Their philosophy was largely the philosophy of life. The two systems which were most popular with them were Epicureanism and Stoicism. The Epicureans believed that happiness was the great end of life. But the high idea of happiness advocated by the Greek philosophers became degraded into the selfish idea of pleasure, which could easily excuse almost any form of indulgence. In Rome we see this idea of life exercising its influence especially upon the wealthy and indolent classes. The Stoics, on the other hand, believed that the end of life is to live according to the highest law of our nature. This doctrine tended to make strong and upright characters. It could not well have a degrading influence; so we find some of the noblest men of Rome adhering to its tenets — such men as Cato, Cicero, Seneca, and Marcus Aurelius. But the study of philosophy was restricted mainly to the educated classes, and had little influence upon the common people. The lower classes still retained their old religious notions, or else were gradually accepting the new teachings of Christianity.

Books and Libraries. — We should no doubt be greatly surprised in going into a Roman library. Instead of seeing many rows of volumes arranged upon shelves, we should see a large number of cabinets, or cupboards, containing circular cases which contained rolls of papyrus or parchment. The librarian would tell us that the papyrus was imported from Egypt, and was made from papyrus plant which grew eight or ten feet high; that the stem of this plant was made up of very thin layers, which could be peeled off and pasted together in the form of sheets. These sheets were written on, as we write, in lines from left to right. In writing, the Romans used a reed, sharpened and split like a pen, and dipped in some kind of coloring matter which served for ink. The sheets were written in columns, so that when the sheets were pasted together in a long roll, they needed to be only partly unrolled to read a single column. The whole roll was a book, or more properly a volume (*volumen*), which means something " rolled up."

READING A VOLUME

There were a number of public libraries at Rome. Julius Cæsar projected such a library, and commissioned Varro to take charge of it; but the scheme was prevented by the death of Cæsar. Augustus founded a Greek and Latin library and placed it in a temple of Apollo on the Palatine hill. The most famous public library of Rome was the Ulpian library, founded by Trajan, and so called from one of his own names, Ulpius. It came to be the fashion for those who wished to appear learned to collect libraries, although they may never have read the titles of the books. Seneca condemns the rage for mere book-collecting and ridicules those who were more pleased with the outside than the inside. There is one person mentioned, a physician, who collected a library of sixty-two thousand volumes. But the number of volumes contained in the ordinary private library rarely exceeded one or two thousand.

IV. THE BEGINNINGS OF CHRISTIANITY

Preparation for Christianity in the Empire. — It was during the early empire that Christianity made its appearance in the world. It was under the first emperor, Augustus, that Jesus was born in Bethlehem, a small town in Judea, and spent his early life in Nazareth, a town in Galilee. It was under the second emperor, Tiberius, that Christ was crucified at Jerusalem, at the hands of Pontius Pilate, the governor of Judea.

There were many things in the Roman Empire at this time which seemed to pave the way for the coming of Christianity. In the first place, there was the world-wide dominion of the empire itself. The empire now took in practically the whole civilized world. It extended from the Rhine and Danube rivers on the north to the cataracts of the Nile and the African desert on the south, from the Atlantic Ocean on the west to the Euphrates River on the east. The bringing together of such a large part of the human race into one single society, bound together by a common feeling of loyalty, and breaking down local prejudices, would prepare the way for a religion which professed to be universal and intended for all mankind. In the next place, the world was now enjoying a reign of peace. The wars that had distracted the republic for a hundred years were now practically over. Men were reconciled to one another, and seemed ready to accept the doctrine of universal brotherhood. Again, the Roman law tended to unify the empire. All men were beginning to be governed by common principles of justice, and to recognize a common standard of right. This would prepare them to recognize the common law of righteousness laid down by the Founder of Christianity. Again, the empire had easy means of communication for travel. The

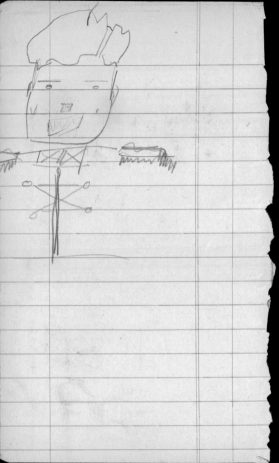

Roman roads connected all the various provinces with one another. Over these roads the early missionaries traveled, carrying the new doctrine into every part of the Roman world. Moreover, the old pagan religion was dying out. Men were losing faith in the old gods of Greece and Rome; and the corrupt religions that were coming in from the Orient were despised by many as having a pernicious influence upon the life of the people. Nearly all intelligent persons of the upper classes were seeking for a refuge in some kind of philosophy which was more inspiring and uplifting than the pagan religion; and the lower classes were longing for a religion which would give them some consolation in the present life, and some hope for the life to come.

Spread of Christianity. — But the spread of Christianity was not due simply to the external conditions which we have noticed. It was due chiefly to the nature of the religion itself, and the appeal that it made to the hearts and consciences of men. It is difficult to explain the early progress made by Christianity in the Roman world, except on the theory that it possessed within itself a vital power capable of overcoming all human opposition. Its beginnings were small and unnoticed by the Roman writers. Jesus himself was a native of Judea, and his early converts were among the Jews. At his death, his followers comprised only a small community in and near the city of Jerusalem. From this beginning new converts were gained among the Jews of other cities. It was in the city of Antioch that they were first called " Christians."

It was at first supposed by the early converts that the new religion was intended only for the Jews. But Saint Peter, the recognized leader of the Twelve Apostles, was persuaded by a vision that the new religion was not for Jews only. It was through his efforts that a Roman centurion was converted — the first Gentile admitted into the church. The work of Peter extended beyond the boundaries of Palestine; and he is believed to have founded the church at Rome. At the same time there appeared

another remarkable man who announced that Christianity
was not a religion intended simply for the Jews, but for the
Gentiles as well; that it was a religion of humanity and intended for all men. This man was the Apostle Paul. He was
a highly educated man, and was well fitted to preach the new
doctrine to other peoples. Setting out from Antioch, he made
missionary tours throughout the eastern provinces, in Asia
Minor, in Thrace, in Macedonia, in Greece, and then even
as far west as Rome. Christian churches sprang up in all
these districts. The new converts were generally from the
lower classes of the people in the cities. For thirty years
Saint Paul labored in preaching Christianity throughout the
Roman empire. When we consider the character and extent
of his work, we must regard him as one of the great men of the
world. After the death of Paul the new religion continued
to spread throughout the provinces of the empire; so that at
the time of Marcus Aurelius, a considerable part of the Roman
world was Christian.

**Attitude of the People and the Government toward the Early
Christians.** — The Christians were for some time regarded
simply as a sect of the Jews. The Roman government professed to be tolerant of all religions, and to permit every one
to worship as he saw fit. As long as the Christians were supposed to be Jews they were not especially molested. They
simply suffered from the ill feeling which the Romans had for
all Jews. But in the process of time the Christians came to
be hated and despised for other reasons. They nearly all, at
first, came from the lower classes, — the tradesmen, the freedmen, the slaves. Being devoted to their religion, they refused
to engage in some of the practices that were commonly followed
by the Romans. They disapproved of the Roman amusements,
the gladiatorial shows, the races in the circus, the plays and
dances in the theaters. They were hence regarded as unsocial,
and "haters of mankind." Their churches were looked upon
as secret societies, which were contrary to the law. They

refused to worship the emperor and the Roman gods, and were charged with disloyalty and impiety and even with atheism.

For these reasons they were despised by many of the Roman people. They were hated and frequently made the subjects of mob violence. Such disturbances were brought to the attention of the provincial governors, and the Christians were often held responsible for the riots that occurred. But it was not until the time of Trajan that the emperor felt called upon to announce some policy with reference to the treatment of the Christians. We have a letter written by Pliny — the governor of Bithynia, a province in Asia Minor — to the emperor Trajan, asking for instructions as to how the Christians should be treated. The emperor replied that they should not be hunted down, and that no attention should be paid to anonymous charges against them; that those only should be punished who openly refused to pay an act of worship to the Roman gods. The immediate successors of Trajan were favorably disposed toward Christianity. Hadrian prohibited all mob violence toward the Christians. The mild Antoninus called upon the people to imitate the piety of the Christians rather than to charge them with atheism. This seems to show that the early prejudice against Christianity was due not so much to the unfriendly attitude of the government as to the malicious hostility of the people.

The Early Persecutions of the Christians. — It is sometimes said that the worst persecutions took place under the best emperors. This is far from true. During the first century there were only two persecutions. They took place under Nero and Domitian, the two worst emperors of this whole period. The tortures inflicted upon the Christians by Nero were quite in harmony with the bloodthirsty character of this prince of despots. They were prompted by no idea of state policy. They were simply the hideous acts of a depraved being who recognized no obligations to God or man. It is said that Peter and Paul were put to death by Nero. Domitian was likewise a tyrant, but of a different type. He professed a desire to reform the Roman religion, and executed those who opposed his so-called reform. He buried alive a vestal virgin on the charge of infidelity. He put to death a consul and banished his own wife on the charge of atheism — that is, of refusing to worship the gods of Rome. He persecuted the Jews as well as the Christians. It may be said to his credit that near the close of his reign he called certain Christians to him, and asked them as to the nature of Christ's kingdom. On being told it was not an earthly, but a spiritual, kingdom, he appeared satisfied and put a stop to the persecutions (Euse'bius, Bk. III., Ch. 20).

These two persecutions, of Nero and Domitian, were confined chiefly to the city of Rome. During the second century there were also two persecutions — those under Trajan and Marcus Aurelius. That under Trajan resulted from the intense popular hatred toward the Christians in Asia Minor. But it is said that when he sent his instructions to Pliny, to the effect that the Christians should not be sought out and no credit should be given to anonymous charges, the number of executions was greatly lessened. The most bitter persecution of the second century occurred during the reign of Marcus Aurelius. It is difficult for us to understand how a prince so wise could have adopted so cruel a policy. The emperor evidently was entirely mistaken as to the real character of the Christians, and misled as to the duty he owed to the state. Executions took place in different cities of the empire, but chiefly in that hotbed of popular hatred, Asia Minor. The most noted and noble victim of these persecutions was Polycarp, the aged bishop of Smyrna. When asked to blaspheme the name of Christ, he answered, " Eighty and six years have I served Him; and He never did me wrong. How can I now blaspheme the name of Him who has saved me? " It was at this time that the historian Eusebius says, " The blood of the martyrs became the seed of the Church."

Selections for Reading

Knowlton, Topic A 27, "Roman Life"; Topic A 28, "Roman Thought" (1).[1]

Seignobos, Ch. 25, "Arts and Sciences"; Ch. 26, "The Christian Religion" (1).

Bury, Roman Empire, Ch. 30, "The Roman World under the Empire"; Ch. 31, "Roman Life and Manners"; pp. 366–373 (the destruction of Jerusalem); ·pp. 438–448 (correspondence between Trajan and Pliny the Younger) (18).

Capes, Early Empire, Ch. 14, "Life in the Provinces"; Ch. 15, "State of Trade" (18).

—— Antonines, Ch. 6, "Attitude of the Imperial Government toward Christians"; Ch. 9, "Administrative Forms of the Imperial Government" (18).

Thomas, Ch. 1, "At Pompeii"; pp. 28–41 (the *graffiti*); Ch. 4, "The Baths and the Games"; Ch. 5 (gifts, peculiar customs of the Romans); Ch. 8, "Country Life"; pp. 190–200 (country houses); Ch. 9, "Schools and Books"; Ch. 14, "A Typical Roman of the Empire, Pliny the Younger" (19).

Mau, Ch. 32, "The Pompeian House"; Ch. 56, "The *Graffiti*" (20).

Preston and Dodge, II., "The House and Every Day Life"; IV., "Food and Clothing" (19).

Inge, Ch. 6, "Grades of Society"; Ch. 9, "Amusements"; Ch. 10, "Luxury" (19).

Merivale, Empire, Vol. IV., Ch. 39, "Unity of the Empire"; Ch. 41, "Life in Rome"; Vol. VII., pp. 58–62 (the eruption of Vesuvius) (18).

Boissier, Rome and Pompeii, Ch. 1, "The Forums"; Ch. 3, "The Catacombs"; Ch. 4, "Hadrian's Villa" (at Tivoli) (20).

Lanciani, Ruins and Excavations, pp. 310–319 (the Forum of Trajan) (20).

Middleton, Vol. I., pp. 343–345 (the arch of Septimius Severus); Vol. II., Ch. 12, "Walls of Aurelianus" (20).

Munro, Source Book, Part XI., "Roman Life and Society" (25).

Tacitus, Annals, Bk. XV., Chs. 38–43 (the burning of Rome); Ch. 44 (persecution of the Christians under Nero) (25).

Suetonius, The Twelve Cæsars (26).

Special Study

ROMAN AMUSEMENTS IN THE EMPIRE. — Guhl and Koner, pp. 553–567 (19); Thomas, Ch. 4 (19); Inge, Ch. 9 (19); Johnston, Ch. 9 (19); Tucker, Ch. 15 (19); Sandys, pp. 503–521 (19).

[1] The figure in parenthesis refers to the number of the topic in the Appendix, where a fuller title of the book will be found.

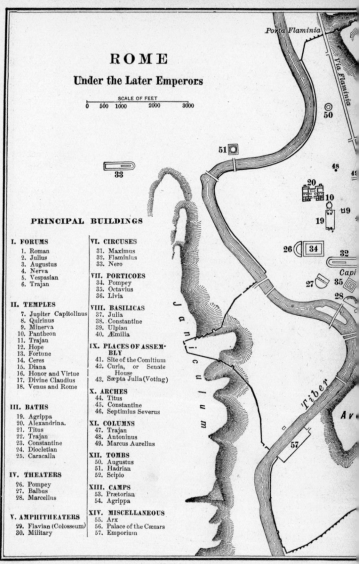

ROME
Under the Later Emperors

SCALE OF FEET
0   500   1000   2000   3000

PRINCIPAL BUILDINGS

I. FORUMS
1. Roman
2. Julius
3. Augustus
4. Nerva
5. Vespasian
6. Trajan

II. TEMPLES
7. Jupiter Capitolinus
8. Quirinus
9. Minerva
10. Pantheon
11. Trajan
12. Hope
13. Fortune
14. Ceres
15. Diana
16. Honor and Virtue
17. Divine Claudius
18. Venus and Rome

III. BATHS
19. Agrippa
20. Alexandrina.
21. Titus
22. Trajan
23. Constantine
24. Diocletian
25. Caracalla

IV. THEATERS
26. Pompey
27. Balbus
28. Marcellus

V. AMPHITHEATERS
29. Flavian (Colosseum)
30. Military

VI. CIRCUSES
31. Maximus
32. Flaminius
33. Nero

VII. PORTICOES
34. Pompey
35. Octavius
36. Livia

VIII. BASILICAS
37. Julia
38. Constantine
39. Ulpian
40. Æmilia

IX. PLACES OF ASSEMBLY
41. Site of the Comitium
42. Curia, or Senate House
43. Sæpta Julia (Voting)

X. ARCHES
44. Titus
45. Constantine
46. Septimius Severus

XI. COLUMNS
47. Trajan
48. Antoninus
49. Marcus Aurelius

XII. TOMBS
50. Augustus
51. Hadrian
52. Scipio

XIII. CAMPS
53. Prætorian
54. Agrippa

XIV. MISCELLANEOUS
55. Arx
56. Palace of the Cæsars
57. Emporium

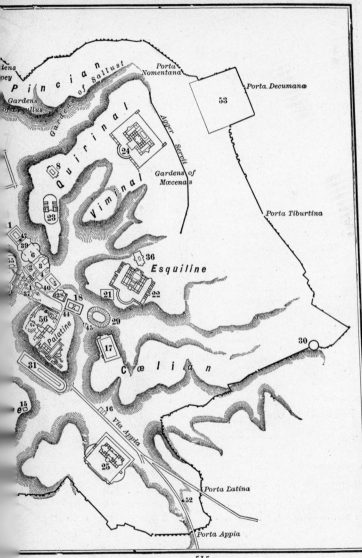

Gardens Pincian
pey

Gardens
of Lucullus

Porta
Nomentana

Porta Decumana

Gardens of Sallust

53

Aggrer Servii

Quirinal

24

8

Gardens of
Mæcenas

23

Viminal

Porta Tiburtina

1

47
39

36

6

55

3

Esquiline

4
5

37
40

21   22

33

18

56   44

45   29

Palatine

17

31

Cœlian

30

15

16

Via Appia

25

Porta Latina

52

Porta Appia

515

CHAPTER XXXI

THE DECLINE AND REORGANIZATION OF THE EMPIRE

Synopsis

I. DECLINE OF THE EARLY EMPIRE (180–284 A.D.). — The Soldier Emperors. — Edict of Caracalla. — Elagabalus and Alexander Severus. — Foreign Dangers of the Empire. — First Invasion of the Goths. — Partial Recovery of the Empire.

II. THE LATER EMPIRE OF DIOCLETIAN (284–305 A.D.). — The New Imperialism. — Diocletian and his Policy. — The "Augusti" and "Cæsars." — The Last Persecution of the Christians. — Effects of Diocletian's Policy.

III. CONSTANTINE AND HIS SUCCESSORS (312–395 A.D.). — Accession and Policy of Constantine. — Conversion of Constantine. — Adoption of Christianity. — The New Provincial System. — The New Military Organization. — The New Capital, Constantinople. — The New Court Organization. — Effect of Constantine's Reforms. — Attempt to Restore Paganism. — Irruption of the Huns and Revolt of the Goths. — Theodosius I. and the Final Division of the Empire.

IV. THE PEOPLE UNDER THE LATER EMPIRE. — Classes of Society. — The Silent Invasions: the Coloni. — Degradation of the Peasantry. — Decay of the Population. — Burdens of Taxation. — Social Effects of Christianity.

I. DECLINE OF THE EARLY EMPIRE (180–284 A.D.)

The Soldier Emperors. — On his deathbed Marcus Aurelius recommended to the senate the appointment of his son, Com'-modus, as emperor (180 A.D.). The appointment was made, but this young prince proved a disgrace to the throne. He claimed the title of Hercules, and had a passion for the sports of the amphitheater. He himself took a part in these sports. It is said that he fought as a gladiator seven hundred and fifty times. After a disreputable reign of thirteen years he was assassinated by one of his own household, assisted by the prefect of the prætorian guard. The prætorians then chose as his successor a distinguished senator by the name of Per'tinax, but within three months they slew him and carried his head in triumph to their camp. They then offered the empire for sale at public auction to the highest bidder. This proved to be an ambitious senator named Julia'nus. But no sooner had he taken possession of the palace than the armies on the frontier put in their claims to appoint an emperor.

Commodus as Hercules

Septimius Seve'rus, an able general, happened to be in command of the army nearest Italy. He was accordingly the first to enter Rome, two months after the accession of Julianus. He put Julianus to death, and had himself proclaimed emperor. His chief act was to disband the old prætorian guard which had opposed him, and to organize a new body of prætorians, made up of forty thousand men from his own soldiers. This was intended to give a stronger support to the government. But, in fact, it gave to the army a stronger influence in the appointment of the emperor. From this time the soldiers came to be the real sovereigns of the empire. Hence, this whole period (down to 284 A.D.) has been aptly called the "period of military despotism." It was a time when the emperors were set up and cut down at the whim of the army. During a period of one hundred and four years, the imperial title was held by twenty-nine different rulers, some of them retaining their places for only a few months.

Edict of Caracalla (212 A.D.). — One event that occurred early in this period is especially worthy of notice. The Roman franchise, which had been gradually extended by the previous emperors, was now conferred upon all the free inhabitants of the Roman world. This important act was done by Caracalla, whose motive, however, was not above reproach. The edict

was issued to increase the revenue by extending the inheritance tax, which rested only upon citizens. Notwithstanding the questionable motive of the emperor, this was in the line of earlier reforms. It effaced the last distinction between Romans and provincials. The name of Caracalla, however, is infamous for his cruel proscriptions, and especially for his murder of Papinian, one of the greatest of the Roman jurists, who refused to defend his crimes. He was himself murdered by one of his own soldiers.

CARACALLA

Elagabalus and Alexander Severus. — We need not dwell upon the different reigns of this dreary period. But we should notice two princes, who represent the most extreme types of the Roman character. The one was Elagab'alus (218–222 A.D.), the most repulsive of the emperors; he took his name from the sun god worshiped in the East, became a devotee of the grossest superstitions and a monster of wickedness, and finally was put to death by the prætorians. The other ruler was Alexander Severus (222–235 A.D.), a prince of the purest and most blameless

ALEXANDER SEVERUS

life. He loved the true and the good at all times. It is said that he set up in his private chapel the images of those whom he regarded as the greatest teachers of mankind, including Abraham and Jesus Christ. He selected as his advisers the famous jurists, Ulpian and Paullus. The most important event of his reign was the successful resistance made to the Persians, who had just established a new monarchy (that of the Sassan'idæ) on the ruins of the Parthian empire. Like so many other rulers at this time, this upright man came to his death at the hands of the army.

Foreign Dangers of the Empire. — Ever since the time of Augustus it had been the policy of the emperors to maintain the frontiers on the Rhine, the Danube, and the Euphrates. This policy was generally carried out with success until about the middle of the third century, when the outside nations began to break over these boundaries. There were several foreign peoples that were now encroaching upon the Roman territory. On the lower Rhine near the North Sea were a number of barbarous German tribes, united under the general name of Franks. On the upper Rhine were other tribes called Alemanni (all men). Across the Danube and on the northern shores of the Black Sea was the great nation of the Goths, which came to be the terror of Rome. On the east beyond the Euphrates was the new Persian monarchy, which was now laying claim to all the Roman provinces in Asia. Under a succession of emperors whose names are unimportant, the Romans were engaged in wars with these various peoples — not now wars for the sake of conquest and glory as in the time of the republic, but wars of defense and for the sake of existence.

First Invasion of the Goths. — The Goths made their first appearance upon the Roman territory in the middle of the third century (250 A.D.). At this time they invaded Dacia, crossed the Danube, and overran the province of Mœsia. In a great battle in Mœsia perished the brave emperor Decius, a descendant of the Decius Mus who devoted his life in battle in the heroic days of the republic (p. 343). His successor purchased a peace of the Goths by the payment of an annual tribute. It was not many years after this that the same barbarians made a more formidable invasion, this time by way of the Black Sea and the Bosporus. Crossing the sea, they besieged and plundered many cities of Asia Minor. They destroyed the splendid temple of Diana at Ephesus; they crossed the Ægean Sea into Greece, and threatened Italy; and finally retired with their spoils to their homes across the Danube.

Partial Recovery of the Empire (268–284 A.D.). — Under the leadership of certain able rulers, — the so-called Illyrian emperors — the empire recovered somewhat from the disasters of the preceding years. It was at this time that the emperor Aure'lian built a new and more extensive wall about the city of Rome to prevent its possible capture by the barbarians. Aurelian was an able prince and did much to restore the authority of Rome. The most famous person who was now defying the Roman power was Zeno'bia, the beautiful queen of Palmy'ra. She claimed descent from Cleopatra, the Egyptian queen. She had set up an independent kingdom with its capital at Palmyra in Syria (map, p. 483), and professed to rule over Egypt and the eastern Roman provinces. She had adorned her capital city with monuments of art that rivaled those of Rome. But her splendid reign was brought to a close by Aurelian, who destroyed the city of Palmyra and carried the queen as a captive to Rome. After she had graced the triumph of the emperor, bedecked as she was with gold and jewels, Aurelian presented her with an elegant villa, where she was permitted to live in peace and seclusion.

The successful efforts of the Illyrian emperors showed that the empire could still be preserved, if properly organized and administered. The events of the third century made it quite clear that if the empire was to continue, and the provinces were to be held together, there must be some radical change in the imperial government. The decline of the early empire thus paved the way for a new form of imperialism.

II. The Later Empire of Diocletian (284–305 A.D.)

The New Imperialism. — It has been said that the early empire of Augustus and his successors was an absolute monarchy *disguised* by republican forms. This is in general quite true. But the old republican forms had for a long time been losing their hold, and at the time of Diocle'tian they were ready to be thrown away entirely. By the reforms of Diocletian and Con'stantine there was established a new form of imperialism — an absolute monarchy *divested* of republican forms. Some of their ideas of reform no doubt came from the new Persian monarchy, which was now the greatest rival of Rome. In this powerful monarchy the Romans saw certain elements of strength which they could use in giving new vigor to their own government. By adopting these Oriental ideas, the Roman empire may be said to have become Orientalized.

Diocletian and his Policy. — The first step in the direction of the new imperialism was made by Diocletian. Born of an obscure family in Dalmatia (part of Illyricum), he had risen by his own efforts to the high position of commander of the

DIOCLETIAN

Roman army in the East. It was here that he was proclaimed emperor by his soldiers. He overcame all opposition, assumed the imperial power, and made his residence not at Rome, but in Nicomedia, a town in Asia Minor. His whole policy was to give dignity and strength to the imperial authority. He made of himself an Oriental monarch. He assumed the diadem of the East. He wore gorgeous robes of silk and gold such as were worn by Eastern rulers. He compelled his subjects to salute him with low prostrations, and to treat him not as a citizen, but as a superior being. In this way he hoped to make the imperial office respected by the people and the army. The emperor was to be the sole source of power, and as such was to be venerated and obeyed.

The " Augusti " and " Cæsars." — Diocletian saw that it was difficult for one man alone to manage all the affairs of a great empire. It was sufficient for one man to rule over the East, and to repel the Persians. It needed another to take care of the West and to drive back the German invaders. He therefore associated with him his trusted friend and companion in arms, Maximian. But he was soon convinced that even this division of power was not sufficient. To each of the chief rulers, who received the title of *Augustus*, he assigned an assistant, who received the title of *Cæsar*. The two Cæsars were Gale'rius and Constan'tius; and they were to be regarded as the sons and successors of the chief rulers, the Augusti. Each Cæsar was to recognize the authority of his chief; and all were to be subject to the supreme authority of Diocletian himself. The Roman world was divided among the four rulers as follows:

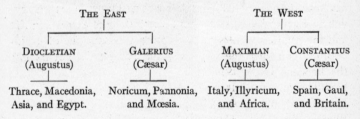

THE EAST		THE WEST	
DIOCLETIAN	GALERIUS	MAXIMIAN	CONSTANTIUS
(Augustus)	(Cæsar)	(Augustus)	(Cæsar)
Thrace, Macedonia, Asia, and Egypt.	Noricum, Pannonia, and Mœsia.	Italy, Illyricum, and Africa.	Spain, Gaul, and Britain.

The Last Persecution of the Christians. — In the latter part of his reign Diocletian was induced to issue an edict of persecution against the Christians. It is said that he was led to perform this infamous act by his assistant Galerius, who had always been hostile to the new religion, and who filled the emperor's mind with stories of seditions and conspiracies. An order was issued that all churches should be demolished, that the sacred Scriptures should be burned, that all Christians should be dismissed from public office, and that those who secretly met for public worship should be punished with death. The persecution raged most fiercely in the provinces subject to Galerius; and it has been suggested that the persecution should be known by his name rather than by the name of Diocletian. Whoever was responsible for this attempt to destroy the Christian religion, it proved a failure. Christianity was strengthened, rather than weakened, by the death of the martyrs.

RUINS OF DIOCLETIAN'S PALACE

Effects of Diocletian's Policy. — The general result of the new policy of Diocletian was to give to the empire a strong and efficient government. The dangers which threatened the state were met with firmness and vigor. A revolt in Egypt was quelled, and the frontiers were successfully defended against the Persians and the barbarians. Public works were constructed, among which were the great Baths of Diocletian at Rome. After a successful reign of twenty-one years Diocletian voluntarily gave up his power (305 A.D.), either on account of ill health, or else to see how his new system would work without his supervision. He retired to his native province of Dalmatia, and spent the rest of his days in his new palace at Salo'na on the shores of the Adriatic. He loved his country home; and when he was asked by his old colleague Maximian to resume the imperial power, he wrote to him, " Were you to come to Salona and see the vegetables which I raise in my garden, with my own hands, you would not talk to me of empire." But before he died Diocletian saw the defects of the system which he had established. Rivalries sprang up among the different rulers, which led to civil war. At one time there were six emperors who were trying to adjust between themselves the government of the empire. Out of this conflict Constantine arose as the man destined to carry on and complete the work of Diocletian.

III. CONSTANTINE AND HIS SUCCESSORS (312-395 A.D.)

Accession and Policy of Constantine. — By a succession of victories Constantine established his authority and became the sole and undisputed ruler of the empire. He was a man of wider views than Diocletian, and had even a greater genius for organization. He in fact gave to Roman imperialism the final form which it preserved as long as the empire existed, and the form in which it exercised its great influence upon modern governments. This fact will enable us to understand the greatness of Constantine as a statesman and a political reformer. His policy was to centralize all power in the hands of the chief ruler; to surround his person with an elaborate court system and an imposing ceremonial; and to make all officers, civil and military, responsible to the head of the empire.

Conversion of Constantine. — Constantine is generally known as the " first Christian emperor." The story of his miraculous conversion is told by his biographer, Eusebius. It is said that while marching against his rival Maxentius, he beheld in the heavens the luminous sign of the cross, inscribed with the words, " By this sign conquer." As a result of this vision, he accepted the Christian religion; he adopted the cross as his battle standard; and from this time he ascribed his victories to God, and not to himself. The truth of this story has been doubted by some historians; but that Constantine looked upon Christianity in an entirely different light from his predecessors, and that he was an avowed friend of the Christian church, cannot be denied. His mother, Hel'ena, was a Christian, and his father, Constantius, had opposed the per-

CONSTANTINE

secutions of Diocletian and Galerius.   He had himself, while he was ruler in the West, issued an edict of toleration to the Christians in his own provinces — the Edict of Milan (313 A.D.).

Adoption of Christianity. — Constantine was therefore prepared, when he became the sole emperor, to reverse the policy of Diocletian and to recognize Christianity as the state religion. The failure of the efforts of Diocletian and his colleague to destroy the new religion was sufficient to convince him that Christianity was already in fact the religion of a large part of the Roman people. How far Constantine himself was a sincere Christian it is not for us to say; but no one can doubt that the adoption of Christianity was an act that showed political wisdom. The recognition of the new religion gave stability to the new government. Constantine, however, in accepting Christianity as the state religion, did not go to the extreme of trying to uproot paganism. He seems to have been far in advance of his age in recognizing "religious liberty." In the Edict of Milan he had said, "Let every man embrace the religion that pleases him, and celebrate its rites freely. In

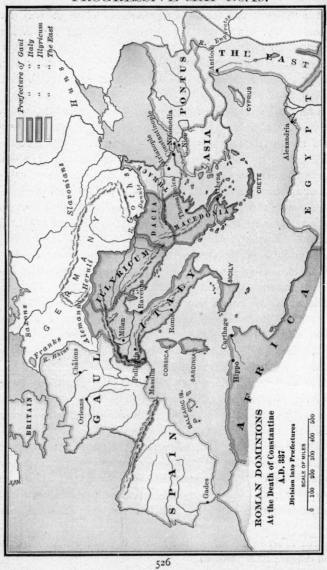

ROMAN DOMINIONS
At the Death of Constantine
A.D. 337
Division into Præfectures

SCALE OF MILES

0   100   200   300   400   500

divine things no one should be forbidden to follow the way that seems to him best." For the purpose of settling the disputes between the different Christian sects, Constantine called (325 A.D.) a general council of the bishops at Nice (*Nicæa*, in Asia Minor), which decided what should be accepted as the Catholic faith.[1]

The New Provincial System. — Another important reform of Constantine was the reorganization of the Roman territory in a most systematic manner. This was based upon Diocletian's division, but was much more complete and thorough. The whole empire was first divided into four great parts, called "prefectures," each under a prætorian prefect subject to the emperor. Each prefecture was then subdivided into dioceses, each under a governor called a vicar, subject to the prætorian prefect. Each diocese was further subdivided into provinces, each under a provincial governor called a consular, president, duke, or count. Each province was made up of cities and towns, under their own municipal governments. The new divisions of the empire may be indicated as follows (p. 526):

(1) The Prefecture of the East — containing the five dioceses of the East, Egypt, Asia, Pontus, and Thrace.

(2) The Prefecture of Illyricum — containing the two dioceses of Dacia and Macedonia.

(3) The Prefecture of Italy — containing the three dioceses of Italy, Illyricum, and Africa.

(4) The Prefecture of Gaul — containing the three dioceses of Spain, Gaul, and Britain.

The New Military Organization. — Scarcely less important than the new provincial system was the new military organization. One of the chief defects of the early empire was the improper position which the army occupied in the state. This defect is seen in two ways. In the first place, the army had

---

[1] This was the doctrine regarding the nature of the Son upheld by Athanasius, as opposed to the doctrine which was held by A'rius and condemned as a heresy, receiving the name of "Arianism."

not been subject to the imperial authority. We have seen how the prætorian guards really became supreme, and brought about that wretched condition of things, a military despotism. In the next place, the military power had not been separated from the civil power. In the early empire, every governor of a province had not only civil authority, but he also had command of an army, so that he could resist the central government if he were so disposed. But Constantine changed all this. He abolished the Roman garrison or prætorian guard. He gave to the territorial governors only a civil authority; the whole army was organized under distinct officers, and made completely subject to the central power of the empire. This change tended to prevent, on the one hand, a military despotism; and, on the other hand, the revolt of local governors.

The military ability of Constantine cannot be questioned. In commemoration of his early victories, the senate erected in the city of Rome a splendid triumphal arch, which stands today as one of the finest specimens of this kind of architecture.

ARCH OF CONSTANTINE

The New Capital, Constantinople. — One very important act of Constantine was to break away from the traditions of the old empire by establishing a new capital. The old city of Rome was filled with the memories of paganism and the relics of the republic. It was the desire of Constantine to give the empire a new center of power, which should be favorably situated for working out his new plans, and also for defending the Roman territory. He selected for this purpose the site of the old Greek colony, Byzantium, on the confines of Europe and Asia. This site was favorable alike for defense, for commerce, and for the maintenance of an Oriental system of government. Constantine laid out the city on an extensive scale, and adorned it with new buildings and works of art. The new capital was called the city of Constantine, or Constantinople.

The New Court Organization. — Constantine believed with Diocletian that one of the defects of the old empire was the fact that the person of the emperor was not sufficiently respected. He therefore not only adopted the diadem and the elaborate robes of the Asiatic monarchs, as Diocletian had done, but reorganized the court on a thoroughly Eastern model. An Oriental court consisted of a large retinue of officials, who surrounded the monarch, paid obeisance to him and served him, and were raised to the rank of nobles by this service. All political authority was exercised through these court officials.

These Oriental features were now adopted by the Roman emperor. The chief officers of the court comprised: (1) the grand chamberlain, who had charge of the imperial palace; (2) the chancellor, who had the supervision of the court officials and received foreign ambassadors; (3) the quæstor, who drew up and issued the imperial edicts; (4) the treasurer-general, who had control of the public revenues; (5) the master of the privy purse, who managed the emperor's private estate; and (6) (7) the two commanders of the cavalry and infantry. The imperial court of Constantine furnished the model of the royal courts of modern times.

Effect of Constantine's Reforms. — If we should take no account of the effects of these reforms upon the financial condition of the empire, we might say that his government was an improvement upon that of Augustus. It gave new strength to the empire, and enabled it to resist foreign invasions. We should also notice the untold advantage that was derived by accepting Christianity as the state religion, and by thus bringing the government into harmony with the religion already adopted by a great part of the Roman people. The empire was preserved for several generations longer in the West, and for more than a thousand years longer in the East. But the expense necessary to maintain such a system, with its elaborate court and its vast number of officials, was great. The taxes were oppressive. The people were burdened and lost their interest in the state. Constantine also, like Augustus, failed to make a proper provision for his successor. At his death his three sons divided the empire between them, and this division gave rise to another period of quarrels and civil strife before the empire was again brought under the sway of a single ruler.

JULIAN

Attempt to Restore Paganism. — The first event of grave importance after the reign of Constantine was the attempt of the Emperor Julian (361–363 A.D.) to restore the old pagan religion, for which attempt he has been called "the Apostate." Julian was in many respects a man of ability and energy. He repelled the Alemanni who had crossed the Rhine, and made a vigorous campaign against the Persians. But he was by conviction a pagan, and in the struggle between Christianity and paganism he took the part of the ancient faith. He tried to undo the work of Constantine by bringing back paganism to its old position. He did not realize that Christianity was the religion of the future, and was presumptuous in his belief that he could accomplish that in which Marcus Aurelius and Diocletian had failed. He may not have expected to uproot the new religion entirely; but he hoped to deprive it of the important privileges which it had already acquired. The religious changes which he was able to effect in his brief reign were reversed by his successor Jovian (363–364 A.D.), and Christianity afterward remained undisturbed as the religion of the empire.

Irruption of the Huns and Revolt of the Goths. — After the death of Jovian the empire was divided for a time between two emperors. It was during this period that a great event occurred which forewarned the empire of its final doom. This event was the irruption of the savage Huns into Europe. Emerging from the steppes of Asia, the Huns pressed upon the Goths living north of the Danube and drove them from their homes into the Roman territory. It was now necessary for the eastern emperor, Valens, either to resist the whole Gothic nation, or else to receive them as friends and give them settlements within the empire. The latter course seemed the wiser, and they were given new homes south of the Danube. But they were soon provoked by the ill-treatment of the Roman officials, and rose in revolt, defeating the Roman army in a battle at Adriano'ple (378 A.D.). They advanced even to the walls of Constantinople; but they were finally reduced to submission through the skill of the new emperor Theodo'sius I.

Theodosius I. and the Final Division of the Empire (379–395 A.D.). — Theodosius I. was a man of great vigor and military ability. He continued the policy of admitting the barbarians into the empire, but converted them into useful and loyal subjects. From their number he reënforced the ranks of the imperial armies, and jealously guarded them from injustice.

When a garrison of Gothic soldiers was once mobbed by the Roman people in Thessaloni′ca, he resorted to a punishment as revengeful as that of Marius and as cruel as that of Sulla. He gathered the people of this city into the circus to the number of seven thousand, and caused them to be massacred by a body of Gothic soldiers. For this inhuman act he was compelled to do penance by St. Ambrose, the bishop of Milan — which fact shows how powerful the Church had become at this time, to compel an emperor to obey its mandates. Theodosius was himself an ardent and Catholic Christian, and went so far as to be intolerant of the pagan religion, and even of the Christian heretics. In spite of his shortcomings he was an able monarch, and has received the name of " Theodosius the Great." He conquered his rivals and reunited for a brief time the whole Roman world under a single ruler. But at his death (395 A.D.), he divided the empire between his two sons, Arca′dius and Hono′rius, the former receiving the East, and the latter the West.

THEODOSIUS

(Statue at Barletta, Italy)

The death of Theodosius marks an important epoch, not only in the history of the Roman empire but in the history of European civilization. From this time the two parts of the empire — the East and the West — became more and more separated from each other, until they became at last two distinct worlds, having different destinies. The eastern part maintained itself for about a thousand years with its capital at Constantinople, until it was finally conquered by the Turks (1453 A.D.). The western part was soon overrun and conquered by the German invaders, who brought with them new blood and new ideas, and furnished the elements of a new civilization.

IV. The People under the Later Empire

Classes of Society. — If we should look over the different classes into which the Roman people were now divided we should find that certain changes had taken place since we last took account of them under the early empire (p. 487). At the top of the social scale we should, of course, still find the emperor and the royal family. But we should see that the emperor was an entirely different kind of person from what he was at the time of Augustus and Hadrian. Instead of seeing a simple, unpretentious officer of the state, we should see a man enthroned in all the dignity and majesty of an Oriental king, crowned with a diadem of jewels, clothed in purple robes, and surrounded by a magnificent court.

Below the emperor we should find a new aristocracy, — no longer a senatorial or equestrian aristocracy as of old, — but an imperial aristocracy, which derived its rank from its official relations to the emperor. Its members were dignified with the class-titles of the *Illustrious*, the *Respectable*, and the *Honorable*. The first class, the Illustrious, included the ministers of the palace, the prefects of the four great prefectures, the masters-general of the cavalry and infantry, who received their orders directly from the emperor. The other classes, the Respectables and the Honorables, included the various governors of the dioceses and provinces, who were thus bound to the emperor by being dignified with an aristocratic rank.

Below this imperial aristocracy was what we may call the middle classes, including the lawyers, the physicians, the large landed proprietors, the traders, and the artisans. The artisans were still organized in guilds, which were under strict supervision, being licensed by the government.

Below these was the peasantry, or the agricultural classes, including the small land owners and the free laborers. In these agricultural classes we might include also the slave population, who were gradually being lifted up to the condition of serfs, that is, persons bound to the soil, not capable of being bought and sold off from the estate where they lived.

The Silent Invasions: the Coloni. — The people within the limits of the empire were now beginning to include other persons than the native Roman population. These foreign persons were, in fact, beginning to form a considerable part of the people subject to the Roman authority. The continual pressure of the outside peoples — especially the Goths on the north — led the emperors to adopt a conciliatory policy, and to grant to these barbarians peaceful settlements within the provinces. Sometimes whole tribes had been allowed to settle upon lands assigned to them. Not only the Roman territory, but the army and offices of the state were open to Germans who were willing to serve the emperor. The most able of the barbarian chiefs were even made generals in the Roman army. This gradual introduction of a barbarian population is sometimes called the " silent invasions."

This subject population was treated in a manner quite different from that which the Romans had been accustomed to adopt in the case of a conquered people. Instead of being sold as slaves, like captives in war, they were given over to large landed proprietors, and attached to the estates as permanent tenants. This class of persons were called *colo'ni*, and were really serfs attached to the soil.

Degradation of the Peasantry. — The degradation of the free agricultural class was one of the deplorable facts connected with the later empire. The ruin of this class of persons was due, in part, to the fact that they were obliged to compete with slave labor. But the truth is that the condition of the slaves was considerably improved during the later period. They were better protected by the law, and they obtained their freedom

more easily than before. But even when freed they were obliged
to obtain their living by settling upon the estates of the great
landlords, who granted them a little plot of ground on condition
of manual labor or a certain amount of produce. Here they
lived from one generation to another; and by being attached
to the soil they became serfs, or *coloni*, like many of the barbarian immigrants. This movement was no doubt beneficial
to the slave population. But the burdens resting upon the
small landowner and the free laborer compelled them also to
drift into this servile condition. The lifting up of the slaves
was thus accompanied by the lowering of the free peasant
classes. In this way a large part of the Roman people was
reduced practically to the condition of serfdom.

Decay of the Population. — Still further, the native population of the empire was continually decreasing in numbers. The
vitality of the Roman people was becoming exhausted. The
upper classes were worn out by a life of luxury and indolence.
The lower classes were exhausted by a constant struggle for
existence under unfavorable conditions. Famines, plagues, and
wars had also reduced the population. The armies, notwithstanding their excellent organization, could not be replenished
by vigorous native soldiers. Domestic life, too, had lost much
of its sanctity; and, as a consequence, the empire lost one of
the conditions of national growth and prosperity. Human life
itself was often held in light esteem. All these causes led to the
depopulation and exhaustion of the later empire. It has been
aptly said that Rome " perished for want of men."

Burdens of Taxation. — The people also suffered from the
grinding system of taxation which existed in the later empire.
The old abuses which prevailed in the republic had been corrected by the reforms of Augustus and his successors. But the
later empire, with its Orientalized form of government and its
elaborate system of bureaus and officials, required a vast amount
of money to support it. This money had to be raised from the
people. The duty of collecting the taxes rested upon the

curiales, that is, the governing class in the cities, which consisted of those holding a certain amount of land. If the *curiales* could not collect the money from the lower classes, they were obliged to furnish it from their own fortunes. They could not evade this responsibility. They could not abandon their position for that of the law or the clergy or the army; nor could they quit the city without the permission of the provincial governor. They became practically an hereditary class, upon which rested largely the financial weight of the empire. The heavy exactions laid upon the people for the support of the government tended to the impoverishment of the empire.

Social Effects of Christianity. — The one strong force remaining in the Roman world was the Christian church. But the mission of the Church was not to save the empire. While the empire was growing weak the church was growing strong. While the government was helpless to improve the material condition of the people, Christianity was doing a great deal to improve their moral and spiritual condition. It was teaching men to look to a kingdom which was not of this world. The influence of Christianity is seen in the development of the spirit of charity and benevolence among the people. Self-denial, in doing good to others, was one of the virtues expected of every Christian. It devolved on the church to see that strangers were entertained, that the sick were nursed, that the poor were fed, that the orphans were protected, that those who were in prison were visited. Contributions were taken up in all the churches for the benefit of the poor. It is said that a single bishop, in the third century, supported two thousand poor people.

The church also set its face against all forms of cruelty, and led to the making of new laws against such practices. To poison a slave, to tear his body with the nails of wild beasts, and to brand him were regarded as equivalent to homicide. The manumission of slaves was encouraged, and the freeing of slaves in the presence of the assembled congregation was regarded as a religious act. The absolute power of the father over his children was taken away. Constantine declared that a father who killed his son should be held guilty of murder. Laws were passed against infanticide. Marriage was transformed from a mere civil contract to a religious sacrament, and the position of women was greatly improved. The moral and social effects of Christianity were seen in almost all the relations of human life.

Selections for Reading

Knowlton, Topic A 24, "The Later Roman Empire" (1).[1]

Seignobos, Ch. 27, "The Later Empire" (1).

Goodspeed, Ancient World, pp. 416–425, "The World-Empire under the Despotism" (1).

Pelham, Bk. VII., Ch. 1, "From the Accession of Diocletian to the Death of Theodosius" (18).

Merivale, General History, Ch. 70, "The Epoch of Diocletian"; Ch. 73, "Reign of Julian"; Ch. 80, "Reflections on the History of Rome" (18).

Gibbon, Ch. 17, "Foundation of Constantinople"; Ch. 23, "The Religion of Julian" (18).

Stanley, Lect. 2, "The Council of Nicæa" (21).

Milman, History of Christianity, Ch. 3, "Foundation of Constantinople" (21).

Seeley, Essays, "The Later Empire"; "Proximate Causes of the Fall of the Western Empire" (18).

Munro, Source Book, Part X., "Christianity and Stoicism" (25).

Special Topic

THE REIGN OF CONSTANTINE. — Merivale, General History, Chs. 71, 72 (18); Gibbon, "Decline and Fall," Chs. 17, 18 (18); Stanley, "Eastern Church," Lect. 6 (21); Encyclopedias, "Constantine."

[1] The figure in parenthesis refers to the number of the topic in the Appendix, where a fuller title of the book will be found.

CHAPTER XXXII

THE GERMAN OCCUPATION OF THE WEST

Synopsis

I. THE GERMANS AND THEIR INSTITUTIONS. — The Barbarian World. — German Characteristics. — The German Political System. — The German Judicial System. — Conversion of the Germans.

II. THE GREAT INVASIONS. — Nature of the Invasions. — Invasion of the Visigoths under Alaric. — Invasion of the Huns under Attila. — Invasion of the Vandals under Genseric. — Fall of the Empire in the West.

III. THE NEW GERMANIC KINGDOMS. — In Italy, the Heruli and Ostrogoths. — In Spain, the Suevi and Visigoths. — In Gaul, the Burgundians and Franks. — In Britain, the Anglo-Saxons.

IV. THE ROMANO-GERMAN SOCIETY. — Effects of the Invasions. — Fusion of the Romans and the Germans. — The New German Kingship. — The New German Nobility. — The Common Freemen. — The Christian Church.

I. THE GERMANS AND THEIR INSTITUTIONS

The Barbarian World. — The glory of the old Roman empire had departed. It had apparently done its great work in the world's history. It was now called upon to furnish homes for other peoples, with fresher blood and simpler customs. We are now to see how the old empire was broken up, and how it became the foundation of a new society and of new states.

This breaking up of the old empire and transformation of Europe were due largely to the encroachments of the barbarian world upon the Roman world. For our purpose we may group the peoples of this outside barbarian world into three great branches: (1) the Germanic or Teutonic peoples, on the north of the Rhine and the Danube; (2) the Slavic or Slavonian peoples, in the central part of what is now European Russia; and (3) the peoples in the central and western parts of Asia,

whom we call, for want of a better name, Scythians or Tura-
nians. The most barbarous of these peoples were the Tura-
nians, of which the Huns were the most warlike and aggressive.
The Slavs were more peaceful and at this time did not make
any important incursions into the empire. The Germans were
nearest to the Roman borders, and also approached most nearly
to the civilized stage. They comprised many tribes — the
Goths, the Vandals, the Alemanni, the Burgundians, the Lombards, the Franks, the Saxons,
and others of less importance. It
was these Germans who made the
first inroads into the empire, and
whose characteristics are the most
important for us to consider.

German Characteristics. — Our
knowledge of the early Germans
is derived mostly from Cæsar and
Tacitus. They are described by
these writers as a vigorous and
warlike race, of gigantic stature,
with fierce blue eyes and long yellow hair, simple in their social and
political life, and inspired with the
spirit of liberty and independence.
They differed from the more civilized Romans in their manners and

GERMAN SLINGERS (Roman relief)

customs, in their political organization, their laws, and their religion. They had no great cities, no splendid architecture, no
fine works of literature, none of the marks of a high civilization. They were, in fact, in that primitive stage of progress in
which the Romans, as well as the Greeks, were at the beginning
of the historical period. Their most striking characteristics were
their love of liberty and their spirit of personal loyalty. Tacitus tells us that their chiefs ruled by persuasion rather than
by authority. The chief was wont to surround himself with a

following (*comitatus*) of young men, who voluntarily attached themselves to him, and shared in his dangers and glory. Though fond of fighting and drinking, the Germans had a respect for women, and were devoted to a pure family life.

The German Political System. — The unit of the German political society was not the city, as in the case of the Romans, but the village community. The Germans, who had been a nomadic people living by war and the chase, were now beginning to settle down to an agricultural life. The most primitive form of agricultural life is the village community — which is simply a collection of families, settled upon a piece of land, and organized into a little body politic. The land upon which the people settled was, for the most part, held in common; upon it every one could pasture his flocks and herds. The arable land was divided into strips, and allotted each year to the householders for cultivation. The land upon which the house and garden were situated was assigned permanently to each family. Thus we have three kinds of land — the common or waste land, the arable land, and the house land.

The village community was governed by an assembly composed of all freemen capable of bearing arms; and hence the village was a pure democracy. It was presided over by a headman, or village chief, who was chosen by the people and who led them to war. A group of villages formed a " hundred," which also had its democratic assembly and its chief. A collection of hundreds made the tribe; and the tribe was also governed by an assembly and a war chief. The tribes were sometimes united into confederations in times of war, under chiefs chosen for their bravery. The political system of the Germans was thus democratic in character, and presented a striking contrast to the imperial system of Rome.

The German Judicial System. — Among primitive barbarians it is customary for injuries to be atoned for either (1) by private redress, in which each one takes the law into his own hands, or (2) by blood revenge, in which a family obtains redress for an injury done to its members. But the Germans had advanced beyond this primitive stage, and the person charged with a crime was allowed a trial before the chief and the whole assembly, or before a number of persons selected to try the case. The guilt or innocence of the culprit was usually determined in one of three ways: (1) by " compurgation," which required that a certain number of persons, called " compurgators," be found who would swear that they believed the accused, when he asserted his innocence; (2) by ordeal, which required that the accused should undergo some dangerous test, like handling red-hot iron, from which, if he escaped uninjured, he was judged to be innocent; or (3) by combat, or a fight between the contesting parties, or their champions. The penalty inflicted upon the guilty party was usually a money compensation, called *wergild*, which varied according to the rank of the injured person. The crimes which

EARLY GERMAN COIN

prevailed among the Germans were chiefly of the character of personal injuries; since the rights relating to property and contracts were scarcely yet recognized. The simple laws of the Germans thus showed a marked difference from the highly developed jurisprudence of the Romans.

Conversion of the Germans. — The early German religion was similar to the primitive worship of the early Greeks and Romans — a polytheistic nature worship. They worshiped Woden, Thor, and Freya — names still preserved in our English names of the days of the week, Wednesday, Thursday, and Friday. Their idea of immortality was based upon what they regarded as most enjoyable in human life. Their heaven was the " Valhalla," the hall of the slain, where valiant heroes shared in the banquets of the gods. But it is

especially important for us to notice that many of the German
tribes were converted to Christianity before they made their
final settlements in the Roman territory. When the followers
of Arius were banished from the Roman empire as heretics,
after the Council of Nice (p. 527), many of them became missionaries to the barbarians. The most distinguished of these
missionaries was Ul'filas, "the apostle to the Goths." By his
efforts the Gothic nation was converted to the Arian form of
Christianity; and his translation of the Bible into their language was the first German version of the Scriptures. From the
Goths Christianity spread among the neighboring tribes, the
Burgundians and the Vandals. The acceptance by the Germans of a religion which was fundamentally the same as that
of the Romans was one of the causes which finally led to the
fusion of the Romans and the Germans into one society.

II. The Great Invasions

Nature of the Invasions. — If we recall what we have already learned, we may realize that the pressure of the northern
barbarians upon the south was not a new thing in the history
of the ancient world. In fact, it represents a long-continued
and almost constant struggle. We have seen long ago the
Gauls invading Italy and destroying Rome (p. 337). We
have seen the Cimbri and Teutones threatening the Roman
republic in the days of Marius (p. 408). We have seen the
frontiers broken in during the decline of the early empire, and
the Goths obtaining a foothold in the provinces (p. 531). These
events show that from the earliest times the barbarian north
had been a constant menace to the civilized south. The invasions were, in their nature, a struggle for the possession of
the earth — or at least for the lands most favorable for human
existence. As long as the Roman empire preserved its original
strength, it was able to maintain itself in this struggle for existence. But when its resources were exhausted, its frontiers

gave way to the barbarian pressure. These invasions were not of the nature of mere military expeditions; they were rather the migration of nations in the search of new settlements. They were the movements of a whole people, men, women, and children, with their horses and wagons and all their effects, in search of new lands from which they might obtain food and plunder. The most important of the great invasions which now took place were those of the Vis'igoths under Al'aric, the Huns under At'tila, and the Vandals under Gen'seric.

Invasion of the Visigoths under Alaric. — The Gothic nation was divided into two parts, the Visigoths or West Goths, and the Ostrogoths or East Goths. The Visigoths were now settled in the Roman territory south of the Danube, and were subject to the Eastern emperor. Under their great leader, Alaric, they revolted (395 A.D.) against the Roman authority; they invaded Macedonia and Greece, and threatened to devastate the whole peninsula. The Eastern emperor, Arcadius, in order to relieve his own territory, pacified the Gothic leader by granting Illyricum to him and making him master-general of that province. Not entirely satisfied with that territory, Alaric soon invaded Italy, and ravaged the plains of the Po. But he was defeated at Pollentia (403 A.D.) by the great Vandal soldier, Stil'icho, who was now enlisted in the service of the Western emperor, Honorius. The generalship of Stilicho was also shown in checking an invasion made by a host of Vandals, Burgundians, and Sue'vi, under the lead of Radagai'sus (406 A.D.). Italy seemed safe as long as Stilicho lived; but he was unfortunately put to death to satisfy the jealousy of his ungrateful master, Honorius (408 A.D.).

With Stilicho dead, Italy was practically defenseless. Alaric at the head of the Visigoths immediately invaded the peninsula, and marched to Rome. He was induced to spare the city only by the payment of an enormous ransom. But the barbarian chief was not satisfied with the payment of money. He was in search of lands upon which to settle his people. Honorius refused to grant his demand, and after fruitless negotiations with the emperor, Alaric determined to enforce it by the sword. He took the city of Rome and sacked it (410 A.D.). For three days the city was given up to plunder. He then overran southern Italy and made himself master of the peninsula. He soon died, and his successor, Adolphus, was induced to find in southern Gaul and Spain the lands which Alaric had sought in Italy.

Invasion of the Huns under Attila. — The next great invasion of the Western Empire was made by the Huns under Attila. This savage people from Asia had already gained a foothold in eastern Europe north of the Danube. They boasted that the grass never grew where their horses' hoofs had once trod. Under their great chieftain, Attila, who has been called " the Scourge of God," they invaded Gaul and devastated the provinces; they laid siege to the city of Orleans, but were finally defeated by the Roman general Aë'tius, with the aid of the Visigoths. This battle was fought near Châlons (shà-lôn'; 451 A.D.), not far from Paris; it has been called one of the great decisive battles of the world, because it relieved Europe from the danger of Scythian domination. Attila later invaded Italy, but retired without attacking Rome. The city was saved through the efforts of the Pope, Leo the Great, — which shows how strong the church had become, that even a barbarian chieftain respected its authority.

Notwithstanding the brilliant service which Aëtius had rendered, he was made the victim of court intrigue, and was murdered by his jealous prince, Valentinian III. The fate of Aëtius, like that of Stilicho before him, shows the wretched condition into which the imperial government had fallen.

Invasion of the Vandals under Genseric. — The Vandals who had fought under Radagaisus had, upon the death of that leader, retreated into Spain, and had finally crossed over into Africa, where they had erected a kingdom under their chief Genseric. They captured the Roman city of Carthage and made it their capital; and they soon obtained control of the western Mediterranean. On the pretext of settling a quarrel at Rome, Genseric landed his army at the mouth of the Tiber, took possession of the city of Rome, and for fourteen days made it the subject of pillage (455 A.D.). The intercession of Pope Leo, which had availed with Attila, did not stay the hand of the Vandal chief, although it prevented the slaughter of the people. The city itself was given over to plunder. Its magnificent buildings and works of art were ruthlessly destroyed — and the word " vandalism " came to be a term of odious meaning.

Fall of the Empire in the West (476 A.D.). — By these and other barbarian conquests, the authority of the Western emperor was now limited to Italy, together with a small part of northwestern Gaul, which still remained under the Roman governor Sya'grius. The emperors themselves were weak and incapable of ruling. The real power was exercised by others. The imperial administration at Rome was, for a time, in the hands of Placid'ia, sister of Honorius and daughter of Theodosius the Great. With the death of Stilicho and Aëtius, the command of the Roman armies fell to Ric'imer, who is known as the " king-maker," since he set up and deposed emperors at his will. Then followed Ores'tes, who was once the secretary of the barbarian chief Attila, and who now commanded the barbarian auxiliaries in Italy. He received the title of Roman " patrician " and attempted to rule after the manner of Ricimer. He placed upon the throne his son, Romulus Augustulus, a boy six years of age, whose reign has no significance, except that he was the last of the Western emperors. His brief reign was brought to an end by a revolt on the part of the barbarian mercenaries, who demanded one third of the lands of Italy. The young prince, Augustulus, was deposed by Odoa'cer, chief of the Her'uli (476 A.D.). Word was sent to the Eastern ruler that there was no longer any need of a separate emperor in the West. Odoacer accordingly received the title of patrician and ruled over Italy as the vicar of the Eastern emperor. The

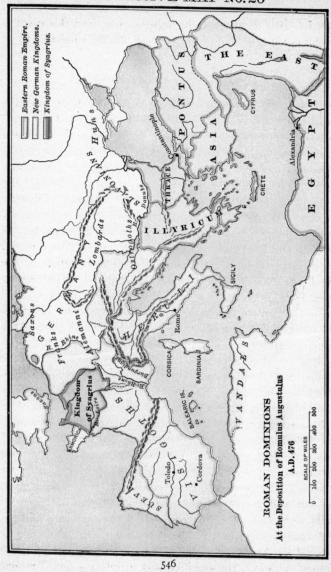

ROMAN DOMINIONS
At the Deposition of Romulus Augustulus
A.D. 476

SCALE OF MILES

0   100   200   300   400   500

West was thus deprived of the imperial title; and this event is usually called the " fall of the Western Roman empire."

III. The New Germanic Kingdoms

In Italy, the Heruli and Ostrogoths. — The West was now theoretically united to the East.   But as the result of the invasions the provinces became the seats of new Germanic kingdoms, which were practically independent of the Eastern emperor.

In order to realize the great changes which were now taking place in western Europe, let us locate on the map (p. 546) the new kingdoms established by the German invaders.   Odoacer, the king of the Heruli, continued to rule over Italy for seventeen years (476-493 A.D.).   Although a barbarian, he respected the forms of the Roman government.   Although an Arian, he did not disturb the Catholic church.   The brief dominion of the Heruli was cut short by the conquest of Italy by the Ostrogoths under Theod'oric.

The Ostrogoths, following their old kinsmen the Visigoths, had settled south of the Danube, and had become allies of the Eastern emperor.   Their chief was Theodoric, who had been brought up as a hostage at Constantinople, and had become familiar with the customs and institutions of the Romans.   To satisfy the demands of his people for better lands, Theodoric obtained from the emperor the authority to take possession of Italy.   After a brief war he became master of the peninsula, and founded the new kingdom of the Ostrogoths (493-552 A.D.).   He acknowledged a nominal allegiance to the emperor at Constantinople, but in fact he ruled as an independent sovereign.   He proved to be a great statesman and civilizer, and may well be regarded as the greatest of the barbarian kings. He restored Italy to a prosperous condition, such as it had not seen since the days of the Antonines.   He drained the marshes, repaired the highways, restored the old monuments, and built splendid edifices.   His ambition was to infuse a new Teutonic vigor into the old civilization of Rome — to preserve the old institutions, while he gave to them a new spirit. He compiled the Roman law for the benefit of his Roman subjects; and, although an Arian, he respected the rights of the Catholic church. He also patronized learning. The chief ornaments of his reign were Boë'thius, who wrote the "Consolations of Philosophy"; and his private secretary, Cassiodo'rus, who wrote

TOMB OF THEODORIC AT RAVENNA

a "History of the Goths" (now preserved only in an abridged form). The last years of Theodoric were disturbed by intrigues and by acts unworthy of a great prince. At his death (527 A.D.), his enemies succeeded in having his ashes scattered; but his tomb at Ravenna remains as a monument of his greatness.

In Spain, the Suevi and Visigoths. — The peninsula of Spain became the seat of two Germanic kingdoms — that of the Suevi and that of the Visigoths. The Suevi had taken part in the great invasion under Radagaisus (p. 543). After the defeat of that barbarian leader by Stilicho, they had found a refuge in Spain. Here they founded a kingdom in the north-western part of the peninsula (409–585 A.D.). They had little influence upon the history of Spain, as they were absorbed into the greater kingdom of the Visigoths.

The Visigoths were led into Spain from Italy by Adolphus, the successor of Alaric (p. 544). Their kingdom lasted for many years (419–711 A.D.), and at one time extended over the entire Spanish peninsula and into southern Gaul as far as the river Loire. Like many other barbarian chiefs, the Visigothic kings had great respect for the Roman institutions which they found among the conquered people. How much Adolphus was under the influence of Rome we may judge from his own statement; he says that while he wished at first to destroy the Roman name, he was convinced that to maintain the Gothic state it was necessary to preserve the Roman institutions. The Visigothic kings respected the rights of their Roman subjects. While one king, Euric, drew up the barbarian laws for the Gothic people, another king, Alaric II., drew up the Roman laws for the Roman people. The tendency in Spain was to preserve the equality of the Romans and the Goths under the common authority of the king, who ruled more like a Roman emperor than like a barbarian chieftain.

In Gaul, the Burgundians and Franks. — In passing to the province of Gaul, we find the southeastern part, along the valley of the Rhone, occupied by the kingdom of the Burgundians (413–534 A.D.). Here, as in Italy and Spain, there was a disposition on the part of the kings to place the Roman and the German people on a plane of equality. For example, one Burgundian king codified the barbarian laws for his own people; and another king drew up a collection of the Roman law for his Roman subjects. The Burgundians were a brave people; and their heroic exploits are sung in *Nibelungenlied* (nē'bē-lōong-en-lēt), the great epic poem of the German race. The kingdom of the Burgundians was continued until it was absorbed by that of the Franks.

The most important of all the new German kingdoms was the
kingdom of the Franks; the founder of this kingdom was
Clovis. This great chieftain led his people across the Rhine
and defeated Syagrius, the Roman governor, at the battle of
Soissons (swä-sôn'; 486 A.D.). He then overcame the neighboring

EUROPEAN KINGDOMS
526 A.D.
SCALE OF MILES
0   100   200   300   400   500

tribes in Gaul, — the Alemanni in the east, the Burgundians in
the southeast, and the Visigoths in the south, — and thus
brought the whole of Gaul under his authority. He recognized
a sort of allegiance to the Eastern emperor by accepting the title
of "consul." During his reign and that of his successors, the
Roman people were respected, their cities were preserved, their
language and laws remained; and many of the Romans were
even selected to assist the Frankish king in his government.

One of the most noteworthy facts in the reign of Clovis was

his conversion to the Catholic form of Christianity, which followed his victory over the Alemanni. It was during a battle with this people that the king made a vow that if he were successful, he would accept the religion of his wife Clotilda, who was a Catholic. After he obtained the victory he was baptized, with three thousand of his followers. The king became the protector of the church, and the church became a support of the king. The death of Clovis was followed by many divisions and reunions of the kingdom; but the policy which he adopted led to the blending of Roman ideas of law with the German ideas of liberty. It also led to an alliance between the church and the state which afterward made the Frankish monarchy the strongest political power in western Europe, as we shall hereafter see.

In Britain, the Anglo-Saxons. — The German conquest of Britain resulted from a series of migrations, which began in the middle of the fifth century (449 A.D.) and extended over a period of a hundred and fifty years. The people whom we generally call the "Anglo-Saxons" included the Jutes, who settled in Kent; the Saxons, who settled in Sussex, Wessex, and Essex: and the Angles, who settled in East Anglia, Mercia, and Northum'berland. These settlements grew into as many king-

ANGLO-SAXON HEPTARCHY

doms, and are often spoken of as the "Anglo-Saxon Heptarchy." Although the province of Britain had previously been a seat of Roman civilization, many of the remains of which exist at the present day, the Teutonic institutions became thoroughly transplanted to English soil; and the German ideas of personal liberty and of local self-government became more firmly fixed there than in any other country of Europe. But still the Roman influence was not entirely destroyed. The Roman cities still remained and preserved some of the municipal institutions of the empire.

When the Anglo-Saxons came to Britain they brought with them their old pagan religion — the same idea of the gods and of the future life that they had had in their native forests of Germany. They still worshiped Woden, Thor, and Freya, gods of the woods and sky and the powers of nature. They still looked forward to Valhalla, where they would drink the blood of their slain victims. It was in the latter part of the sixth century that the great missionary Pope, Gregory I., sent Au'gustine to Britain to preach the gospel to the Anglo-Saxon people. He landed in Britain with nearly forty other monks. He first appealed to the king of Kent. This prince had already married a Frankish princess, Bertha, who was a Christian. Through the persuasion of Augustine, the king accepted the religion of his wife, and was baptized with his people. From that day Christianity took a firm root in England. There was then need of a man to organize the British churches. The Pope chose for this purpose Theodore, who came from Tarsus, the native city of Saint Paul. Under his supervision the churches were united, and he was made archbishop. He formed new dioceses, appointed new bishops, and established monasteries, which provided peaceful centers where learning, art, agriculture, and the sciences were encouraged. The church thus obtained a national unity before the Saxon kingdoms were united into a single nation.

IV. The Romano-German Society

Effects of the Invasions. — The period of the invasions was a period of disorder and anarchy. The successive waves of barbarism which had flowed over the western provinces had left in their wake scenes of destruction and desolation. The city of Rome itself had been sacked three times during this period. Buildings had been demolished, libraries had been destroyed, works of art had been mutilated. Except in the carnage of battle, the Roman people, however, were generally unmolested. But the barbarians had no taste for the finer arts of life. They cared little for the culture which the Romans had developed. The boasted civilization of Rome which had flourished for over two centuries in the midst of peace and prosperity was now threatened with destruction. But when the invaders were fairly settled in their new homes they began to show a desire for improvement. They came under the influence of the church, which was a civilizing force. They even began to adopt some of the ideas of the people whom they had conquered. So that when the chief invasions are over, we begin to see some evidences of progress. From the disorder and darkness of this period, we may see a tendency toward the formation of a new society.

Fusion of the Romans and the Germans. — The society which grew up in the new barbarian kingdoms was partly Roman and partly German. It is a great mistake to suppose that the Roman population was destroyed as the result of the barbarian conquests. The Romans were, it is true, no longer masters of themselves, for they were now subject to their German conquerors. But the Roman people still remained. In fact, they formed in many places the larger part of the population. They still spoke the Latin language. They still preserved their own laws. Both their language and their laws were highly respected and even imitated by the Germans who came into contact with them. The two peoples lived side by side in the same territory — the Romans in the old municipalities, and the Germans, generally speaking, in the rural districts, in villages or upon great estates. Being thus brought together under the same authority, they were necessarily influenced by each other. Their institutions, although diverse in origin and different in character, were modified by their mutual contact. This resulted in a system which possessed both Roman and German elements. One of the chief results of the invasions, therefore, was the fusion of the two peoples, the mingling to a great extent of their political and social institutions, their languages, and to a certain degree their systems of law. There was thus gradually forming a new society, a Romano-German society.

The New German Kingship. — We can see how the old Germans were becoming different from what they were in their ancient forests. The chiefs of the old tribes had little authority, but ruled rather by persuasion. The chiefs of the new kingdoms became kings with something of an imperial dignity and authority. They assumed the imperial insignia — the crown, the imperial scepter, and the purple robe. They surrounded themselves with household officers, like an imperial court. They governed their territory in a manner similar to that of an imperial province. Thus the royal power, by appropriating the old imperial ideas of Rome, gradually became much stronger than among the primitive German people.

The New German Nobility. — A new nobility also sprang up, which included both a German and a Roman element. It depended primarily upon the German principle of the *comitatus* (p. 540), or the personal relation between the chief and his followers. Those who were closely related to the king were his companions, and shared something of his dignity. Besides this personal nobility, there was what might be called an official nobility, made up of the military chiefs, or dukes, and the territorial governors, or counts. Persons were admitted to this privileged class, whether they were Germans or Romans; and this fact tended to break down the distinction between the two peoples.

The Common Freemen. — The growth of the new kingship and the new nobility tended to degrade the condition of the common freemen. The pure democratic institutions of the primitive Germans became somewhat changed. In the old German society, before the invasions, all the freemen had been accustomed to meet together in their assemblies, and had had a real share in the government. It is true that after the invasions the kings sometimes called the people together; but the national assemblies were more often made up of the nobles than of the common freemen. Moreover, the freemen who were excluded from the nobility were obliged to live upon the soil; and many of them gradually descended to the condition of the old Roman *coloni*, or serfs.

The Christian Church. — During the period of the invasions the church was growing in authority and influence. By its splendid organization, it was able to maintain its power, while the rest of society was breaking up and becoming reorganized. The clergy formed the most intelligent and influential class in the community. They not only exercised a great influence over the people, but became the advisers of the kings, and, to a large extent, shaped their laws and administration. Moreover, the church, by bringing within its communion and under its authority both the German and the Roman population, became a powerful agency in fusing the two peoples together and breaking down their race prejudices. Finally, the division between the Arians and the Catholics gradually passed away by the triumph of the Catholic faith. On this account the church came to be united, and formed the greatest single power in western Europe.

Selections for Reading

Knowlton, Topic A 25, "The German Peril" (1).[1]

Emerton, Ch. 2, "The Two Races"; Ch. 3, "Breaking of the Frontiers"; Ch. 8, "Germanic Ideas of Law" (the Salic law) (24).

Curteis, Ch. 6, "Alaric and the Visigoths"; Ch. 7, "Genseric and the Vandals"; Ch. 8, "Attila and the Huns" (24).

[1] The figure in parenthesis refers to the number of the topic in the Appendix, where a fuller title of the book will be found.

Thatcher and Schwill, Ch. 4, "The Migration of Nations" (24).

Adams, Ch. 3, "Additions of Christianity"; Ch. 4, "The German Conquest and Fall of Rome" (24).

Milman, Latin Christianity, Vol. II., Bk. III., Ch. 2, "Conversion of the Teutonic Races" (Saint Columban; Saint Boniface); Ch. 3, "Theodoric the Ostrogoth" (21).

Robinson, Ch. 3, "The German Invasions and Break-up of the Roman Empire" (24).

Oman, Dark Ages, Ch. 8, "The Visigoths in Spain" (24).

Bémont and Monod, Ch. 7, "Institutions in Gaul after the Invasions" (24).

Ogg, Source Book, Ch. 1, "The Early Germans"; Ch. 5, "The Angles and Saxons in Britain"; Ch. 6, "Development of the Christian Church" (25).

Robinson, Readings, Vol. I., pp. 52–55 (conversion of Clovis as told by Gregory of Tours) (25).

Special Study

THE REIGN OF THEODORIC. — Duruy, "Middle Ages," Ch. 2 (24); Oman, "Dark Ages," Ch. 2 (24); Milman, "Latin Christianity," Bk. III., Ch. 3 (21); Hodgkin, "Life of Theodoric" (27).

CHAPTER XXXIII

THE FATE OF THE EMPIRE IN THE EAST

Synopsis

I. RECOVERY OF THE EMPIRE BY JUSTINIAN. — The Eastern Empire before Justinian. — The Reign of Justinian. — Recovery of Africa from the Vandals. — Recovery of Italy from the Ostrogoths. — The Codification of the Roman law.

II. NEW BARBARIAN INVASIONS OF THE EMPIRE. — Conquest of Italy by the Lombards. — Slavic Settlements in the Eastern Provinces. — Heraclius and the Declining Empire.

III. THE RISE OF MOHAMMEDANISM. — Arabia before Mohammed. — Mohammed and his Religion. — The Mohammedan Scriptures : the Koran. — Mohammedan Conquests in the East and West. — Dismemberment of the Caliphate. — Mohammedan Civilization.

I. RECOVERY OF THE EMPIRE BY JUSTINIAN

The Eastern Empire before Justinian. — While the Roman and the Teuton were uniting to build up a new society in the West, the old Roman empire still continued in the East. The emperor at Constantinople still claimed to be the rightful ruler of the whole Roman world, and had succeeded in gaining the nominal allegiance of most of the German kings; but his real authority was confined to the provinces east of the Adriatic. It is true that the East was relieved of such invasions as had destroyed the Western provinces. Still the government at Constantinople was very weak, often in the hands of incapable men and under the influence of intriguing women. The capital and the other cities of the empire were distracted by political dissensions and religious discord. Not till we come to the reign of Justinian do we see anything like a revival of the old Roman spirit.

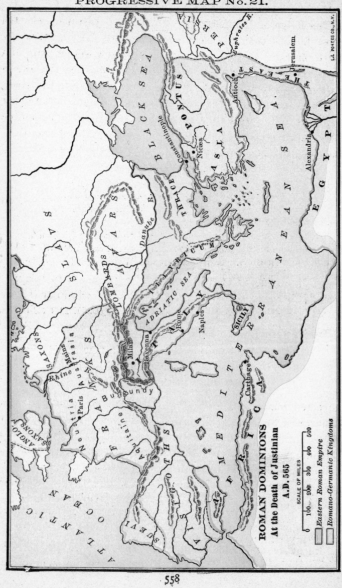

ROMAN DOMINIONS
At the Death of Justinian
A.D. 565

SCALE OF MILES

0 100 200 300 400 500

☐ Eastern Roman Empire
☐ Romano-Germanic Kingdoms

The Reign of Justinian (527–565 A.D.). — Justinian was the most famous ruler of the Eastern Empire. A barbarian by birth, he came to Constantinople while yet a young man, and there received an excellent education. He married the famous dancer Theodo′ra, who afterward became an orthodox Christian, and who at times aided the emperor by her keen intellect and her vigorous spirit. In spite of many stories which detract from the personal character of Justinian, his reign was, after that of Constantine, the most brilliant in the history of the East. He con-

CHURCH OF ST. SOPHIA AT CONSTANTINOPLE

structed many public buildings, chief among which was the Church of St. Sophia, dedicated to Wisdom; after the fall of Constantinople, about 900 years later, it was turned into a Mohammedan mosque. During his reign the culture of the silkworm was introduced into Europe, the eggs being stealthily brought from China, it is said, by being concealed in a hollow staff. But the greatest renown of Justinian rests upon his partial recovery of the western provinces, and his codification of the Roman law.

Recovery of Africa from the Vandals (534 A.D.). — The great desire of Justinian was to restore the grandeur of the old Roman empire. To accomplish this, it was necessary not only to maintain the frontiers against the hostile Persians in the East, but also to recover the provinces in the West from the hands of the barbarian kings. The most hated and aggressive of the barbarians were the Vandals in Africa. They had swept the Mediterranean with their fleets, and had even threatened Constantinople. Unlike other tribes that had accepted Arian Christianity, the Vandals were intolerant in religion, and persecuted the members of the Catholic church. To rescue this province Justinian placed his greatest general, Belisa'rius, in command of a naval expedition to Africa. After a campaign of three months, the Vandals were conquered. Africa was restored to the empire, and placed under an " exarch," or governor, appointed by the emperor.

Recovery of Italy from the Ostrogoths (535–552 A.D.). — Justinian soon found a pretext for invading Italy. But the conquest of the Ostrogoths proved a more serious undertaking than that of the Vandals. Belisarius was dispatched with an expedition to Sicily. After the conquest of that island, Naples and Rome were taken. But Belisarius was himself shut up in the Roman capital and besieged for a year by the Gothic armies. When the siege was finally raised, he pursued the Goths to Ravenna, and compelled the surrender of that city. In the midst of his victories, he was recalled to Constantinople and sent against the Persians. While he was away the Ostrogoths recovered Rome and a large part of the Italian peninsula. Belisarius was a second time sent into Italy. He succeeded in recapturing Rome; but he was feebly supported by the emperor and again recalled to Constantinople. The final conquest of Italy was left to another general, Narses. With the fall of the Ostrogothic kingdom, Narses was appointed exarch, with his capital at Ravenna. By these conquests in Africa and Italy — to which the southern part of Spain was added — the authority of the empire was reëstablished over a large part of the western provinces.

The Codification of the Roman Law. — To the transient fame which resulted from the wars of Justinian was added the more permanent glory which came from his compilation of the Roman law. The emperor appointed the famous lawyer Tribo'nian, with the aid of a commission of jurists, to collect the laws of the empire. These consisted of the imperial " constitutions " — that is, the laws issued by the emperors — and the writings of the jurists. The newly codified body of the civil law was called the *Corpus Juris Civilis*, and consisted of four parts. (1) The *Code* was a collection of the imperial constitutions issued since the time of Theodosius — who had already made a collection of the previous constitutions. (2) The *Digest*, or *Pandects*, comprised extracts from the writings of thirty-nine of the greatest Roman jurists — including Gaius, Ulpian, Paullus, Modestinus, and Papinian. It was the boast of the commission that three million lines had been reduced to one hundred and fifty thousand. (3) The *Institutes* was a textbook, containing the general principles of the law and intended for the use of students. (4) The *Novels* contained the later laws of Justinian issued after the publication of the Code. This compilation was perhaps the greatest legacy of Rome to the modern world. " It was in this form," as Savigny says, " that the Roman law became the common law of Europe."

II. New Barbarian Invasions of the Empire

Conquest of Italy by the Lombards (568 A.D.). — The empire, which had recovered so much of its former greatness during the reign of Justinian, was after his death again exposed to barbarian incursions. The first great disaster was the loss of Italy, which had just been recovered by Belisarius and Narses. It is said that Narses — now the exarch at Ravenna — was illtreated by the authorities at Constantinople; and that he, in revenge, invited the Lombards to come to Italy. The Lombards had already settled in Pannonia. Under their leader, Al'boin, they descended into the valley of the Po, and afterward overran nearly the whole of Italy. The principal seat of their power was in the north, their capital being at Pavia. In the south they established a number of duchies — such as that of Spole′-tum and that of Beneventum. The Eastern Empire was able, however, to hold the territory about Ravenna and about Rome;

and this territory remained under the authority of the exarch of Ravenna and of the Eastern Empire. The Lombards were oppressive and cruel. Unlike the Ostrogoths, they had little respect for the Roman people or for Roman institutions. They had adopted the Arian form of Christianity; but they were intolerant and were open enemies of the Catholic church, and had little respect for the Pope.

Slavic Settlements in the Eastern Provinces. — The invasion of the Lombards was the beginning of a new period of encroachments upon the Eastern Empire. We saw some time ago that the early Germans had been pushed forward upon the frontiers by the pressure of the Huns from Asia (p. 531). So now the Slavic peoples were being pressed forward by other Asiatic tribes, the Avars and Bulgarians. The Slavs were thus brought into somewhat the same relation to the East as the Germans had been to the West. They did not, however, succeed in overthrowing the empire in the East, as the Germans had practically done in the West. But still there came to be established at least four new barbarian states south of the Danube. These were Servia, Croatia, Carinthia, and Bulgaria (map, p. 567). The first three of these were founded by the Slavs; the last was founded by the Bulgarians, originally a "Turanian" people, who, however, having mixed with the Slavs, adopted the language and customs of the latter, and became themselves practically a Slavic people.

Heraclius and the Declining Empire. — The loss of these territories in Italy and on the Danube was a painful evidence of the weakness of the government at Constantinople. The Persians also renewed their wars and overran the provinces in the East. They took possession of Egypt and Syria, invaded Asia Minor, and their armies encamped within sight of Constantinople. From this dangerous condition the empire was temporarily rescued by the heroic efforts of Heracli′us (610–641 A.D.), an emperor whose warlike deeds remind us of Justinian. He boldly attacked the enemy, rescued Asia Minor and Egypt, and carried the war into the Persian territory. But the vigorous reign of Heraclius was hardly more than a parenthesis in the general movement toward decay and degeneracy. The Eastern Empire continued to exist for more than eight hundred years and to render some service to civilization. It protected Europe from the encroachments of Asiatic peoples, and preserved the fruits of ancient learning to modern times.

III. The Rise of Mohammedanism

Arabia before Mohammed. — There was a solitary land in Asia which had scarcely yet been touched by the great civilized peoples of the world. It had never been conquered by the Assyrians, by the Persians, or by the Romans. This was Arabia, a peninsula lying between the Persian Gulf and the Red Sea. It lay in a tropical climate. It had no great rivers. It had few towns. Its inhabitants were a barbarous people, scattered about in numerous tribes. They got their living from their flocks and herds, or from a primitive kind of agriculture. Some of these people were brigands, gaining a livelihood by plundering the caravans that crossed the Syrian desert on their way from the Euphrates to the coasts of the Mediterranean. They were skilled in the use of arms, and were expert horsemen. They had no common government, and were frequently at war with one another. They belonged to the Semitic race, and were the brothers of the Babylonians, the Assyrians, the Phœnicians, and the Hebrews. At the appearance of Mohammed they were, for the most part, gross idolaters, worshiping various gods and goddesses. But other religions were finding their way into Arabia. Many Jews had come there, especially after the destruction of Jerusalem. Many Christians, also, had found there a refuge during the early persecutions.

Mohammed and his Religion. — Mohammed was born at Mecca, a town in western Arabia not far from the shores of the Red Sea. He shared the general ignorance of his countrymen, and was not able to read and write. He started in life as a shepherd and became a camel driver and finally a merchant. He entered the service of a rich widow, whom he afterwards married. In his journeys he found his way into a Christian monastery, and was impressed with the teaching of the monks. Mohammed was a sincere seeker after truth, and possessed a deeply religious mind, bordering upon superstition. He was accustomed to withdraw into a neighboring mountain and to pass the time in meditation and prayer. Sometimes, he declared, he saw the angel Gabriel and heard himself saluted as prophet of God. In such ecstatic visions he professed to receive revelations from heaven, which he committed to memory. These experiences he confided to his wife, who became his first convert. Other converts were then made, from whom he chose twelve apostles, after the example of Christ, to propagate his religion.

Opposition soon sprang up in his native city; and he was driven out of Mecca and took refuge in the neighboring city of Medi'na. This flight of Mohammed is called the "Heg'ira," from which date (622 A.D.) begins the Mohammedan era. In Medina was erected the first mosque, at which Mohammed labored with his own hands, and in which he preached his first sermon. Hostilities soon broke out between Mecca and Medina. At this time the prophet first took the sword, and at the head of 10,000 followers captured the city of Mecca, destroying 300 idols that were worshiped there. With sword in hand he conquered all Arabia. When next he made his pilgrimage to Mecca he was accompanied by 100,000 Mohammedans. After having thus brought his native country to accept his religion, he died at Medina just ten years after his flight from Mecca.

The Mohammedan Scriptures: the Koran. — The Bible of the Mohammedans is the Koran'. This is said to be made up of the revelations received by Mohammed from heaven, and taken down by his followers, on pieces of pottery, the shoulder bones of sheep, and other fragile substances. These were collected together after his death and copied into the book called the Koran. The doctrine of Mohammedanism is known as "Islam," meaning "submission to God." The creed of this religion is summed up in the words, "There is no God but Allah, and Mohammed is his prophet." The Koran is divided into 114 chapters or "suras," beginning with the longest.

The Koran teaches the doctrine of predestination, — that a man's destiny is fixed even before he is born — that a man will die only when his time has come. A belief in this doctrine takes away the fear of death in battle. The Koran also teaches four cardinal duties: (1) to pray five times every day with the face turned toward Mecca; (2) to keep the sacred month, called Ramadan', as a fast; (3) to give in charity one tenth of one's income; (4) to make at least one pilgrimage to Mecca during one's lifetime. The teaching of the Koran no doubt tended in many ways to improve the peoples of the East. But with all its worthy precepts it encourages a most barbarous practice, namely the extension of religion by the sword. The Koran decrees: " Kill infidels wherever you find them."

Mohammedan Conquests in the East and West. — The conquests begun by Mohammed were carried on by his successors,

MOSQUE OF OMAR, JERUSALEM

the "caliphs," as they were called. Of these the greatest warrior, and the real founder of the Arabian supremacy in the East, was Omar. He united all the people of Arabia under his banner, and entered upon a remarkable career of conquest. He defeated Heraclius, as that emperor was returning from a victorious campaign against Persia; he wrested Syria and Palestine from the empire, and erected an Arabian mosque at Jerusalem on the site of Solomon's Temple. He then defeated the Persians and overthrew their rulers. He invaded Egypt, and, after besieging Alexandria for fourteen months, became master of that country. With this beginning under Omar, the Arabians continued to push their conquests, under other caliphs, in northern Africa to the Atlantic. They then crossed into Spain and destroyed the kingdom of the Visigoths (711 A.D.). They invaded Gaul and threatened to overrun all the countries of western Europe, and even to destroy Christianity itself.

MOHAMMEDAN DOMINIONS, 750 A.D.

From this disastrous fate Christian Europe was rescued by the Franks under Charles Martel' at the famous battle near Tours (toor), which may well be called one of the decisive battles of the world. In a single century, from the death of Mohammed (632 A.D.) to the battle of Tours (732 A.D.), the Arabians, or Saracens, had established an empire extending from the Indus River to the Atlantic Ocean.

Dismemberment of the Caliphate. — By the middle of the eighth century the Mohammedan power had reached its greatest extent under the dynasty called the Ommi'ads, who made their capital at Damascus. From this time the caliphate gradually fell to pieces. The Ommiads were overthrown by a new dynasty, called the Abbas'sids, who removed their capital farther east, to Bagdad. One of the Ommiads, named Abd-er-Rah'man, escaped and fled to Spain, where he established an independent caliphate, with its capital at Cor'dova. It was not long before another independent caliphate arose in Africa, with its capital at Cairo, under the rule of the Fat'imites, who traced their descent from Fa'tima, the daughter of Mohammed. In spite of these and subsequent divisions, the Mohammedan religion continued to prevail over these countries.

Mohammedan Civilization. — By their conquests the Mohammedans came into contact with the higher civilizations of

Persia and the Eastern Empire. While western Europe was under the shadow of the German invasions, and the Eastern Empire was going into decline, Bagdad and Cordova, and other Mohammedan cities, became the centers of learning and culture. The Arabians studied philosophy, cultivated mathematics, and excelled in medicine. They obtained their chief ideas of architecture from the cities of the Eastern Empire; but they developed a new and beautiful style of ornamentation, called " arabesque," which is made up of lines and curves, and dispenses with the forms of living beings. The Arabians were not very original; but they took up much of the culture of the East and afterward transmitted it to the peoples of western Europe.

Selections for Reading

Knowlton, Topic A 26, "Rise of the New Empire" (1).[1]

Bémont and Monod, Ch. 8, "The Roman Empire in the East"; Ch. 11, "The Arabian Empire" (24).

Duruy, Ch. 4, "The Greek Empire"; Bk. II., "The Arab Invasion" (24).

Curteis, Ch. 10, "The Emperor Justinian"; Ch. 11, "The Empire in Relation to the Barbarians of the East" (24).

Gibbon, Ch. 40, "The Reign of Justinian"; Ch. 41 (career of Belisarius); Chs. 50–52 (extension of the Mohammedan power); Ch. 51 (Saracen conquest of Spain); Ch. 52 (siege of Constantinople) (18).

Stanley, Lect. 8, "Mahometanism in its Relation to the Eastern Church" (21).

Milman, Latin Christianity, Bk. III., Ch. 4, "Justinian" (21).

Morey, Roman Law, pp. 158–163, "The Final Codification by Justinian" (22).

Ogg, Source Book, Ch. 7, "Rise of Mohammedanism" (25).

Special Study

THE REIGN OF JUSTINIAN. — Duruy, "Middle Ages," Ch. 4 (24); Church, "Beginning of Middle Ages," Ch. 6 (24); Gibbon, "Decline and Fall," Ch. 40 (18); Milman, "Latin Christianity," Bk. III., Ch. 4 (21).

[1] The figure in parenthesis refers to the number of the topic in the Appendix, where a fuller title of the book will be found.

CHAPTER XXXIV

THE REVIVAL OF THE WESTERN ROMAN EMPIRE

Synopsis

I. THE PAPACY AND THE LATIN CHURCH. — The Growth of the Papacy. — Western Monasticism. — The Papal Missions. — The Popes and the Lombards.

II. THE ALLIANCE OF THE FRANKS AND THE PAPACY. — The Frankish Monarchy; Mayors of the Palace. — Pepin the Short and the New Dynasty. — Pepin's Defeat of the Lombards. — The "Donation of Pepin" and the Temporal Power of the Popes.

III. THE ROMANO-GERMAN EMPIRE OF CHARLEMAGNE. — Accession of Charlemagne. — Consolidation of Central Europe. — Coronation of Charlemagne as Roman Emperor. — Charlemagne and his Imperial Government. — The Capitularies of Charlemagne. — Charlemagne and European Civilization.

I. THE PAPACY AND THE LATIN CHURCH

The Growth of the Papacy. — We have seen the breaking up and decline of the old Roman empire. We are now prepared to look at the events which led to the reorganization of western Europe. Our attention must first be directed to that power which was most influential in bringing about this result — namely, the papacy, the chief authority in the Latin church.

PAPAL EMBLEMS

The bishop of Rome — or the "Pope" (*papa*, father) as he was now called — had been acquiring new power and dignity during the whole period of the invasions. This was due to a number of causes, which we may briefly enumerate as follows: (1) the

569

belief that the Roman bishop was the lineal successor of Saint Peter; (2) the prestige of Rome as the previous capital of the world; (3) the recognition of the Roman church as the "mother church" in the West; (4) the custom of appealing to the Roman bishop upon moral and ecclesiastical questions; and (5) the personal influence of three great bishops — Innocent I., Leo I., and Gregory I.,— whose ability as statesmen and whose vigorous policy gave to the bishop of Rome a commanding position throughout the Christian world.

The papacy was now the strongest power in western Europe. Its influence was on the side of order and good government. It tended to repress the anarchy which followed the barbarian invasions. It was also the most efficient agent in the reorganization of European society.

Western Monasticism. — An institution which tended to strengthen the church and the papacy was monasticism. This is the kind of life in which people separate themselves from the world to cultivate a religious spirit. Such a life had been common in the East, where men lived as hermits, sometimes retiring to the desert, providing themselves with the scantiest food and clothing, and spending their time in prayer and meditation. But when transplanted to the West, monasticism assumed a more practical and philanthropic character. Under the rule of Saint Benedict, who established a monastery at Monte Cassino in Italy (529 A.D.), it became a beneficent feature of the Western church. The "rule of Saint Benedict" required the taking of three vows — poverty, chastity, and obedience. It also required the performance of three daily duties — prayer, study, and manual labor. The monastic system spread throughout the countries of Europe, and exercised an important influence, not only in strengthening the church, but also in improving the condition of society. By encouraging manual labor, the monks restored the waste lands in different countries, and gave a new dignity to agricultural pursuits. By their copying of manuscripts, they preserved from destruction many works of ancient literature, and encouraged learning and scholarship. By their hospitality, they furnished a peaceful refuge for the weak, the sick, and the distressed, and presented to the world worthy examples of Christian charity.

The Papal Missions. — The influence of the Latin church was also extended by the encouragement given by the Popes to missionary work. We have already seen how Augustine was sent by the Pope to Britain to rescue that island from paganism and to bring it under the authority of the church (p. 552). The Irish monk and missionary, Saint Columban, was also sent to the countries about the upper Rhine, where his work was continued by his disciple, Saint Gall, the founder of one of the great monasteries in central Europe. But the greatest of the papal missionaries was Saint Boniface, who was sent by the Pope as the " apostle to the Germans." His work resulted not only in the conversion of many German tribes, but also in the reform of the Frankish church and in bringing it more completely under the papal authority. In this work he received the aid of Charles Martel, the great Frankish general, who had now come to be looked upon as the champion of Christendom and the faithful supporter of the Pope.

The Popes and the Lombards. — The people of western Europe who seemed to have the least respect for the dignity and authority of the Pope were his nearest neighbors, the Lombards. The Lombard kings desired to unite the whole of Italy under their own power. This would require, in the first place, the conquest of the Exarchate of Ravenna, which was still subject to the Eastern emperor. It would require, in the next place, the occupation of the city of Rome, the seat of the papal power. If this were accomplished, the Pope would be obliged to submit to the authority of the Lombard king — a master more distasteful than the emperor, who had refused to recognize the papal claims. In the face of such a warlike people as the Lombards, the Pope was practically helpless, unless he could find some military support. The only people of Europe who could give him the necessary aid were the Franks — the people who had already saved Christendom by their victory over the Mohammedans (p. 567). The Pope, therefore, first turned for help to Charles Martel, the hero of the battle of Tours; but this great general died before the desired aid could be given. This appeal of the Pope for military assistance against the Lombards was an important step, which finally led to the alliance of the Franks and the papacy — an event of great significance in the history of Europe.

II. The Alliance of the Franks and the Papacy

The Frankish Monarchy; Mayors of the Palace. — We may ask why the Pope called for help upon Charles Martel and not upon the Frankish king. The fact is the Frankish kings had ceased to possess any real authority. The governing power had passed into the hands of an officer of the king's household, called " mayor of the palace." It is true that the early kings — such as Clovis, the founder of the Merovin'gian dynasty, and Dag'obert, who consolidated the Frankish power — were able rulers. But after the time of Dagobert, the crown was worn by feeble men, who *reigned* but did not *rule*. It was said by an old writer, " There was nothing left for the king to do but to be content with his flowing hair and long beard, and to sit on the throne and play the ruler " (Eginhard). The later Merovingian kings are hence known as " do-nothing " kings. But in spite of the weakness of these so-called kings, the Frankish people found able rulers in the mayors of the palace. These officers had succeeded in making the Franks the strongest nation of Europe. Charles Martel was mayor of the palace when he defeated the Mohammedans at Tours; and it was to him as the defender of Christendom, that the Pope now appealed for help against the Lombards.

Pepin the Short and the New Dynasty. — At his death Charles Martel was succeeded by his two sons, one of whom soon retired to a monastery. This left the other son, Pep'in (or Pippin), surnamed the Short, as the sole mayor of the palace. Pepin was not disposed to exercise the real power of king without also having the title of king. He needed only some moral support to depose his feeble sovereign, and to reign in his stead. He therefore appealed to the Pope as the supreme arbiter of moral questions. The Pope replied, " It seems better that he who has the power in the state should be king, and should be called king rather than he who is falsely so called." With this sanction Pepin deposed the last Merovingian, assumed the royal title, and was raised on a shield, according to the German custom. He was also anointed with the holy oil, according to the Jewish custom, by Saint Boniface, now archbishop of Mainz. This ceremony was intended to give a religious sanction to the royal power, and to indicate that the king reigns " by the grace of God." In this way was established a new line of Frankish kings, called the Carolin'gian dynasty (752 A.D.). The effect of this revolution was to cement more closely the alliance of the Franks with the papacy, and to give to the Popes the military support which they desired.

Pepin's Defeat of the Lombards. — The Pope could now urge upon Pepin his duty to protect the church from the encroachments of the Lombards. The Lombards had already conquered the Exarchate of Ravenna ; they had also overrun the central part of Italy, and were laying siege to the city of Rome. The Pope fled to Gaul and besought the new Frankish king to come to his aid. Pepin was quick to respond. He crossed the Alps with his army, marched to Rome, and relieved the city. Thinking that his work was accomplished, he then returned to Gaul. On his departure from Italy the Lombards again beseiged Rome with a larger force than before. A second time the Pope appealed to the Frankish king ; and a second time Pepin led his army into Italy. The king was now determined to make a more thorough settlement of the Italian trouble. He not only raised the siege of Rome, but drove the Lombards from all the territory they had recently captured. He also extorted from their king a promise to respect thereafter the rights of the church.

The " Donation of Pepin " and the Temporal Power of the Popes. — The question now arose as to what should be done with the territory rescued from the hands of the Lombards. This territory was claimed by the Eastern emperor as his rightful possession. But Pepin replied to this demand that his expedition into Italy was not made in the interests of the emperor, but in the interests of the church ; that he himself had no desire for these lands, and that they should be given to the Pope. The whole territory — comprising the Exarchate of Ravenna, the Pentap'olis, and the Duchy of Rome (map, p. 562) — was therefore turned over to the church as the " patrimony of Saint Peter " (756 A. D.). This gift is called the " Donation of Pepin," and it laid the foundation of the temporal power of the Popes. From this time the Pope became a temporal sovereign in Italy, exercising a political as well as an ecclesiastical authority. This authority over the States of the Church the Pope continued to exercise until recent times (in 1870). But quite as important was the fact that the donation of Pepin established more firmly the alliance between the Franks and the papacy, by which each was bound to assist the other in their respective spheres of authority.

III. The Romano-German Empire of Charlemagne

Accession of Charlemagne. — The movements which we have already considered resulted finally in the establishment of a Romano-German empire under the Carolingian rulers. The founder of this empire was Charles the Great, who was the son of Pepin, and who is generally known as Charlemagne (shär'lemän). Charlemagne was not only the greatest man of his age, but one of the great men of history. After the death of Pepin (768 A.D.) he ruled for a short time with this brother Car'loman ; but at the death of Carloman he became the sole ruler of the

Frankish nation. He proved himself to be a born king and statesman. He was a man of gigantic stature, of imposing presence, and of broad ideas. His mode of life was simple. He was temperate in eating and drinking. He was fond of manly sports, particularly of hunting. He generally wore the simple ancient costume of his own people; but on state occasions he soon began to wear the imperial robes of a Roman emperor. As a man, he was thus proud of his German race; but as a ruler, he was inspired by Roman ideas. His great ambition was to consolidate the peoples of central Europe into one great Christian state, and to lift them to a higher plane of civilization.

Consolidation of Central Europe. — A considerable part of his reign was occupied with wars with outlying peoples, and with efforts to organize them under his authority and to bring them under the influence of the church. We can only briefly refer to

these wars: (1) He invaded the kingdom of the Lombards, to settle another quarrel between this people and the Popes; he conquered their territory, and was himself crowned with the " iron crown of the Lombards," [1] thus annexing this kingdom to his own. (2) He invaded northern Spain to free

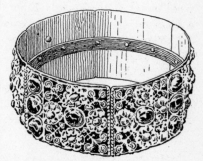

THE IRON CROWN OF THE LOMBARDS

Christians from the yoke of the Saracens (Mohammedans). On his retreat the rear guard of his army was attacked in the pass of Roncesvalles (rŏn-thĕs-väl′yäs), where the heroic warrior Roland

[1] This famous crown takes its name from a small fillet of iron within the broad band of gold and jewels which protects it. The piece of iron is said to have been wrought from a nail taken from the true cross, and to have been owned by Constantine and Pope Gregory the Great before it passed into the hands of the Lombard kings. The crown was afterward used by Charlemagne and Napoleon. It is now in the church of Monza, a town in northern Italy.

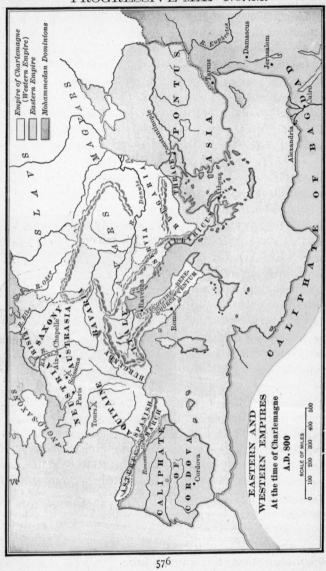

EASTERN AND
WESTERN EMPIRES
At the time of Charlemagne
A.D. 800

SCALE OF MILES
0 100 200 300 400 500

was killed; but this disaster did not prevent Charlemagne from annexing the northern part of Spain, which he did under the name of the " Spanish March." (3) He made war upon the barbarous nations on the eastern frontier — the Avars and Bavarians; he drove back the Avars, and added to his territory the land of the Bavarians, who had hitherto remained independent. (4) He made many expeditions against the Saxons on the north of the Rhine, who long resisted his power; but they were finally reduced to his authority and brought under the influence of Christianity.

By these conquests the dominions of Charlemagne were extended over a large part of central Europe. They included the following chief provinces: Saxony and Frisia, Austrasia and Neustria, Bur'gundy and Aquitaine, Lom'bardy (northern Italy) and Bavaria, together with the Spanish March on the south, and the Avaric March on the east. This extensive dominion seemed to need only the sanction of the Pope to make it in name, as well as in fact, an empire.

Coronation of Charlemagne as Roman Emperor (800 A.D.). — At this time the imperial title at Constantinople was held by a woman — the empress Irene — whose authority

CHARLEMAGNE

(Mosaic in the Lateran, Rome)

was not recognized in the West. It needed only a suitable occasion to confer the title upon Charlemagne, who was now the most conspicuous ruler in Europe and the ablest defender of Christianity. The occasion soon presented itself. When the Pope was driven from Rome by an insurrection, Charlemagne, with his army, entered the city and reinstated him. As a reward for this service, the Pope on Christmas Day, in the Church of St. Peter, placed upon Charlemagne's head a golden crown, and saluted him as " Charles Augustus, crowned of God, great and pacific emperor of the Romans." The Roman people who witnessed this impressive ceremony in the church shouted their approval, and the Frankish soldiers outside the building joined in the acclamation. In describing this memorable event, Mr. Bryce says: " In that shout, echoed by the Franks without, was pronounced the union, so long in preparation, so mighty in its consequences, of the Roman and the Teuton, of the memories and the civilization of the South and the fresh energy of the North, and from that moment modern history begins." Charlemagne himself professed to be surprised by this act of coronation; but he nevertheless gracefully accepted the title which was thereby conferred.

Charlemagne and his Imperial Government. — Charlemagne was now both Frankish king and Roman emperor. But it is difficult for us to separate these two functions, since his government, like that of his predecessors, was made up of both German and Roman features. In looking at the political organization of Charlemagne's empire we may distinguish between the central government and the local government.

(1) The central government consisted of the emperor himself, the officers of the palace, and the national assemblies. The emperor was of course the supreme head of the empire somewhat like the old Roman prince. His authority extended over all the affairs of the state. He was assisted by the officers of the palace, called the " pal'atines," each one of whom had charge of some particular branch of administration, such as the issuing of the royal decrees, the administration of justice, the care of the imperial household. One of the peculiar features of

Charlemagne's government was the preservation of the old
German assemblies, in which the people had some share of political authority. There were two of these assemblies held each
year. The larger one, which met in the spring and was called
the " Field of May," was made up not only of the nobles, but of
a large part of the common freemen. This assembly generally
met in the open air, and approved the laws submitted to it by
the emperor. The smaller assembly, which met in the autumn,
was a gathering of the various officers of the empire for the purpose of giving an account of their administration, and of laying
out the work for the coming year in accordance with the wish
of the emperor.

(2) The local government consisted of a large number of
officers who exercised authority within the different provinces
or districts. There were several kinds of such local officers.
There were two kings, the sons of Charlemagne, who ruled
over Aquitaine and Italy. Then there were several dukes, the
chiefs of barbarian tribes, who were permitted to govern their
own people, subject to the imperial will; such were the dukes
of Brit'tany in Gaul, and of Spoletum and Beneventum in
Italy. But the largest number of these local officers were
counts, or " grafs," — there were about three hundred of these,
— who were appointed directly by the emperor to carry out
his will in their separate districts or counties. The districts on
the borders of the empire were called " marks," and were
placed under officers called " margraves." Bishops also were
appointed over the various dioceses to supervise the affairs of
the church. But all these officers, whatever their rank, were
subject to the supreme authority of the emperor. To keep a
strict control over all these local governors, and to protect the
interests of the people, Charlemagne appointed special officers
called *missi dominici*, who were sent in pairs — a count and a
bishop — through the various provinces for the purpose of in-
specting the affairs of each locality, of correcting abuses, and of
administering justice. These last-named officers formed a sort

of connecting link between the central and local governments. In the political system which he organized, Charlemagne showed his great ability as a statesman and an efficient administrator.

The Capitularies of Charlemagne. — The comprehensive mind of Charlemagne is seen in the vast number of laws passed by him for the government of his people. These laws were called " capit'ularies," and related to all matters which concerned the interests of his subjects. More than eleven hundred of such laws have been collected and preserved to us; so that we can learn much from them not only regarding the high ideals of Charlemagne, but regarding the condition of European society during this time. These laws emanated from the emperor himself or from his immediate counselors, and were prepared so as to meet the approval of the assemblies, to which they were generally submitted. They related to the duties of officers, the administration of justice, the punishment of crime, the regulation of industry, the suppression of beggary, the encouragement of religion, and a multitude of other matters, all of which indicate the great concern which the emperor had for the welfare of his people.

Charlemagne and European Civilization. — Charlemagne's greatest distinction lies in the fact that he was a promoter of civilization. He brought about a union of the German and the Roman people, and laid the basis of a new European society. He encouraged habits of industry among his people, and published rules for the cultivation of the soil. He encouraged the revival of learning and of art. The long period which had elapsed since the beginning of the invasions had been a period of intellectual decline. But Charlemagne was a man who appreciated culture. He gathered about him the most learned men from all parts of Europe, and encouraged them in their scholarly pursuits. He also looked after the education of his subjects. He established schools in connection with the cathedrals and monasteries, as well as a " school of the palace " under the supervision of the famous scholar, Al'cuin, archbishop of York. He promoted a taste for architecture, and built many churches, one of which was the cathedral at his capital, Aix-la-Chapelle (āks-lä-shà-pěl'), where he was at last buried (814 A.D.). Charlemagne was the most efficient agent in uniting the German and the western Roman world, and in laying the basis of a new Romano-German society, and thus in furnishing a broader foundation for the states which were to be formed from the ruins of the old Roman empire. Although his empire fell to pieces after his death, the beneficial results of his policy and work have remained as a heritage to modern Europe.

References for Reading

Duruy, Bk. III., "The Carolingian Empire" (24).[1]

Emerton, Ch. 9, "Rise of the Christian Church"; Ch. 12, "The Franks from Charles Martel to Charlemagne"; Ch. 14, "Foundation of the Mediæval Empire" (24).

Thatcher and Schwill, Ch. 5, "The Franks" (24).

Curteis, Ch. 13, "The Popes and the Franks in Italy"; Ch. 14, "The Franks and the Papacy" (24).

Robinson, Ch. 4, "The Rise of the Papacy"; Ch. 7, "Charlemagne" (24).

Bémont and Monod, Ch. 12, "The Fainéant Kings"; Ch. 13, "Empire of the Franks" (24).

Adams, Ch. 6, "The Formation of the Papacy"; Ch. 7, "The Franks and Charlemagne" (24).

Oman, Ch. 16, "The Lombards and the Papacy"; Ch. 22, "Charles the Great and the Empire" (24).

Bryce, Ch. 4, "Restoration of the Empire in the West"; Ch. 7, "Theory of the Mediæval Empire" (24).

Milman, Latin Christianity, Vol. II., Bk. III., Ch. 6, "Western Monasticism"; Ch. 7, "Gregory the Great" (21).

Ogg, Source Book, Ch. 9, "The Age of Charlemagne" (25).

Special Study

THE REIGN OF CHARLEMAGNE. — Duruy, "Middle Ages," Ch. 9 (24); Adams, "Middle Ages," Ch. 7 (24); Milman, "Latin Christianity," Bk. V., Ch. 4 (21); Bryce, "Holy Roman Empire," Ch. 5 (24); Eginhard, "Life of Charlemagne" (27).

---

[1] The figure in parenthesis refers to the number of the topic in the Appendix, where a fuller title of the book will be found.

CHAPTER XXXV

THE GIFTS OF ROME TO CIVILIZATION

Synopsis

I. THE MONUMENTS OF ROME. — Remains of Roman Civilization. — The Monuments of the Kingdom. — The Monuments of the Republic. — The Monuments of the Empire.

II. THE LATIN LANGUAGE AND LITERATURE. — Character of the Latin Language. — Preservation of the Roman Alphabet. — The Latin and Modern Languages. — Permanence of Roman Literature. — Roman Element in Modern Education.

III. THE POLITICAL SYSTEM OF ROME. — Roman Genius for Organization. — Preservation of Roman Political Ideas. — The Roman Imperial Idea. — The Roman Provincial Government. — The Roman Municipal System.

IV. THE ROMAN LAW. — Character of Roman Jurisprudence. — Influence of the Roman Jurists. — Preservation of the Roman Law. — Revival of the Study of the Roman Law. — The Roman Law in Modern Countries.

V. THE CHRISTIAN CHURCH. — The Church and the Empire. — The Church Fathers, Chrysostom and Augustine. — Conversion of the Barbarians. — The Church succeeds the Empire. — Conclusion.

I. THE MONUMENTS OF ROME

Remains of Roman Civilization. — We have now followed the career of Rome from the foundation of the city to the revival of the Western Empire. We have seen how a small Latin village on the Palatine grew into the seven-hilled city on the Tiber; and how this city became the controlling power of Latium, of Italy, and of the whole Mediterranean world. We have also seen how the Romans, with their growing conquests, gradually developed the capacity to govern the countries of the Mediterranean better than they had ever been governed before. Moreover, we have seen how the Roman people, as they came into contact with their neighbors, became more and more civilized, gathering up the ideas of the Etruscans, the Carthaginians, the Greeks, and the countries of the East, and molding them into a new civilization.

But we are interested not only in what Rome did for herself, but in what she has done for others; not only in what she gathered up from the ancient world, but in what she has given to the modern world. It is the gifts of Rome to civilization that make her history especially important to us. Her real greatness must be judged not by that which perished with her fall, but by that which remained after her empire passed away; for this forms a part of the world's possessions to-day.

The Monuments of the Kingdom. — The first and most striking relics of Rome that appeal to us are the monumental buildings and other structures, the pictures of which every traveler brings home from his foreign tour. The person who visits the city on the Tiber to-day sees everywhere the evidences of Rome's greatness and power. The various stages of her growth and progress are recorded in works of stone. There still remain to us the monuments of her kings, which suggest to us the time and place of her birth. As we stand in the Forum to-day, we are standing on the site where the Latins and Sabines found a common meeting place, and where the political life of Rome really began. We may see fragments of the original wall which was erected upon the Palatine, and which is known as the " Wall of Romulus " (see p. 311). We may see portions of the Servian fortifications, which show to us the greatness of the city under the later kings. Close by the Capitol, under the walls of a modern church, we may descend into the Mamertine prison, where criminals were confined ages ago. If we walk to the banks of the Tiber, we may see the mouth of the Cloaca Maxima, the great sewer constructed by the later kings (p. 321).

The Monuments of the Republic. — There also remain monumental relics of the republic, which show how the Forum became embellished with public buildings. Near the center of this

Arch of Septimius Severus Temple of Saturn Foundations of the Basilica Julia

RUINS OF THE ROMAN FORUM

open space we may see three beautiful pillars, which belonged
to the temple of Castor and Pollux originally dedicated to the
twin gods after the battle of Re-
gillus (p. 307). Cicero speaks of
this temple as the most celebrated
in Rome in his day; it was afterward rebuilt by Tiberius (6 A.D.).
Close by the Palatine is the site of
the temple of Vesta, where the
sacred fire of the city was kept.
Near the Capitoline stand eight
massive columns, a part of the
temple dedicated to Saturn, the
ancient god who presided over that
hill. On the south side of the Forum we may still see the solid
foundations of the Basilica Julia,
the great hall of justice, or court-
house, built by Julius Cæsar and
finished by Augustus. Beneath

RUINS OF THE TEMPLE OF CASTOR
AND POLLUX

our feet we can see the pavement of the Sacra Via, over
which the victorious armies of the republic marched in triumph to the Capitol. Outside the city, stretching away to the
south, can still be seen the Appian Way, begun by Appius
Claudius during the wars with the Samnites (p. 353).

The Monuments of the Empire. — The empire has, of course,
left us the largest number of architectural monuments. The
old Forum itself received new buildings. New forums were
also constructed by the emperors. In the Forum of Trajan
rises the column dedicated to that emperor, and decorated with
a vast number of figures representing scenes in the Dacian
wars (p. 480). On the Palatine hill we may wander among
the extensive ruins which mark the site of the palaces of the
Cæsars (p. 472). Everywhere in Rome to-day the evidences
of the empire meet the visitor's eye — the great dome of the

MAUSOLEUM OF HADRIAN (Castle of St. Angelo)

Pantheon erected by Agrippa (p. 464) — the immense circle of the Colosseum (p. 501) — the imposing mausoleum of Hadrian, transformed into the Castle of St. Angelo — the triumphal arches of Titus, of Septimius Severus, and of Constantine (pp. 584, 528) — the ruins of the great Baths of Trajan, of Caracalla, and of Diocletian. And also throughout the countries of Europe, especially in the West, in Italy, in Spain, in France, and in England, are scattered similar monuments, which show the greatness of a people who have passed away, but whose influence still remains.

II. THE LATIN LANGUAGE AND LITERATURE

Character of the Latin Language. — But the most important remains of Roman civilization are not ruins. When we think how many words we use to-day that are derived from the Latin language, we may realize that the Romans have given to us some of the means by which we are able to express our thoughts. Just as the Latin people became the ruling people of Italy and of the Mediterranean, so the Latin speech became the ruling speech of Italy and the most important language of the Mediterranean world, especially of the western provinces. The Romans gave to the Latin tongue its dignity and power. Into it they breathed the spirit of patriotism.   Over the countries which they conquered they made it an instrument of dominion.   And from their more civilized neighbors they derived a refining influence which made it a medium of culture.

Preservation of the Roman Alphabet. — We may, perhaps, get some idea of the permanence of the Latin language by looking at the way in which the Roman alphabet has been preserved. The letters which the Romans used in writing were for the most part derived directly from old forms used by the Greek colonies in southern Italy ; and these in turn came remotely from the Phœnicians. But the Romans gave to these characters more definite forms, which have been substantially preserved by a great many modern nations. The accompanying table may indicate how the Romans learned their letters from the Greeks and Phœnicians, and also how closely these letters are related to our modern alphabet. By comparing the last two columns we may understand what Professor Whitney means when he says, " The Latin alphabet has become the common property of nearly all the enlightened nations of modern times whose civilization is derived from that of Greece and Rome."

Phœnician.	Old Greek.	Old Roman.	Modern Roman, English, etc.
⩜	A	A	A
⅁	B	B	B
⟩	C	‹C	C
△	▷D	D	D
⅂	Ɛ	E	E
Y	⟨	F	F
		C	G
⊟H	⊟H	H	H
⇂	I	I	I
			J
⅄	K	K	K
⌐	ⴽ	⅃L	L
M	M	M	M
Ч	N	N	N
O	O	O	O
⊃	Ⲅ	⌐P	P
φ	ϙ	ϙQ	Q
⌐	PR	R	R
⩗	⩒⅃	⩒S	S
↑	T	T	T

GROWTH OF THE
ALPHABET

The Latin and Modern Languages. — Not only the letters which the Romans used in their writing, but the words with which they expressed their thoughts, have also become the common property of the world. The Latin language was preserved by the Church after the fall of the empire, and it became the language of Christian worship, the language in which the ritual was read by the priests, in which the hymns were written, in which theological discussions were carried on. Moreover, what are to-day called the Romance languages — the Italian, the French, the Spanish, the Portuguese, and the Roumanian — are based chiefly upon the Latin language spoken by the Roman provincials. The English language, also, has obtained many additions from the Latin, by means of the Norman Conquest, and in other ways. While the Saxon people in England were using the crude words of their barbarian ancestors, the Norman aristocracy was employing the more refined and dignified speech derived from the Latin. And after a while these two forms of speech became fused together into the English language; so that to-day we can scarcely utter a sentence without using some words which were once spoken by the old Roman people.

Permanence of Roman Literature. — Again, not only the letters and words, but the writings which made up the great body of Roman literature, have also become the common heritage of mankind. How much we owe to the Romans is seen in the fact that we are able to read to-day the thoughts which once amused, instructed, and inspired that great people in the times of the republic and the empire. We can still read the comedies of Plautus and Terence, the historical works of Cæsar and Sallust, of Livy and Tacitus, the poems of Lucretius and Vergil, the satires of Horace and Juvenal, and the masterly orations, the versatile letters, and the philosophical essays of Cicero. And these writings have exercised a wonderful influence upon nearly all the great authors of modern times.

Roman Element in Modern Education. — Still further, by the preservation of the Latin language and literature the modern world has acquired some very important means necessary for mental culture and education. When, for example, in the fifteenth and sixteenth centuries, Europe waked up to the need of a higher education, Latin and Greek became the most important studies in the schools and universities; and it was believed that these studies were necessary for the best scholarship. We all know that these studies hold an important place in modern education. The boy who is preparing for college still studies the make-up of Latin words, the syntax of Latin sentences, the rhythm of Latin verses, and the thoughts of Latin authors. But Latin is not simply a study for schoolboys; every literary man feels that his power to write his own language is not fully developed until he has obtained some culture by the study of the Latin language and literature. So it is that while the Roman state has passed away, the language, the thoughts, and the spirit of the Roman people still remain to enrich the intellectual life of the world.

III. The Political System of Rome

Roman Genius for Organization. — There are other gifts of Rome to the world which are quite as important as her alphabet, her language, or even her literature. The possessions which we have already noticed she obtained in large measure from her predecessors, the people whom she conquered, and passed them on to the nations which succeeded her. But we should remember that we have received from Rome other valuable gifts, which she did not borrow from her predecessors, but which she may be said to have created. It is in her political system that we may see the special marks of her genius. No nation, before the Romans, had developed a system of government so well suited to maintain an authority over such a wide territory, and to hold together so many different kinds of people. The great glory of Rome does not rest upon her conquests, but upon the way in which she maintained her conquests in time of peace. It is in her genius for organization that her greatness chiefly consists. We have seen how her ideas of government were slowly developed and expanded with the expansion of her territory; how she gradually " incorporated " her subjects, and made of them loyal citizens, having equal rights and inspired by her own spirit and ambition; and how successfully she governed her provinces for hundreds of years. Although we have seen many instances of corruption and bad administration, yet there can be no doubt that before the growth of modern ideas of representation and constitutional law, the Roman system of government was the most highly developed that the world had ever seen.

Preservation of Roman Political Ideas. — If we should study the condition of Europe after the fall of the empire, we should find that the political ideas of Rome continued to exercise an influence after she herself had ceased to rule. The new German settlers from the north, it is true, brought with them certain ideas of freedom and democracy; but they hardly knew what was meant by an efficient and well-organized government. They therefore adopted Roman ideas. Their kings aspired to rule like Roman monarchs. Their officers received Roman titles, and exercised powers like Roman officials. Although the Germans introduced some important principles regarding personal liberty and local self-government, still it is true that the chief states of modern Europe have derived their ideas of a strong central authority and an efficient administration from the political system of Rome.

The Roman Imperial Idea. — We may illustrate how the political ideas of Rome were preserved in Europe after the fall of the empire by the way in which the idea of " imperialism " continued to influence men's minds. The Romans, as we know, came to believe that the highest political power must be exercised by one man, the Cæsar, who personified the nation. To him all must look as the highest source of authority. This idea floated before the minds of the barbarian kings after they had destroyed the empire; and when they built up their new states they aspired to the position and to the name of emperor. Thus it came to pass that Charlemagne, the great king of the Franks, had himself crowned as emperor, and established a new Roman Empire in western Europe. So, afterward, the German kings were crowned as Roman emperors, and their dominions were called the Holy Roman Empire. The influence of this imperial idea which was associated with the name of "Cæsar," we see still preserved in the names of the German "Kaiser" and the Russian "Czar."

The Roman Provincial Government. — One of the chief features of the Roman government was the division and subdivision of the territory for purposes of administration. These provincial districts, whatever they might be called, were controlled by officers sent out from the capital city; and thus the central authority was maintained throughout the whole Roman domain. This method of maintaining the central power over a large territory, by local divisions and subdivisions, has been adopted by modern states. In this way every modern European country has, to a greater or less extent, modeled its administrative system upon Roman provincial methods. This is perhaps least true as regards England; but even here the English government, in the administration of its crown colonies, has adopted methods quite similar to those employed in the Roman provinces.

The Roman Municipal System. — In many respects the most important elements of the whole political system of Rome were the municipalities, or the cities. It has been said that the Roman Empire was a "collection of cities." The conquests which Rome made were conquests of cities. The government which she established was a government over cities. Her life and activities were concentrated in cities. And when the provinces were finally overrun and the last emperor was deposed, the cities still remained with their government and their institutions. On this account the cities of Rome may be regarded as the most permanent features of her political organization. The Roman city was what we should call to-day a "municipal corporation," established by a charter, having the right to elect its own officers and to be governed by its own city council. This idea of the city has descended to modern times, and forms nearly as important an element in our own political system as it did in that of the Romans.

As we look at these various features of the Roman government which have exercised such influence in the formation of modern states, we may not be so strongly impressed by them as we are by the architectural monuments and the literary remains; but we must remember that they have been, none the less, important contributions to the world's civilization.

IV. The Roman Law

Character of Roman Jurisprudence. — If one were asked what was the most valuable gift of Rome to the modern world, the correct answer would be that it was none of the things which have thus far been mentioned — but her jurisprudence, or system of law. When we remember that our lives, our personal security, and our property are protected only by means of the law, we can appreciate how important it is that a nation's laws should be founded upon broad ideas of justice. It was in the development of just and liberal laws, by which the rights of Roman citizens were protected in their relations with one another, that the Romans showed their greatest ability, and have exercised their most powerful influence upon modern nations. When the Romans began their career on the banks of the Tiber, they had very crude and meager ideas of law and justice. But as they established their authority over other peoples, they gradually learned that it would be the best policy to put their new subjects upon a plane of equality with their older citizens; to regard all men as equal before the law; and to protect them all alike in their rights of person and property. By extending this policy throughout Italy and the provinces, the Romans were able to create a body of just laws, such as the ancient world had never before seen, and from which the modern world has drawn a large part of its jurisprudence. While we must admit that the government of Rome was often corrupt and despotic in its political and financial administration, we must not lose sight of the spirit of fairness and equity which almost uniformly marked her legal system.

Influence of the Roman Jurists. — If we believe that the greatness of men is to be measured by the extent of their influence, we must believe that the greatest men that Rome produced were not her warriors, her poets, her historians, or even her statesmen — but her lawyers and jurists. It is a question whether Cicero or Cæsar, whose names are so familiar to us, has exercised so great an influence upon the world as some other Romans, not so famous, — Gaius, Ulpian, Paullus, and Papinian. These were the men who, with others like them, gave to the Roman law its liberal and scientific character, and laid its foundations upon the broad principles of justice. Like the framers of our own Declaration of Independence, they believed that all men are created equal, and that they are all alike entitled to the rights of life and property. With such ideas of right and justice they settled a vast number of legal questions, such as naturally arise among the people of every country. They thus built up a noble system of jurisprudence suited to the wants of those nations which sprang up and became civilized in Europe after the Roman Empire had passed away.

Preservation of the Roman Law. — In order to understand how the Roman law was preserved after the fall of the empire, we must bear in mind what we have already learned, that the empire at the death of Theodosius was divided into two parts, the western part and the eastern part. We must also remember that it was the Western Empire that was overrun and destroyed by the barbarians from the north, while the Eastern Empire remained intact. The Roman people who still lived in the West, that is, in Italy, Spain, and Gaul, found themselves now subject to the new German rulers, and living side by side with the new German people who had conquered their territory. The new German kingdoms were thus made up of two kinds of people, the Romans and the Germans. But the German kings, while ruling their German subjects according to their old barbarian customs, permitted their Roman subjects still to be judged by the laws of Rome. How liberal these barbarian kings were is seen in the fact that they even took the pains to make special collections of the Roman law by which to govern their Roman subjects. They also permitted the Christian clergy to retain the Roman law in the tribunals of the Church.

While the Roman law was thus preserved in the West after the barbarian conquest, it was also preserved in the East in quite as remarkable a way. The Emperor Justinian, when he was ruling at Constantinople, saw the importance of gathering together the great mass of laws, which had been growing up for centuries, and of putting it into a complete codified form (p. 561). It was in this codified form that it descended to modern times.

Revival of the Study of the Roman Law. — The Roman law never lost its hold upon Europe after the fall of the Western Empire. It was preserved in the cities, in the courts where the Romans were tried, and in the tribunals of the Church. But after the twelfth century, when there came to be a greater demand for scientific education, a renewed interest was shown in the Roman law, and it became the object of eager study. It came to be expounded by learned men in Italy, in Spain, in France, in Holland, in Germany, and in England. Students flocked from all parts of Europe to the great centers of learning to listen to the teachers of the Roman law. And to this day, in the great universities of Europe this important subject has never lost its place as a liberal and scientific study.

The Roman Law in Modern Countries. — By the preservation of the Roman law after the fall of the Western Empire, by its codification by Justinian, and by the revival of its scientific study, it has become in fact the basis of the modern laws of Europe. Professor Bryce says, " Being studied by all the educated men, the poets, the philosophers, the administrators of the Middle Ages, it worked itself into the thoughts of Christendom; it became the common property of the world." By appreciating this fact the student who reads Blackstone will be able to understand what that writer means when he says that the revival of the Roman law " established in the twelfth century a new Roman Empire over most of the states of the Continent." In various ways which cannot be reviewed here, the legal principles worked out by the Roman jurists and embodied in the " Digest " of Justinian, have found their way into the laws of nearly all modern countries, and are to-day practiced in nearly every European court. If Rome had done nothing else in the long course of her history, she would be entitled to the gratitude of the world for the noble body of laws which she has left us.

V. The Christian Church

The Church and the Empire. — To complete our brief review of the gifts of Rome to civilization we should notice, finally, the influence which she has continued to exercise through the organization of the Christian Church. We must remember that Christianity became the religion of the Roman Empire before it became the religion of the modern world. It may therefore be regarded as one of the valuable possessions which Rome received from her subjects, and which she bequeathed to her descendants.

In the organization of the Church we may see especially the influence of the imperial system. Upon the territorial divisions of the empire were modeled the divisions of the Church. For example, in the town was organized the parish church, at first under its own bishop, afterward under a presbyter, or priest; the diocese furnished the subsequent field of the bishop; the province was the district over which presided the archbishop, or metropolitan; and the great cities of the empire, such as Constantinople, Antioch, and Alexandria, formed the seats of the patriarchates, the largest ecclesiastical divisions. The organization of the empire was thus, to a certain extent, impressed upon the organization of the Church; and with the adoption of Christianity by Constantine the Church became a part of the imperial system. We may, therefore, say that as the Roman Empire became Christianized, the Christian Church became Romanized; and with the preservation of the Church were also preserved the Roman features of its organization.

The Church Fathers, Chrysostom and Augustine. — Moreover, as the empire became Christian, many of the leaders of Roman thought became the leaders and expounders of the new religion. The names which stand out with marked prominence in the literature of the later empire are those of Chrys'ostom and Augustine, the former the greatest of the Greek fathers, and the latter the greatest of the Latin fathers. Chrysostom received the education of a Roman lawyer; but giving up the bar he became the most eloquent preacher of his day — some say of the world — on account of which he received his name, " the golden-mouthed." Leaving his native city of Antioch, he became the archbishop of Constantinople, and his eloquence became the terror of evil-doers. His enemies obtained his banishment, but from his retreat he continued his work, and became one of the most voluminous writers of the early Church.

Augustine received the training of a Roman rhetorician, but afterward became the bishop of Hippo (a town in Africa), and one of the most distinguished expounders of the Christian religion. His most noted work, the " City of God," was intended to defend the Christian faith against those pagans who asserted that the capture of Rome and the other calamities of the time were a judgment of the gods upon the new religion. He showed that the kingdom of God was more enduring than the empire of Rome. Thus it happened that in the midst of moral decay and of external dangers Rome gave to the Church some of her brightest minds and her strongest defenders.

Conversion of the Barbarians. — Not only did Christianity become the religion of the Roman Empire; it also became the religion of the barbarians who were invading and destroying the empire. When the Goths invaded the provinces they carried back with them numbers of Roman captives who were Christians, and who succeeded in converting their new masters. It is said that Chrysostom, while archbishop of Constantinople, founded an institution in which the Goths might be trained to preach the gospel to the barbarians. From the Goths the new religion spread among the neighboring tribes of the Vandals and Burgundians. It should be noticed that the barbarians who settled within the empire before its fall, had accepted the Arian form of Christianity; that is, the form which had been condemned as a heresy by the Council of Nice. But in the course of time this form gave way to the prevailing Roman form, or the Catholic faith. It may be said, then, that Rome not only accepted Christianity herself, but was instrumental in giving it to other nations.

The Church succeeds the Empire. — By taking advantage of Roman principles of organization, by appropriating the best intellect of the empire, by adopting rules of the Roman law, and by extending her influence over the invading nations, the Church attained a great degree of solidity and strength. Moreover, the prestige of the city of Rome was one of the reasons that gave to the bishop of that diocese a commanding position in the West. These were some of the causes which prepared the Latin Church, at the close of the fifth century, to take the place of the Roman Empire as the ruling power in western Europe. When the empire at last fell, the Church remained standing, and assumed the duty of helping to organize and control the new nations which were coming into existence. The spirit of Rome thus remained in the Church, and continued to exercise its powerful influence in the reorganization of European society.

Conclusion. — As we consider the influence of Rome upon civilization, we must conclude that there is much truth in the statement of Professor Freeman that " the history of Rome is in truth the same as the history of the world." It is certainly true that the history of Rome touches at some point or other the history of nearly every other people, ancient and modern. Every important nation of the ancient world seems to have contributed something to her civilization. The more we study the origin of our modern life and institutions, the more shall we be convinced that nearly everything of value which has come to us from antiquity has come to us through Rome. She has thus been one of the great *civilizing* nations of the world. While we think of the events of her history as belonging to ancient times, we must think of her civilization as something which has not passed away, but which remains a permanent possession for all time. This idea of Rome's continued influence is well expressed in the eloquent words of a great French jurist: " The mighty destinies of Rome have not yet been accomplished; she reigns throughout the world by her reason after having ceased to rule by her authority."

Selections for Reading

Gibbon, Decline, Ch. 71, "Ruins of Rome" (18).[1]

Freeman, Essays, 2d Ser., "Mommsen's History of Rome" (3).

—— Comp. Politics, Lect. on "The Unity of History" (3).

Whitney, Language and the Study of Language, pp. 462–467, "The Latin Alphabet."

Ramsay and Lanciani, Ch. 9, "Roman Law and the Administration of Justice" (19).

Morey, Roman Law, pp. 192–216, "Roman Element in Modern Jurisprudence" (22).

Merivale, Gen. Hist., Ch. 80, "Reflections upon the History of Rome" (18).

Special Study

ROME OF TO-DAY. — Hare, Walks in Rome (20); Burn, Rome and the Campagna (20); Lanciani, Ruins (20); Middleton, Remains (20); Encyclopædias, article " Rome."

[1] The figure in parenthesis refers to the number of the topic in the Appendix, where a fuller title of the book will be found.

CHRONOLOGICAL SUMMARY

A. THE ORIENTAL PEOPLES

I. **The Tigris-Euphrates Valley.**   B.C.

  1. *The Early Babylonian Empire.*

    Semitic occupation of Babylonia . . . (?) 5000

    The age of Sargon, King of Akkad . . (?) 3800 or 2800

    The age of Hammurabi . . . . (?) 1950

  2. *The Assyrian Empire.*

    The first Assyrian Empire . . . (?) 1120–745

    The second Assyrian Empire . . . 745–606

    Destruction of Babylon 688

  3. *The Later Babylonian Empire.*

    Destruction of Nineveh 606

    Reign of Nebuchadnezzar . . . 605–561

    Conquest of Babylonia by Persia . . 538

  4. *Rise of the Persian Empire.*

    Reign of Cyrus the Great . . . 558–529

    Reign of Cambyses 529–522

    Reign of Darius 521–484

    Reign of Xerxes 484–465

II. **The Valley of the Nile — Egypt.**

  1. *The Old Empire* . . . . (?) 3400–2160

    Menes, first king of Egypt . . . (?) 3400

    The pyramid builders . . . (?) 3000–2800

  2. *The Middle Empire* . . . . (?) 2160–1580

    The rule of the Hyksos . . . (?) 2080–1580

  3. *The New Empire* . . . . (?) 1580–525

    Reign of Rameses II . . . (?) 1292–1225

    Conquest of Egypt by Persia . . . 525

III. **The Syrian States.**

  1. *Phœnicia.*

    Flourishing period of Phœnicia . . . about 1100

C. THE ROMAN PEOPLE

A.D.

A CLASSIFIED LIST OF IMPORTANT BOOKS UPON ANCIENT HISTORY[1]

I. GENERAL AND MISCELLANEOUS WORKS

(1) Ancient History, General.

Ducoudray, G. History of Ancient Civilization. Ed. by J. Verschoyle. N. Y. 1889.

Goodspeed, G. S. History of the Ancient World. N. Y. 1909.

Knowlton, D. C. Illustrated Topics for Ancient History. Phil. 1913.

Myres, J. L. Dawn of History. Lond. and N. Y.

Ploetz, C. Epitome of Ancient, Mediæval, and Modern History. Part I. Ancient History. Bost. 1884.

Seignobos, C. History of Ancient Civilization. Tr. by A. H. Wilde. N. Y. 1906.

Souttar, R. Short History of Ancient Peoples. Lond. 1904.

(2) Anthropology and Ethnology.

Clodd, E. Childhood of the World. Lond.

Haberlandt, M. Ethnology. Lond. 1900. (Primer.)

Hoernes, M. Primitive Man. Lond. 1901. (Primer.)

Joly, N. Man before Metals. N. Y. 1883.

Keary, C. F. Dawn of History. N. Y.

Peschel, O. Races of Man. N. Y. 1876.

Tylor, E. B. Primitive Culture. 2 vols. N. Y. 1874.

—— Early History of Mankind. Bost. 1878.

—— Anthropology. N. Y. 1881.

Starr, F. Some First Steps in Human Progress. Meadville. 1895.

(3) Miscellaneous Works.

Bourne, H. E. Teaching of History and Civics in the Elementary and Secondary School. N. Y. 1902.

Clarke, J. F. Ten Great Religions: an Essay in Comparative Theology. Bost. 1871.

[1] The books contained in this list have been selected with special reference to their educational value in connection with the work of secondary schools. More complete lists may be found in the author's "Outline of Greek History" and "Outlines of Roman History."

Committee of Seven. American Historical Association. Study of History in Schools. N. Y. 1903.

Freeman, E. A. Historical Essays. Second Series. Lond. 1873.

—— Comparative Politics: with Lecture on the Unity of History. N. Y. 1874.

Rawlinson, G. Religions of the Ancient World. N. Y.

Whitney, W. D. Language and the Study of Language. N. Y.

II. THE ORIENTAL PEOPLES

(4) Oriental History, General.

Boughton, W. History of Ancient Peoples. N. Y. 1897.

Hommel, F. Civilization of the East. N. Y. 1900. (Primer.)

Lenormant, F., and Chevallier, E. Ancient History of the East. 2 vols. Phil. 1871.

Maspero, G. C. C. Life in Ancient Egypt and Assyria. N. Y. 1892.

—— Dawn of Civilization. Egypt and Assyria. Lond. 1894.

Rawlinson, G. Five Great Monarchies. 3 vols. N. Y. 1871.

Sayce, A. H. Ancient Empires of the East. N. Y. 1889.

Smith, P. Ancient History of the East. N. Y. 1871. (Students' Series.)

(5) Babylonia and Assyria.

Budge, E. A. W. Babylonian Life and History. Lond. 1891.

Goodspeed, G. S. History of the Babylonians and Assyrians. N. Y. 1904.

Jastrow, M. Religion of Babylonia and Assyria. Bost. 1898.

Murison, R. G. Babylonia and Assyria. Edin. (Primer.)

Ragozin, Z. A. Story of Chaldea. N. Y. 1891.

—— Story of Assyria. N. Y. 1891.

Sayce, A. H. Social Life among the Assyrians and Babylonians. Lond. 1893.

(6) Egypt.

Breasted, J. H. History of Egypt from the Earliest Times to the Persian Conquest. N. Y. 1905.

Erman, A. Life in Ancient Egypt. Lond. and N. Y. 1894.

Mariette, A. Monuments of Upper Egypt. Rev. by L. Dickerson. Boston. 1890.

Maspero, G. C. C. Egyptian Archæology. N. Y. 1891.

Murison, R. G. History of Egypt. Edin. (Primer.)

Newberry, P. E., and Garstang, J. Short History of Ancient Egypt.
Lond. 1904.

Petrie, W. M. F. History of Egypt. 6 vols. N. Y. 1905.

Rawlinson, G. History of Egypt. 2 vols. Lond. 1881.

—— Story of Egypt. N. Y. 1892.

Weigall, A. E. P. B. Treasury of Ancient Egypt. 1911.

Wendel, F. C. H. History of Egypt. N. Y. 1890. (Primer.)

(7) Phœnicia and Palestine.

Day, E. Social Life of the Hebrews. N. Y. 1901.

Hosmer, J. K. Story of the Jews. N. Y. 1891.

Kent, C. F. History of the Jewish People. N. Y. 1899.

—— History of the Hebrew People. 2 vols. N. Y. 1899–1901.

Ottley, R. L. Short History of the Hebrews. N. Y. 1901.

Petrie, W. M. F. Egypt and Israel. Lond. 1911.

Rawlinson, G. History of Phœnicia. Lond. and N. Y. 1889.

—— Story of Phœnicia. N. Y. 1896.

Sayce, A. H. Early History of the Hebrews. N. Y. 1897.

(8) Media and Persia.

Benjamin, S. G. W. Story of Persia. N. Y. 1891.

Ragozin, Z. A. Story of Media, Babylon, and Persia. N. Y. 1891.

Vaux, W. S. W. Persia, from the Earliest Period to the Arab Conquest. Lond.

(9) Sources of Oriental History.

Baum, H. M., and Wright, T. B. Records of the Past. 6 vols.
Washington, 1902–1907.

Hammurabi, Code of. Tr. by C. H. W. Johns. Edin. 1903. Same
tr. by R. F. Harper, Chicago, 1904.

Josephus, F. Works. Tr. by W. Whiston. Lond. 1870.

Old Testament. Revised Version.

Sayce, A. H. Records of the Past. 6 vols. Lond. 1888–92.

III. THE GREEK PEOPLE

(10) Greek History, General.

Abbott, E. History of Greece. 2 vols. N. Y. 1888–92.

Allcroft, A. H. History of Greece. 5 vols. Lond.

Bury, J. B. History of Greece (one vol. edition). N. Y. 1900.

Butcher, S. H. Some Aspects of the Greek Genius. Lond. and
N. Y. 1893.

Cox, G. W. General History of Greece. N. Y. 1894. (Students' Series.)

—— The Greeks and the Persians. N. Y. (Epochs.)

—— The Athenian Empire. N. Y. (Epochs.)

Curteis, A. M. Rise of the Macedonian Empire. N. Y. 1887. (Epochs.)

Curtius, E. History of Greece. 5 vols. N. Y. 1875.

Felton, C. C. Greece, Ancient and Modern. 2 vols. Bost. 1893.

Gardner, P. New Chapters in Greek History. Lond. and N. Y. 1892.

Grote, G. History of Greece. 12 vols. N. Y. 1857. Same 10 vols. Lond. 1888.

Holm, A. History of Greece. 4 vols. Lond. and N. Y. 1894–1898.

Mahaffy, J. P. Survey of Greek Civilization. Meadville. 1896.

—— Story of Alexander's Empire. N. Y. 1897.

—— Greek Life and Thought from the Age of Alexander to the Roman Conquest. Lond. and N. Y. 1887.

Oman, C. W. C. History of Greece. Lond. and N. Y. 1901.

Shuckburgh, E. S. Short History of the Greeks. Camb. 1901.

Smith, Wm. History of Greece, with supplementary chapters on the History of Literature and Art. N. Y. (Students' Series.)

(11) Greek Antiquities. Public and Private Life.

Becker, W. A. Charicles. Lond. 1866.

Blümner, H. Home Life of the Ancient Greeks. Tr. by A. Zimmern. Lond. 1893.

Davidson, T. Education of the Greek People. N. Y. 1894.

Gardiner, E. N. Greek Athletic Sports and Festivals. Lond. 1910.

Gilbert, G. Constitutional Antiquities of Sparta and Athens. Lond. and N. Y. 1895.

Greenidge, A. H. J. Handbook of Greek Constitutional History. Lond. and N. Y. 1896.

Guhl, E., and Koner, W. Life of the Greeks and Romans. Lond. 1889.

Gulick, C. B. Life of the Ancient Greeks. N. Y. 1902.

Harper's Dictionary of Classical Literature and Antiquities. N. Y. 1897.

Mahaffy, J. P. Old Greek Life. N. Y. 1876.

—— Social Life in Greece. Lond. and N. Y. 1890.

Smith, Wm. Dictionary of Greek and Roman Antiquities. 3d Edition. 2 vols. Lond. 1890.

Tucker, T. G. Life in Ancient Athens. Lond. and N. Y. 1907.

Whibley, L. Political Parties in Athens. Camb. 1889.

—— Companion to Greek Studies. Cambridge. 1906.

(12) Greek Archæology and Art.

Butler, H. C. Story of Athens. N. Y. 1902.

Collignon, M. Manual of Greek Archæology. N. Y. 1886.

Fowler, H. N., and Wheeler, J. R. Handbook of Greek Archæology. N. Y. 1909.

Gardner, E. A. Handbook of Greek Sculpture. Lond. and N. Y. 1897.

—— Ancient Athens. N. Y. 1902.

Harrison, J. E. Introductory Studies in Greek Art. Lond. 1904.

Mitchell, L. M. History of Ancient Sculpture. N. Y. 1883.

Murray, A. S. History of Greek Sculpture. 2 vols. Lond. 1890.

—— Handbook of Greek Archæology. N. Y. 1892.

Richardson, R. B. History of Greek Sculpture. N. Y. 1911.

Tarbell, F. B. History of Greek Art. Lond. 1896.

(13) Prehistoric Greece.

Baikie, J. Sea-Kings of Crete. Lond. 1910.

Hall, H. R. The Oldest Civilization of Greece. Lond. and Phil. 1901.

Hawes, C. H. and H. B. Crete, the Forerunner of Greece. Lond. and N. Y. 1909.

Mosso, A. Dawn of Mediterranean Civilization. N. Y. 1906.

Schuchhardt, C. Schliemann's Excavations. Lond. and N. Y. 1891.

Tsountas, C., and Manatt, J. I. The Mycenæan Age. Bost. 1897.

(14) Homer and the Homeric Age.

Keller, A. G. Homeric Society. N. Y. 1902.

Lang, A. Homer and his Age. N. Y. 1906.

Leaf, W. Companion to the Iliad. N. Y. 1892.

Warr, G. C. W. The Greek Epic. Lond. and N. Y. 1895.

Weissenborn, E. Homeric Life. Eng. trans. N. Y. 1903.

(15) Greek Literature and Philosophy.

Benn, A. W. Philosophy of Greece in Relation to the History and Character of the People. Lond. 1898.

Croiset, A. and M. Abridged History of Greek Literature. N. Y. 1904.

Fowler, H. N. History of Ancient Greek Literature. N. Y. 1902.

Lawton, W. C. Introduction to Classical Greek Literature. N. Y. 1903.

Mayor, J. B. Sketch of Ancient Philosophy. Camb. 1881.

Wright, W. C., and Smyth, H. W. Short History of Greek Literature. Lond. 1910.

Zeller, E. Outlines of the History of Greek Philosophy. N. Y. 1886.

(16) Greek Religion and Mythology.

Bulfinch, T. Age of Fable. (New Edition.) Phil. 1898.

Collignon, M. Manual of Greek Mythology in relation to Greek Art. Lond. 1890.

Fairbanks, A. Handbook of Greek Religion. N. Y. 1910.

Gayley, C. M. Classical Myths. Bost. 1893.

Guerber, H. A. Myths of Greece and Rome. N. Y. 1893.

Murray, A. S. Manual of Mythology. Phil. 1895.

(17) Sources of Greek History.

Æschylus. Tragedies. Tr. by E. H. Plumptre. N. Y. 1868.

Aristotle. Athenian Constitution. Tr. by F. G. Kenyon. Lond. 1891.

Arrian. Anabasis of Alexander. Tr. by E. J. Chinnock. Lond. 1893.

Demosthenes. Orations. 5 vols. (Bohn.) . . . 2 vols. (Harpers.)

Herodotus. Tr. by G. Rawlinson. 4 vols. N. Y. . . . Tr. by H. Cary. (Bohn.) . . . Analysis and Summary by J. T. Wheeler. (Bohn.)

Homer. Iliad. Tr. by W. C. Bryant. Bost. 1870. . . . Tr. by Lang, Leaf, and Myers. Lond. 1893.

—— Odyssey. Tr. by W. C. Bryant. Bost. 1872. . . . Tr. by Butcher and Lang. Lond. 1893.

Thucydides. Tr. by B. Jowett. 2 vols. N. Y. . . . . Analysis and Summary by J. T. Wheeler. (Bohn.)

Xenophon. Cyropædia and Hellenics. Tr. by J. S. Watson and H. Dale. (Bohn.)

IV. THE ROMAN PEOPLE

(18) Roman History, General.

Allcroft, A. H., and Masom, W. F. History of Rome. 5 vols. Lond.

Bury, J. B. History of the Roman Empire from its Foundation to the Death of Marcus Aurelius. N. Y. 1893. (Students' Series.)

Capes, W. W. The Early Empire. N. Y. (Epochs.)

—— The Age of the Antonines. N. Y. (Epochs.)

Gibbon, E. History of the Decline and Fall of the Roman Empire. Ed. by Milman. 6 vols. Phil. . . . Ed. by Bury. 7 vols. Lond.

Heitland, W. E. Roman Republic. 3 vols. Camb. 1909.

How, W. W., and Leigh, H. D. History of Rome to the Death of Cæsar. N. Y. 1896.

Ihne, W. Early Rome. N. Y. (Epochs.)

Jones, H. S. Story of the Roman Empire. N. Y. 1908.

Liddell, H. G. History of Rome. N. Y. 1890. (Students' Series.)

Merivale, C. History of the Romans under the Empire. 7 vols. N. Y. 1866.

—— General History of Rome. N. Y. 1880. (Students' Series.)

Mommsen, T. History of Rome. Tr. by W. P. Dickson. 4 vols. N. Y. 1871. Same abridged by Bryans and Hendy. N. Y. 1889.

Pelham, H. F. Outlines of Roman History. N. Y. 1893.

Seeley, J. R. Roman Imperialism and other Lectures and Essays. Bost. 1871.

Shuckburgh, E. S. History of Rome to the Battle of Actium. N. Y. 1894.

Smith, Wm. Smaller History of Rome. N. Y. Revised ed. by A. H. J. Greenidge. 1899.

(19) Roman Antiquities. Life and Manners.

Abbott, F. F. The Common People of Ancient Rome. N. Y. 1911.

Church, A. J. Roman Life in the Days of Cicero. N. Y. 1890.

Dill, S. Roman Society from Nero to Marcus Aurelius. Lond. 1905.

—— Roman Society in the Last Century of the Western Empire. Lond. 1898.

Fowler, W. W. Social Life at Rome in the Age of Cicero. N. Y. 1909.

Friedländer, L. Town Life in Ancient Italy. Tr. by W. E. Waters Bost. 1902.

Guhl, E., and Koner, W. Life of the Greeks and Romans. Lond. 1889.

Harper's Dictionary of Classical Literature and Antiquities. N. Y. 1897.

Inge, W. R. Society in Rome under the Cæsars. N. Y. 1888.

Johnston, H. W. Private Life of the Romans. Chicago. 1905.

Preston, H. W., and Dodge, L. Private Life of the Romans. Bost. 1894.

Ramsay, W., and Lanciani, R. Manual of Roman Antiquities. Lond. 1894.

Sandys, J. E. Companion to Latin Studies. Cambridge. 1910.

Smith, Wm. Dictionary of Greek and Roman Antiquities. 3d Edition. 2 vols. Lond. 1890.

Thomas, E. Roman Life under the Cæsars. N. Y. 1899.

Tucker, T. G. Life in the Roman World of Nero and St. Paul. N. Y. 1910.

(20) Roman Archæology and Art.

Boissier, G. Rome and Pompeii: Archæological Rambles. Lond. 1896.

Burn, R. Ancient Rome and its Neighbourhood. Lond. 1895.

Hare, A. J. C. Walks in Rome. 2 vols. N. Y.

Lanciani, R. A. Ancient Rome in the Light of Recent Discoveries. Bost. 1891.

—— Ruins and Excavations of Ancient Rome. Bost. 1897.

Mau, A. Pompeii: its Life and Art. Tr. by F. W. Kelsey. N. Y. 1899.

Middleton, J. H. Remains of Ancient Rome. 2 vols. Lond. 1892.

Parker, J. H. Architectural History of the City of Rome. Oxford and Lond. 1881.

(21) Christianity and Rome.

Carr, A. The Church and the Roman Empire. Lond. and N. Y 1887.

Fisher, G. P. Beginnings of Christianity. N. Y. 1878.

—— History of the Christian Church. N. Y. 1887.

Hardy, E. G. Christianity and the Roman Government. Lond. and N. Y. 1894.

Hatch, E. Organization of the Early Christian Churches. Lond. 1881.

Milman, H. H.   History of Christianity.   N. Y.   1872.
—— History of Latin Christianity.   8 vols. in 4.   N. Y.   1881.
Ramsay, W. M.   The Church and the Roman Empire.   N. Y.
 1893.
Schmidt, C.   Social Results of Early Christianity.   Eng. trans.
 Boston.   1885.
Shahan, T. J.   The Beginnings of Christianity.   N. Y.   1903.
Stanley, A. P.   History of the Eastern Church.   N. Y.   1884.
Uhlhorn, G.   Conflict of Christianity with Heathenism.   N. Y.
 1879.

(22) Roman Constitution and Law.

Abbott, F. F.   History and Description of Roman Political Institu-
 tions.   Bost.   1902.
—— Society and Politics in Ancient Rome.   N. Y.   1909.
Arnold, W. T.   Roman System of Provincial Administration.   Lond.
Granrud, J. E.   Roman Constitutional History.   Bost.   1902.
Greenidge, A. H. J.   Roman Public Life.   Lond.   1901.
Hadley, J.   Introduction to Roman Law.   N. Y.   1880.
Morey, W. C.   Outlines of Roman Law.   Revised Ed.   N. Y.
 1913.
Muirhead, J.   Historical Introduction to the Private Law of Rome.
 Lond.   1899.
Taylor, T. M.   Constitutional and Political History of Rome.
 Lond.   1899.

(23) Roman Literature.

Cruttwell, C. T.   History of Roman Literature.   N. Y.   1887.
Lawton, W. C.   Introduction to Classical Latin Literature.   N. Y.
 1904.
Mackail, J. W.   Latin Literature.   Lond.   1896.
Simcox, G. A.   History of Latin Literature.   2 vols.   Lond.   1883.
Tyrrell, R. Y.   Latin Poetry.   Bost.   1895.

(24) Mediæval Period.

Adams, G. B.   Civilization during the Middle Ages.   N. Y.   1894.
Bémont, C., and Monod, G.   Mediæval Europe from 395 to 1270
 A.D.   N. Y.   1902.
Bryce, J.   Holy Roman Empire.   6th Edition.   Lond.   1899.
Bury, J. B.   History of the Later Roman Empire from Arcadius to
 Irene (395–800 A.D.).   2 vols.   Lond. and N. Y.   1889.

Church, R. W. Beginnings of the Middle Ages. N. Y. 1877.

Curteis, A. M. History of the Roman Empire, 395–800 A.D. Phil. 1875.

Duruy, V. History of the Middle Ages. N. Y. 1891.

Emerton, E. Introduction to the Study of the Middle Ages. Bost. 1888.

Mohammed. The Qur'ân (Koran). Tr. by E. H. Palmer. Oxford.

Oman, C. W. C. The Dark Ages, 476–918 A.D. N. Y.

Robinson, J. H. Introduction to the History of Western Europe. Part I. (The Middle Ages.) Bost. 1902.

Thatcher, O. J., and Schevill, F. Europe in the Middle Age. N. Y. 1896.

(25) Sources of Roman History.

Greenidge, A. H. J. Sources for Roman History. Oxford.

Munro, D. C. Source Book of Roman History. Bost. 1904.

Ogg, F. A. Source Book of Mediæval History. N. Y. 1908.

Robinson, J. H. Readings in European History. Bost. 1904.

Thatcher, O. J., and McNeal, E. H. Source Book for Mediæval History. N. Y. 1905.

Ammianus Marcellinus. Roman History. (Bohn.)

Appian. Roman History. Tr. by H. White. 2 vols. N. Y. 1899.

Cæsar. Commentaries. (Harpers.)

Livy. History of Rome. 2 vols. (Harpers). . . . 4 vols. (Bohn.)

Marcus Aurelius. Meditations. Boston.

Polybius. Histories. Tr. by E. S. Shuckburgh. 2 vols. Lond. 1889.

Tacitus. Works. Oxford translation. (Bohn.)

Sallust. Works. (Harpers.) (Bohn.)

Vergil. Æneid. Tr. by C. P. Cranch. Bost. 1897.

V. BIOGRAPHY

(26) Biography, Collected.

Collins, W. L. (Ed.). Ancient Classics for English Readers. 28 vols. Edin. and Phil. 1879–88.

Cox, G. W. Lives of Greek Statesmen. 2 vols. N. Y. 1885.

Oman, C. W. Seven Roman Statesmen of the Later Republic. Lond. 1903.

Plutarch. Lives. Tr. by J. Dryden. 3 vols. N. Y. . . . Ed. by A. H. Clough. Bost. 1881. . . . Tr. by A. Stewart and G. Long. 4 vols. N. Y. 1889.

Suetonius. The Twelve Cæsars. (Bohn.)

(27) Biography, Individuals.

Alexander. By T. A. Dodge. Bost. 1890.
—— By R. Steele. Lond. 1894.
—— By B. I. Wheeler. N. Y. 1900.
Augustus Cæsar. By J. B. Firth. N. Y. 1903.
—— By E. S. Shuckburgh. Lond. 1903.
Charlemagne. By Eginhard (Einhard). N. Y.
—— By H. W. C. Davis. N. Y. 1900.
—— By T. Hodgkin. Lond. 1897.
Constantine. By E. L. Cutts. Lond. 1881.
Cicero. By G. Bossier. Lond. 1897.
—— By W. L. Collins. Phil. 1871. (Anc. Classics.)
—— By W. Forsyth. 2 vols. in one. N. Y. 1871.
—— By J. L. Strachan-Davidson. N. Y. 1894.
Demosthenes. By Brédif. Chicago. 1881.
—— By S. H. Butcher. N. Y. 1882.
Hannibal. By J. Abbott. N. Y.
—— By T. A. Dodge. Bost. 1890.
—— By W. O. Morris. N. Y. 1897.
Julian. By A. Gardner. N. Y. 1895.
Julius Cæsar. By J. Abbott. N. Y.
—— By T. A. Dodge. Bost. 1892.
—— By W. W. Fowler. N. Y. 1892.
—— By J. A. Froude. N. Y. 1880.
Marcus Aurelius. By P. B. Watson. N. Y. 1884.
Mohammed. By W. Irving. 2 vols. N. Y. 1868.
—— By Sir W. Muir. Lond. 1888.
Nero. By B. W. Henderson. Phil. 1903.
Pericles. By E. Abbott. N. Y. 1891.
Tiberius. By J. C. Tarver. N. Y. 1902.
Theodoric. By T. Hodgkin. N. Y. 1896.
Zoroaster. By A. V. W. Jackson. N. Y. 1890.

VI. HISTORICAL FICTION

(28) Oriental.

Arnold, E. L. L.   Phra the Phœnician.
Ebers, G. M.   Daughter of an Egyptian King.   (6th century B.C.)
—— The Sisters.   (2d century B.C.)
—— Uarda.   (Time of Rameses II.)

(29) Historical Fiction, Greek.

Church, A. J. Heroes and Kings. (Mythical age.)
—— Stories from Homer. (Mythical age.)
—— Stories from Herodotus. (5th century B.C.)
—— Callias. (5th century B.C.)
—— Young Macedonian in the Army of Alexander. (4th century B.C.)
Haggard, H. R., and Lang, A. The World's Desire. (Trojan war.)
Hawthorne, N. Tanglewood Tales. (Mythical age.)
—— Wonder Book. (Mythical age.)
Kingsley, C. The Heroes. (Mythical age.)
Lamb, C. Adventures of Ulysses. (Trojan war.)
Landon, R. Fountain of Arethusa. (5th century B.C.)
Landon, W. S. Pericles and Aspasia. (5th century B.C.)
Leatham, E. A. Charmione. (5th century B.C.)

(30) Historical Fiction, Roman.

Bulwer-Lytton. Last Days of Pompeii. (1st century A.D.)
Church, A. J. The Hammer. (2d century B.C.)
—— The Burning of Rome. (1st century A.D.)
—— To the Lions. (2d century A.D.)
—— The Count of the Saxon Shore. (5th century A.D.)
Eckstein, E. Prusias. (1st century B.C.)
—— Nero (1st century A.D.)
—— Quintus Claudius. (1st century A.D.)
Farrar, F. W. Darkness and Dawn. (1st century A.D.)
Kingsley, C. Hypatia. (4th century A.D.)
Lee, E. B. Parthenia. (4th century A.D.)
Pater, W. Marius, the Epicurean. (2d century A.D.)
Sienkiewicz, H. Quo Vadis. (1st century A.D.)
Wallace, L. Ben-Hur. (1st century A.D.)

INDEX

Diacritic marks: ä as in father; e, eh as in cart, chasm; N, the French nasal; ô as in lord; single Italic letters are silent. The long and short marks used with vowels have their usual meaning. In the names in this index, c and g followed by e, i, or y have respectively the sounds of s and j (except Elgin); followed by a, o, or u, however, c has the sound of k, and g is sounded as in the word go.

Index